PSYCHOEDUCATIONAL DIAGNOSIS
OF
EXCEPTIONAL CHILDREN

Psychoeducational Diagnosis of Exceptional Children

(Second Printing)

By

MILTON V. WISLAND, Ed. D.

CHARLES C THOMAS • PUBLISHER

Springfield • Illinois • U.S.A.

Published and Distributed Throughout the World by
CHARLES C THOMAS · PUBLISHER
Bannerstone House
301-327 East Lawrence Avenue, Springfield, Illinois, U.S.A.

© *1974,* by CHARLES C THOMAS · PUBLISHER
ISBN 0-398-02843-5
Library of Congress Catalog Card Number: 73–4660

First Printing, 1974
Second Printing, 1977

Printed in the United States of America
M-3

Library of Congress Cataloging in Publication Data

Wisland, Milton V
   Psychoeducational diagnosis of exceptional children.
   1. Exceptional children—Diagnosis. I. Title.
[DNLM: 1. Child, Gifted. 2. Handicapped. 3. Mental retardation. 4.
Psychological tests—In infancy and childhood. 5. Psychology, Educational.
WS 105 W814p 1973]
BF723.E9W57   371.9′042   73–4660
ISBN 0–398–02843–5

CONTRIBUTORS

Mary K. Bauman, M.S.
Director of Personnel Research and Guidance, Inc.
Philadelphia, Pennsylvania

Sam D. Clements, Ph.D.
Professor, Department of Child and Adolescent Psychiatry
Executive Director, Child Study Center
University of Arkansas Medical Center
Little Rock, Arkansas

Calvin O. Dyer, Ph.D.
Associate Professor of Education
Director, School Psychological Examiner Program and
Coordinator, Field Placement and School Psychology Training
University of Michigan
Ann Arbor, Michigan

Joseph L. French, Ed.D.
Head, Department of Special Education
Chairman, Interdisciplinary Graduate Program in
School Psychology
Director, Center for Educational Diagnosis and Remediation
Pennsylvania State University
University Park, Pennsylvania

Tom J. Hicks, M.S.
Coordinator, Special Education
Arkansas Department of Education
State Capitol
Little Rock, Arkansas

Max Mueller, Ph.D.
Bureau of Education for the Handicapped
U. S. Office of Education
Regional Office Building, Room 2012
7th and D Streets, S.W.
Washington, D.C.

McCay Vernon, Ph.D., Professor
Department of Psychology
Western Maryland College
Westminster, Maryland

Milton V. Wisland, Ed.D.
Director of Special Services
Bellingham Public Schools
Bellingham, Washington

David E. Yoder, Ph.D.
Chairman, Department of Communicative Disorders
University of Wisconsin
Madison, Wisconsin

PREFACE

THE PAST DECADE has generated sufficient information to demonstrate the multiplicity of problems associated with exceptional children. It is now generally accepted that the problems precipitated by the child demonstrating aberrant development is no longer the sole responsibility of a single professional group or discipline but rather the cooperative effort, pooling of knowledge and consultations of many disciplines working together to resolve these problems. It is the desire of these authors that this text emphasize the contributions to be made by the psychoeducationally oriented professions.

In reviewing the manuscripts submitted by contributing authors, it became readily apparent that there was some overlapping between chapters in that several tests were discussed repeatedly by different authors. This was not, however, considered a problem in that various writers considered these tests for different types of exceptional children. This divergence is considered a strength rather than a weakness.

This book is intended for several audiences. First, it should be a useful text for junior and senior undergraduates as well as graduate students concerned with problems of assessment of exceptional children, particularly students majoring in such fields as psychology, sociology and education. Students in peripheral fields such as clinical psychology, pediatrics, general education, nursing, and social work will also increase their understanding of the problems of diagnosing exceptional children.

Second, it is intended as an introductory text in specialized professional training programs designed to prepare students for careers within the behavioral sciences and peripheral fields dealing with exceptional children. Students majoring in special education, clinical and school psychology will find this text a beneficial reference in their programs.

Third, professional persons already in the field who have not had the benefits of specific training with exceptional children will find this a useful text. Staff members working in child guidance clinics, schools, pediatric clinics, public health and rehabilitation services, and institutions for exceptional children also will find new material to help them develop improved diagnostic skills, prepare better reports, and perform with greater skill in staffings, as well as gain more insight into problems of exceptional children.

In writing this book, recognition must be given to several people who helped with the seemingly endless correspondence, providing encouragement, and professional guidance. Without the aid of Helen Jacobs and Cheryl Brown who typed and retyped the many revisions of this manuscript, this text would never have been completed. To my wife, Elizabeth, who also typed, edited, and encouraged me, a great deal of the credit is due.

In addition to those directly involved in the writing of this book, a debt of gratitude is due the National Institute of Child Health and Human Development as well as the Bureau of Educational Studies and Testing of Indiana University for supporting services and resources. Both Richard Pugh and David Vore, Indiana University, contributed many professional ideas to this text.

CONTENTS

PSYCHOEDUCATIONAL DIAGNOSIS
OF
EXCEPTIONAL CHILDREN

CHAPTER I

INTRODUCTION TO TESTING

Milton V. Wisland

What is a Diagnosis?

THE CHALLENGES FACING professional individuals concerned with aberrant child health and human development can be grouped into three main categories: identification, diagnosis, and remediation. The reasoning behind this categorization is obvious in that first a problem must be identified before any professional assistance can be given. Usually identification procedures involve rather crude measurements that are plagued with problems of over and under referrals that require more refined and extensive examinations before the actual diagnosis can be made.

The term *diagnosis* is of German origin meaning to decide, or in the case of diagnosing the art of or the act of deciding. The term diagnosis can be further defined as the act of determining the nature of the child's problem or the decision that has been reached concerning this problem. The term diagnosis also can mean the art of distinguishing one problem from another or the process of determining the nature of the problem. Various modifying terms can be used to extend the meaning of diagnosis; for example, we have various professional diagnoses such as medical, educational, psychological, etc.; or we can have deductive diagnoses, clinical or differential diagnoses depending upon the process used to reach the decision or the kinds of decisions that were reached.

If we regard the diagnostic process as the art of, or act of, deciding, it becomes readily apparent that it would be wise to establish basic assumptions that can be used to guide and assist us in formulating a diagnosis. Although there are other assumptions that can be made, the following appear to be most basic or generic in the formation of a diagnosis:

(1) A diagnosis is not simply a classification process but rather a description of a condition or problem from which a hypothetical model is derived which provides for a prognosis as well as treatment procedures.

(2) Such a model should explain the interrelationships of established variables, as well as make inferences to assumed variables or propositions.

(3) The diagnostic process should begin with the identication of identifiable variables as well as measurement of measurable variables, through processes involving empirical and clinical or controlled observations.

(4) The usefulness of a diagnosis is enhanced through the recognition of the whole individual including the dynamic effect of adverse and influential physical, mental, and social variables.

(5) Diagnosticians should attempt to establish a hierarchical order of influence for contributing variables to provide some degree of order and structure to the therapeutic process to clarify the responsibilities of various professional groups involved.

(6) The ultimate purpose of the diagnostic process is to expedite understanding as well as communication between remedial specialists to enhance and improve the remedial process.

It is becoming more apparent to specialists in this field that no one profession or discipline contains all the skills and knowledge necessary to make an adequate diagnosis. Today there is a shift from a focus on a single to multiple causation in the diagnostic process as well as in the remediation of problems. There is an increasing awareness that we are no longer dealing with simply a neurological impairment, an emotional distortion, or an inability to learn to read, but rather it is frequently a combination of these.

What is a Test?

The word *test* is used in this text to mean, *the objective as well as standardized evaluation of a sample of behavior made on a small and carefully chosen sample of an individual's behavior.* Obviously, an educator or psychologist cannot possibly accumulate all the information that is known about an individual nor obtain a complete inventory of what he may know on a given subject at a given time; consequently, behavioral scientists proceed in much the same way as a physicist or chemist who examines electricity or magnetic forces by analyzing samples of the particular force he is observing. The adequacy of the sample the examiner takes, of course, depends upon the nature of the problem, the amount of time and expense one is able to use in coming up with a decision or diagnosis as well as the consequences of the decisions that must be reached.

If one is working with human subjects rather than raw materials, other problems arise in obtaining adequate samples; for instance, one is certainly limited in what he can do to human subjects to obtain a sample. An example of this is the simple problem of fatigue which one frequently encounters after working only a few minutes with some exceptional children.

The diagnostic value of a procedure depends upon the degree to which it serves as an indicator of a relatively broad and significant area of behavior or knowledge. It also should be called to the attention of the reader that the particular samples of behavior do not necessarily have to resemble the kind of behavior the test is attempting to evaluate. It is only important that an empirical relationship or correlation be established between the two variables. The above statement may be particularly true in working with handicapped children in that a child may not necessarily be able to perform or demonstrate a particular skill or task the examiner is trying to evaluate. Frequently, handicapped children are given substitute tasks that are assumed to have predictive or diagnostic value while in actuality may have only descriptive value. An educator or psychologist working with an exceptional child will be limited in many instances to the sensory modality the child is capable of responding with, or he will be limited to the motor control or development a particular individual has when attempts are made to evaluate his adaptive behavior.

Purpose of Testing

Before a diagnosis can be determined, the characteristics of an individual must be systematically examined. This is basically the purpose for psychological or educational measurements. Measurement is essentially concerned with the problem of providing a quantitative and qualitative description of the individual or child who is manifesting problems (Newland, 1963). It is, therefore, important that we understand something of the process of examining children and the nature and use of these instruments.

Many measuring instruments have been devised for measuring the general characteristics of children. However, as one begins to work with deviate children or children with aberrant development, it becomes apparent that the process of systematic comparisons is extremely complicated in that these children do not readily fit into established systems of measurement. It is also obvious that the descriptions of the behavior encountered are going to be varied and in some ways contradictory to descriptions we have of normal children. Many instruments available today are useful as they currently exist, whereas, others must be subjected to further evaluation to make necessary transformations or modifications to provide more meaningful and useful scores for diagnosis and evaluating exceptional children (Birch, 1964).

Who uses Tests?

Every professional person working with children uses tests if we take a broad interpretation of the definition of tests previously described. Nearly everyone makes comparisons between individuals and situations that he faces professionally in his day-to-day contact with children. One example of this can be found in our daily contact with individuals we meet. We are constantly evaluating forms of greetings, degrees of friendliness or kinds of expressions that individuals have in making a greeting.

In the professional instruments we use, we certainly employ a greater degree of sophistication in our observations than we have in our casual, unstructured relationships with people. The more structured and involved the system of evaluation becomes, the more skilled one must become to administer and skillfully interpret a given instrument. There are a number of instruments on the market today that are currently being used with exceptional children that are not within the realm of experience of the classroom teacher or the psychologist. For example, various types of audiometric examinations or visual acuity tests require highly specialized training to be able to skillfully administer and interpret them. It appears imperative that individuals working with exceptional children recognize their professional limitations, including their limited proficiency in using many highly developed and technical tests.

Taking a narrower point of view, it appears to be rather obvious that anyone who attempts to evaluate and diagnose exceptional children should have a rather thorough and comprehensive understanding of the exceptionality to be evaluated as well as a correspondingly thorough working knowledge of the instrument to be utilized. For example, it would not appear reasonable to find one individual who can relate equally well to preschoolers, adolescents, and adults, as well as blind, retarded, gifted, and cerebral palsied children, and all of the instruments having relevance to their problems.

Only a brief survey of the literature reveals the great proliferation of instruments occurring on the market today measuring many characteristics of children. A great deal of the diagnostic quality of an instrument, however, is dependent upon the individual using a given test, and his knowledge of the handicap of the particular group of children he is evaluating.

Historical Background of Tests

Although exceptional children have been acknowledged in the writings of man for a period of twenty-five hundred years, attempts to measure or evaluate these children with a standardized instrument were delayed until the first part of the nineteenth century which witnessed a strong awakening of interest in a humane treatment of the feebleminded and the insane. Prior to this time, mistreatment in the form of neglect, ridicule, and even torture was not uncommon. Out of a growing concern for the proper identification and classification of mental retardation, there developed an interest in designing some form of uniform criteria for diagnosing and classifying these individuals. It was also during this time that institutions for the retarded began to appear on the scene requiring that admission requirements be established, particularly to differentiate between the psychotic, neurotic, and mentally retarded individual.

Esquirol (1772–1840) : It was in 1838 that one of the first pioneers attempted to formulate an explicit statement differentiating between the mentally retarded and those whom we would classify today as pseudo-mentally retarded. In his two-volume work he recognized that there are many degrees of retardation ranging from normal to what he referred to as *low-grade idiocy*. In his attempt to develop an instrument for diagnosing mental retardation, he considered physical measurements, particularly the size and proportion of the skull, as important variables (Anastasi, 1968). Through his efforts, Esquirol concluded that the best indicator of intellectual development was probably that of language rather than physical criteria (Freeman, 1962). It is interesting that his hypothesis is still supported today by many investigators. Using a language criteria he differentiated between two grades of imbecility and three grades of idiocy. He further stated that in the higher degrees of imbecility, speech is employed readily and easily, whereas in the lower grade imbecile, speech is more difficult and vocabulary more limited. He defined the highest grade of idiot as one who uses only a few words or very short phrases, the second level was able to utter only monosyllables and cries, and the lowest level of idiocy had no language. Thus, Esquirol was one of the first scientists to attempt to differentiate between various levels of mental retardation.

Seguin (1812–1880) : A French physician was another pioneer in the training of the mentally retarded. Seguin experimented for many years with what he described as the physiological method of training and in 1837 he established the first school devoted to the education of mentally retarded children. He rejected the prevailing notion that mental retardation was incurable. In 1848 he migrated to the United States where his ideas were given wide recognition. Many of the sense and muscular training techniques currently in use in institutions for the mentally retarded were originated by Seguin (Robinson and Robinson, 1965). He advocated sensory discrimination tests and development of motor control among low grade, mentally defective children. Some of his ideas are currently being used in performance or nonverbal tests of intelligence. An example of this is the very famous Seguin form board (DuBois, 1970), used in the Stanford-Binet intelligence scale in which an individual is required to insert three red blocks of various shapes into correspondingly shaped green recesses.

FRANCIS GALTON (1822–1911): An English biologist was the first scientist to undertake systematic and statistical investigations of individual differences and introduce them into the field of psychology (Freeman, 1962). Many historians would probably state that he is the father of the testing movement and primarily responsible for launching this type of investigation (Watson, 1963). Because of his background in biology he was strongly influenced by the development of the biological science then ascendent among British scientists, although he was also interested and influenced by the psychological work of his predecessors. Galton assumed that the simpler and measurable sensory capacities were significantly correlated with intelligence. This hypothesis, at least, was reflected in the subjects he selected for study in that they represented individuals of extreme differences of mental ability in order to learn whether the differences in sensory discrimination corresponded with the known differences in their mental ability. Although it has been known for a long time that sensory and sensory motor tests have little predictive value for the study of the higher and more complex intellectual processes called intelligence, these ideas are actively being pursued today in analysis of brain damage and its effect on cognitive processes.

In 1882, Galton established an anthropometric laboratory in South Kensington Museum in London where, by the payment of a small fee, individuals could be measured in certain physical traits and could undergo tests of keenness of vision and hearing, muscular strength, reaction time, and other simple sensory motor functions (DuBois, 1970). With this large body of information, he was able to demonstrate that human psychological traits distributed themselves statistically in the normal probability curve (Misiak and Sexton, 1966). Galton's work did strongly affect the course taken by testing experimenters during the 1900's until about the beginning of 1900 when the influence of Alfred Binet, a French psychologist, became prominent.

JAMES McKEEN CATTELL (1860–1944) : Cattell was the American counterpart of Francis Galton who introduced psychometrics into this country in his article *Mental Tests and Measurements,* 1890. He may be considered, by some, the actual originator of psychometrics (Misiak and Sexton, 1966) in that he was strongly interested in measuring sensory abilities that involved keenness of eyesight and hearing, color vision, perception of pitch and weight, perception of time intervals, and sensitivity to pain. As one examines Cattell's range of interests, we find a strong interest in perceptual skill in the involvement of understanding the use of perception in sensory skills, rather than measuring keenness of perception *per se.* Cattell's interest in reaction time was an important part of his early contributions to differential psychology, for much of the subsequent interest in reaction time experiments are contributed to Cattell's early work in this area. The use of the term *mental test* was seen for the first time in psychoanalytic literature as used by Cattell in 1890 (Freeman, 1962). The article describes a series of tests which were being administered annually to college students in an effort to determine their intellectual ability. Again he found that the study of reaction time had little or no value in estimating intellectual abilities. The time variable alone played a minor role in most mental tests except in those devised specifically to measure speed of performance, usually in a restricted type of activity, for a specific purpose, such as the task frequently used in measuring clerical aptitude. Cattell and his collaborators realized that the more complex mental processes should be measured, but they were aware of the fact that much research analysis had yet to be done before adequate mental tests could be devised for the measurement of these processes.

ALFRED BINET (1857–1911) : From a historic point of view, Binet was one of the chief founders of psychometrics, particularly in the area of intelligence evaluation. Binet and his colleagues spent many years developing ingenious methods and ways of measuring intelligence. Although his scale first appeared in 1905, it was preceded by ten years of research and trial testing. They used many approaches including the measurement of physical traits, handwriting analysis, and palmistry. However, these results led to a growing conviction that the direct measurement, though crude, was the only approach that appeared to be capable of measuring the complexity of intellectual functioning. In October 1904, the Minister of Public Instruction appointed a commission to study procedures for educating mentally retarded children attending the Paris schools (DuBois, 1970). This represented a real opportunity to develop Binet's ideas on intellectual assessment. It was in meeting this task that Binet, in his collaboration with Simon, prepared the first Binet-Simon scale which is now known as the 1905 scale. Although we find that Binet included perceptual tests, which to some extent reflects the thinking of Galton and Cattell, he provided a much greater proportion of verbal content than was found in most instruments of this type at this time.

In the experimental model presented as the 1905 scale, no precise objective method for evaluating a total score had been formulated. In the second instrument, which was developed in 1908, the number of items were increased, unsatisfactory tests from the earlier scale were eliminated, and all items were grouped into age levels. To do this, all items that were passed by normal three year olds were placed at the three-year-old level; items passed by normal four year olds were placed at the four year level; etc., up to age thirteen (Watson, 1963). This provided the basis for expressing a child's score in terms of mental age; in other words, a child was compared with the performance of normal individuals (Anastasi, 1968). It was from this test that mental age norms were developed and achieved considerable popularity in subsequent stages of psychological testing.

In 1911 a third revision appeared with no radical changes made at this time, only slight changes and some relocation of special items. Additional items were placed in several year levels as well as extending the scale to the adult level.

From the beginning the Binet scale drew considerable interest by other investigators in the field. His first 1905 scale was tried by Decroly in Belgium, Goddard in the United States, and Ferrari in Italy. Binet used their findings and criticisms in revising the 1911 scale, which was Binet's final contribution to the field of mental testing as he died the same year.

Since 1911, several revisions and adaptations of the scale have been made in a number of countries. Most of the changes have been in the way of expansions, modifications, and improvements on the 1911 scale. The latest revision of this instrument has been the 1960 revision done by Merrill and Terman. The 1960 scale incorporates a single form designated as form LM, which includes the best subtests from both forms of the 1937 scale. The selection of subtests included in the 1960 edition was based on records of tests administered during the five-year period from 1950 to 1954. The greatest change made at this time was the conversion from a ratio intelligence quotient to a deviation intelligence quotient which will be explained later in the text. Another innovation has been the extension of the IQ tables to include chronological ages 17 and 18. The reasoning for this change has been the research supporting the test findings that mental development, as measured by the Stanford-Binet, continues longer than formerly believed.

EMIL KRAEPELIN (1856–1926): A German psychiatrist, who had been one of Wundt's first pupils, was concerned with a program of applying the methods of psychology to psychopathology. Through the efforts of his students, he proposed and developed a comprehensive system of comparative testing of the sane and the insane. His plan involved the use of items taken from everyday life to examine such personal characteristics as mental ability, trainability, memory, sensitivity, ability to recover from fatigue, depth of sleep, and distractibilty. Through his concern for standard procedures in testing, he stressed the need to examine each case a sufficient number of times so that chance variations would be avoided (DuBois, 1970).

Specific items included counting letters singly and in groups of three, memory span for digits and nonsense syllables, adding single digits to obtain sums of one hundred, writing from dictation, and reading aloud. His goal, of course, was to obtain data on normal subjects for comparative purposes. With experience, the test was extended to include color naming, reading digits, letters and words, as well as classifying nouns as either living or non-living objects. Although he and his students were creative, the results of their efforts were admittedly disappointing.

WILHELM STERN (1871–1938) : In his work *Uber Psychologie der Individuellen Differenzen (On the Psychology of Individual Differences,* 1900) , Stern introduced psychometrics to Germany (Misiak and Sexton, 1966) . A major contribution on his part was the intelligence quotient which was used with the Binet test. Stern recognized that the amount of retardation expressed in years or months alone had different implications, depending upon the age of the individual. For example, being retarded six months is much more serious for a two-year-old child than a fifteen year old in that it represents a greater proportion of the child's total development. He suggested the establishment of a *mental quotient* which is found by dividing the mental age by the chronological age. This, he stated, would be relatively constant during his period of mental growth (DuBois, 1970) .

L. L. THURSTONE (1887–1955) : The great American pioneer of factorial methods, Thurstone is also known as the first to bridge the gap between psychophysics and psychometrics. In addition to developing the centroid method of factor analysis, he suggested the concept of simple structure, a procedure used in rotating factors to obtain a maximum amount of zero loadings between factors; thus describing each test with as few factors as possible. In 1920, Thurstone and others developed the *Multiple-Factor* theory which was in contrast to Spearman's *Two-Factor* theory which will be discussed later. Thurstone was of the opinion that a number of group factors existed within tests, the amount varying between different tests. That is, a verbal factor may be found within several if not all of the subtests of a particular instrument. Tests loading on this factor are assumed to be measuring this verbal factor; those not loading or having little loading are assumed to be measuring other factors.

Although substantial disagreement developed around these factorial issues, many of the issues have been resolved today. Thurstone's purpose was to describe complex performances as being derived from simpler performances. To do this he was of the opinion that test scores could be broken down into more simple, fundamental component parts. This was accomplished by developing tests that were relatively pure in their loadings, that is having a high loading in just one factor. Out of this effort came a most extensive factorial investigation of human abilities. Thurstone and his associates studied both adults and children to develop what they called *primary mental abilities*. These factors which have been commonly referred to by Thurstone and others are as follows:

NUMBER FACTOR (N) : This is primarily a factor of speed and accuracy in numerical calculations such as addition or multiplication.

VERBAL COMPREHENSION FACTOR (V) : Here we find a factor that is heavily loaded in vocabulary, as well as reading comprehension, verbal analogies and reasoning, disarranged sentences, and matching proverbs for similar meaning.

SPACE FACTOR (S) : This involves tasks in which the subject manipulates an object imaginarily in space.

WORD FLUENCY FACTOR (W) : Here the subject is asked to think of isolated words at a rapid rate, usually in tests involving anagrams, rhyming, giving words beginning with a certain letter, etc.

REASONING FACTOR (R) : This factor involves tasks requiring the subject to discover a rule or principle from a series or groups of letters. Both inductive and deductive reasoning are involved, although it appears that induction is the stronger.

PERCEPTUAL SPEED FACTORS (P) : Tests measuring this factor require quick and accurate grouping of visual details or the rapid recognition of similarities and differences.

ASSOCIATIVE MEMORY FACTOR (M) : This factor involves tests of rote memory for paired associates.

Many other identified factors can be added to this list and inevitably other factors will be added for future test construction.

CHARLES SPEARMAN (1863–1945) : A British psychologist, should be mentioned here because of his contributions to statistics, particularly the measurement of intelligence, his contributions to factorial analysis, and his famous two-factor theory of intelligence. In this theory, he states that in human capacities it is possible to distinguish one general factor *g*, which he identifies with intelligence, and several independent specific factors *s*, he referred to as *special abilities*. This is, of course, conflicting with Thurstone's *multiple-factor* theory which became a topic of heated discussion for decades.

Spearman is well known for the technique he developed and called the *tetrad* equation. This method analyzes tests in sets of four, hence the name *tetrad*. Intercorrelations among sets of four tests yield three tetrad equations as follows:

$$t_{1234} = r_{12}r_{34} - r_{13}r_{24}$$
$$t_{1243} = r_{12}r_{34} - r_{14}r_{23}$$
$$t_{1342} = r_{13}r_{24} - r_{14}r_{23}$$

With these equations he demonstrated that when all three tetrads are equal to zero within their sampling areas, the intercorrelations among the four tests can be attributed to a single common factor. After conducting many studies applying the tetrad criteria he concluded that the intercorrelations among all tests of ability could be explained in terms of a single common factor which he designated *general factor*. This two-factor theory depends upon two classes of factors to explain performance on any test, the general factor *g*, and many specific factors *s*. Tests heavily loaded with specific factors will yield low intercorrelations, those highly saturated with general factors will yield high intercorrelations.

Contemporary Model Builders

On the contemporary scene investigators have attempted to develop new tests that evolve from theoretical models. Examples of this are the efforts of Kirk and McCarthy who have taken Osgood's psycholinguistic model, developed from Hull's theory of learning, to develop a test which attempts to diagnose psycholinguistic problems in children. Although this test was originally designed for working with mentally retarded children, it is a test that is believed to have considerable potential for working with aphasic children as well as children with cerebral palsy. (This will be discussed in further detail in the text.)

Another model builder is Guilford who has developed a *structure-of-intellect* model from his factorial studies to determine

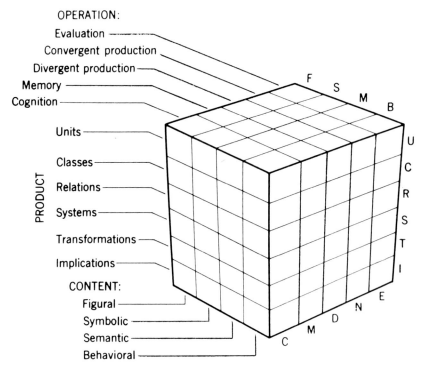

Figure I.1. Guilford's structure-of-intellect model. (Guilford, 1967; reproduced with permission.) From *The Nature of Human Intelligence* by Guilford, 1967, McGraw-Hill, Inc.

the factorial content of a wide range of ability tests. Like Thurstone, he has followed the *multiple-factor* theory, proposing a large number of primary factors which make up a scheme to simultaneously incorporate all the known primary factors of cognitive behavior, as well as establish a framework to explain existing factors that are as yet undiscovered.

His model is a three dimensional rectangular block as shown in Figure I.1. Guilford's model is organized into three schemes of classification with each of the many primary factors of human intelligence being represented by a *cell* in the model. Each cell contains a blend of three variables: *content, products,* and *operations.* Each variable is further broken down, as one can see from the model. Content of materials represents classes of stimuli or general information; operations represents major kinds of intellectual activities or processes used by individuals to handle raw stimuli. Products are in turn achieved as the result of processing the stimuli; thus, within each cell we have content, product, and operational variables.

Classification of Tests

Tests may be classified in many ways. The following discussion will cover methods for classifying tests using such categorical areas as administrative procedures used to give the test, medium or materials used in giving the test, what is measured by the test, as well as kinds of items used in the test construction.

GROUP AND INDIVIDUAL TESTS: Administrative tests can be classified into *group tests* which implies that the test may be given to many individuals at one time. The only limitation to the number is the communication problem as well as monitoring the test. In contrast there are *individual tests* which are only given to one person at a time. Historically, through Binet's influence, individual testing was given a strong position in the field of psychometrics. Around the year of 1916 a most significant occurrence in this field took place with the development of group tests. It became apparent to school and military personnel that individual tests were too time consuming and expensive to give individually when large numbers of individuals were involved in the classification and diagnostic process. This was particularly true because of the pressures created during World War I when large numbers of men were coming into military service. At this time the government agreed that it would be desirable to examine newly drafted men to evaluate their general mental capacity and fitness for service using the best available methods and techniques. It was obvious that group testing was the answer to this problem, so from this effort the well known Army Alpha and Beta tests were developed; the former being verbal in content and the latter non-verbal. It was from this early development that many group tests appeared on the scene, tests for measuring achievement, intelligence, or the readiness of children to learn.

Today there are large numbers of group tests designed for use at the kindergarten level all the way through the university. One of the problems, as far as exceptional children are concerned, has been the fact that nearly all of these have been developed and standardized for use in working with normal individuals rather than exceptional individuals. This point will be discussed in further detail later in the text. Group tests can be highly reliable and have good validity if used with the right group of individuals, and if considerable care is given to the administration and interpretation of the test results.

As mentioned above, tests may be grouped by the medium used and by the materials consumed. We have some tests that are referred to as *paper and pencil tests* which implies, of course, that these tests involve the use of paper and pencils. There are *television tests* which can be administered through television sets after the test has been recorded on video tape, as well as other simple types of classifications including the scoring procedure used, for example *true-false tests,* or *multiple choice tests.*

SPEED VERSUS POWER TESTS: One classification that is not as common as those above is *power and speed tests.* Power tests are usually designed with easier items being placed in the beginning of the test, and more difficult items toward the end, with the level of difficulty increasing gradually from the beginning to the end of the test. Theoretically, a test of this type that is well designed for the group it is being used with, will have items that are easy enough for all participants to pass as well as having sufficient power to challenge all members of the group including the most capable. The time requirement for power tests is more for convenience than necessity; that is, the score an individual receives is dependent upon his knowledge of the subject rather than the amount of time allowed to finish the test. Stated another way, the element of time should not change his score, unless of course, he has too little time to react to each item, or sufficient time has not passed for the subject to change (acquire new knowledge).

In contrast, the pure speed test contains items that are of uniform level of difficulty throughout the test, usually quite easy. Given sufficient time, all items would normally be successfully completed. Here time is the variable that determines the score the individual receives. An example of a speed test can be seen

(Here the student is requested to place an x in each circle within a specified period of time. Obviously the student would receive the same score on the odd and even items if separated into two tests.)

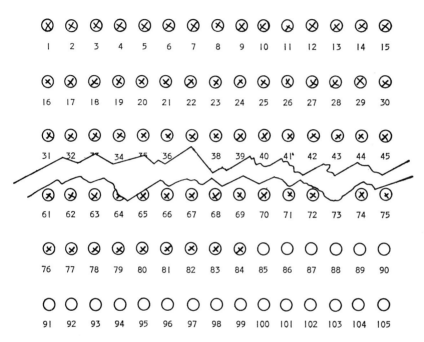

Figure I.2. A demonstration of the split-half type of reliability on a speed test.

in Figure I.2, where the individual is required to place an X in each circle. One can see that if two minutes are provided to place as many X's as possible in these circles, time alone will determine the final score.

Frequently, the variables of speed and power are found in combination in the same test. It is also true that for exceptional children, the test that is recognized as a speed test for normal children with adequate perceptual and neurological processes, may be for all practical purposes a power test for a cerebral palsied child who has neurological complications. Thus, the explanation of speed and power tests becomes complicated when working with exceptional children. This certainly becomes an area for needed research and future test development.

PERFORMANCE TESTS: Psychologists and educators soon recognized the need for an instrument that was not heavily loaded with verbal material to evaluate some of the learning problems of children and adults. Consequently, we find the *performance test* developing to meet this need and to provide a way of examining individuals with language handicaps as well as the deaf and the blind. Normally, performance tests provide perceptual tasks in which the individual is required to manipulate items such as blocks, beads, pictures, etc. Performance tests may involve the actual object which may be handled and manipulated, or the test may use a more abstract method through use of pictures, diagrams, and illustrations. Both types of tests are currently on the scene and used extensively. Examples of these are the performance scale of the Wechsler tests, the Grace-Arthur, and the Pintner-Paterson tests. Some tests, such as the Grace-Arthur and the Pintner-Paterson, are entirely performance tests, whereas, the Wechsler scales have been developed into basically two tests, one a performance test and another the verbal test.

VERBAL TESTS: As the term implies these instruments contain subtests that require the individual to either do a great deal of speaking, reading, or writing. Specific items on a verbal test would require that an individual define words, interpret meanings, answer questions to short stories, or follow verbal instructions.

APTITUDE TESTS: Another instrument that is frequently used in assessing an individual's capacity for learning or performance is the aptitude test. These instruments, unlike the general ability instrument, are intended to measure an individual's ability to perform a specific task. Examples of this are tests of mechanical aptitude or clerical aptitude, musical aptitude, language aptitude, etc. The need to have instruments of this type evolved from the Army's need to select individuals who would be able to carry out a specific task with a minimum amount of investment, as far as training is concerned and with a maximum amount of production on the part of the individual. Employment offices use aptitude tests a great deal to determine the right person for a specific kind of job. Vocational rehabilitation has relied on the use of aptitude tests in working with handicapped individuals to determine their vocational potential. Extensive use of aptitude tests has been made by school counselors to program children into courses most suited to their abilities.

The term aptitude tests has been applied to intelligence tests, for intelligence tests evaluate one's aptitude for learning. For example, aptitude tests can be given to determine the ability an individual may have for acquiring a foreign language, or for profiting from a precollege sequence of courses, or an advanced course in mathematics.

OCCUPATIONAL INTEREST INVENTORIES: These are sometimes referred to as interest tests and are used in a supplementary way along with aptitude tests and intelligence tests to assess an individual's interest in entering into a particular occupational area. Normally these scales are made up of a series of preference statements to which the subject is asked to react. His reactions to these statements are compared to individuals within specific vocational areas. If he develops a similar pattern to that of lawyers, for example, the assumption is made that he has an interest in the area of law.

ACHIEVEMENT TESTS: Because of the extensive use of achievement tests, they have been frequently referred to as a type of test having their own specific category. These tests are not tests for diagnosing learning problems, nor are they particularly involved in making predictions. Instead, they are intended to sample one's actual knowledge of a given subject at a specific period of time in his instruction. They have been valuable in evaluating school programs, for example, determining the adequacy of curriculum, evaluating the effectiveness of teaching, as well as planning the progress of an individual child.

PERSONALITY TESTS: As the term implies, personality tests have been used to evaluate an individual's personality, using the term in an analytical sense. Generally, these instruments are developed to expose *deeper* personality traits and, if possible, to assist in differentiating among various kinds of psychosis, neurosis, etc. These instruments usually contain word association tests or reactions to statements as well as reactions to pictures and abstract designs.

A large number of personality tests are now available in varying quality from those being very poorly conceived to those being well designed with adequate validating research. Individuals working with tests in this area need to take a close look at the supporting research.

RATING SCALES: Rating scales are not considered tests by some individuals in that the person being evaluated does not interreact with the scale, but rather is rated by a person who is reasonably familiar with his performance or behavior. Rating scales were first tried out and used during World War I before they were formalized and refined by statistical methods and psychological analysis to develop scales relevant to specific situations. Rating scales have been used extensively in working with retarded children and to some extent with blind children. Some of these instruments, however, are out of date and in some instances inappropriate for many situations. Some concern needs to be given to developing better scales in this area.

One type of rating scale that is sometimes given specific recognition in textbooks of this type is the self-rating inventory that can be used by an individual to rank himself as he perceives his standing in a particular profession or job. Sometimes these inventories are used as personality tests to screen out individuals with questionable personalities or behavioral symptoms indicative of maladjustment. Sometimes these instruments are used in place of personal interviews or are used to supplement the personal interview approach to selecting individuals for particular vocational or military occupations.

PROJECTIVE TESTS: In the early 1930's another type of instrument appeared on the scene becoming prominent particularly among American psychologists. The projective test of personality is a much more subtle type of instrument usually involving a person-to-person relationship with a psychologist who is highly trained in the interpretation of the instrument. The test usually provides a greater flexibility as far as response is concerned, requiring a great deal of skill on the part of the person administering the instrument to interpret the wide range of unstructured responses.

The Rorschach inkblot test published in Switzerland in 1921, is probably the best known of the instruments in this area, although it was not introduced into the United States until the early 1930's. Rorschach was a Swiss psychiatrist who began his experimentation with ink blots as a means of stimulating and evaluating imagination. Another popular form of this test is the Thematic Appreciation Test (TAT) introduced and developed by H. A. Muray and C. D. Morgan in 1935. This test contains three pictures, each on a separate card and one blank card. The person or child being examined is asked to make up a story about the picture giving his reactions and interpretations to what is taking place.

Although the Rorschach and the TAT, as it is frequently referred to, are the most common or well-known types of projective techniques, many others have been introduced into the field of testing in recent years. Many of these tests have considerable value in working with emotionally disturbed children and are of interest in this text. They will be discussed in more detail.

Tests of Typical versus Maximum Performance: Another classification of tests that users of these instruments should recognize when working with exceptional children is *tests of typical and maximum performance*. Tests of maximum performance are designed to measure the best performance a subject is capable of producing on a particular task or in a certain area. Tests of this type include intelligence tests, aptitude tests, and achievement tests. Usually tests of this type are designed to provide the most desirable environment possible to build motivation and interest, reduce distracting and competing stimuli, as well as other contributing factors to assist the subject in obtaining a maximum level of performance. For example, in working with exceptional children, it may be desirable to arrange for a temporary reduction in the amount of drugs used to control seizures or behavior to get this level of maximum ability, or it may be necessary to amplify the auditory or visual stimulation the child receives to achieve this goal. A great deal more will be said about this in a later chapter.

The second classification involves tests measuring typical performance which involves the measurement of behavior the individual normally or habitually displays. These tests usually include interest tests, rating scales, as well as personality tests. Individuals using these instruments are at times hard pressed to state whether or not they are obtaining maximum or typical levels of behavior, depending upon what the test is designed to do. A testing situation is not one where individuals normally will give typical kinds of behavior for obvious reasons such as fear of the examiner; the consequences of the test often motivate or inhibit behavior making it difficult for the examiner to evaluate the performance he is getting. Obviously, a great deal of skill and training is required to make these kinds of assessments. Working with exceptional children or handicapped children makes it extremely difficult to evaluate typical or maximum behavior in that the norms for behavior are not as well defined; consequently, individuals working with these children are required to spend a great deal of time observing the type of handicapped behavior being evaluated to be able to assess whether he is getting typical or maximum behavior (Freeman, 1962).

DIAGNOSTIC VERSUS CLASSIFICATION TESTS: The differentiation between diagnostic and classification tests should be recognized by professional users of tests. In essence, classification tests are instruments that group individuals into classes or categories. A large majority of the instruments in use today are of this type. For instance, intelligence tests group by intelligence quotient; achievement tests group by grade level; interest tests group by professional interest, etc. The separation of classification from diagnosis in a practical sense is difficult because the treatment one receives is frequently determined by the label attached or the level one is assigned to; yet the act of classification is more apt to be limited to a grouping process having generic overtones, while the diagnostic instrument usually *takes the problem apart*, separating it into significant areas that are susceptible to remedial treatment. Diagnostic instruments do not confine their results to one definite question, but rather come up with multidimensional profiles.

State of the Art

Although the writer has not stressed unique problems within specific tests, it is readily apparent that there are many inadequacies in the tests currently on the market concerning their use or value in diagnosing and evaluating handicapped children. Many of the instruments currently being used by educators and psychologists are being adapted for evaluating exceptional children; thus, making a diagnosis, classification, or evaluation difficult in as much as these instruments were originally designed and standardized on normal children. Although the science of testing and evaluating children has come a long way from the time of Binet, and many promising new instruments are beginning to appear, we still have a long way to go in perfecting and developing diagnostic instruments for children demonstrating various types of aberrant growth patterns. Specific implications inherent in this comment will be expanded further in the following chapters.

REFERENCES

Anastasi, Anne: *Psychological Testing,* 3rd ed. New York, Macmillan Co., 1968.

Barclay, James R.: *Controversial Issues in Testing—Guidance Monograph Series III.* Boston, Houghton Mifflin Co., 1968.

Birch, H. G.: *Brain Damage in Children: The Biological and Social Aspects.* Baltimore, Williams & Wilkins, 1964.

DuBois, Philip H.: *A History of Psychological Testing.* Boston, Allyn and Bacon, Inc., 1970.

Freeman, Frank S.: *Theory and Practice of Psychological Testing,* 3rd ed. New York, Holt, Rinehart and Winston, 1962.

Kirk, Samuel A.; Johnson, G. Orville: *Educating The Retarded Child.* New York, Houghton Mifflin Co., 1951.

Misiak, Henryk; Sexton, V. S.: *History of Psychology.* New York, Greene and Stratton, 1966.

Newland, T. Ernest: *Psychological Assessment of Exceptional Children and Youth,* in W. M. Cruickshank (ed.), *Psychology of Exceptional Children and Youth.* Englewood Cliffs, N. J., Prentice Hall, 1963.

Robinson, Halbert B.; Robinson Nancy M.: *The Mentally Retarded Child.* New York, McGraw-Hill Book Co., 1965.

Thurstone, L. L.: *Multiple-Factor Analysis.* Chicago, University of Chicago Press, 1947.

Watson, Robert I.: *The Great Psychologists.* New York, J. B. Lippincott Co., 1963.

CHAPTER II

SCORING

MILTON V. WISLAND

Meaningful observations and measurement of behavior require a method of record keeping as well as objective interpretation to enable the examiner to describe with accuracy what was measured. To do this a numerical description is used to represent the frequency, degree, or amount of behavior a subject manifests during the period of observation. This expression of measurement is referred to as *scoring* which is described in this chapter.

Raw Score

A raw score usually represents the actual number of responses answered correctly by the individual in the examination. Alone, this score does not impart a great deal of information. Understandably, the raw score is dependent upon the number of items in a given test. For instance, one test may have 50 items, another 200 items, and another 25 items. If one were to report the raw scores only, they would be of little value until we know the following things: 1) who else took the test, 2) the high and low scores, and 3) the average level of performance. With this kind of information we can begin to evaluate the score of any one given individual. For example, if we know that an individual obtained a score of 25 on an arithmetic test, 90 on a reading test, and 35 on a spelling test, we still do not know how well this

26

person has performed on these given tests until we have the kind of information indicated above.

A raw score of 25 on an arithmetic test would be considered very good if it were the highest score obtained by any individual in the class, as well as indicating that the individual only missed two out of a total possible 27 points. If we look at the arithmetic score of 90, this could be rather poor if 75 per cent of the individuals in that class were above him and he had obtained only 90 correct items out of a possible 200. It readily becomes clear that if scores are to obtain some level of meaning we must have some basis for comparison which will express the relative significance of a given score or indicate what is known as its relative rank among the individuals taking this test or those who have taken it in the past. Recognizably, many other examples can be selected to illustrate the inadequacy of a raw score alone as well as demonstrating the need for a facilitating process for interpretation. Normally this is provided through tables giving normative data for raw scores. By normative data we mean either age equivalent or grade equivalent scores (Cronbach, 1960), showing the individual's ranking among individuals as previously mentioned by giving the percent of individuals above or percent of individuals below the person in question. Usually these scores are reported as percentile ranks, decile ranks, quartile scores, or as standard scores, depending upon the instrument's purpose as well as the use to be made of the information obtained from the test. These scores are also referred to as norm reference scores which will be discussed later.

Norms

Norms can be defined as raw scores expressed as transformed scores or as an average or typical score on a particular test made by a specified population. Transformations are empirically established by determining how well a representative group of individuals actually do on a test; for example, the average achievement test score in reading for a group of third grade children, or the average score of a group of fifth grade students on a test of arithmetic. A table of normative data enables us to compare an individual's performance with other children who have taken the same test. Thus, any individual's raw score is then compared with the distribution of scores obtained by the standardization sample to show where he falls in such a distribution. Normative scores also enable an examiner to compare an individual with other groups that have taken the same test.

In selecting a test for classifying or diagnosing an individual's problem, it is therefore necessary that the test be standardized on populations that are valuable for comparative purposes. The adequacy of these groups is not necessarily related to the size. Inexperienced users of tests and test data are frequently overly impressed with the size of the normative population upon which the norms have been established. It is true that the number of individuals is important. However, some populations involving one or two thousand students who have been carefully selected may be a great deal more desirable and useful than a population of 25,000 students who have not been appropriately selected or do not apply to the particular problem the diagnostician is working with. This is especially true when working with exceptional children, particularly if the diagnostician wishes to compare the performance or behavior of one child with others having similar problems, such as sensory, motor, or neurological. Further examples of normative data are found in Table II.1 where the scattering of score data for several groups can be easily seen. The total number of cases reported in each group can be seen in the bottom of the table along with the mean score and amount of variability (standard deviation) for each group. If an achievement test were given to a fifth grade class and the diagnostician wanted to compare a fifth grade child with other fifth grade children who had taken this test in the past, he would compare this child with the normative data supplied with this test. Thus, if one assumes that the child in question has a raw score of 45, the data in Table II.1 reveals that he is slightly below the average level of performance of the other fifth grade students who have taken this test. More specific and detailed comparisons are possible, but because of the complexity involved, this will be discussed in greater detail later in this chapter.

Table II.1. An Illustration of Norms Reported for Different Groups on an Achievement Test.

Grade Level

Scores	4th	5th	6th	7th	8th
175–179					1
170–174					1
165–169					2
160–164					1
155–159					4
150–154				1	6
145–149			1	2	7
140–144			2	1	7
135–139			1	1	8
130–134			2	5	7
125–129		1	3	4	9
120–124		1	4	6	12
115–119		2	6	7	10
110–114		4	7	10	26
105–109		3	7	9	25
100–104		4	9	11	26
95–99		6	10	14	26
90–94	1	8	9	21	27
85–89	2	9	10	22	30
80–84	1	7	11	27	32
75–79	4	13	27	29	33
70–74	6	14	29	28	31
65–69	7	17	30	30	27
60–64	11	20	31	32	22
55–59	9	22	32	31	21
50–54	14	27	36	27	19
45–49	17	29	27	22	17
40–44	21	31	21	17	12
35–39	27	32	19	12	7
30–34	32	27	14	9	9
25–29	36	19	9	4	4
20–24	33	12	7	1	2
15–19	19	3		2	1
10–14	12	1		1	
5–9	3	2			
0–4	1				
N =	256	314	364	386	472
Mean =	36.6	54.0	65.7	72.9	86.5
SD =	17.3	23.1	24.9	25.4	30.3

The characteristics of a set of norms are dependent upon the number of factors controlled in the standardizing process used to develop the normative data. Comparisons that can be made are dependent upon the population used in establishing a set of norms, the proportion of boys and girls, geographical and socio-economic status of the families of the children, as well as the age distribution of the sample. If the purpose in testing is to compare an individual with his peer group to determine if he is making normal progress, then ideally the norms should be derived from a population having the same characteristics as the group or individual being examined. In that this is possible in theory only, the next best thing is to use norms derived from a population possessing similar characteristics. Unfortunately economic pressure has forced most test designers and publishers to create tests having the largest market, which accounts for the large number of tests on the market with norms on normal children instead of children with aberrant developmental patterns.

Diversification within norms appears to be very advantageous because it provides examiners with more latitude in their diagnostic appraisals of exceptional children; for instance, norms used in the fifth grade achievement test may be divided into three ability groups with the low groups having IQ scores from 60 to 90, the median group 91 to 110, and the high IQ group from 110 on up. With this kind of normative data, a school system using a multitrack system can compare the achievement of the superior students with their peer groups or retarded students with their peers, etc. The advantage of such a system can be demonstrated with superior children where it is not uncommon to find students who will perform on an average level in academic achievement when compared with children in general, but below average when compared with their peer group. To state that such a student is making normal progress may be entirely misleading when in fact he is performing considerably below his potential. It is also possible that a school district with superior students may want to compare their students with other districts having comparable populations. These few examples readily illustrate the need for diversification within norms supplied with standardized tests.

Ideally the desired population should be defined in advance of the test construction in terms of the objectives of the test. Not only do exceptional children require unique norms for comparative purposes, but frequently require unique items and overall test design as well. In working with exceptional children it is imperative that we have these instruments to form meaningful diagnoses for blind children, deaf children, as well as neurologically impaired, mentally retarded, socially and culturally deprived, and others. Because of a continued lack of tests in this area, it appears to be most essential that individuals doing extensive diagnostic and evaluation work attempt to develop their own norms for tests and instruments with which they are currently working. This requires extensive long term planning and is hampered by the frequent turnover of personnel working in a specific job or location. Extensive records in some instances may require the coordinated efforts of several clinics or teams working together in various parts of the country.

Another point which should be emphasized is that tables of norms derived for tests classified under the same name and intended for the same purposes are not necessarily comparable. Before an examiner decides upon the particular test he intends to use, it is always necessary to know the characteristics and composition used to standardize the test. It is essential that a diagnostician have this kind of information to determine the appropriateness of the test. In selecting normative supporting data for a test it is important that the norms include not only single values or scores but the average of the distribution as well as the range of values, including such statistics as the variance or standard deviation of the group involved.

It also seems to be imperative at this point that we discuss the difference between norms and standards. As previously mentioned, norms enable an examiner or diagnostician to compare an individual taking a test with the performance of other individuals who have taken this test in the past. The standards, on the other hand, are the desired goals or objective that an individual or group may be working toward which may or may not be the same as the average level of performance of individuals who have taken the test. Obviously, a diagnosis would involve norms as well as standards for a particular individual. In other words, it is imperative that we know not only where the individual ranks in comparison with other individuals who have taken this test, but it is also important that we determine the standard or the potential for development that this particular individual may have, should have, or will have.

Age Scores

Many tests used with handicapped children transform raw scores into age scores (or grade scores which are very similar). Grade scores are usually converted to age scores by simply adding five to the grade scores. For example, an individual who is doing first grade work in reading would have an age equivalent in reading of six years, which is the normal age of first graders. Examples of age scores are social age, mental age, and developmental age. Most achievement test scores are reported in terms of grade age but intelligence test scores and developmental scales frequently report the score in terms of the particular developmental task being evaluated. Thus, if linguistic skills are being measured they may be reported in terms of a linguistic age, or if social skills are being evaluated the scores may be reported in terms of social age.

In actual practice age equivalent scores are usually determined by counting the number of correct items to obtain the raw scores. The raw score is then converted to an age equivalent score by the use of a conversion table. The computation of the raw score may be determined in one of two ways. One is to simply count all the correct items and the other method is to first determine the *basal age.* This is usually defined in power tests as the highest item below which all tests are passed. The basal age is normally found on developmental scales where the items are presented in increasing level of difficulty, the easiest item being associated with early development and more difficult items associated with more advanced development. Frequently the individual test items are grouped together within specific age levels with individual items being given credit for so many months of development. Following the basal age a certain number of test items will fall within an area called the *scatter*. The scatter range is from the basal age where the individual passes all of the items up to that level or point where he fails all of the items, again assuming that the items are given in order of increasing level of difficulty. Stated another way, the scatter is that part of the individual's test scale where he begins to miss items, up to a point where he can no longer pass any of the items, which is called the *ceiling*. To determine an individual's total raw score, the number of correct items in the scatter area of the test are added to the basal score instead of counting all of the items. This reduces the amount of time required for counting the total number of raw scores. The scatter area is also considered to be of some diagnostic value by a few investigators in the field, although the research support for this idea is weak.

Ratio Scores

In order to provide a score which, unlike mental age or age scores, permits a uniform interpretation regardless of the age of the subject, the intelligence quotient (IQ) was introduced. The need for such a ratio measure was originally indicated by Stern and Kuhlman; however, the IQ was first employed in the 1916 form of the Stanford-Binet. This IQ is frequently referred to as the *ratio IQ* and is actually a ratio of the mental age to the chronological age. The fraction is then multiplied by 100 to avoid the use of decimals. This formula:

$$IQ = \frac{MA}{CA} \times 100 \qquad\qquad 2.1$$

may still be used to convert an individual's IQ into a mental age even though a deviation IQ has been used instead of the ratio IQ.

Formula 2.1 can be used to find the mental age by using the following arrangement:

$$MA = \frac{IQ}{100} \times CA \qquad\qquad 2.2$$

For example, if a child's chronological age is 12 years six month, and his IQ is 75, substituting in Formula 2.2 we would have:

$$MA = \frac{75}{100} \times 150 = 112.5$$

After converting 12 years and six months to a total of 150 months and then multiplying this figure by .75 we have a mental age of 112.5 months or nine years, four and a half months.

Although the IQ in theory is comparable at different ages, complications develop with advanced age in that the mental age unit shrinks in direct portion with age. This condition must be provided for if the IQ is to be consistent for the more advanced ages of the individual. The ratio IQ assumes a linear relationship between mental development and chronological age for an indefinite period. Research has for some time shown that this is not true; consequently, the ratio IQ is not a realistic IQ for older individuals. Mental growth does not continue to develop at the same rate throughout the life span of the individual. Like physical growth there is a natural tapering off starting around the age of 13 or 14 with a gradual reduction in rate of development into the early twenties. At this point mental development appears to be to some extent dependent upon the individual's intellectual activity. Those who push themselves intellectually will show a gradual but much slower increase in mental age, particularly in vocabulary skills, until senility occurs and there is a decline in mental capacity.

Two other quotients should be mentioned at this time, one of which is an *educational quotient*. This quotient indicates the ratio of educational achievement to chronological age. The simple formula is:

$$EQ = \frac{EA}{CA} \times 100 \qquad\qquad 2.3$$

where EA stands for educational age, which is equivalent to grade age plus five years. A child who is reading on a second grade level will have an educational age equivalent of seven years in reading. In that there is no fixed or uniform list of school subjects for which educational ages have been computed, they are not necessarily comparable. Another problem is that standardization processes used for determining achievement age are not always comparable. An educational quotient indicates whether or not a pupil's knowledge of a group of school subjects is commensurate with his chronological age. It determines whether or not he is performing at a level expected for an individual of this particular age.

Another quotient frequently used in working with children is the *achievement quotient*. The formula for this is:

$$AQ = \frac{EA}{MA} \times 100 \qquad 2.4$$

Although this ratio is now very rarely encountered, it does appear from time to time in the literature and is included in this text in that it has had a place in the history of testing; therefore, the student should have some familiarity with it. In this formula the mental age is used as a valid index of the pupil's learning capacity and the educational age is used as an index of the student's current level of achievement. Dividing the educational age by the mental age yields the quotient indicating whether or not the individual is working up to his mental capacity as determined by the intelligence test that was given to determine the mental age.

There are serious defects in this ratio which virtually accounts for its abandonment after being initially introduced in 1920 by Franzen. One problem with this index is that all individual students do not obtain a level of educational achievement equal to their mental age in that some children are found to be working below their capacity to learn. For example, we do not find that all children with mental ages of seven are reading even though the achievement age or educational age accompanying a mental age of seven would indicate that the individual should be reading, or is reading. To get an AQ of 100 an individual with a mental age of seven would have to have an educational achievement age of seven which would indicate that the individual was reading. Under achievement is found in superior children as well as in mentally retarded children. Another defect in the AQ is that the population norms upon which the achievement tests have been standardized are not always comparable with the norms of the intelligence tests; consequently, they are not comparable groups. A third defect is the fact that many achievement tests do not differentiate as well as general intelligence tests; that is, the standard error of measurement is generally greater in achievement tests than in intelligence tests. A fourth problem found in working with exceptional children is that adequate norms are not always available for making desirable comparisons on academic achievement. The picture is further complicated in that children of similar mental ages do not necessarily have comparable intellectual development. If one examines the items that retarded individuals pass and fail with those of superior individuals, we find that retarded children consistently pass and fail different kinds of items implying that there are differences in their cognitive abilities even though they may have the same mental ages.

All of these variables must be considered when working with the type of indexes indicated above. In spite of the above criticism, the EQ and AQ have some association value in diagnosing an individual's school achievement; however, additional supplemental information should accompany such an index.

Percentile Scores

A very common way of describing people, finances, and even politics is to state the proportion of other individuals a given person exceeds in the characteristic being measured, as well as the proportion of individuals making a certain income. Another example we frequently find in newspapers and magazines is an expression stating that a person described therein exceeds 70 percent of the population of the United States in his income, or we state that 40 percent of the people are at this time in favor of the democratic party. The above examples illustrate the kinds of exposure that people in general are experiencing in their everyday lives. Statements of percentages of persons exceeded then is a familiar means of quantitative description and are immediately meaningful to parents and the lay public alike.

The percentile rank of a score is the percentage of persons in the same group with those who earn lower scores. Therefore, if an individual earns a raw score of 32 on a given test and his score is higher than the scores earned by 75 percent of the persons in the normative group it is said that his percentile rank is 75. It is important that the reader recognize that percentile ranks are expressed as percentage figures. In contrast, percentiles are expressed as score values. To illustrate the example given above, one may say that the 75th percentile is 32. The value 32 is a score value. One may also say that the percentile rank of 32 is 75. Here the number 75 is a percentage figure.

The computation of percentiles can be accomplished from either grouped or ungrouped data. An example of ungrouped test scores can be seen in Table II.2. Here the reader will note that the scores must be arranged in ascending or descending order; however, the procedure shown in the table is preferred in that we are always trying to find the percent of individuals below a given point or rank in the distribution.

We will first consider the computation for percentile scores in ungrouped data. Initially the reader must assume that this is continuous data with score values being reported to the nearest whole number. The assumption is that the score could be reported to the nearest tenth, but for simplicity's sake or other reasons the score is rounded to the nearest whole number; consequently, it is imperative that we define the exact limits of any given score as being 0.5 above and below the score in question. For example, the score of 85 has the integral limits of 84.5 and 85.5. This is the same procedure we use in working with group data which has been grouped into specific class intervals. A more detailed description of class intervals will follow in the discussion of percentile computations of grouped data.

For illustration purposes let us calculate the tenth percentile point abbreviated as P_{10}, a point below which 10 percent of the individuals fall. As one can see from Table II.2 the total number of subjects tested is 60, that is N equals 60. Thus, 10 percent of 60 is 6. This sixth individual has a raw score of 80. The upper limit of this score value is 80.5 which is the point on the raw score scale below which 10 percent of the individuals fall. Thus, P_{10} equals 80.5.

Instances where the percentile point involves several individuals with the same raw score, a slightly different procedure is used to determine the percentile point. To illustrate this we will calculate P_{50}. Fifty percent of 60 equals 30; consequently, a score value is required below which 30 individuals fall. It will be noted that four individuals have the score value of 103 so it is necessary that we establish a point value within the range of these scores as the percentile point we are seeking. Again, the theoretical range of this score value is from 102.5 to 103.5. It is necessary that we establish this percentile point one fourth of the distance between these two values; thus, the distance is 103.5 minus 102.5 equals 1.0. One fourth of this distance is 0.25, which is then added to the lower limit of the raw score containing the percentile point so P_{50} is equal to 102.5 plus 0.25 which equals 102.75.

The computation of percentile scores in grouped data involves the following formula:

$$P_p = L + \frac{(pn - cf)}{fi} h \qquad\qquad 2.5$$

where:

P_p = any percentile point

p = portion corresponding to the i percentile point (thus, if p equals 90, p equals 0.90)

L = exact lower limit of the interval containing P_p

n = total number of children involved

cf = cumulative frequency of all scores below L

fi = frequency of interval containing P_p

h = class interval.

Table II.2. Computation of Percentiles and Percentile Ranks

From Ungrouped Data

Individual	Score	Individual	Score
1.	75	31.	103
2.	76	32.	103
3.	78	33.	103
4.	78	34.	105
5.	78	35.	105
6.	80	36.	105
7.	81	37.	105
8.	82	38.	105
9.	84	39.	111
10.	85	40.	111
11.	87	41.	111
12.	87	42.	111
13.	87	43.	111
14.	90	44.	113
15.	91	45.	114
16.	91	46.	115
17.	92	47.	115
18.	93	48.	115
19.	93	49.	117
20.	94	50.	118
21.	97	51.	119
22.	97	52.	120
23.	97	53.	120
24.	97	54.	121
25.	99	55.	124
26.	101	56.	127
27.	102	57.	129
28.	102	58.	130
29.	102	59.	131
30.	103	60.	133

For example, let us calculate P_{90} again looking at Table II.3 showing grouped data. Here N equals 150, 90 percent of 150 equals 135. An examination of the cumulative frequency column in Table II.3 (Column 4) reveals that the 135th individual (counting from the bottom of the distribution up) has a raw score value of 28, which has an upper and lower theoretical interval limit of 27.5 to 28.5. Figure II.1 shows an expanded view of this score value illustrating the upper and lower score values with dash lines. The small x's represent the individuals having the same score value of 28. Column 3 of Table II.3 shows that 12 individuals have a score of 28; thus, we have 12 small x's representing these individuals

Table II.3. Computation of Percentiles and Percentile Ranks from Grouped Data

Grouped Raw Score (1)	Theoretical Interval Limits (2)	Frequency (3)	Cumulative Frequency (4)	Cumulative Percentage (5)
31	30.5–31.5	0		
30	29.5–30.5	1	150	100
29	28.5–29.5	5	149	99.3
28	27.5–28.5	12	144	96.0
27	26.5–27.5	15	132	88.0
26	25.5–26.5	22	117	78.0
25	24.5–25.5	30	95	63.3
24	23.5–24.5	24	65	43.3
23	22.5–23.5	16	41	27.3
22	21.5–22.5	13	25	16.7
21	20.5–21.5	4	12	8.0
20	19.5–20.5	5	8	5.3
19	18.5–19.5	2	3	2.0
18	17.5–18.5	1	1	0.7
17	16.5–17.5	0	0	0.0

N = 150

who are evenly distributed throughout the interval in a linear relationship to each other. Our task at this point is to determine where we are going to place our percentile point on the gray vertical line, (see Fig. II.1) between the lower and upper limits of this score value. Again, knowing that 132 individuals fall below the score value of 28 we see that (135 minus 132 equals 3) we are three cases away from the 135th individual we need to find the score value equal to P_{90}. The distance we then need to go into this interval is 3/12th of the total distance. In this example the class interval is one. If the interval had been five, the distance into the class would have been 3/12th of five. Converting this to a decimal figure we have 3 ÷ 12 = 0.25; adding 0.25 to the lower limit of 27.5 gives us the 90th percentile point of 27.75 (27.5 + 0.25). Substituting the same information into the above formula we get:

$$P_{90} = 27.5 + \frac{135 - 132}{12} \times 1 = 27.75$$

The main difference between the computation of percentile points in grouped and ungrouped data is the use of the cumula-

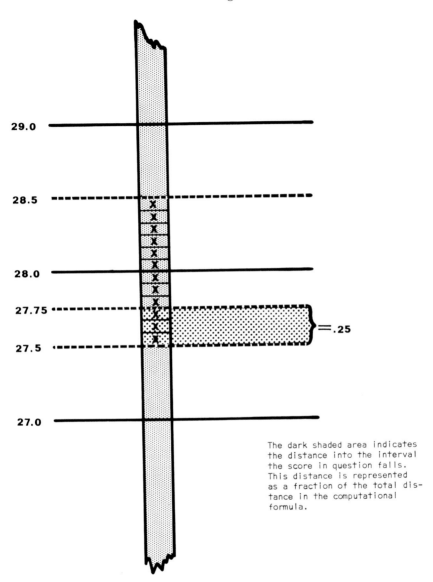

Figure II.1. An expanded view of the interval 28 showing an even hypothetical distribution of the raw scores (X's in the shaded area) from the lower to upper interval limits.

tive frequency column in grouped data. Instead of numbering each individual as we do in ungrouped data, we add the frequencies of each class interval together starting with the lowest class and accumulating the totals as we move up the scale. Thus, we add the frequency of one for the score value 18 to the frequency of 2 for the score value 19, giving us a cumulative total of 3. This process is repeated for each class interval. If we have added these frequencies together correctly, the top value should equal N, the total number of individuals in the group.

The calculation of percentile ranks can be considered as the reverse of the computation of percentile points. Again, following the same procedure we used for calculating percentile points, we will determine the computation of percentile ranks first for ungrouped and then grouped data. For an example of computing percentile ranks in ungrouped data, let us take the raw score value of 127 in Table II.2. This individual is 56th in rank order from the bottom of the distribution. The number of individuals scoring below 127 is 55. This position can be expressed as a percentage by dividing 55 by N which give us $55 \div 60 \times 100 = 91.67$ percent of the individuals falling below this point. The number scoring above 127 is 4 which represents 6.67 percent of the total population ($\frac{4}{60} \times 100 = 6.67$ percent) . It is obvious that these two percentage figures do not add to 100 $(91.67 + 6.67 = 98.34)$. The reason for this is that individual 56 occupies 1/60th of the total scale or 1.67 percent ($\frac{1}{60} \times 100 = 1.67$) . (This adds up to $98.34 + 1.67 = 100.01$, which is slightly over 100 because of a rounding off error.) This student's percentile rank falls between 91.67 and 93.34 $(91.67 + 1.67)$. Taking the midpoint of this interval as the required percentile rank, the percentile rank corresponding to score 127 then becomes

$$91.67 + \frac{1.67}{2} = 92.51.$$

This manipulation assumes that any percentile rank covers the interval between plus and minus 0.5 of the score in question.

Frequently, we have several individuals having the same score value. For example, if the reader examines Table II.2 he will find that we have four individuals with the raw score of 105. In this example we note there are thirty-three individuals below the raw score of 105, which represents 55 percent of the total number of students taking this test. The number of individuals scoring above 105 is 22, which equal 22/60 or 37 percent of the total number of students. There are five individuals with a raw score of 105, which represents 5/60 or 8.33 percent of the group. The percentile rank then may be taken as the midpoint of the interval containing the raw score of 105 as being equal to $\dfrac{8.33 + 55}{2} = 59.17$

Percentile rank also may be found by using the following with ungrouped data:

$$PR = \frac{100 \times R - 0.5}{N} \qquad 2.6$$

where:

R = the rank of the individual counting from the bottom up

N = the total number of individuals being tested.

In examples like the one above where more than one individual obtains the same raw score, an average is computed for the number of individuals of the same score. An example of this can be seen again with the raw score of 105. Using an average rank order of 36 for the five scores, we have the following substitution in formula 2.6:

$$PR = \frac{100 \times 36 - 0.5}{60} = 59.17\%$$

In that percentile ranks ordinarily are rounded to the nearest whole number, the percentile rank of 59.17 becomes 59.

Calculating percentile ranks in group scores is very similar to the procedure described above, with the exception of a cumulative percentage column that is usually compiled from grouped figures. Table II.3, Column 5 shows a cumulative percentage column. The corresponding cumulative percentage associated with a given class interval represents the percentile rank of the upper limit of the class interval with which it is associated. For example, the value 88 in column 5 represents the percentile rank of a raw score of 27.5, which is the theoretical upper limit of the class interval 26.5 to 27.5 for the raw score 27. Converting the raw score between the lower and upper interval limits of a given class to a percentile rank can be done in either one or two ways. One is to work with the cumulative percentage column or the cumulative frequency column. Since the procedure involving the cumulative frequency column is used more frequently, this will be described in detail at this time. For example, to determine the percentile rank of a raw score of 27, we subtract the lower limit of this class interval which is 26.5 from 27, obtaining a difference of 0.5. Our next task is to take 0.5 of the interval size, which will represent the distance the score in question is from the lower limit of the interval. In this case the class interval is one; consequently, our score lies 0.5 of the distance between, or half way between, 26.5 and 27.5. The frequency for this class interval is 15. Again, assuming that the scores are evenly distributed throughout this interval, we take half of this frequency (which would be 7.5) ; adding this to the cumulative frequency just below this raw score of 26.5 we have 117 + 7.5 which equals 124.5. When 124.5 is divided by 150 and multiplied by 100, we have the percentile rank of the raw score of 27 which equals 83 percent. The following formula can be used to make these computations:

$$PR = 100 \times \frac{fc + \left(\dfrac{RS - L}{i}\right)fw}{N} \qquad 2.7$$

where:

fc = cumulative frequency up to but not including the interval containing the raw score

L = lower limit of the interval containing the raw score

RS = frequency within the interval containing the raw score

i = interval size

fw = raw score

N = total number of subjects taking the test.

This procedure is essentially the same as the first, with the exception that one is working with proportions of percentages instead of frequencies. Several variations of the percentile score are frequently used. Probably the most common is the *quartile,* which is abbreviated as Q_1 for the first quartile (twenty-fifth percentile), Q_2 the second (fiftieth percentile), and Q_3 the third quartile (seventy-fifth percentile). Percentiles are abbreviated as P_{10}, P_{23}, P_{46}, etc. for the tenth, twenty-third, and forty-sixth percentile. *Deciles* are used occasionally to designate percentiles in tenths; such as, D_1, D_2, D_3, represent the tenth, twentieth, and thirtieth percentiles. Thus, through various abbreviations, the fiftieth percentile may be represented the following ways:

P_{50}, Q_2, Md. (Median), and D_5.

Standard Scores

Although the meaning of standard scores is generally less obvious than that of percentile ranks, at least as far as the lay public is concerned, standard scores probably have more importance in the field of psychometrics and in the areas of research than percentile scores.

Standard scores indicate in terms of standard deviations how far a particular individual is removed from the mean of the distribution. The mean is taken as a zero point and standard scores are given as plus or minus. As mentioned earlier, percentile scores are rank positions and do not represent equal units of individual differences. It is possible, however, to have scales that provide units approximating equal size as well as comparability of means, dispersion, and form of distribution.

Standard scores may be obtained by using either a linear or a nonlinear transformation of the original raw score data. Normally, a linear transformation is made enabling the examiner or test developer to retain the exact numerical relationship of the original raw scores to the newly computed standard scores in that they are determined by subtracting a constant (the mean) from each raw score and then dividing the result by another constant (the standard deviation). The distances between standard scores derived by this type of a linear transformation corresponds exactly to the distances between the raw scores.

The formula for finding the standard deviation involves the

computation of a mean which is subtracted from each score in the distribution. In that these distances are both positive and negative, the algebraic sum of these distances add to zero; consequently, the distance is squared. The sum of the squared distance is then obtained and divided by the number of individuals taking the test, and then the square root of the mean of these squares is determined to return the data to its original form. Before we take the square root of the formula we have the total variance; after taking the square root we have a standard deviation. The formula for making these computations is as follows:

$$SD = \sqrt{\frac{\Sigma(X - \overline{X})}{N}} \qquad 2.8$$

where:

SD = standard deviation
Σ = sum of
$\overline{X}$ = mean
X = raw score

Because formula 2.8 is time consuming in its computation, the following formula is used to save time for ungrouped data:

$$SD = \sqrt{\frac{\Sigma X^2 - \dfrac{(\Sigma X)^2}{N}}{N}} \qquad 2.9$$

and the following formula for grouped data:

$$SD = i \sqrt{\frac{\Sigma fd^2}{N} - \left(\frac{\Sigma fd^2}{N}\right)} \qquad 2.10$$

where:

i = interval size
d = distance of each class from the mean
f = frequency within each interval.

A slight variation of formula 2.10 is used when the mean is not known and an assumed mean is used.

Standard scores are derived from Z-scores which have the disadvantage of being both positive and negative as well as involving decimal points; consequently, they are frequently converted to other standard score values. The formula for computing Z-scores is as follows:

$$\text{Z-score} = \frac{X - \overline{X}}{SD} \qquad\qquad 2.11$$

where:

X = raw score

$\overline{X}$ = mean

SD = standard deviation.

The conversion of Z-scores described above to more workable score units has several advantages: 1) to eliminate the positive and negative scores; 2) to eliminate decimal points; 3) to work with score values or units of various sizes. For example, we can work with scores involving one, two, or three digits. The diagnostician or researcher may have various kinds of motivation for requiring different size score units. If the standard error of measurement is fairly large, it is rather presumptuous to use a scale that pretends to distinguish to one-tenth or one-hundredth of a standard deviation when the standard error of measurement is much larger than this. Another reason for varying the number of digits in the reported scores is that more digits require more work in recording as well as more space for storage, which can be important if, for example, one is limited in the number of columns one can use on an IBM card for computer analysis of test scores.

The T-score is probably the most well-known conversion of Z-scores from raw scores. The *T* stands for E. L. Thorndike who, as we mentioned, was an early leader in measurement. The symbol was originally applied by one of his students. The conversion of Z-scores to T-scores is a very simple process. In converting to T-scores, the standard deviation is converted to 10 units per standard deviation, which is simply done by multiplying any Z-score value by ten, which is then added to the mean, which is converted to a value of 50 regardless of the raw score value of the mean. Thus, to convert a Z-score of +1.0 to a T-score, one would simply multiply 1.0 times ten and add this to a mean value of 50, which

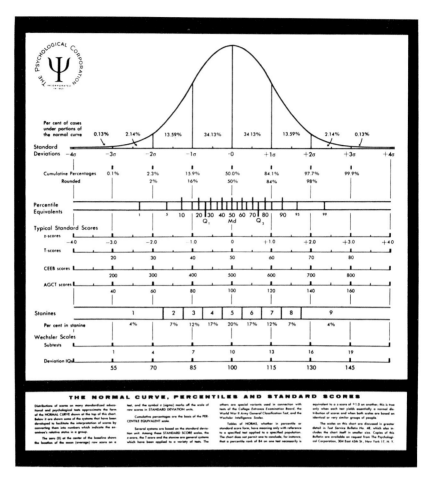

Figure II.2. A comparison of cumulative percentages and typical standard scores. (The Psychological Corporation Test Service Bulletin No. 48 reproduced with permission.)

would give a T-score of 60. Likewise, a Z-score value of -1.5 would convert to a T-score of 35 as follows:

$$50 + (10 \times -1.5) = 35$$

The formula for calculating a T-score is:

$$\text{T-score} = 50 + 10 \left(\frac{RS - M}{SD}\right) \qquad 2.12$$

As mentioned above, different kinds of standard scores are frequently used in tests. If the student will examine Figure II.2, he can readily see the comparisons of cumulative percentile scores and typical standard scores, including stanine scores. Stanine scores are found the same way T-score values are, with the exception that the raw score mean value here is made equivalent to 5 and the standard deviation value is 1.96. This computation formula then becomes:

$$\text{Stanine score} = 5 + 1.96 \left(\frac{X - \overline{X}}{SD} \right) \qquad 2.13$$

This particular scale was developed during World War II by the United States Army Air Force Aviation Psychological Program. The term *stanine* is a contraction of *standard nine*. One of the benefits derived from nine units rather than ten or more is that such scores occupy only one column on a computer punch and record system for research purposes. There is a slight grouping error involved with large intervals, as can be seen in Figure II.3,

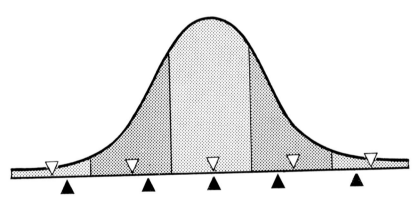

▲   Mean of class interval

△   Mid-point of class interval

Figure II.3. An illustration of grouping errors, showing the difference between the mean and midpoint of class intervals located at different locations in the distribution.

which illustrates the difference between the midpoint value of the class interval and the mean of that class interval. The student will note that the mean value has a tendency to be pulled toward the mean of the distribution. This is caused by the greater frequency of the scores within the class interval on that side of the interval facing the center of the entire distribution or the mean of the entire distribution. In that all of the individuals falling within the class interval are assumed to have a value of the midpoint of that interval, the difference between the midpoint and the mean of that interval represents the amount of error in that interval. The reader will also note that the interval that is equally distributed on both sides of the mean of the entire distribution has a midpoint and mean located at the same point within the class interval implying that there is no grouping error within this interval. Generally, we can state that the grouping errors tend to enlarge the estimate of the standard deviation. The coarser the grouping (that is the larger the interval), the greater the systematic error becomes. For research purposes it sometimes becomes necessary to apply a correction for the error involved using *Sheppard's* formula which was developed for this purpose. The formula for this correction is:

$$SDc = SD^2 - \frac{i}{12} \hspace{3cm} 2.14$$

where:

   SDc = corrected standard deviation
   SD = standard deviation
   i   = class interval

   Statisticians working with this kind of grouping error have found that for large samples twelve class intervals are required as a minimum for the accurate computation of a standard deviation. To summarize then, the use of Sheppard's correction depends upon three things: 1) the size of the sample, 2) the number of intervals to be used, and 3) the use we intend to make of the standard deviation.

   Another scale that has been recommended by J. P. Guilford is very similar to the stanine scale in that the range of scores is from 0 to 10 with a mean value equal to 5 and a standard deviation

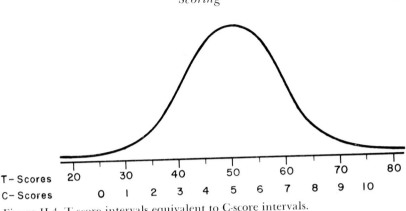

Figure II.4. T-score intervals equivalent to C-score intervals.

equal to 2.0. In this scale an interval of one unit on the C-scale corresponds to five units on the T-scale. Figure II.4 shows the T-score equivalent to C-score intervals. An evaluation of the C-scale reveals that it has many of the advantages of the T-scale in that it refers obtained scores to a common scale that is related to the normal distribution. Since it does not have the refinement or small units of the T-scale it comes closer to representing the accuracy and discrimination actually being made by educational and psychological instruments. For diagnostic purposes, the use of the C-scale has a serious fault in that it may imply that the individual obtained a zero score on the lower end of the scale when in fact this is not actually true. To avoid this problem Guilford recommends that the score range be extended from 1 to 11 instead of 0 through 10 (Guilford, 1965). An additional problem arises in the selection of students for special classes in that a greater degree of sensitivity is required at the extreme ends of the scale, particularly when working with gifted or trainable mentally retarded children. This same criticism applies to the T-scale even though its range is greater than the C-scale. It would be impossible to discriminate to any degree among these children without extending these scales at least one, or better yet, two standard deviations beyond their existing limits.

Normalizing Scores

All distributions resulting from the administration of an examination or test do not always result in a normal distribution of the particular attribute being examined. In fact, the curve of the distribution may vary all the way from leptokurtic to platykurtic as well as from negatively and positively skewed distributions. When scores on a test are skewed it is sometimes desirable to change the distribution to a normal, or at least change it so that it closely approaches the shape of a normal distribution. Transmitting raw scores to other values which are normally distributed may be done in four different ways involving techniques which have been developed for normalizing a given set of scores. These four techniques are: 1) Using a function of the raw scores such that the distribution becomes normal, such as a square, square root, logarithm, reciprocal, or some other function of the raw score values; 2) transmitting rankings into scale values in a normal distribution; 3) using areas corresponding to a base line interval of equal size; and 4) using area means corresponding to base line intervals of unequal size.

Some texts refer to techniques 3 and 4 above as area transformations. To demonstrate this procedure we will use the data in Table II.4 to transform raw scores in column 1 to normalized T-scores in column 7. The step-by-step procedure is as follows:

1. Establish an interval size that will provide between 10 and 20 classes. (column 1)
2. Indicate the upper real limits of each class. (column 2)
3. Determine the number of scores below each class. (column 4)
4. Divide each value in column 4 by N or 140 to find its percentile rank. (column 5)
5. Using a set of tables providing statistical values for normal curves, determine the normalized Z-scores associated with these percentile ranks. (column 6)
6. These values may be converted to T-scores by using the following formula $T = 10(Z) + 50$. If the table in step five above provides T-score values, this step may be omitted. (column 7)

Figure II.5 shows a histogram associated with the scores in Table II.4. One can see that the scores are positively skewed in the histogram but normally distributed under the normal curve. The

Table II.4. Frequency Distribution Employed in Area Transformation Using Real Limits for Conversion.

Raw Score (1)	Upper Real Limit (2)	f (3)	No. of Scores Below, Upper Real Limit (4)	Percentile Rank of Upper Real Limit (5)	Normalized Scores Z-scores (6)	Normalized Scores T-scores (7)
42	42.5	1	140	100		
41	41.5	2	139	99.3	+2.46	75
40	40.5	3	137	97.9	+2.03	70
39	39.5	4	134	95.7	+1.72	67
38	38.5	4	130	92.9	+1.47	65
37	37.5	6	126	90.0	+1.28	63
36	36.5	9	120	85.7	+1.07	61
35	35.5	10	111	79.3	+0.82	58
34	34.5	10	101	72.1	+0.59	56
33	33.5	14	91	65.0	+0.39	54
32	32.5	17	77	55.0	+0.12	51
31	31.5	24	60	42.9	−0.18	48
30	30.5	27	36	25.7	−0.65	43
29	29.5	7	9	6.4	−1.52	35
28	28.5	2	2	1.4	−2.20	28

effect of area transformations or normalizing is very evident in this example. The dash lines indicate the location of the real limits of score values on the histogram and the converted T-scores equivalents on the normal curve. The area associated with the

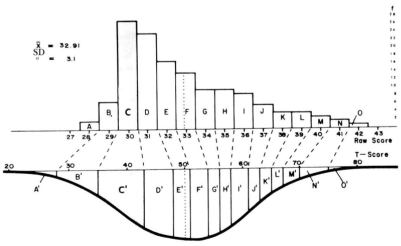

Figure II.5. An illustration showing the effect of normalizing raw scores. Intervals are matched to equate areas under histogram to area under normal curve. This illustration shows why this process is called area transformation.

raw score of 30 is designated as *C* in the histogram. The area associated with that same score after the area transformation is now *C'*. This process ensures that the areas A, B, C, . . . , O correspond in the same proportions that they occupy to area A', B', C', . . . O'. One can see that the raw score values represent equal distances in the histogram but unequal distances on the normal curve. If the raw scores are converted to T-score values as indicated in Figure II.5, the T-score values will, however, be equally distributed along the base of the normal curve. The illustration, in addition to showing the spreading effect where scores are concentrated (on the lower end of this curve), also pulls the skewed scores toward the mean.

We know that the form of a sample distribution is not necessarily the same form as that of the population it was taken from. If the population trait is normally distributed then our transformed scores provide more meaning than the original scores.

Problems may develop, however, when exceptional children are involved. For example, a difficult instrument used with mentally retarded subjects may result in a skewed distribution similar to the one in Figure II.5. An attempt to normalize these scores would be an inappropriate use of this technique. Anastasi (1961) recommend that transformations be carried out only when the sample is large and representative or from minor irregularities in the test itself. In general it is more desirable to obtain a normal distribution of raw scores through the proper adjustment of the difficulty level of test item, for example, than by attempting to normalize a severely non-normal distribution.

Although the above example uses the real limits of each class to show the effect of area transformations, in actual practice it is better to use the mid-point of each class to make this transformation. Table II.5 shows the changes required to make this change. One can see that the percentile rank of the mid-point of each class is found instead of the lower real limits. When the class interval is one, and each possible raw score is recorded, this procedure will provide a conversion for each raw score. However, if scores cover a large range, the use of a curve may be desirable (see Blommers, 1960).

Table II.5. Frequency Distribution Employed in Area Transformation Using Mid-point of Each Class for Conversion.

Raw Score	f	No. of scores below each class	No. of scores below mid-point of each class	Total No. of scores below mid-point	P.R. of each score	Normalized score T-scores	Z-scores
(1)	(2)	(3)	(4)	(5)	(6)	(7)	(8)
43	0	140	0.0	140	100		
42	1	139	0.5	139.5	99.6	2.65	77
41	2	137	1.0	138.0	98.6	2.20	72
40	3	134	1.5	135.5	96.8	1.85	69
39	4	130	2.0	132.0	94.3	1.58	66
38	4	126	2.0	128.0	91.4	1.37	64
37	6	120	3.0	125.0	89.3	1.24	62
36	9	111	4.5	114.5	81.8	.91	59
35	10	101	5.0	106.0	75.7	.70	57
34	10	91	5.0	96.0	68.6	.48	55
33	14	77	7.0	84.0	60.0	.25	53
32	17	60	8.5	68.5	48.9	−.03	50
31	24	36	12.0	48.0	34.3	−.40	46
30	27	9	13.5	22.5	16.1	−.99	40
29	7	2	3.5	5.5	3.9	−1.76	32
28	2	0	1.0	1.0	0.7	−2.46	25
27	0	0	0	0	0.0		

REFERENCES

Blommers, Paul; Lindquist, E. F.: *Elementary Statistical Methods.* Boston, Houghton Mifflin Co., 1960.

Cronbach, Lee J.: *Essentials of Psychological Testing,* 3rd ed.: New York. Harper and Brothers, 1960.

Guilford, J. P.: *Fundamental Statistics in Psychology and Education,* 4th ed. New York, McGraw-Hill Book Co., 1965.

Guilford, J. P.: *Psychometric Methods,* 2nd ed. New York, McGraw-Hill Book Co., 1954.

Wert, James E.; Neidt, Charles O.; Ahmann, J. Stanley: *Statistical Method* New York, Appleton-Century-Crofts, Inc., 1954.

CHAPTER III

CRITERION FOR SELECTING TESTS

MILTON V. WISLAND

USING AN APPROPRIATE test and gathering significant information is imperative for the formation of any diagnosis. Today when the number and variety of tests is rapidly expanding, it has become even more essential that individuals extend their knowledge and develop sufficient skills to select and use the appropriate instrument. The problem becomes more complex when the subject being diagnosed is an exceptional child.

Although in recent years test publishers as well as test producers have attempted to develop better instruments for exceptional children, there are still severe weaknesses in many of the tests widely used. It is also not uncommon to find tests that simply do not measure what their title or author intended them to measure, particularly when applied to unique populations. A wise procedure currently in practice utilizes initially an experimental edition or form, implying that the instrument has not been adequately researched to publish the final edition. However, because of the pressure that frequently exists in public school systems to diagnose aberrant learning problems, many instruments are being pressed into use even though they have not been adequately developed, or are known to have limited value or specific weaknesses.

The ability to evaluate tests is important for many people who may never be involved in direct use of tests. For example, administrators are often involved in the purchasing of tests though they may not necessarily use them; and on the other side of the fence, teachers who regularly use tests may be surprisingly inadequate in their ability to analyze a good test. It is the intent of this chapter to develop some degree of sophistication in diagnosing exceptional children through the selection and utilization of appropriate tests.

VALIDITY

Indubitably, the most important criteria of any instrument used to evaluate ability is its validity; in other words, the extent to which the test actually measures what it has been designed to measure. The construction and design of a test implies that the instrument has been evaluated against a criteria regarded by experts as the best evidence of the trait that is to be measured by the test. The utilization of appropriate criteria and demonstration cannot be overemphasized in establishing validity in psychological and educational tests, particularly if exceptional children are to be involved.

Normally external criteria is used to establish validity. An attempt to do this is made by comparing the test results with an outside criterion which may take several different forms. Let's take a specific illustration. If a test is designed for screening visually handicapped children, this particular instrument is administered to a given population that is described in terms of age, degree, or type of handicap, etc. This same population is evaluated by experts in the field, such as ophthalmologists and optometrists, who thoroughly examine the same population to determine the incidence of visually handicapped children. Their diagnosis is compared with that of the screening instrument. If there is extensive agreement between the diagnosis of professionals and the screening instrument, this test is said to have a great deal of validity in diagnosing children who are visually handicapped. The diagnosis of the expert then becomes the outside criteria. The correlation between the screening test and diagnosis is a mathematical expression indicating the relationship between the diagnosis and the obtained scores on the screening instrument. The validity coefficient, as it is sometimes referred to, tells us what the test is measuring. Through the examination of this kind of information, we can objectively determine what the test is measuring. Several procedures used to establish various types of validity have been identified in the literature. A brief description of these procedures as well as their strength and weaknesses will be given in the discussion that follows, particularly their relevance to populations involving exceptional children.

Face Validity

Probably the simplest type of validity is that of face validity, which is a term used to describe test items that are included in the test. The expression that is usually used here is that the items *appear* to measure what the author desires to measure; that is, the items *look* as if they are relevant to the variable being measured. Frequently, face validity is determined by a panel of specialists who know the field or the problem an individual is trying to measure. Face content is usually based upon some psychological knowledge or insight the test designer or panel of experts may have for evaluating the items included in the test as well as the characteristics of the population involved. Frequently, face validity involves the problem of anticipating the reaction subjects may have toward the test and its items such as:

1) Are the items appropriate for the interest levels of the subjects. For example, are retarded adult men being asked to participate in inappropriate or degrading activities by requesting them to count dolls, balls, etc.

2) Do items appeal to the available senses of the subjects. For instance, are colors attractive, complimentary, are sounds tolerable.

3) Are the items frightening, fearsome, or offensive. The decision to include an item in a test is often based upon an objective, mathematical relationship of item to the total test performance rather than considering the subject's reaction to materials.

The question that should be asked in determining this type of validity is, does the task or material appear to be appropriate to measure whatever the test designers have proposed to measure?

Content Validity

Content validity is known by other terms such as logical validity and validity by definition. Generally, content validity refers to the content of the items in the test, particularly achievement tests. An example of content validity may be found in an achievement test covering a specific body of information. The question usually asked here is, does the collection of test items reflect the curriculum content of that area of knowledge? Specifically, content validity assesses whether or not the items adequately sample the body of knowledge the test proposes to cover. An example of poor content validity would be a history test proposing to cover the entire Civil War that is primarily limited to items relating to General Grant, ignoring the rest of the issues of the Civil War. Another example of content validity might be in an elementary mathematics test involving simple addition and subtraction problems. If all of the problems involve only digits 2, 3, and 4 and single digit combinations, one can hardly say that this is an adequate sampling of broader mathematical skills. Consequently, one would say that this test is lacking in content validity. Content validity, like face validity, normally is not established through a mathematical relationship, but with a simple visual examination of the items to determine their suitability and adequacy in terms of the overall test objective; in other words, does the test measure what it is supposed to measure.

Content validity may be extended beyond the ideas expressed above through a statistical analysis of the items. For example, the following kinds of information can be obtained on each item in the test:

1) Determine the discriminating value of a specific item by computing the percentage of individuals passing or failing each item which, in essence, is the level of the difficulty for a given time.

2) Determine the percent of individuals passing a given item from one school grade to the next or one age level to another if the test covers a wide range developmental concept.

3) Determine the correlation of each item with educational progress or with general educational performance.

This kind of information can be used to refine the original selection of items that may be included in an instrument. This procedure, also, can be used to revise an old test by removing items that are no longer discriminating items while entering new items that do have discriminating ability. In other words, an item that everyone passes or fails has little value in a test. Also, if an instrument proposed to measure a developmental concept such as school achievement, it should not contain items that do not predict school achievement.

Criterion-related Validity

Criterion-related validity refers to the technique of studying the relationship between the test scores and an independent external measure or criterion. Many writers distinguish two kinds of criterion-related validity, concurrent and predictive validity. The type of validity the reader should be interested in depends upon whether or not he is interested in prediction of current or future behavior.

Concurrent Validity

Determines the extent to which an instrument is measuring what it proposes to measure at the time the test is administered or within a reasonably short period of time, such as a week or two. In other words, does the test measure a given psychological or educational trait or characteristic at the time the test is administered? For example, does it measure the subject's current status in achievement or his current level of intelligence? Concurrent validity is determined by establishing a correlation coefficient between measurements on a given test and some other criterion the test is believed to be measuring. For instance, if it is measuring school achievement the test results may be compared with a current teacher evaluation, school marks, etc. If the test is measuring mechanical aptitude one can compare test scores with the supervisor's daily ratings or his level of performance on a particular job, such as an assembly line, etc.

Predictive Validity

In contrast with concurrent validity, we have another concept of validity called predictive validity, which refers to the test's ability to predict future performance or ability. This type of validity is determined by administering a test and then following this administration for possibly a period of several years, correlating the testee's performance with the test that was initially given. An example of this can be found in interest tests. A child taking an interest test at the age of twelve should have a similar profile of likes and dislikes ten years later if the test has high predictive validity. Another example can be given for tests predicting clerical aptitude. An individual taking such a test may be interested in predicting her ability to perform in a secretarial school. The test may be given prior to entering high school with a follow-up after the individual has finished post high school secretarial training school to see if the test correlates with overall rating in the secretarial school. If there is a high correlation, one would assume that this particular test has high predictive validity concerning secretarial training.

Construct Validity

Construct validity is one of the most difficult types of validity concepts to understand and establish. The establishment of construct validity is an attempt to prove or disprove or show an association between a hypothetical concept or model around which the test may be developed. An example of this might be found in the following theoretical example. One may hypothesize that an individual with central nervous system damage is unable to accurately perceive certain visual symbols. An inability to do this would be hypothesized as indicating the presence of central nervous system damage. The establishment of construct validity would then require that an individual's score on this instrument be validated against an outside criterion, such as a neurological examination or medical history of the subject, to establish the relationship of test response to brain damage. Another example of construct validity could be established using the same geometric symbols, the hypothetical construct being that an individual who is capable of reproducing these geometric or abstract symbols from memory with a certain degree of accuracy will predict artistic ability or, for instance, architectural ability.

Again, to establish this type of construct validity one must take the scores that have been obtained on this instrument and validate them by comparing each individual's test scores with his artistic ability or his success as an architect, as determined by his professional peer group. In many cases, construct validity is hard to establish in that the hypothetical concept that the test is attempting to measure is difficult to compare with an outside criteria. This is easily seen in tests of creativity which are extremely difficult to validate.

Factor Validity

Factorial validity is particularly important for those working with exceptional children in that we have less confidence in what is being measured when we apply diagnostic instruments. Thurstone (1947) has quite clearly stated that factors cannot be expected to be *invariant* from one population to another. A specific vocabulary test of moderate difficulty may be a measure of reasoning for normal elementary school children, but a measure of perceptual speed for gifted children as well as a word fluency test for mildly retarded children. The process used to solve a problem may also change at different points along the learning curve; consequently, different factors may be measured by specific tests or test items at different points along the learning curve, or during various stages of development; thus, given items may measure different factors with the populations described above.

Factorial validity is determined through the statistical manipulation of underlying variables measured by numerous items and subtests located within the instrument. It is a method or procedure for analyzing a given set of observations (test scores) from their intercorrelations to determine if observed variations can be reduced to a fewer number of basic categories than initially observed. Thus, a large number of observations may be explained with fewer reference variables. Factorial validity may be stated as being a method used to extract common factor variance from sets of measures through statistical procedures to determine k underlying variable factors from n sets of test items, k usually being less than n. Thurstone (1947) has developed a formula for estimating

Table III.1. Minimum Number of Subtests (*n*) Needed to Determine (*r*) Factors

n	*r*
3	1
5	2
6	3
8	4
9	5
10	6
12	7
13	8
14	9
15	10

the maximum number of factors that can be formed from a given number of *n* sets of test items:

$$n \geq \frac{(2k + 1) + \sqrt{8k - 1}}{2} \qquad 3.1$$

where:

n = number of subtests
k = number of factors

Table III.1 shows the relationship between the minimum number of subtests and factors as expressed in the above formula.

It is generally agreed that it is desirable to overdetermine the number of factors through the involvement of more than the minimum number of tests in a factorial problem. Although there is no exact method for determining when to stop extracting factors contained in a correlation matrix, several empirical procedures have been developed, such as Tucker's Phi, Humphrey's Rule, Coomb's Criterion (Frutcher, 1954).

Factors themselves should be considered as constructs or a hypothetical entity assembled to underlie tests and test performance. In simpler terms, a psychological or educational trait may be defined or identified by analyzing the interrelationships among many measures of behavior.

The procedure used in factor analysis involves the administration of many tests or test items to a selected group of individuals; usually the number of individuals involved is fairly large, including anywhere from two hundred to four hundred or more subjects. Although Guilford (1954) states that fewer subjects may be

Test Numbers	1	2	3	4	5	6	7	8	9
1		.76	.81	.67	.06	.01	.08	.91	.92
2	.76		.71	.74	.31	.16	.06	.87	.81
3	.81	.71		.81	.00	.01	.11	.07	.13
4	.67	.74	.81		.03	.09	.13	.14	.07
5	.06	.31	.00	.03		.81	.80	.73	.12
6	.01	.16	.01	.09	.87		.71	.81	.06
7	.08	.06	.11	.13	.80	.71		.72	.00
8	.91	.87	.07	.14	.73	.81	.72		.01
9	.92	.81	.13	.07	.12	.06	.00	.01	

Figure III.1. Correlation matrix showing coefficients of correlation among nine tests.

used, he indicates that two hundred individuals normally are the minimum number required when Pearson r's are used in a factorial study.

The first step in determining factorial validity is to find the correlation of each test with every other test yielding a correlation matrix. An example of a correlation matrix may be seen in Figure III.1. As one can see from the table, certain clusters or groupings appear among the correlations in the matrix.*

Factor validity implies two questions: How many factors are there, and what are these factors? The factors are reflected in cor-

---

* Students should note that a matrix is a rectangular arrangement of numbers. Correlation matrices are always square and symmetrical. This is caused by the duplication within the matrix in that the upper right portion (separated by a diagonal of blank spaces from upper left to lower right) is the same as the lower left, except for a mirror arrangement of the scores. This is further explained by the fact that two combinations are given for each possible correlation. We find, for example, the same correlation (.76) between row 1 and column 2, as well as between row 2 and column 1. The blank spaces in the diagonal occur because a test cannot be correlated with itself.

relation coefficients. If two or more tests are substantially correlated, then these two tests are sharing a common variance. In fact, they are stated as having common factor variance, implying that they are measuring something in common. It is not difficult to show a mathematical basis for a factor; it is, however, difficult to identify or explain the characteristics of a factor once it has been identified.

In that many of the concepts of validity are explainable on the basis of factor theory, some time will be spent discussing the basic features of factor theory to enable the student to better understand the problems and methods involved. A detailed discussion will not be attempted regarding the statistical procedures used for computation. Students interested in the statistical procedures in more detail are referred to Harmon, 1960.

Elementary Assumptions in Factor Theory: Certain basic assumptions are necessary to establish a foundation for the logic of validity. One of these is the fact that a test score may be regarded as containing three kinds of component variances: 1) *Common Variance*—variances made up of one or more common factors. The term common factor is used here to imply that these factors appear in more than one test; 2) *Specific Variance*—variance that is unique to the test itself and to its equivalent forms; and 3) *Error Variance*. These assumptions can be expressed in the following formula:

$$\sigma_t^2 = \sigma_{co}^2 + \sigma_s^2 + \sigma_e^2 \qquad 3.2$$

where

σ_t^2 = total variance in the test

σ_{co}^2 = common factor variance (variance shared by two or more measures)

σ_s^2 = specific variance (variance of the test that is not shared with any other test)

σ_e^2 = error variance

Common factor variance σ_{co}^2 can be further divided into additional sources of variance. For example σ_{co}^2 equals $\sigma_a^2 + \sigma_b^2 + \sigma_c^2 + \cdots + \sigma_n^2$ where σ_a^2 and σ_b^2 stand for factors that may be identified in a given test. For example σ_a^2 may stand for a visual decoding factor, σ_b^2 and auditory decoding factor, and

σ_c^2 may represent an auditory sequential factor, etc. Formula 3.2 may be expanded to:

$$\sigma_t^2 = \sigma_a^2 + \sigma_b^2 + \sigma_c^2 + \cdots + \sigma_n^2 + \sigma_s^2 + \sigma_e^2 \qquad 3.3$$

Common factor variance, frequently referred to as the *communality* of the test, as well as the validity component of the measure, is labeled as h^2 and represented by:

$$h^2 = \sigma_a^2 + \sigma_b^2 + \sigma_c^2 + \cdots + \sigma_n^2 \qquad 3.4$$

It is this part of the total factor variance that gives a test a mathematical basis for correlating with other tests, thus providing the empirical basis for establishing a relationship with an outside criteria which is required in demonstrating validity.

Reliability on the other hand is represented by both common factor variance and specific variance. A mathematical expression of reliability is as follows:

$$r_{XY} = \frac{\sigma_t^2}{\sigma_t^2} - \frac{\sigma_e^2}{\sigma_t^2} \qquad 3.5$$

$$r_{XY} = 1 - \frac{\sigma_e^2}{\sigma_t^2} \qquad 3.6$$

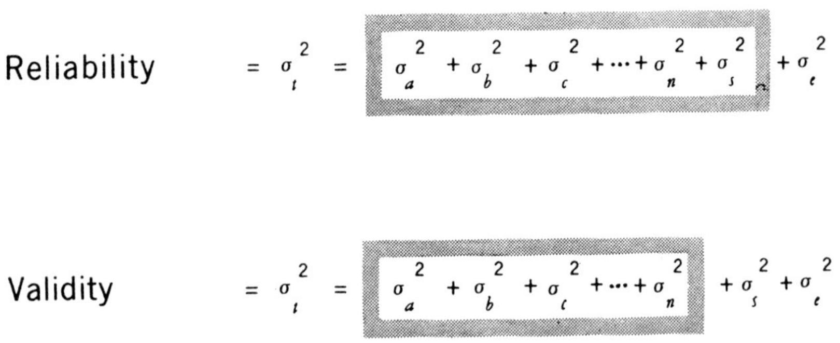

Total Variance $= \sigma_t^2 = \boxed{\sigma_a^2 + \sigma_b^2 + \sigma_c^2 + \cdots + \sigma_n^2} + \sigma_s^2 + \sigma_e^2$

Reliability $= \sigma_t^2 = \boxed{\sigma_a^2 + \sigma_b^2 + \sigma_c^2 + \cdots + \sigma_n^2 + \sigma_s^2} + \sigma_e^2$

Validity $= \sigma_t^2 = \boxed{\sigma_a^2 + \sigma_b^2 + \sigma_c^2 + \cdots + \sigma_n^2} + \sigma_s^2 + \sigma_e^2$

Figure III.2. Relationship of reliability and validity to the total variance of a test.

	COMMON FACTOR VARIANCE*					Specific Variance σs^2	Error Variance σe^2	Communality h^2	Reliability rxx
	A	B	C	D	E				
Test 1	(.40) .16	(.30) .09	(.50) .25	(.10) .00	(.20) .04	.01	.53	.54	.47
Test 2	(.20) .04	(.10) .00	(.20) .04	(.10) .00	(.10) .00	.83	.08	.08	.92
Test 3	(.40) .16	(.10) .00	(.90) .81	(.10) .00	(.10) .00	.01	.02	.97	.98
Criterion	(.50) .25	(.30) .09	(.70) .49	(.20) .04	(.20) .04	.03	.01	.91	.99

*Common factor loadings are given in parenthesis. Note that the common factor loadings squared equals the common factor variance.

Table III.2. An Illustration of Common Factor, Specific and Error Variance in Three Tests Inducing On Outside Criterion As Well As the Communelity and Relibility of Each Test.

The relationship of validity to reliability can be seen in Figure III.2. Here the reader should note that the common factor variance (communality) is a part of both reliability and validity. However, it is possible for a test to have very little or no communality and yet be quite reliable. A test with no communality would not correlate with anything else unless by chance the error variance should be correlated with an outside criteria. In contrast, one can see that a test may also have very low reliability and still have substantial validity if the common factor variance (h^2) correlates with an outside validating criteria. Examples of this can be seen in Table III.2 where test one has rather low reliability (.47) but a validity coefficient of .70 with the outside criterion. (See formula 3.7 for the computation of this coefficient.) It is also possible to see how a high reliability can be obtained even though the common factor variance is almost non-existent in test two in Table III.2. Test three also shows a high reliability with a low specific variance.

Another basic assumption in factor theory that is important in establishing empirical evidence for validity is that the correlation of a test with an outside criterion is equal to the sum of the cross products of their common factor loadings. The equation for representing this relationship is:

$$r_{XY} = a_x a_y + b_x b_y + c_x c_y + \cdots + n_x n_y \qquad (3.7)$$

where:

a_x = loading of factor a on test x

a_y = loading of factor a on criterion

If the reader will examine Table III.2 he can see the application of this formula in the correlation of test one with the outside criterion where:

(.40) (.50) + (.30) (.30) + (.50) (.70) + (.10) (.20) + (.20) (.20) = .70

Factor Loading:

Factor loading or factor saturation indicates the extent to which a test measures a given factor. If the test measures only one factor it is said to be *factorially pure*. In factor analysis we attempt to determine the extent to which a test is factorially pure and the degree to which it is saturated with a given factor. Normally, however, a test is not factorially pure in that it is also evaluating other factors at the same time. In this case a test is saturated with more than one factor and it is said to be *factorially complex*. A factor matrix which is developed in the final steps of factor analysis shows the coefficients that express the relationship between the tests and the underlying factors which we referred to as *factor loadings*. The correlation between two experimental variables such as test and an outside criteria is equal to the sum of the cross products of their common factor loadings, as expressed above. (See formula 3.7.)

In that factor analysis involves a spatial and geometrical orientation to factor loading, some attempt will be made here to develop this concept. A table of correlations or a correlation matrix can be represented through the use of vectors and angles. To do this we treat the row entries of a factor matrix as coordinates and plot them in geometric space. A factor matrix shown in Table III.3 will be used to demonstrate this concept. At this point it is probably sufficient to state that a factor matrix is a table of coefficients that is developed in the computation process to express the relationship between tests and underlying factors. The row

Table III.3. A Factor Matrix Showing the Loadings of Five Factors on Seven Tests.

Variables	Common		Factors			
	A	B	C	D	E	h^2*
Test 1	.95	.10	.17	.02	.21	.986
Test 2	.35	.90	.22	.06	.06	.988
Test 3	.25	.25	.71	.01	.41	.797
Test 4	.20	.95	.08	.13	.11	.978
Test 5	.85	.15	.01	.41	.02	.914
Test 6	.80	.10	.09	.42	.21	.879
Test 7	.25	.75	.03	.41	.36	.924
Criterion$_J$	.20	.65	.10	.72	.07	.996

*h^2 the sum of each factor squared, thus h^2 for test 1 equals $(.95)^2 + (.10)^2 + (.17)^2 + (.02)^2 + (.21)^2 = .986$

entries of this factor matrix are used as coordinates to plot each test. To demonstrate the plotting process, factor A and B of Table III.3 were plotted at right angles orthogonally to each other along what is called the reference axis. Each axis represents a factor as can be seen in Figure III.3. Factor loadings are indicated on each axis. To illustrate the factor loading of test 2, it has been plotted in Figure III.3 by going out to .90 on factor B and .35 on factor A. (See dash lines on Figure III.3.) Each test has been located in a similar fashion. Numerical expressions of factor loadings are easily interpreted in that they range from -1.00 through 0 to $+1.00$, similar to correlation coefficients.

The last column of Table III.3 contains the communalities of each test. The communality of test one is:

$$h^2 = (.95)^2 + (.10)^2 + (.17)^2 + (.02)^2 + (.21)^2 = .986$$

Thus, we can again see that the sum of the squares of factor loadings equal the communality of that test or variable.

It should be noted at this time that the above discussion refers to the plotting of two factors at a time. Though it is possible to plot more than this, it is difficult to graphically represent complete multidimensional structures. Also, it is important to note that the axes employed in Figure III.3 are known as *orthogonal axes* in that they are at right angles to each other. Some factor analysts are of the opinion that this is the most desirable way as it provides a simpler illustration of the trait relationship. An orthogonal relationship implies that the factors are uncorrelated. As one can see, a change in values on one factor does not affect

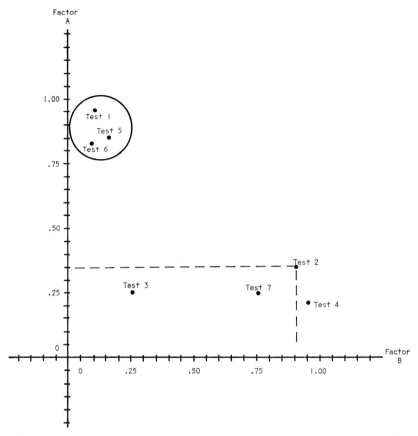

Figure III.3. A demonstration of factorial loading, illustrating the clustering of tests one, five, and six on factor A.

the values on the other factor. Other investigators are of the opinion that *oblique axes* should be used in that they may fit the data better because many meaningful factorial categories are correlated. In fact, there have been increasing tendencies to favor oblique transformations over the years.

Another factorial concept that should be explained here is the principle of *simple structure*. Normally, factorial analytic methods supply row data in the form of a factor matrix that is different or impossible to interpret without some type of additional manipulation. This manipulation is normally referred to as *rotation*, which involves the movement of the reference axes to obtain what is called *simple structure*. One can say that simple structure has been established when there is a maximum of zero loadings on the reference axes. Thurstone (1947) has listed more specific criteria for simple structure, which are as follows: 1) Each row of the rotated factor matrix should have at least one zero. This means that each test is of complexity less than *r*, the number of common factors. 2) Each column of the rotated factor matrix should have at least *r* zeroes. 3) For every pair of columns in the rotated factor matrix, there should be a number of tests having zeroes in the one column matched with non-zeroes in the other. 4) For every pair of columns, there should be a number of pairs of zero loadings. 5) For every pair of columns, there should be very few pairs of loadings of substantial size. Thurstone (1947) was of the opinion that simple structure provides psychological meaning to rotated factors in that he was also of the opinion that simple structure is a principle of order in psychological nature.

These factorial transformations are applied more easily using oblique rather than orthogonal rotations because of the flexibility it provides. As one can see in Figures III.4 and III.5, orthogonal procedures are limited to an angle of 90° between references axes; whereas, the oblique rotation has considerable fluctuation concerning the degree of this angle.

Several methods have been developed to transform arbitrary factor matrices to the criteria of simple structure: 1) A graphic method using a plotting procedure similar to the one above described in Figure III.4 and Figure III.5 which involves the plotting of every vector of factor loadings against every factor. Here a visual rotation is made to obtain simple structure which is extremely time consuming and not adaptable to objective computation procedures; consequently, a great deal of personal judgment is left to the person making the transformation. 2) Another procedure is based on a *priori hypothesis* when the investigator has a preconceived hypothesis as to which variables should have high factor loadings and which should not. This is sometimes called the *hypothesis method of transformation.* 3) The last method involves an analytical or mathematical criteria for transformations. This procedure uses a mathematical function of the

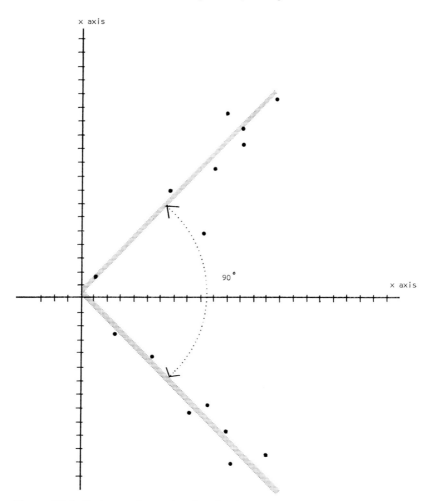

Figure III.4. Orthogonal rotation for simple structure.

transformed factor loadings which are to be optimized. This procedure is referred to as an *analytical method of transformation*.

Some of the basic concepts of factorial theory have been given to establish a logical foundation for validity. In brief, factorial validity of a test is a correlation between that test and the factor common to a group of tests or other measures of behavior. Up to this point we have seen that this is dependent upon the test's common factor variance or its communality (see Tables III.2 and

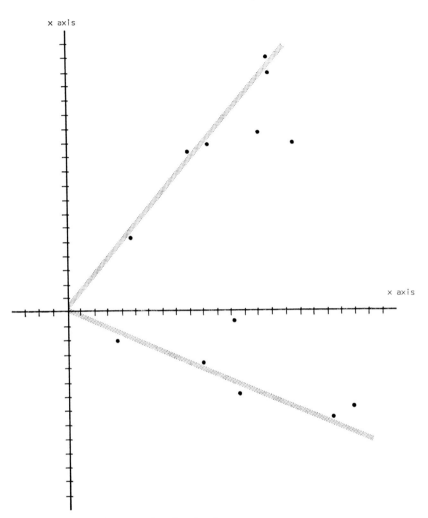

Figure III.5. Oblique rotation for simple structure.

III.3). More specifically, we can again state that the correlation between two tests is equal to the sum of the cross products of their common-factor coefficients or factor loadings. In actual practice, the factor loadings are estimated by first computing the factor analysis. The assumption taken in this text is that the factor loadings are known for illustrative purposes only.

From the previous examples it can be seen that a given test and criterion must have at least one factor in common or the test will have a zero coefficient of validity for predicting that criterion. We should also note that factorial validity of a test may be established by simply studying the extent to which a given test has *factor loading* for a particular factor in question. Some individuals have argued that factor validity provides the clearest description of what a test measures; consequently, they feel that this method of establishing validity should be used in preference over other methods (Anatasia, 1968). As the student should now be aware, validity must be established by correlating test scores with other indices of performance. These indices may be other tests, school achievement, job performance, or any criteira that can be assumed to be related to the criteria of the instrument in question.

In that newer and better designed tests may be better controlled and more precise in measuring a given criteria than the validating criteria itself, it would appear logical that a better indicator of validity could be established through factorial validity than through the use of outside criteria that may be less adequate in measuring the criterion in question than the test itself. This may be particularly true in working with exceptional children in that outside criteria is not always available in sufficient quantity or quality. An example of this is readily apparent in examining the effects of brain damage on learning. One of the existing problems has been our inability to measure or precisely define brain damage itself; consequently, our attempts to measure its effects on learning or its existence may be best accomplished through the instruments we develop. Thus, physiological and neurological examination might well be validated against psychoeducational instruments rather than the reverse of this. In other words, behavior may be the best criterion for establishing brain damage rather than physiological or neurological phenomena, particularly when the extent of the damage is minimal or subtle rather than extensive. Therefore, an outside criterion may be less adequate than the instrument itself (Birch, 1964).

It is also possible through factorial procedures to have empirical evidence of the *extent* to which factors are being measured by an instrument. In actual practice it is difficult to develop a test that is factorially pure. However, through factor analysis it is possible to minimize the influence of factors, by developing a test with a minimum of ambiguity. In forming a diagnosis it is desirable to eliminate undesirable criteria and concentrate on criteria that will, when combined, enable one to make the most accurate diagnosis possible. This, of course, implies that the individual is working with relatively pure tests covering significant aspects of the diagnosis.

Unfortunately, at the present time relatively few factorial studies have been made on the many instruments that are currently in use, particularly with exceptional children. In the absence of such data the use of other forms of validity may prove misleading. An error the diagnostician may make is assuming that a given battery of tests include all the factors that are important in making a diagnosis. Educational and psychological diagnoses are extremely complicated because of the many factors that may influence a particular problem. It is also important to note in evaluating factorial validity studies that without an outside criteria, the investigator cannot be assured that a test is a valid predictor of any practical criteria (Anastasia, 1968).

Another difficulty in the interpretation of factorial studies is that different investigators may in fact use the same terminology to identify a given factor, yet the factors themselves may not be identical; that is, factor labels do not always accurately describe the factor itself; consequently, a factor must be defined in terms of the test battery in which it is identified. For this reason some factorial investigators have recommended that a standard reference test be selected for the most clearly established factors in order to establish greater uniformity in the interpretation of factors (Anastasia, 1968). In general, one can state that the results of factor analysis are not yet sufficiently uniform nor systematic to allow wide application of the concept of factorial validity exclusively to test designs for general use.

RELIABILITY

Theory of Reliability

The theory of reliability is also dependent upon variance. As previously mentioned, reliability is concerned with the fluctuation or variability of the obtained scores. For this reason, it is logical to assume that we would use a statistical concept related to variability to describe it. To do this each obtained measurement must be thought of as containing two parts, 1) a true measurement of the characteristic being measured, and, 2) an error measure. This may be expressed as follows:

$$X_t = X_\infty + X_e \qquad\qquad 3.8$$

which implies that the total score (X_t) obtained by any single individual is equal to a true score (X_∞) and an error score (X_e). Obivously, the difficulty inherent in this equation is determining what part of the total score is true score or the genuine value this individual should have on this particular instrument. It is also obvious that this value is never known to the examiner. A definition of this true score is that if it is the mean score that one has obtained for an individual then we could administer the instrument a large number of times without changing the subject in the process. This assumes that the subject would not learn from repeated administrations of the test or change during the period of time required to give this test many times. It is also assumed that the errors involved in his scores are random errors; that is, they are both positive and negative and equally

Table III.4. The Effect of Adding Error Scores to True Scores to Obtain Total Score.

	Total Scores X_t	True Scores X_∞	Error Scores X_e
	2	4	+2
	1	2	+1
	7	6	−1
	6	7	+1
	4	3	−1
	3	4	+1
	6	6	0
	8	8	0
	9	8	−1
	4	2	−2
	—	—	—
Σ	50	50	0
M	5	5	0
Σx^2	62	48	14
σ^2	6.20	4.80	1.40
σ	2.49	2.19	1.18

distributed above and below his true score. This implies that the mean of the error scores obtained from each administration of the test would be equal to zero.

Table III.4 demonstrates the effect of adding error scores to true scores to obtain the total score. Note that the sum and mean of the error scores are equal to zero. Because there is a zero correlation between the error scores and the true scores (errors are randomly distributed), the variance of the total scores is equal to the sum of the variance of the true score and error score. In that the sum of the variance of the true and error scores equals the sum of the variance for the total scores, equation 3.8 can be converted to a more useful equation using variance terms:

$$\sigma_t^2 = \sigma_\sim^2 + \sigma_e^2 \qquad\qquad 3.9$$

where:

σ_t^2 represents the variance of the total group of scores,

$\sigma_\sim^2$ variance of the true score, and,

σ_e^2 variance of the error scores.

The application of this formula can be seen in Table III.4 where the error variance 1.40 plus the true variance 4.80 is equal to the total score variance of 6.20. To further explain the theory of reliability, one can show that reliability is expressed as a ratio between the total variance and error variance by first dividing each term of equation 3.9 by the total variance we have:

$$\frac{\sigma_t^2}{\sigma_t^2} = \frac{\sigma_\sim^2}{\sigma_t^2} + \frac{\sigma_e^2}{\sigma_t^2} = 1.00 \qquad\qquad 3.10$$

where 1.00 represents the total variance $\dfrac{\sigma_t^2}{\sigma_t^2}$

and reliability is represented by $1 - \dfrac{\sigma_e^2}{\sigma_t^2}$ or the ratio $\dfrac{\sigma_\sim^2}{\sigma_t^2}$

In equation form it becomes

$$\mathbf{r}_{xy} = \frac{\sigma_\sim^2}{\sigma_t^2}$$

or

$$\mathbf{r}_{xy} = 1 - \frac{\sigma_e^2}{\sigma_t^2} \qquad\qquad \text{(same as formula 3.6)}.$$

Theoretically, the more reliable instrument has less error variance; consequently, with repeated use we would expect less fluctuation in the scores. Using the information in Table III. 4, to substitute in the two formulas for reliability just given we have:

$$r_{xy} = \frac{4.80}{6.20} = .77$$

$$r_{xy} = 1 - \frac{1.40}{6.20} = .77$$

Standard Error of Measurement

Another approach to the theory of reliability is through the statistical concept, *standard error of measurement*. This concept is dependent upon the standard deviation of the distribution of the measured score values and upon the reliability coefficient of the instrument used to obtain these scores. To show the relationship between the standard error of measurement and reliability we start with formula 3.6 which, remember, contained error variance. With a little algebraic manipulation we can demonstrate that

$$r_{xy} = 1 - \frac{\sigma_e^2}{\sigma_t^2} \text{ is equal to}$$

$$r_{xy}\,\sigma_t^2 = \sigma_t^2 - \sigma_e^2 \text{ is equal to}$$

$$\sigma_e^2 = \sigma_t^2 - r_{xy}\,\sigma_t^2 \text{ is equal to}$$

$$\sigma_e^2 = \sigma_t^2\,(1 - r_{xy}) \qquad\qquad 3.11$$

where the error variance (σ_e^2) equals total variance (σ_t^2) times the quantity one minus the reliability coefficient $(1 - r_{xy})$. The square root of this statistic is a *standard error of measurement* (SE$_{mea}$) which is algebraically defined as:

$$\text{SE}_{mea} = \sigma_e = \sigma_t\,\sqrt{1 - r_{xy}} \qquad\qquad 3.12$$

where we can see that the square root of the error variance (σ_e^2) is equal to the standard error of measurement. The variance of this error score (formula 3.11) sometimes is called the *standard variance of measurement* or *standard variance of error measure-*

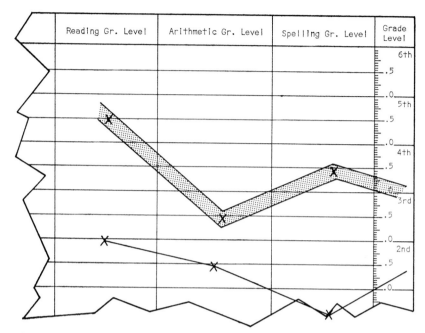

Figure III.6. A profile chart showing the standard error of measurement as being 0.2 of a grade level wide.

ment. The square root of this statistic (formula 3.12) is the standard error of measurement.

This concept is being used more frequently in expressing test reliability as well as reporting test scores. An example of this can be seen in Figure III.6 where achievement test scores are recorded as grade equivalent values. An *X* has been plotted on the profile chart for each value measured by this instrument with a connecting line being drawn between each point on the chart. The width of this line has been extended to one standard error of measurement above and below the measured value reported on the profile. The implication of this extended width is that the frequency of errors is normally distributed and, for this reason, predictable in terms of probability associated with the normal curve. Values obtained by a given instrument are assumed to be true values or scores for this individual. If the error variance is zero, obviously the assumption is true that the obtained value is the true score for the individual being examined. However, the larger the error variance, the greater the chances are that the obtained value does not represent the true score. This chance is expressed in terms of probability as reflected in the standard error of measurement, which is interpreted as being equivalent to a standard deviation unit on the normal curve. Thus, one standard error of measurement above and below the obtained scores implies that the probability is two chances out of three that the true score falls within this area. (This probability represents the area in the normal curve within one standard deviation of the mean.) If this area is extended, for example, to two standard errors of measurement, we can then state that the chances are ninety-five out of one hundred that the true score falls within two standard error units of the obtained score.

To illustrate this concept, the reader is referred to Figure III.6 where arithmetic achievement is reported to be on a 2.5 grade level. If the standard error of measurement is 0.2, this implies that two chances out of three the true achievement for this child is between 2.3 and 2.7, which is reflected in the extended width of the line.

In that nearly all tests have less than perfect reliability, it would appear most desirable to report test scores in terms of probable ranges instead of specific scores which implies a degree of accuracy to which the test is not capable. In the above example one would state that the odds are 2 to 1 that his true score in this area will not exceed 2.7 or fall below 2.3. The narrow line above implies that there is no variation in the score values represented.

EMPIRICAL PROCEDURES FOR ESTABLISHING RELIABILITY

Four procedures are normally used to establish reliability. These are as follows: 1) The correlation coefficient obtained from scores derived from repeated administration of the same test. 2) The correlation coefficient obtained from scores on comparable parts of the test. 3) The correlation coefficient obtained from scores on parallel forms of the test. 4) Intercorrelations obtained from elements within the test.

The procedures used as well as an evaluation of these methods will be given, particularly as they relate to exceptional children.

Repetition of the Same Test

This procedure is frequently called the test-retest method which involves the administration of the test at least twice to the same group of individuals. The two groups of scores are then used to compute the intercorrelations among the scores which are taken as the reliability coefficient, or, as it is sometimes called, the stability coefficient. Many factors may influence this type of reliability such as the length of interval between tests, memory, changes in the subject resulting from everyday experiences, and intervening practice. To minimize changes in the individual a short time interval is used; however, if too short an interval is used, the subject is apt to remember the test items. Consequently, one can see that the test-retest method of establishing a reliability coefficient may contain several sources of error that lowers the reliability. On the positive side, the test-retest procedure does use the identical test each time eliminating sources of errors caused by differences between forms of tests.

Parallel Forms

Many tests on the market today may have two or more equivalent forms. To be equivalent they should, of course, measure the same thing; therefore, alternate forms must cover the same material. In the case of achievement tests equivalent forms should have similar items, the same range of difficulty, and so forth. The correlation between forms provides a reliability coefficient or self-correlation of the test. By using equivalent forms we avoid the problem referred to above, that is, the effect of memory. However, the use of parallel forms does require that an interval of time take place between tests. It does not provide for changes in the individual that may take place.

Measure of Internal Consistency:

COMPARABLE PARTS: This method is frequently referred to as the split-half method of determining reliability. The problem of splitting a test into two equivalent halves is complicated and involved. One common procedure for developing two equivalent halves is to arrange all of the items in the test into increasing levels of difficulty for each item, normally starting out with the easiest items first and the more difficult items being toward the end of the test. The odd numbered items are then placed into one form and the even numbered items placed into the other form. One way of determining the level of difficulty for each item is to administer the test and determine the percent failing each item which provides an index of difficulty. Care must be taken in splitting the test to make sure that the subject content is equally distributed between the two forms which we might refer to as a and b. For example, if the test is an achievement test involving arithmetic, spelling and reading, one should make certain that in the process of splitting the test in two equivalent halves that an equal number of arithmetic, spelling and reading items fall within each form as well as items in the other subjects. This, of course, involves stratified grouping.

After the two equivalent halves have been established a correlation coefficient is computed between the two halves to provide an estimate of the reliability coefficient for the whole test. In that the length of a test affects the reliability, it is necessary to correct the obtained reliability coefficient by the use of the Spearman-Brown formula which provides an estimate of the reliability of this instrument for its original length. For example, if the original test contained 100 items in the process of establishing two equivalent forms using the split half method we would have established two tests of 50 items each. The correlation between these two tests is lower than the reliability of the original instrument because we have reduced its length in half. The Spearman-Brown formula provides an estimate of the reliability of 100 items. The formula is as follows:

$$r_{xy} = \frac{2r_{ab}}{1 + r_{ab}} \qquad 3.13$$

in which r_{xy} = the reliability of the whole test.

r_{ab} represents the correlation between the two halves a and b. For illustration purposes, assume that in a test of 100 items we find after splitting it into two halves, the correlation coefficient between the two halves is .75. To estimate the reliability of the original 100 item test we substitute into formula 3.13 as follows:

$$r_{xy} = \frac{2\,(0.75)}{1\,+\,0.75} = .86$$

Here we can see that the reliability of the 100 item test is estimated to be 0.86. If the correlation between the two halves had been 0.85, the reliability coefficient for the whole test using formula 3.13 would have been:

$$r_{xy} = \frac{2\,(0.85)}{1\,+\,0.85} = .92$$

The reliability of a test of any given length can be determined by using the general Spearman-Brown formula for reliability of a test of n length which is:

$$r_{xy} = \frac{n r_{ab}}{1\,+\,(n\,-\,1)\,\,r_{ab}} \qquad 3.14$$

where:

r_{xy} = reliability coefficient of a test after adjusting its length

n = the number of times the test is to be lengthened (a decimal if the test is to be shortened)

r_{ab} = coefficient of correlation between the first and second half.

Using formula 3.14, we can take the correlation coefficient of .86 calculated in the example above and estimate the reliability for this test if it were half as long. An example of this is as follows:

$$r_{xy} = \frac{.5\,\,(0.86)}{1\,+\,(.5\,-\,1)\,\,(0.86)} = .75$$

This gives us again an estimated correlation coefficient of .75 which is what we started with initially.

It is possible to use the Spearman-Brown formula to determine the number of times a test must be lengthened to reach a decimal level of reliability. Rewriting formula 3.14 we have:

$$n = \frac{rn \ (1 - r'_{xy})}{r'_{xy} \ (1 - rn)} \qquad 3.15$$

where:

n = the number of times the test is to be lengthened
rn = proposed level of reliability
r_{xx} = given level of reliability

Additional discussion on this topic will be given toward the end of the chapter under Length of the Instrument.

This formula is based upon the following assumptions:

1. That the material in the two halves is homogenous, that is, similar in type of content, level of difficulty, form, time per element.

2. That the SD's of the two half scores are equal which will be true if the above criteria are met.

3. That such things as fatigue, etc., do not enter into longer tests.

The advantages of the Spearman-Brown formula for determining reliability are quite obvious. After being given only once to a group of individuals, a repeat performance is not required at a later time, thereby eliminating one of the criticisms described above, in that there will be no changes within individuals over a period of time. Also, by administering the test once, we have reduced expenses involved in determining the reliability as well as minimizing the amount of exposure the population at large is given to this particular test.

This procedure is not applicable to certain tests such as speed tests where we would obtain nearly the same score for each half for each individual, giving close to a perfect correlation coefficient between the two halves which would obviously give us an artificially high correlation. Figure I.2 demonstrates this very clearly. Here the student can see an example of a speed test where the subject is asked to place as many X's as possible within the circles in a two minute time period. As the illustration shows, the subject completed eighty-four items. Taking the odd items for one test and the even for the other would give us forty-two correct items in each test. As one can see, this would result in a perfect correlation if everyone finished an even number of items.

The Spearman-Brown formula has particular significance for exceptional children in that an examiner frequently finds that tests used with normal children are too long and fatiguing for some exceptional children. With formula 3.14, it is possible to estimate the level of reliability one would have if the test were shortened to reduce fatigue. Of course the same assumptions that apply to shortening a test apply to lengthening it. That is, the quality of the item must remain the same in both the long and short tests.

KUDER-RICHARDSON: Another procedure to be described in this text is based upon the consistency of the individual's responses to each item in the test. This provides a form of reliability that combines the advantages of the split-half procedure, as well as looking at inter-item consistency.

The most familiar procedure used in determining inter-item consistency has been developed by Kuder and Richardson. This procedure involves a single administration of a test similar to that used in split-half methods of determining reliability. However, rather than requiring two half scores as the split-half method requires, this technique is based upon the examination of the performance of each subject on each item in the test in question. Several formulas have been developed to do this; however, the preferred formula developed by Kuder and Richardson has been K-R20 which is as follows:

$$r = \left(\frac{n}{n-1} \right) \left(\frac{\sigma_t^2 - \Sigma pq}{\sigma_t^2} \right) \qquad 3.16$$

where:

n = number of items in the test

p = proportion of subjects responding correctly to an item

q = $1 - p$

σ_t^2 = variance of the total test scores

Σpq = the sum of the proportions of persons who pass (p) and proportion who fail (q) each item.

Table III.5. An Item Score Matrix Showing the Scores of Ten Subjects on Eight Test Items. (Subjects are arranged by level of ability, items by level of difficulty.)

		Kuder — Richardson Method									Rulon's Method			
		Test Items								$\sum\limits_{j=1}^{n} s\,i = X$				
		a	b	c	d	...	t	...	n		X_E	X_O	d	d^2
Subjects	1	0	0	0	0	0	0	0	0	0	0	0	0	0
	2	1	1	0	0	0	0	0	0	2	1	1	0	0
	3	1	1	1	0	0	0	0	0	3	1	2	1	1
	4	1	1	1	1	0	0	0	0	4	2	2	0	0
	5	1	1	1	1	1	0	0	0	5	2	3	1	1
	6	1	1	1	1	0	1	0	0	5	3	2	1	1
	.	1	1	1	0	1	0	1	0	5	1	4	3	9
	i	1	1	1	1	1	1	1	0	7	3	4	1	1
	.	1	1	1	1	1	1	0	1	7	4	3	1	1
	N	1	1	1	1	1	1	1	1	8	4	4	0	0
$\sum\limits_{j=1}^{N} s_i$		9	9	8	6	5	4	3	2	$46 = \Sigma X$	21	25		14
pi		.9	.9	.8	.6	.5	.4	.3	.2	$4.6 = M$				
$pi\ qi$		.09	.09	.16	.24	.25	.24	.21	.16	$1.44 = \Sigma\ piqi$ $\sigma_t^2 = 5.44$ $\sigma_t = 2.33$		σ_d^2		1.4

Table III.5 shows the procedure one would use to get the information needed in formula 3.16. Students and items have been arranged by level of ability and level of difficulty to help the reader see essential computational relationships. In actual practice, this arrangement is not required. The score for each item is 1 for a correct answer and 0 for an incorrect answer. In the example all subjects attempted all questions.

The total score for each subject (X) is determined by summing each row, while the sum of each column indicates the number of correct responses to each test item. The total sum of correct responses in this artificial example is 46. (The sum of N row and n column should equal each other.) Dividing the sum of each column by N gives the proportion of subjects passing each item or (p). The proportion failing each item is $1 - p$; consequently, to determine pq for item a, we make the following computation: $.9 \times .1 = .09$

In our example $\Sigma pq = 1.44$, total variance $\sigma_t^2 = 5.44$, and $n = 8$ which when substituted in formula 3.16 we have:

$$r = \left(\frac{8}{8 - 1} \right)\left(\frac{5.44 - 1.44}{5.44} \right) = (1.14)\ (.735) = .84$$

RULON METHOD: The Rulon Method computes the standard error of measurement from differences in scores on two halves of a test, either alternate forms or a split-half procedure can be used. Again, referring to formula 3.6:

$$r_{xy} = 1 - \frac{\sigma_e^2}{\sigma_t^2}$$

Rulon has devised a procedure for computing σ_e^2 directly from differences between scores made by subjects, or odd and even items from the same test.

The equation is $\sigma_e^2 = \dfrac{\Sigma d^2}{N}$

Thus, the Rulon formula becomes:

$$r_{xy} = 1 - \frac{\dfrac{\Sigma d^2}{N}}{\sigma_t^2} \qquad\qquad 3.17$$

Substituted from Table III.5 the formula becomes:

$$r_{xy} = 1 - \frac{1.4}{5.44} = 1 - .26 = .74$$

This estimate is less than the K-R20 formula. In that it is based on the odd-even scores, we would expect it to be close to the odd-even procedure described previously. It is important to note that the Rulon procedure, however, is based on the whole test; consequently, the Spearman-Brown reliability coefficient will have to be adjusted for a test half as long (see formula 3.14).

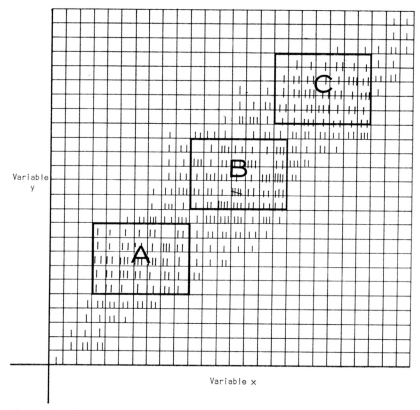

Figure III.7. A scatter diagram showing the effects of a wide range of ability upon the correlation coefficient.

HOYT'S ANALYSIS OF VARIANCE PROCEDURE: Because of vast differences in exceptional children, we find an extensive range of responses to tests. Because exceptional children are found in all areas of society and in all populations, including those used to standardize tests, it appears to be essential that we devise procedures for estimating levels of reliability for those exceptional populations. Analysis of variance is well-suited to this task in that this statistical model is particularly sensitive to variances between and within various stratified or subdivided populations while relating these variances to total variance.

As discussed previously, the coefficient of reliability of a given test provides an estimate of true variance. Although this procedure gives precisely the same result as the Kuder-Richardson formula 20 previously described, it has additional advantages in that the sources of variance, either in the instrument itself or in the subjects, may be subdivided or broken down for further examination as indicated by Winer, Wert, Neidt, and Ahmann. For example, two or more equivalent forms administered to the same group of students could produce a practice effect. Another example highly relevant for this text is the fact that the total standardizing population may be divided into retarded, normal, and superior as illustrated in Figure III.7, to identify the variance associated with these unique populations which may be used in establishing test reliability for these groups (Hoyt, 1941).

The computational procedure used in a simple analysis of variance has been illustrated in Table III.6. Although the procedure looks difficult, the reader will note that the only data needed to compute the reliability are the number of correct responses for each item and the total score for each subject. These values are obtained in Part I of Table III.6 where the statistical arrangement of subjects and test items may be seen. Here the symbol (X) represents a subject's response to a test item. The first subscript refers to the row (subject's number) and the second subscript to the column (test item number). The symbol (T) represents the sum of scores for test items, while the summation of all the T's equals (G) or total number of correct responses. The symbol (P) represents the total number of correct responses or the test score for each subject. It should be noted that the summation of all the P's equals G. At this point a good check on computational procedures is G. The total sum of P's and T's should both equal G. In formula form:

$$\Sigma T_j = \Sigma P_i = G \qquad\qquad 3.18$$

Part II of Table III.6 displays the statistical values needed to complete the computation required for this analysis of variance. Part III indicates how these values are combined to find the sum of squares and mean square. For example, to find the sum of squares between subjects, subtract statistical values (1) from (4):

$$SS_b = \frac{\Sigma P_i^2}{k} - \frac{G^2}{kn} \qquad\qquad 3.19$$

Table III.6. Computational Procedures Used in Analysis of Variance to Determine Reliability.

	Subjects	Test Items					Subjects Test Scores
		1	2	... j	...	k	
	1	X_{11}	X_{12}	X_{1j}		X_{1k}	P_1
	2	X_{21}	X_{22}	X_{2j}		X_{2k}	P_2
	.	.	.	.		.	.
	.	.	.	.		.	.
	.	.	.	.		.	.
I	i	X_{i1}	X_{i2}	X_{ij}		X_{ik}	P_i
	.	.	.	.		.	.
	.	.	.	.		.	.
	.	.	.	.		.	.
	n	X_{n1}	X_{n2}	X_{nj}		X_{nk}	P_n
	Item Total Score	T_1	T_2	... T_j	...	T_k	G

$$\text{(1)} \quad \frac{G^2}{kn}$$

$$\text{(2)} \quad G$$

II

$$\text{(3)} \quad \frac{\Sigma T_j^2}{n} = \frac{T_1^2 + T_2^2 + \cdots T_k^2}{n}$$

$$\text{(4)} \quad \frac{\Sigma P_i^2}{k} = \frac{P_1^2 + P_2^2 + \cdots P_k^2}{k}$$

	Source of Variance	Sum of Squares (SS)		Degrees of freedom (df)	Mean Square (MS)
	Between Subjects	SS_b	(4)-(1)	$n-1$	$\frac{SS_b}{df}$
	Within Subjects	SS_w	(2)-(4)	$n(k-1)$	$\frac{SS_w}{df}$
III	Items	SS_i	(3)-(1)	$k-1$	$\frac{SS_i}{df}$
	Residual	SS_r	(2)-(3)-(4)+(1)	$(n-1)(k-1)$	$\frac{SS_r}{df}$
	Total	SS_t	(2)-(1)	$kn-1$	$\frac{SS_t}{df}$

To find SS_w subtract (4) from (2), for SS_i subtract (1) from (3). Degrees of freedom (df) are found as follows:

$n - 1$ = number of subjects minus one

$n(k - 1)$ = multiply the number of test items minus one by the number of subjects

$k - 1$ = number of test items minus one

$(n - 1)(k - 1)$ = number of subjects minus one times the number of test items minus one

$kn - 1$ = number of test items times number of subjects minus one.

Mean square values are obtained by dividing the sum of squares by their degrees of freedom. For example:

$$MS_p = \frac{SS_b}{n - 1} \qquad 3.20$$

Mean square for this discussion represent a *type of variance* that is used in computing reliability coefficient which is as follows:

$$r = \frac{MS_b - MS_r}{MS_b} \qquad 3.21$$

The reader should note that the MS_r represents the amount of uncontrolled or error variance. The error of measurement in this case should be interpreted as a measure of the extent to which people having the same test scores do not have identical profiles of correct responses, (Winer 1962). For subject 1, the profile of responses is X_{11}, X_{12}, X_{1k}. In the numerical example given in Table III.7 we find MS_b to be .756, and MS_r .121. Substituting in formula 3.21 we have:

$$r = \frac{.756 - .121}{.756} = \frac{.635}{.756} = .84$$

Here the reader should note, as indicated earlier, that this procedure gives the same reliability coefficient as the K–R 20 formula with the added advantage discussed above. The matrix in Tables III.5 and III.7 contain identical data to demonstrate this similarity.

It should be noted at this point in our discussion that certain assumptions are essential in using this procedure. In the example it is assumed that:

Table III.7. Numerical Examples Used in Analysis of Variance to Determine Reliability.

	Subjects	Test Items								Subjects Test Score
		1	2	3	4	5	6	7	8	
	1	0	0	0	0	0	0	0	0	0
	2	1	1	0	0	0	0	0	0	2
	3	1	1	1	0	0	0	0	0	3
	4	1	1	1	1	0	0	0	0	4
	5	1	1	1	1	1	0	0	0	5
I	6	1	1	1	1	0	1	0	0	5
	7	1	1	1	0	1	0	1	0	5
	8	1	1	1	1	1	1	1	0	7
	9	1	1	1	1	1	1	0	1	7
	10	1	1	1	1	1	1	1	1	8
	Item Total Score	9	9	8	6	5	4	3	2	46

II

$$(1)\quad \frac{G^2}{kn} = \frac{46^2}{80} = \frac{2116}{80} = 26.45$$

$$(2)\quad G = 46$$

$$(3)\quad \frac{\Sigma T_j^2}{n} = \frac{9^2+9^2+8^2+6^2+5^2+4^2+3^2+2^2}{10} = \frac{316}{10} = 31.6$$

$$(4)\quad \frac{\Sigma P_i^2}{k} = \frac{0^2+2^2+3^2+4^2+5^2+5^2+5^2+7^2+7^2+8^2}{8} = \frac{266}{8} = 33.25$$

(1) *n* subjects represent a random sample from a potentially infinite population.

(2) The characteristic being measured is a random variable normally distributed (such as intelligence) and that it

remains constant across all measurements made (all items.) In other words, the correlation between items is constant.

(3) Error variance remains constant between items and is normally distributed within each test item with a mean of zero.

The analysis of variance model, especially, must not be used to estimate reliability when the true score changes irregularly from one measurement to the next; for example, if a practice effect should be introduced in some nonsystematic manner (Winer, 1962). If changes are introduced in a systematic manner and constant for all subjects, it is then possible to make adjustments for this change by eliminating variance due to change from the within-subject variance (Winer, 1962). In the above example all students are exposed to multiple forms in establishing reliability, the practice effect variance can be removed in this model. It is also possible to identify the practice effect variance associated with the retarded, normal, or superior by simply subdividing the subjects (Wert, Neidt, Ahmann, 1954). For example, refer to Table III.8 where a computational model has been developed for the reader's examination. Each matrix in this model may be related to our previous example in Table III.7. In other words, a reliability coefficient may be determined for those score values in matrix I using the same procedures we described in Tables III.6 and III.7. In this example, however, the dimensions have been expanded to involve five other matrices. The same basic symbol system has been retained with the following additions:

R   retarded population
N   normal population
S   superior population
A   test form A
B   test form B

G still represents the total sum of scores (in this example for all matrices). G_{RA} for sum of scores in matrix I, G_R for matrix I and II, etc. In the bottom row $n = $ total number of subjects in R.N., and S populations above. $T_{A1} = $ total sum of scores for item 1 in test A for all populations. Thus, the total correlation coeffi-

Table III.8. Showing a computational model with multiple forms and subpopulations

Subjects	Test		Forms		Subject
Retarded	A		B		Test Scores
1	x_{RA11}	p_{RA1}	x_{RB11}	p_{RB1}	p_{R1}
2		p_{RA2}		p_{RB2}	p_{R2}
R i	Matrix I	p_{RAi}	Matrix II	p_{RBi}	p_{Ri}
n_R	x_{RAjk}	p_{RAn}	x_{RBjk}	p_{RBn}	p_{Rn}
	$T_{RA1}+T_{RA2}\cdots T_{RAj}\cdots T_{RAk}$	G_{RA}	$T_{RB1}+T_{RB2}\cdots T_{RBj}\cdots T_{RBk}$ G_{RB}		G_R
Normal					
1	x_{NA11}	p_{NA1}	x_{NB11}	p_{NB1}	p_{N1}
2		p_{NA2}		p_{NB2}	p_{N2}
N i	Matrix III	p_{NAi}	Matrix IV	p_{NBi}	p_{Ni}
n_N	x_{NAjk}	p_{NAn}	x_{NBjk}	p_{NBn}	p_{Nn}
	$T_{NA1}+T_{NA2}\cdots T_{NAj}\cdots T_{NAk}$	G_{NA}	$T_{NB1}+T_{NB2}\cdots T_{NBj}\cdots T_{NBk}$ G_{NB}		G_N
Superior					
1	x_{SA11}	p_{SA1}	x_{SB11}	p_{SB1}	p_{S1}
2		p_{SA2}		p_{SB2}	p_{S2}
S i	Matrix V	p_{SAi}	Matrix VI	p_{SBi}	p_{Si}
n_S	x_{SAjk}	p_{SAn}	x_{SBjk}	p_{SBn}	p_{Sn}
	$T_{SA1}+T_{SA2}\cdots T_{SAj}\cdots T_{SAk}$	G_{SA}	$T_{SB1}+T_{SB2}\cdots T_{SBj}\cdots T_{SBk}$ G_{SB}		G_S
n	$T_{A1}+T_{A2}\cdots T_{Aj}\cdots T_{Ak}$	G_A	$T_{B1}+T_{B2}\cdots T_{Bj}\cdots T_{Bk}$ G_{BA}		G

cient for all subjects in all populations for both forms may be determined using the total number of correct responses for each item in both forms and the total score for each subject for combined forms A and B. We would use the (P) values in the last column and (T) values in the bottom row and proceed as explained in Tables III.6 and III.7. It is obvious now that there are additional benefits to be derived from this expanded model. We can now determine the reliability for each matrix, each population, each form, or the total. Again, we can estimate how reliable this test is with retarded or superior children for either form, or we can determine the reliability for combined forms. For example, the reliability for matrix I may be too low for the diagnostic problem involved; consequently, we can find the extent to which reliability will be increased if we use the combined forms by simply expanding k of the R population, to include both forms in one matrix. We could also use the Spearman-Brown formulas 3.14 or 3.15 to estimate this value.

It is possible in this computational model to construct or observe the change in variance between the various matrices. For instance, a practice effect variance that may occur between form A and B could be eliminated by subtracting a constant from each P value in matrix II equal to the difference between the overall mean values of the two groups. This procedure would eliminate the increase in score values caused by a practice effect, changing the within-subjects variance, while leaving between-subjects variance the same (Kerlinger 1965; Winer, 1962).

It is important that educators and psychologists understand the conditions affecting the reliability of their diagnostic instruments. In general, they can be grouped into the following categories: 1) range of ability in the population samples; 2) length of the instrument; 3) judgment of the examiner; and 4) speed versus power tests. These conditions and important considerations that may alter the reliability of an instrument, particularly those associated with exceptional children, will be considered in the discussion that follows.

RANGE OF ABILITY IN THE POPULATION SAMPLE: The composition of the population involved in the computation of the reliability coefficient can greatly alter the level of reliability reported for a test. An illustration of this can be found in Figure III.7 where it readily can be seen that reliability of homogenous groups is less than the reliability of heterogenous groups. This concept is particularly important for professional groups working with exceptional children in that they represent a specific homogenous group within the general population. In Figure III.7, for example, group A may represent retarded children, group B normal children, and group C superior children in a particular school system. Obviously, this particular instrument in the example shown would have a high reliability coefficient for the entire group, but limited reliability for specific groups within.

A mathematical demonstration of this can be derived from the

reliability formula (3.6) where: $r = 1 - \dfrac{\sigma_e{}^2}{\sigma_t{}^2}$

Here one can see that if the error variance for a certain test remains constant and the total variance decreases, the error ratio obviously increases, causing the reliability to decrease. In other words, the larger the proportion of error variance to total variance the lower the reliability will be.

Another example can be seen from the error of measurement formula 3.12 where:

$$SE_{mea} = \sigma_t \sqrt{1 - r_{xy}}$$

If we assume that the error of measurement (SE_{mea}) remains constant and total variance is increased (σ_t), then the reliability coefficient will increase (r_{xy}). Or the reverse of this is true if σ_t decreases, r_{xy} obviously decreases.

LENGTH OF INSTRUMENT: In general we can state the the longer a test is the more reliable it becomes. Of course, the honesty of this statement is dependent upon two things. One is the element of fatigue which assumes that the subjects taking the test do not tire of the longer test, and second, it is assumed that all items added to the test are homogenous to the initial pool of items to which they have been added. By homogenous it is understood that the new items are all of similar level of difficulty as well as possessing a high level of intercorrelation with the initial items.

A psychoeducational diagnosis frequently requires measurements that involve a sampling process. For example, if a diagnostician is interested in evaluating a child's perceptual skills, he will take samples of the child's behavior with various kinds of perceptual activity, assuming in the process that his sample is representative of the child's repertoire in this area. Obviously, the smaller the sample the greater the chance for error. A more specific example of this can be made in evaluating a person's knowledge of the Civil War. If one were asked two questions of a very narrow aspect of the war and he failed to answer both questions it cannot be assumed that he has no knowledge of the Civil War. It is more reasonable to assume that the sample was inadequate and does not represent his knowledge in this area. Here one can see that the fewer the number of items the greater the chances are for an error in diagnosis. The more items a test has, the more adequately it samples a specific area of behavior or knowledge or some other aspect of the individual the diagnostician is interested in.

In that exceptional children may tire more easily than normal children when taking tests, it is frequently desirable to shorten examinations or give an examination in several sessions over a longer period of time. It is possible to estimate the reliability of tests of varying lengths through the use of the Spearman-Brown formula. The general formula, given earlier (3.14), was:

$$r_{xy} = \frac{n \, r_{ab}}{1 + (n - 1) \, r_{ab}}$$

where the student will remember that r_{ab} equals the reliability of the existing test and r_{xy} equals estimated reliability of the revised test n times as long. If the known reliability of the existing test is 0.95 the estimated reliability of a revised test half as long would be determined by substituting in the above formula .5 for (n) as follows:

$$r_{xy} = \frac{.5 \, (.95)}{1 + (.5 - 1) \, .95} = .90$$

with r_{xy} equal to .90. Likewise, if we wish to estimate the reliability of the same test if it were twice as long $(n=2)$, we would find the reliability equal to .97. It is also possible to estimate the extent to which a test must be either lengthened or shortened to obtain a desirable level of reliability. For example, if one is of the opinion that a reliability of .90 is adequate for screening purposes and the particular test in question has a reliability of .98 but takes too long to administer, one can estimate how much this test can be shortened and still have the required level of reliability. Again, using Spearman-Brown formula 3.15:

$$n = \frac{rn \ (1 - r'_{xy})}{r'_{xy} \ (1 - rn)}$$

Assuming that a test had a given reliability of .80, we can determine how much longer this test must be to have a reliability of .90 by substituting in the above formula we have:

$$n = \frac{.90 \ (1 - .80)}{.80 \ (1 - .90)} = 2.25$$

We can see that this test must be 2.25 times longer to have a reliability of .90. If the test had 40 items initially it must be increased to 90 items to obtain a reliability coefficient of .90. Normally the above example is typical in that the reliability of a particular test is too low and the investigator is interested in lengthening the test to obtain a higher level of reliabiilty. However, the reverse may be true if a screening instrument is needed to locate retarded children in a given school district, before administering a more expensive diagnostic instrument. If we reverse the above problem by stating that the existing reliability is .90 and we only need .80, we would find:

$$n = \frac{.80 \ (1 - .90)}{.90 \ (1 - .80)} = \frac{.08}{.18} = .44$$

that $n = .44$ which means the test may be decreased to less than half its original length and still have adequate reliability for screening purposes. This, of course, could result in a considerable savings if several thousand children are involved. Again, if the original test had 100 items, it could be reduced to 44 items.

JUDGMENT OF THE EXAMINER: Human judgment can greatly alter the reliability of an instrument particularly when subjects with aberrant developmental patterns are involved requiring unique instructions and responses. Many exceptional children are multiple-handicapped, resulting in complicated sensory limitations as well as deviant motor control. These fluctuating variables result in many unique combinations that make standardization of instructions as well as interpretation of behavior difficult. Following the instructions given for normal children may result in absurd findings when they are applied to exceptional children. In some cases instructions are provided both for normal and specific types of exceptional children with separate norms for interpretation. However, this does not resolve the problem of the multiple-handicapped child.

Administering or giving a test to exceptional children requires unique skills and understanding. Directions must be easily perceived by the child and adaptable to the sensory pathways most receptive of the external environment, yet amenable to standardization. Considerable practice is required on the part of the examiner to develop the skills necessary to give such a test.

Interpretation requiring subjective judgment on the part of the examiner introduces considerable error variance into the total score value. Any scoring procedure which enables the examiners to differ in their interpretation of the responses will provide a source of error into the scoring procedure and result in lowering the reliability of the instrument. Responses required of exceptional children are frequently limited, so the test requires the simplest response, simple in interpretation as well as *emissivity* (skill required of the child to give required response). Frequently, scoring directions will give a variety of detailed, sample responses the child may give, all of which are acceptable, easily interpreted, and easily scored. This appears to be a must for exceptional children to minimize the idiosyncrasies of examiners.

SPEED VERSUS POWER TESTS: One can quickly illustrate that the type of test and procedure used to determine the level of reliability can result in an artifact rather than the instrument's true estimate of reliability. After examining the effect of using a split-half type of reliability with a speed test, it must be remembered that the score or performance to be evaluated on this instrument is primarily dependent upon the speed of the examinee to do the task required. In a pure speed test, time is the only factor preventing the examinee from getting all the items correct except for possibly careless errors. Stated another way, if the examinee is given sufficient time he should get a perfect score without acquiring any further skill or knowledge in the required task. The effect of using a split-half type of reliability has been discussed and illustrated in Figure I.2. One can easily see that each individual would have nearly the same score in each half. Obviously, the correlation coefficient between these two halves would be exceedingly high. In expanding this discussion, a suggested alternative procedure is to split the test into different time blocks. To do this, the above example could be split into two time periods of one minute each with a short time interval between the two time periods to reduce the effect of fatigue or practice. This, in effect, is giving two forms each half the length of the original test. The Spearman-Brown formula would then be used to estimate the reliability of the total test. Another alternative procedure is to actually use two separate forms or, in the event that two time periods are not possible, the normal test period may be divided into quarters, using the first and fourth quarter as one half, the second and third as the other half. The assumption operating here is that the division equalizes the fatigue and practice effects in the two halves.

An obvious problem inherent in the above discussion is that of determining when a test is considered a speed test. Recognizably, tests possess various degrees of speed and power components. The shorter the test period the more influence speed has on the final score. Invariably, the more difficult the items the more the instrument becomes a power test; thus, we find various degrees of power and speed factors between tests. The problem of determining when a test has too much emphasis on speed to question the split-half type of reliability becomes a judgmental problem. It should also be called to the student's attention that tests are not equally weighted on a speed or power variable for all populations. In other words, if tests were rated on a continuum with power ratings falling on the left and speed on the right, we would have the following illustration to show the extent to which a test is a speed or power test:

$$-6 \quad -5 \quad -4 \quad -3 \quad -2 \quad -1 \quad 0 \quad +1 \quad +2 \quad +3 \quad +4 \quad +5 \quad +6$$

Tests with a rating of zero would have an equal amount of power and speed weighting; plus 6 would indicate all speed while a minus 6 all power. For some children, a small amount of speed creates a test strongly weighted on power. For example, a child with neuro-muscular problems involving eye-hand control may not be able to respond to a speed test. For the average child the test may have a rating of +3 but for the child above a −6. Therefore, we cannot assume that tests are invariant on this variable for all populations.

REFERENCES

Anatasi, Anne: *Psychological Testing*, 3rd ed. New York, Macmillan Co., 1968.

Birch, H. G.: *Brain Damage in Children: The Biological and Social Aspects*. Baltimore, Williams and Wilkins, 1964.

Fruchter, Benjamin: *Introduction to Factor Analysis*. Princeton, N. J., D. Van Nostrand Co., 1954.

Guilford, J. P.: *Fundamental Statistics in Psychology and Education,* 4th ed. New York, McGraw-Hill Book Co., 1965.

Guilford, J. P.: *Psychometric Methods*. New York, McGraw-Hill Book Co., 1954.

Harman, H. H.: *Modern Factor Analysis*. Chicago, University of Chicago Press, 1960.

Hoyt, Cyril: Test reliability estimated by analysis of variance. *Psychometrika,* 6:153–160, June, 1941.

Kerlinger, Fred. N.: *Foundations of Behavior Research*. New York, Holt, Rinehart and Winston, Inc., 1965.

Thurstone, L. L.: *Multiple-Factor Analysis*. Chicago, University of Chicago Press, 1947.

Wert, J. E.; Neidt, C. O.; Ahmann, J. S.: *Statistical Methods in Educational and Psychological Research*. New York, Appleton-Century-Crofts, 1954.

Winer, J. B.: *Statistical Principles in Experimental Design*. New York, McGraw-Hill, 1962.

CHAPTER IV

MENTAL RETARDATION

MAX W. MUELLER

IT IS THE PURPOSE of this chapter to explore psychoeducational appraisal as it is applied in the field of mental retardation. This exploration will proceed by first defining the concept
of mental retardation and considering associated systems of classification. The major task of the chapter is to present data on the
appropriateness of a number of psychometric instruments for
identifying mental retardates, studying behavioral characteristics
of the retarded, and evaluating response to educational efforts.
This section will be limited largely to tests of current interest for
which a body of data dealing specifically with the retarded is
available. Finally, some conjecture regarding probable future
development of the field will be braved.

Definition and Classification

The most widely accepted definition of mental retardation
is currently that of the American Association of Mental Deficiency (AAMD).

"Mental retardation refers to subaverage general intellectual functioning which originates during the developmental
period and is associated with impairment in adaptive
behavior" (Heber, 1961).

For the purposes of delineating the scope of this chapter,

---

1 This chapter was prepared by the author acting in his private capacity. No
official support or endorsement by the Office of Education or the Department of
Health, Education, and Welfare is intended or should be inferred.

three elements of this definition are critical. Since mental retardation is defined as *subaverage intellectual functioning,* a major focus of the presentation will be on tests of intelligence. Since it is *associated with impairment in adaptive behavior,* measurement in this area will also be emphasized. Since it is defined as *arising during the developmental period,* the majority of the discourse will be on tests appropriate for use within this period.

This definiton has attained wide acceptance in the various disciplines which relate to the field. This acceptance appears to stem largely from the fact that it incorporates the major features of most previous definitions with the exception of two features which enhance its utility. It does not, as did many previous definitions, imply that mental retardation is an irreversible condition, nor does it suggest that a low score on an intelligence test is sufficient evidence to warrant a diagnosis of mental retardation. There is ample empirical evidence that the once common idea that IQ remains stable over time is not viable. As recently as 1946 a study (Schmidt, 1946) suggesting that intelligence is an educable aspect of human behavior raised considerable controversy. Today studies indicating the educability of intelligence are too numerous to warrant discussion in the present context. These data also bear on the inappropriateness of establishing a diagnosis of mental retardation on the basis of IQ score alone. More important, there simply seems to be little reason to stigmatize an individual on the basis of a very limited sample of behavior when he is adequately meeting the demands of his environment.

As a final point, the AAMD definition is accepted as an appropriate basis for the development of this chapter since it is essentially a psychometric approach to the condition. That is, the major dimensions of the condition, intellectual functioning and adaptive behavior, are generally amenable to psychoeducational measurement.

Working with this definition, it is logical to also use the AAMD system of classifying retarded behavior. This system, described more fully by Heber (1961), independently considers *measured intelligence and adaptive behavior.* On both dimensions the fact is emphasized that the classification is based on current

Table IV.1. Levels of Measured Intelligence

Level of Retardation	Range of Level in Standard Deviations	Approximate Range of Level in IQ *
Borderline	−1.01 to −2.00	70 to 84
Mild	−2.01 to −3.00	55 to 69
Moderate	−3.01 to −4.00	40 to 54
Severe	−4.01 to −5.00	25 to 39
Profound	−5.01 or more	24 or less

*Actual range of IQ depends on the standard deviation of the test used to determine measured intelligence. The scores presented assume a standard deviation of 15.

measurement of appropriate behaviors by objective instruments designed for the purpose. Classification is then based on the standard deviation of scores derived from such an instrument.

The five levels of measured intelligence which fall in the category of mental retardation are presented in Table IV-I. Unfortunately, this system of classifying deficits in measured intelligence is not as straightforward in interpretation as it is in theory. In theory, the measured intelligence of a severely retarded child should represent similar behavioral deficit regardless of the test used to determine IQ. To the extent that equally representative standardization of all intelligence tests can be assumed, the AAMD system assures optimal similarity of intellectual performance of similarly classified individuals. However, interpretation of measured intelligence has traditionally been communicated in terms of IQ rather than levels of retardation. This factor raises several problems when the classification system is viewed in the light of presently available instruments for the measurement of intelligence. The standard deviation is not the same for all tests. Many of the available tests to derive IQ have a standard deviation of 15, but others, including the popular Stanford-Binet, have deviations of different magnitude. Thus a given IQ score may signify one level of retardation if derived from the Wechsler Scales and quite another if derived from the Columbia Mental Maturity Scale. Furthermore, the reported standard deviation of a test is frequently an average figure based on all age levels, while the true value may vary considerably from age group to age group. Even more critical, some tests in fairly broad use do not provide sufficient information on standard-

Table IV.2. Levels of Adaptive Behavior

Level of Retardation	Range of Level in Standard Deviations
Mild	−1.01 to −2.25
Moderate	−2.26 to −3.50
Severe	−3.51 to −4.75
Profound	−4.76 or more

ization to determine an appropriate value to use in transforming the obtained IQ score. These problems do not detract from the potential value of this mathematically sound classification system. They do serve to alert us to the need for careful interpretation of IQ scores in a field attuned to the absolute value of the IQ while using tests with only marginally adequate standardization.

The AAMD classification system provides for four levels of retardation in adaptive behavior which are identified in Table IV.2. According to Heber (1961) this dimension . . . "refers to the effectiveness with which the individual copes with the natural and social demands of his environment." He proceeds to identify two major components of adaptive behavior:

"(1) The degree to which the individual is able to function and maintain himself independently, and

(2) the degree to which he meets satisfactorily the culturally-imposed demands of personal and social responsibility."

In contrast to the large number of instruments designed for the measurement of intelligence, there are very few tests available which correspond directly to this dimension of the classification, however, numerous instruments are available to measure specific aspects of adaptive behavior or to provide more general measurement within specific age groups.

From the standpoint of psychoeducational appraisal the most important aspect of adaptive behavior, and fortunately the one for which measuring instruments are most readily available, is academic achievement. The importance of this aspect of adaptive behavior is paramount in two respects. First, it provides data which can be directly translated into treatment programs designed to ameliorate the effects of behavioral deficit. Second, it is quite generally useful in view of the relatively high prevalence of retardation during the school years. Indeed many persons function in the retarded range only as a result of the academic demands of the school system, demonstrating near normal adaptive behavior in other settings.

Measurement of adaptive behavior remains a critical problem. Instrumentation for use with the severely and profoundly retarded is extremely limited. Many of the tests which are available can be used over only a relatively narrow age range. Even the measurement of achievement is complicated by inappropriateness of instruments for use with the retarded.

As indicated previously, the AAMD definition and classification system has been taken as a basis for this chapter as a matter of convenience and consistency, and because this system incorporates the most salient features of most competing systems. The relationship of this classification scheme to the most common educational classification terminology merits specific consideration.

The majority of our states classify retardates, for educational purposes, as educable or trainable, frequently using the term custodial to describe those children who are too severely retarded to benefit from educational efforts. This classification system is IQ based, though the system frequently incorporates adaptive behavior on an informal level inasmuch as an individual is unlikely to be referred for testing unless there is an apparent and significant degree of impairment in adaptive behavior. The exact IQ limits set on these three classifications vary from state to state and even from school to school. However, it is generally true that the educable classification encompasses approximately the same population identified as borderline or mildly retarded in AAMD terminology. Moderately retarded and trainable are also terms which refer to much the same population. Custodial retardates would then correspond with severely and profoundly retarded. Lack of correspondence between groups defined by the two systems will most commonly occur among borderline severely retarded children who may benefit from programs for the trainable.

Overall, the AAMD system of definition and classification

provides an adequate basis for discussing psychoeducational appraisal in mental retardation. Evaluation of intellectual functioning and adaptive behavior will be considered in terms of an analysis of available instruments, and trends and projections related to development in the field.

INTELLIGENCE TESTS

An extremely large number of tests are available which are designed to measure intelligence. An additional substantial pool of instruments are purported to provide data on intelligence in connection with the evaluation of related variables. The Test Information Retrieval System at Michigan State University, for example, includes data on 268 instruments for the measurement of intelligence. It is obvious from even a cursory inspection of the Mental Measurement Yearbook (Buros, 1965) that a complete discussion of all such tests is beyond the scope of this chapter. Thus it is necessary to select certain instruments for consideration, recognizing that equally good instruments may be omitted. The tests which are considered were selected on the basis of the following criteria:

(1) specifically intended to measure intelligence;
(2) readily available through standard channels of publication;
(3) reasonable data available on the use of the test with retardates;
(4) evidence of reasonably broad acceptance in the field; and
(5) adequate validity, reliability, and utility to expect continued interest in the instrument.

Stanford-Binet Intelligence Scale

The S-B (Terman & Merrill, 1960) is a standardized, individual intelligence test yielding scores for mental age and deviation IQ's. Items are grouped into age levels, according to difficulty, ranging from age two to superior adult, and ranging from simple manipulation of objects to abstract reasoning. Although a number of performance type items are included, particularly at lower age levels, the test is essentially verbal in nature. Reliability and validity of the scale have been extensively studied. The broad use of the S-B in its many editions attests to its usability and general acceptability. Surveys by Silverstein (1963), Weise (1960), and Swassing (1969) suggest that it is one of the most widely used tests for evaluating the intellectual functioning of the retarded.

Studies of the S-B with retardates have been primarily with earlier editions of the test. Collman and Newlyn (1958) reported test-retest reliability of 0.93 on a group of 182 retardates over an inter-test interval of one year. Stott (1960) reported a test-retest reliability of 0.80 for S-B scores of a group of 942 retardates. Inter-test interval was not held constant in this study, ranging from one month to ten years. Silverstein (1963) reported a reliability of 0.95 for the 1960 S-B, but his source for this figure is not clear.

Miller (1960) in a review article suggests that research evidence concerning the use of the S-B with retardates indicates a high degree of stability of IQ scores over time, particularly when standard scores are compared. One validity study (Rohns & Haworth, 1962) on the 1960 S-B reported correlations of 0.69 with WISC verbal IQ and 0.72 with WISC full scale IQ. Moss (1962) reported correlations for the S-B with several measures of achievement ranging from 0.44 to 0.68. Validity of the S-B has also been evaluated in terms of correlations with Vineland social age (SA). Goulet and Barclay (1963) reported correlations of 0.78 between MA and SA. Mueller (1965) reported correlations of 0.49 to 0.88 between the S-B and other ability tests with educable mental retardates of early elementary school age. That study also reported concurrent validity of 0.76 taking a battery of achievement and learning tasks as the criterion. This same study was followed up after two years to obtain estimates of the validity of the S-B in predicting school achievement. Predictive validity coefficients ranged from 0.12 to 0.70 on specific criteria, with a coefficient of 0.52 against a pooled score representing overall academic achievement.

Overall, the S-B must be viewed positively as an instrument

for evaluating intellectual functioning among retardates. Estimates of reliability have been consistently good. Validity for a wide variety of purposes has been reasonably demonstrated. The extent to which the test is used documents its utility. The quality of the test is further documented by the frequency with which it is used as a criterion in the development of new tests of intelligence. A fairly extensive bibliography of studies of the Binet with the retarded is available in Mental Retardation Abstracts (1964).

Certain limitations of the S-B should be pointed out despite the general excellence of the scale. A number of factors militate against the use of the S-B at least in certain situations. General criticisms include the lack of suitability for the measurement of differential abilities, lack of discrimination at higher levels of functioning (not frequently critical in testing MR subjects), and the heavy loading of verbal functions. With reference to this last point, Anastasia (1961) suggests that the test is primarily one of scholastic aptitude, and may well be inappropriate in situations where intelligence is being measured for reasons unrelated to academic variables. It has also been suggested (Saltzman, 1940; Kennedy, *et al*, 1959) that performance on the S-B is unduly influenced by cultural factors such as ethnic background and socio-economic status. Data along this line tend to suggest that the Binet scores tend to underestimate potential for learning in subjects from atypical backgrounds, which could include many retardates.

The Binet also suffers by comparison with newer tests in terms of utility. Administration tends to require about an hour which frequently pushes the limits of subject attention. The subjective nature of test administration and scoring requires a relatively high level of training for examiners. Expensive personnel and administration time combine to make the use of the test too expensive for some applications.

Wechsler Scales

The Wechsler scales are a widely accepted group of instruments for the measurement of intelligence. Three scales developed by

Wechsler are currently in broad use: the Wechsler Adult Intelligence Scale (WAIS; Wechsler, 1955), the Wechsler Intelligence Scale for Children (WISC; Wechsler, 1949), and the Wechsler Preschool and Primary Scale of Intelligence (WPPSI; Wechsler, 1962). Though a number of minor differences exist among these scales, they are sufficiently similar to warrant discussion as a group. As the test titles suggest, the major distinction among these scales is the age level for which they are appropriate. These scales are made up of several subtests designed to measure more or less specific areas of intellectual function. These subtests are grouped into two principal subscales of verbal and performance items. Standard scores and IQ scores are available for the Verbal Scale, Performance Scale, and Full Scale. These scales have been carefully and extensively standardized and have generally been found to be highly reliable and valid. With the exception of the WPPSI which is quite recent, extensive research beyond the standardization population attests to the validity and reliability of these instruments. A complete review of the reliability of these scales is beyond the scope of this presentation, but in general reliability estimates range from the high .80s into the .90s except for test-retest estimates which fall into the .70s. Reliabilities of individual subtests is generally lower, as might be expected, but still quite adequate. Validity studies have also been largely confirmatory of the excellence of these scales. While the principal purpose of the Wechsler scales has been to measure general intellectual functioning, the format of the test has also led to considerable study of the potential diagnostic value of differences between subscales and among subtests. While some promising results have been obtained, the interpretation of subtests and subscale differences has not received wide acceptance.

Though the Wechsler scales have been very widely used with retarded populations, the extent to which their characteristics have been studied in relation to the performance of retardates has been somewhat limited. Baumeister (1964) in a review of the use of the WISC with mental retardates concluded that reliability and validity of the WISC with retardates were *not unpromising*. A fairly substantial number of more recent research efforts have been generally confirmatory of the quality of the

WISC and other Wechsler scales. Indeed, the tests are sufficiently accepted that they frequently appear as criteria for congruent validity studies of other instruments. Additional detail regarding studies of the Wechsler scales is available in the Baumeister (1964) article and in Mental Retardation Abstracts (1964).

Usability of the Wechsler scales sometimes presents a major problem. The scales require roughly an hour to administer and examiners must be highly trained. Neither administration nor scoring are entirely objective. The scales are not generally felt to be appropriate for very low functioning retardates. The manuals present IQ scores only down into the mid-40s. Though others (Ogden, 1960; Silverstein, 1963; and Silverstein, 1968) have provided extrapolated scores, the variance in raw scores at these levels is so small that they should be used only with the greatest caution.

In summary, the Wechsler scales are among the most widely used general intelligence tests. Though still more study of the tests, especially the WPPSI, with retarded populations would be desirable, these tests are not easy nor economical to use. It seems reasonable to assume that these problems will continue to be of little consequence except in certain limited situations.

Peabody Picture Vocabulary Test

The PPVT (Dunn, 1959) is an individually administered test yielding an estimate of intelligence based upon the measurement of hearing vocabulary. The subject is required to indicate which of four response pictures correctly depicts a stimulus word presented orally by the examiner. There are 150 items on the total test, but it is necessary to administer only a critical span from the point where a subject makes eight consecutive correct responses, to the point where success is down to a chance level (six of eight consecutive responses incorrect). The PPVT is appropriate for persons from age two years and three months to age 18 years, is avaliable in two forms, and generally requires only ten to fifteen minutes to administer. Derived scores can be obtained for MA, IQ, and percentile rank.

The test was standardized on approximately 4,000 Caucasian

subjects in the Nashville, Tennessee area. The test manual (Dunn, 1965) reports alternate form reliability coefficients ranging from 0.67 to 0.84 for various age levels across the full spectrum of intelligence with a median value of 0.77. The manual also reports validity coefficients ranging up to 0.94 in comparisons with various other intelligence tests. In general, the standardization of the PPVT was carefully and adequately done. However, the use of a local sample and of group testing at some age levels has been criticized.

The use of the PPVT has been studied extensively with retarded populations. Reported results are relatively inconsistent, but a sufficient body of data exists to be of considerable value in determining whether the test should be used in various situations. Indeed, the recent literature on mental retardation includes more studies of the characteristics of the PPVT than of the better established Binet and Wechsler scales.

Several studies dealing specifically with estimates of the reliability of the PPVT with retarded groups have been reported. Budoff and Purseglove (1963) reported a correlation of 0.85 for equivalent forms and 0.87 for stability of MA scores over an inter-test interval of one month. An alternate form reliability of 0.86 was reported by Kimbrell (1960) for PPVT IQ scores. Moss (1962) obtained coefficients of 0.68 for IQ scores with a time lapse of three years and 0.54 over an interval of two years. Kahn (1966) reported on stability of PPVT raw scores for retests over a period of four years. Obtained correlations ranged from 0.71 to 0.90. The largest number of scores (228) were available over a time lapse of one year and yielded a coefficient of 0.82.

A study by Blue (1969) considered both alternate form and test-retest reliability on the basis of scores of 116 trainable retarded subjects. Estimates of temporal stability over a period of one year and alternate form reliability were calculated for the total sample and for three subgroups established on the basis of age. Obtained coefficients ranged from 0.76 to 0.93 and were essentially equivalent for both types of reliability estimates. While the results were interpreted as generally supportive of the reliability of the PPVT, they were least reliable for the youngest age group (78 mos. to 120 mos.). Overall, these investigations suggest quite adequate reliability for the PPVT in use with the retarded. Test-retest reliability is particularly good when one considers the time lapse over which some of these estimates were obtained, and the consequent changes in absolute scores. The majority of the studies of alternate form reliability have been limited to correlation studies, however, the data reported suggest that obtained scores are essentially equivalent for the two forms. One small study (Gardner & Birnbrauer, 1968) did suggest possible differences in scores from alternate forms with younger children performing better on Form B and older ones on Form A.

A large number of studies have dealt directly with the question of the validity of the PPVT with mentally retarded subjects. Budoff and Purseglove (1963) found correlations ranging from 0.83 to 0.88 between the two forms of the PPVT and two forms of the S-B administered to a group of forty-six institutionalized, adolescent retardates. In this study the mean MA on the PPVT was eight months below that on the Binet. Burnett (1964) reported a study comparing PPVT, Wechsler-Bellevue, and S-B scores on 238 residents of a state school for the mentally retarded, ranging in age from 8 to 21 years. Correlations involving the PPVT ranged from 0.27 with Wechsler-Bellevue performance IQ's to 0.47 with Wechsler-Bellevue verbal IQ's. It should be noted in connection with this study that the use of IQ scores on a sample of restricted IQ range and the use of Wechsler and S-B scores from existing records on the subjects may be factors in the relatively low correlations which were obtained. Kicklighter (1964) compared PPVT and S-B scores of a group of 66 educable mentally retarded children, ranging in age from 6–7 to 16–24, obtaining correlations of 0.87 for MA's and 0.71 for IQ's. In a study of institutionalized retardates from 10.5 to 15.8 years of age Kimbrell (1960) found correlations between IQ's derived from the PPVT and WISC ranging from 0.30 to 0.43. Again it should be pointed out that the restricted range of IQ (40–62) may have depressed these coefficients to a considerable extent. A correlation of 0.71 between MA scores derived from PPVT and S-B on institutionalized retardates was reported by Mein (1962). Moss (1962) reported on a comparison of PPVT, S-B, and PMAT scores of 51 seven year old educable mentally retarded children. MA scores from the PPVT correlated 0.66 with those from the S-B and 0.82 with those from the PMAT. PPVT and WISC scores of 107 retarded adults were compared by Tobias and Gorelick (1961). They obtained correlations ranging from 0.42 with WISC performance scores to 0.66 with WISC verbal scores. A study of 101, primary age, educable retardates (Mueller, 1965) produced correlations of from 0.42 to 0.57 with several other ability tests. Shaw, Matthews, and Klue (1966) obtained substantial correlations between PPVT and WISC scores for a group of 83 subjects, but questioned the agreement of the tests for the retarded. Koh and Madow (1967) also obtained high estimates of congruent validity btween the PPVT and the Binet (0.84 to 0.94), but also noted that PPVT scores exceeded Binet scores significantly except at very low age levels. Data from McArthur and Wakefield also indicated substantial correlations (0.55 to 0.85) between PPVT scores and scores from the Binet and WISC. PPVT scores in this study were equivalent to Binet scores, but exceeded those from the WISC. A series of related studies (Rice & Brown, 1967; Brown & Rice, 1967; and Carr, Brown & Rice, 1967) indicated consistently low congruent validity for the PPVT with the Binet, WISC, and Illinois Test of Psycholinguistics Abilities.

Clearly, there is a great deal of variability in these many estimates of the congruent validity of the PPVT. Overall, these results seem to indicate reasonable validity for the PPVT in terms of its correlation with other measures of intelligence, though relatively low correlations and significant differences between scores have been found in some studies.

Several recent studies show promise of leading to clarification of the congruent validity of the PPVT. Two studies (Wells & Pedrini, 1967; and Shotwell, O'Conner, Gabet, & Dingman, 1969) indicate satisfactory congruent validity for the PPVT in terms of predicting Binet scores. Development of adequate, cross validated regression equations may at least reduce some of the problems of equivalence of scores. Further clarification may also result from continued efforts to identify factors effecting the equivalency of tests. One initial effort in this area (Hommill & Irwin, 1967) suggest, for example, the PPVT and Binet scores are quite comparable for TMR subject and young EMR subjects, but less so at higher ability levels.

In studies utilizing measures of achievement (concurrent and predictive validity) as the criterion score, the PPVT has faired less well. Kimbrell (1960) obtained a correlation of only 0.04 between PPVT MA and grade placement as measured by the Gray-Votaw-Rodgers Achievement Test with a group of 62 institutionalized retardates. Moss (1962) obtained concurrent validity coefficients ranging from 0.32 to 0.66 and predictive validity coefficients of 0.22 to 0.43, using the Metropolitan Achievement Test and Illinois General Information Test as criteria. He also noted that both the S-B and PMAT produced higher correlations with these criteria. Utilizing the WRAT as a criterion measure, Tobias and Gorelick (1961) found a correlation of 0.52 between PPVT raw score and WRAT reading scores, and Wolfensberger (1962) found that PPVT MA's correlated 0.52 with reading, 0.33 with spelling, and 0.35 with arithmetic scores from the WRAT. Mueller (1965, 1968) found the PPVT to be significantly poorer than the Binet, Pictorial Test of Intelligence, and Primary Mental Abilities Test in terms of both concurrent and predictive validity using the Wide Range Achievement Test and the New York Achievement Tests as criteria.

Some data are also available regarding the use of the PPVT for less specific purposes. Hammill and Irwin (1965) present data on 76 subjects which suggest the performance on the PPVT does not differentiate among various diagnostic categories in institutionalized retardates. Allen, Haupt, and Jones (1964) have presented data that the PPVT and WISC are equally appropriate measures of intellectual efficiency among subjects whose visual-perceptual ability is appropriate to their mental age. However, the PPVT yielded higher scores than the WISC in subjects with perceptual impairment. These data suggest a possible diagnostic value of the PPVT as well as a caution regarding use of the test.

Overall, it appears that PPVT validity coefficients are consistently lower utilizing achievement criteria than using other intelligence tests as criteria. It also appears that the PPVT is less valid than the S-B, Wechsler Scales, and PMAT, when tested achievement is the criteria, although in one study (Tobias &

Gorelick, 1961) the PPVT was demonstrated to be superior to the WISC.

In terms of usability, the PPVT is extremely good. It generally requires less than fifteen minutes to administer, and procedures for administration and scoring are sufficiently objective that examiners require a minimum of training. Thus, the PPVT may prove to be practical in many cases where less efficient tests are not.

In summary, the PPVT does not appear to be a completely adequate substitute for Binet or Wechsler testing for general appraisal of the retarded. Findings regarding the reliability of the test with the retarded are promising, and, despite some contrary data, congruent validity seems to be adequate. Unfortunately, there is very little data to suggest that the test is an adequate predictor in many situations where intelligence tests are used. Nevertheless, reasonable correspondence with other tests has been demonstrated in a number of situations. Thus, in situations where cost, administration time, and examiner sophistication represent critical considerations, the PPVT may prove a reasonable compromise for some testing purposes.

Pictorial Test of Intelligence

The PTI (French, 1963) was designed to provide an easily administered, objectively scored, individual test for assessing the intelligence of children between the ages of three and eight years. Items are divided into six subtests (Picture Vocabulary, Form Discrimination, Information and Comprehension, Similarities, Size and Number, and Immediate Recall), and are presented in order of difficulty within each test. All responses by the subject are made by simply indicating one of four symbols on a large response card which correctly depicts the answer to various stimulus questions. The test purports to measure intelligence in terms of verbal comprehension, perceptual organization, and ability to manipulate spatial and numerical symbols.

Standardization of the PTI was carried out on a total sample of 1,830 cases. The procedure used in selecting the cases assured that the standardization sample was comparable to 1960 census data as to regional area, community size, and occupational level of the father. The manual reports Kuder-Richardson reliability estimates for the full scale ranging from 0.87 to 0.93 for various age levels. Test-retest reliabilities for periods of two to six weeks yielded coefficients ranging from 0.90 to 0.96, and one study of test-retest reliability with a time lapse of between four and five years yielded a coefficient of 0.69. It should be noted that all studies involving test-retest reliability were done on rather small samples. Several validity studies, also on small Ns, are reported in the manual. In general, the coefficients obtained in these studies ranged from the high 50's to the low 80's when PTI scores were correlated with results of other intelligence tests. One independent evaluation (Pasework, Sawyer, Smith, Wasserberger, Dell, Brito, and Lee, 1967) compared the PTI to the WISC and Large-Thorndile as well as several measures of achievement in kindergarten and second grade children. Congruent validity with the WISC was satisfactory (0.75, K; 0.71, 2nd.), but other coefficients ranged from 0.35 to 0.51. The authors concluded that the PTI was a reasonable predictor of WISC scores, but not satisfactory as a predictor of reading and academic achievement.

Only very limited data on the use of the PTI with retardates are available at this writing. One study, reported in the test manual, compared PTI and the Binet scores of twenty-one mentally retarded children. A correlation of 0.44 was obtained and there was no difference between the mean IQ scores on the two instruments. Mueller (1965) included the PTI in an extensive psychometric study of 101 EMR children from age 7–11. Results indicate reasonable congruence with the Binet (0.72) and the Primary Mental Abilities Test (0.88) as well as mean scores identical to those on the Binet. Estimates of concurrent validity with a number of academic achievement criteria ranged from 0.27 to 0.75 (median 0.59) and were equivalent to validities for the Binet and PMAT. A follow-up study of achievement in this group after two years (Mueller, 1969) yielded coefficients of predictive validity only slightly below concurrent estimates, and again essentially equivalent to the validity demonstrated by the other instruments. In a similar study with fifty-one institutionalized EMR subjects (Bonfield, 1968), MA scores from the PTI correlated 0.39 ($p < 01$) with arithmetic achievement but failed to demonstrate significant relationships with reading or an overall achievement score. For the same group IQ scores correlated significantly with arithmetic (0.41) and overall achievement (0.51), but again failed to predict reading ability.

In terms of usability, the PTI falls somewhere between the Binet and Wechsler and the several tests designed especially for quick administration. In general, administration requires about one-half hour, and does not require a level of examiner sophistication as high as the Binet or Wechslers. The excellent manual and objective scoring are plus factors on this dimension.

In summary, the PTI appears to be one of the more promising new tests of intelligence, but it has not yet been thoroughly evaluated. In terms of usability it strikes a fair compromise between traditional instruments and quick screening tests. The reliability of the test is high, though data are not yet available to determine if this reliability holds up with retarded populations. The limited data available show mixed results, but clearly document some promise.

Full Range Picture Vocabulary Test

The FRPVT (Ammons and Ammons, 1948) was designed as a quickly administered test of intelligence based on measurement of verbal comprehension. The subject is required to indicate which of four alternate response pictures represents a stimulus word presented orally by the examiner. Norms for mental age are provided from age 2 through 16, and for percentiles at adult level.

The basic standardization population was made up of a carefully controlled sample of 589 children and adults. Additional normative data on rural, Spanish-American and Negro populations are available. Reliability coefficients ranging from 0.86 to 0.99 with a median of 0.93 are reported, some estimates being based on split-half and some on alternate form derivations. Various studies of congruent validity have yielded coefficients ranging from 0.46 to 0.91 against the Binet and Wechsler scales. Procedures for standardization and resulting estimates of reliability and validity appear to be generally satisfactory.

Though the FRPVT appears in a substantial number of studies

related to the retarded, relatively few investigations of the test's characteristics with a retarded population have been published. Sloan and Bensberg (1954) reported congruent validity of 0.76 with the Binet for a sample of sixty male retardates. However, they also observed a significant difference of 6.9 points with the FRPVT yielding higher scores. In another study of congruent validity (Cordell, 1959) correlations of 0.73 with an abbreviated Binet and 0.04 with WISC performance were obtained. However, this study involved only twenty-two retarded Indian children. Ho and White (1963) compared FRPVT and Binet scores of a sample of one hundred retarded children age 4 to 18 years. They obtained a coefficient of congruent validity of 0.87 but again a tendency for obtaining higher scores on the FRPVT was observed. When the sample was divided into two age groups only the younger group (CA 4-11) attained significantly higher scores on the FRPVT. Conversely, Fisher, Shotwell, and York (1960) observed that older retardates (CA 35 and over) attained significantly higher scores on the FRPVT than on the WAIS. Overall, the limited study of the FRPVT with the retarded suggests satisfactory reliability and congruent validity. However, users of the test should keep in mind the strongly suggestive findings that derived scores may not be equivalent to those from other instruments, and the lack of investigation of concurrent and predictive validity.

The usability of the test does represent a generally positive feature. Cost of the test is low, administration time short, scoring reasonably objective, and the format permits use with severely handicapped children. These advantages are partially offset by the lack of an adequate manual.

In summary, the FRPVT must be viewed as promising on the basis of its usability and consistently high reliability. However, lack of sufficient research specifically with the retarded, questions regarding validity, and availability of more adequately studied instruments represent major cautions regarding its use.

Quick Test

The QT (Ammons and Ammons, 1962) is designed as a simple, quick individual intelligence test based on perceptual-verbal performance. The subject is required to select from an array of four response pictures, the one which best represents a stimulus word presented orally by the examiner. A single response plate is used for the administration of each of three presumably equivalent forms. Norms are provided for MA, IQ, and percentile rank for subjects from two years to adulthood. Administration can usually be accomplished in 10 minutes or less.

The QT was standardized on a sample of 458 subjects controlled for age, sex, educational level, and occupation. The standardization sample yielded mean interform reliabilities ranging from 0.60 to 0.96 (median 0.72) for various populations. Several independent studies demonstrated reliability in the same range. Congruent validity with the FRPVT is reported as ranging from 0.62 to 0.93 for the three froms of the QT with various populations. Most of the lower validity coefficients can be accounted for, at least in part, by the fact that they represent samples of relatively restricted range.

Limited research on the use of the QT with retardates is available. Bibb (1964) compared the QT with the WISC and the Columbia Mental Maturity Scale on a sample of thirty-nine educable mental retardates. Alternate form reliabilities for the three forms of the the QT ranged from 0.69 to 0.81, comparable to results with normal subjects. Comparisons with other tests were made in terms of discrepancies in scores rather than correlations. This analysis indicated that the QT was superior to the CMMS in terms of estimating WISC scores, but still a tendency for the QT to yield scores below those from the WISC was observed. The variability of discrepancy scores was, however, extremely large, raising some questions as to how meaningful this analysis is. An interesting sidelight of this investigation was the recording of administration time. Mean time for administration of all three forms was five minutes and twenty-six seconds. Lamp and Barclay (1969) investigated the comparability of the QT and the WISC with a sample of 40 EMR children. The obtained correlations of 0.53 with Verbal IQ, 0.32 with Performance IQ, and 0.50 with Full Scale IQ suggest moderate validity in view of the restricted range of scores, but it was noted that QT scores were significantly higher than WISC Verbal and Full Scale scores. Methvin (1964) compared the WAIS and the QT with a sample of eighty-four institutionalized retardates. Obtained correlations ranged from 0.56 to 0.63, but QT IQ scores were significantly lower than those derived from the WAIS. Bonfield (1968) found that neither MA nor IQ scores from the QT correlated significantly with achievement in reading and arithmetic.

There is no question as to the usability of the QT. The test is economical in terms of material costs, examiner time, and level of skill needed by examiners. The manual is generally satisfactory allowing objective administration and scoring.

In summary, the QT represents one of the most appealing of several new tests in terms of usability and reliability. Unfortunately, almost no validity data is yet available, and even less data derived from retarded populations. No studies dealing with the reliability of the QT with the retarded were noted in the literature. The few studies of validity suggest adequate congruent validity but essentially no information is available regarding its value as a predictor of achievement.

Columbia Mental Maturity Scale

The current version of the CMMS (Burgemeister, Blum, and Lorge, 1959) is designed as an individually administered test of intelligence for children of 3 to 10 years. It consists of 100 plates each with several designs from which the subject must select the odd figure.

The test was standardized on a sample of 1,352 children from which MA norms were developed. Deviation IQ scores are not available. The authors report split-half reliabilities mostly in the low 0.90s, and congruent validity with the Binet ranging from 0.39 to 0.70 for various age groups. Independent investigators (Bligh, 1959; Smith, 1961) have obtained coefficients of congruent validity in that same range against Binet and WISC scores. Considering the very restricted range of many of these validation samples, congruent validity appears quite satisfactory.

Some information is available regarding the use of the CMMS with retarded subjects. The test authors report congruent validity coefficients of 0.65 for MA and 0.56 for IQ taking Binet scores as criteria. Dunn and Harley (1959) reported concurrent validity with ratings of achievement of 0.89 for arithmetic and 0.93 for reading. This study also produced coefficients of congruent validity with the PPVT, FRPVT and VanAlstyne Picture Vocabulary Test ranging from 0.80 to 0.87. It should be noted, however, that these data were derived from only 20 subjects distributed over a fairly wide age range.

Usability of the test is quite favorable. Administration requires approximately fifteen minutes for most subjects and demands on examiner skill are not great. Response demands are quite limited, thus making the test appealing for use with speech and motor impaired subjects. The lack of deviation IQ scores is a serious weakness in some situations, especially in view of the extremely large standard deviations observed in some investigations.

In summary, the CCMS seems to demonstrate reasonable reliability and validity with normal populations, and a high degree of utility especially for severely handicapped children. No information on the reliability of the test with the retarded was discovered, but estimates of validity, including prediction of academic performance, appear satisfactory. The available data are too limited to recommend the test generally, but it is worthy of detailed study especially for use with severely involved subjects.

Progressive Matrices

The Matrices are a series of instruments developed by J. C. Raven as tests of perceptual intelligence. The basic 1938 version of the test and the 1947 Coloured Progressive Matrices (CPM) are of primary interest in evaluating mental retardation. The tests are designed to measure Spearman's *g* factor in intelligence. The tests consist of three to five sets of 12 matrices or designs each with one part removed. The subject selects the correct missing part from six or eight alternatives. The test is untimed and quite simple to administer, usually requiring about fifteen minutes in examination time.

The 1938 Matrices were standardized on over 3,000 children and 5,700 adults, though it should be noted that the standardization sample was British and Argentine. Test-retest reliability ranging from 0.83-0.93, and congruent validity of 0.92 with Terman-Merrell scores are reported but for much smaller samples. The 1947 test is available in two forms which are identical except for mode of presentation, one using a board matrix with actual pieces to be filled in and the other printed replications of these matrices. Standardization of the board form was carried out on 291 children aged 5 to 10 years, and of the book form on 608 children from 5 to 11½ years of age. Norms are presented separately for the two forms but these are extremely inadequate by American standards, yielding only percentile ranks in large steps at half year intervals.

Though the reliability and validity of the 1938 matrices have been demonstrated by extensive research, similar data for the CPM is relatively limited. The manual reports test-retest reliabilities ranging from 0.65 for children under seven to 0.90 over the full range of the test. It also reports a correlation of 0.50 with the Stanford-Binet for children less than seven years of age. Martin and Weichers (1954) compared the CPM with the WISC on a group of 100 children between nine and ten years of age. Correlations of 0.91 with full scale IQs, 0.84 with verbal IQs and 0.83 with performance IQs were obtained. Correlations between the CPM and WISC subtest scores ranged from 0.74 to 0.47. Green and Ewert (1955) obtained a correlation of 0.78 with the Otis Intelligence Test with a group of 192 children ranging in age from 6–6 to 12–5 and correlations with California Mental Maturity Test IQs and Kuhlmann-Anderson IQs for small groups at different age levels ranging from 0.28 to 0.56. On the basis of these limited data, it cannot be said that the validity or reliability of the test has been adequately demonstrated, but results suggest that the test shows some promise for general use. An extensive review of literature related to the Progressive Matrices is available (Burke, 1958).

Several studies are available dealing with the validity of the CPM and the standard Matrices with mentally retarded children. Stacey and Carleton (1955), reporting on a study of 150 institutionalized mental retardates, reported that the CPM correlated 0.54 with chronological age, 0.69 with S-B MA, 0.71 with S-B IQ,

0.62 with WISC full-scale scores, 0.55 with WISC full scale IQ, 0.52 with WISC performance IQ, and 0.54 with WISC verbal IQ. Correlation with WISC subtest weighted scores ranged from 0.28 to 0.48. Using a sample of 172 sub-normal adults, Stacey and Gill (1955) obtained correlations of 0.86 with the S-B, 0.51 with Wechsler-Bellevue performance IQ and 0.56 with Wechsler-Bellevue verbal IQ. Malpass, Brown and Hake (1960) found that the CPM correlated about 0.50 with scores from various other intelligence tests. Mueller (1965, 1969) found the CPM to be significantly inferior to the Binet, Pictorial Test of Intelligence, and Primary Mental Abilities Test in terms of congruent, concurrent, and predictive validity in a sample of 101 young retardates. Klauer (1964) also concluded that the CPM did not differentiate adequately between normal and retarded children.

The strength of this test lies primarily in its short administration time, simple administrative procedures, and the interest which the plates engender in most subjects. The test is also of interest of a relatively pure measure of *g*, though some critics (Burke, 1958) have suggested that it is not nearly so pure a measure of this factor as Raven intended. Weaknesses of the CPM include lack of sufficient reliability and validity data, lack of norms comparable to most American tests, and use of only a single type of task. Finally, the manual is extremely inadequate, lacking a number of essential characteristics.

Though the high reliability and usability make this test appealing, available data suggest that it is not an appropriate substitute for other general intelligence tests with mentally retarded children. This is not to say that the test may not be useful in some contexts. Dils (1960) suggests potential value if the test is an indicator of brain damage, and Cronbach (1960) suggests that the Matrices could play a major role in identifying children with adequate reasoning ability within groups which score low on more verbal measures of ability. Budoff (1969) has also discussed the possible utility of the Matrices as an indicator of learning potential among retardates.

Goodenough-Harris Drawing Test

Over the years a number of attempts have been made to measure the intellectual development of children by analysis of their drawings designs, human figures, etc. Perhaps the best developed system for such evaluation is that espoused by Goodenough and Harris (1963) based on earlier work by Goodenough (1926). As presently constituted the test is administered by asking the subject to make three drawings: a man, a woman, and himself. The only other stipulation is that the drawings be of the entire person in each case.

Standardization of scoring procedures was based on 2,975 children controlled for age, location, and occupational status of the family. Norms are available for percentile and deviation IQ scores. Estimates of reliability tend to fall in the 0.80s and 0.90s. Both Goodenough and Harris claim that the test is a valid index of intelligence up to about age 12.

Including work with the older Draw-A-Man Test, there has been considerable research into the characteristics of this technique with the retarded. Tobias and Gorelick (1960) report test-retest reliability of 0.93 over a two year period. Alternate form reliability (male x female) estimates are reported by Taylor (1966) as 0.84 and by Byrd and Springfield (1969) as 0.83. Wells and Pedrini (1967) obtained correlations of 0.94 for a substantial MR sample of 277 subjects. Byrd and Springfield further reported coefficients of congruent validity with WISC Full Scale IQ scores ranging from 0.34 to 0.57 at ages 12 through 15, and correlations with Verbal and Performance IQs ranged from 0.24 to 0.66. Wells and Pedrini (1967) compared the Goodenough-Harris with the Binet and PPVT with a sample of 180 male retardates and 97 females. With both groups, the PPVT proved to be the better predictor of Binet scores though moderate correlations (males, 0.56; females, 0.62) were obtained for the Goodenough-Harris as well. Fine and Tracy (1968) found the Goodenough-Harris to be superior to the FRPVT at identifying mental retardates. Overall, the evidence for the reliability of the test with the retarded is very compelling. Evaluation of congruent validity with other intelligenct tests shows mixed results, but is not unpromising.

Usability of the test is reasonably good. Administration time is brief and requires no outstanding skill. Scoring is somewhat subjective though Harris' scoring system and guidelines provide a fair measure of objectivity. Studies of interscorer reliability tend to yield coefficients in the 0.90s further suggesting reasonable objectivity.

In summary, the usability and reliability of the test recommend its use. Estimates of congruent validity are variable, but generally acceptable. Evidence for validity against criteria other than other intelligence tests, however, is lacking.

Primary Mental Abilities Test

The PMAT (Thurstone & Thurstone, 1962) is designed to provide both multi-factored and general measurement of intelligence. The 1962 revision of the test consists of five levels yielding four to five specific factor scores depending on level, as well as a general or total IQ score. A typical form of the PMAT consists of five subtests (Verbal Meaning, Spatial Relations, Number Facility, Perceptual Speed, and Reasoning) and yields an intelligence quotient and MA based on each factor as well as an IQ score for the total test. The test is designed for group administration, generally requiring slightly over an hour to complete, and it is suggested that this examination period be divided into two sections on successive days.

The PMAT was standardized on a group of 31,919 students from kindergarten through age 12, stratified on the basis of regional location and school size. Stability estimates are reported by grade level with test-retest intervals of one and four weeks. Median values over all grade level were: total score 0.91; Verbal Meaning, 0.89; Spatial Relations, 0.78; Number Facility, 0.81; Perceptual Speed, 0.67; and Reasoning, 0.83. Predictive validity of PMAT IQ scores was evaluated in comparison with school grades after a time lapse of approximately fourteen months. Coefficients ranged from a low of 0.03 to 0.74 for the subtests and 0.30 to 0.78 for total score. Median coefficients were: total score, 0.53; Verbal Meaning, 0.40; Spatial Relations, 0.30; Number Facility, 0.56; and Perceptual Speed, 0.46. Correlations between PMAT scores and grades in various subject areas are reported for all grade levels combined. Coefficients for the total PMAT score were in the .50s and .60s and essentially equal for all subject areas.

The PMAT was also compared with the Kuhlman-Anderson for a group of 45 second grade children. This comparison yielded coefficients of 0.66 for the total score, 0.40 for Verbal Meaning, 0.50 for Spatial Relations, 0.65 for Number Facility, and 0.45 for Perceptual Speed. Overall, the reliability and validity of the PMAT appear to be adaquate and the estimates reported suggest that the reliability and validity of the tests are highest at younger age levels.

Information regarding the characteristics of the PMAT with retarded children is extremely limited. Moss (1962) indicated that the test-retest reliability of the PMAT is below that of the S-B for a sample of 51 educable retardates, but he did not report these coefficients. This study yielded a correlation of 0.82 between MAs derived from the PMAT and the S-B. In addition, the PMAT was superior to both the Binet and PPVT in predicting reading and artihmetic achievement. Mueller (1965, 1969) reported on congruent, concurrent, and predictive validity of the PMAT in comparison with several other ability tests. These data suggested that the PMAT was equal to the Binet in terms of congruent and concurrent validity and superior in terms of predictive validity. Based on a study of fifty-one institutionalized educable mental retardates, Bonfield (1968) compared the PMAT with several other intelligence tests as a predictor of gains in arithmetic and reading achievement. The PMAT was equivalent to the Binet in prediction of arithmetic achievement, but correlated poorly with reading achievement and overall achievement. Both Bonfield and Mueller carried out supplementary multiple regression analyses in connection with their investigations, and in both cases the results of these analyses suggested that the predictive value of the PMAT resulted primarily from the contributions of the Number Facility and Perceptual Speed subtests.

The PMAT is designed to provide differential measurement of intellectual abilities as well as overall intellectual efficiency. However, factor analysis of data from the Bonfield and Mueller studies obtained high loading of all subtests on general factors. Substantial intercorrelations among PMAT subtests were also demonstrated by Junkala (1966) for a sample of seventy-nine retarded subjects. Minimal support for the construct validity of the test was obtained by Money and Alexander (1966) when PMAT protocals of sixteen subjects with Turner's syndrome demonstrated differential ability consistent with previous findings using the Wechsler scales.

Usability of the PMAT ranks very well. It is one of very few group administered tests of intelligence which has been accepted to any extent for evaluating the intellectual functioning of the retarded. Group administration, of course, generally leads to substantial economy in testing time. In addition, administration does not require highly trained examiners. However, one is less likely to obtain potentially valuable clinical data from a group examination, and there is an increased probability that one may be measuring test-taking ability rather than the variables which the test sets out to evaluate.

In summary, it cannot yet be said that the PMAT is a proven intelligence test for use with the retarded, or that it is a reasonable substitute for the better established instruments. Almost no information is available regarding the reliability of the test with a retarded population, but general estimates of reliability are satisfactory. Studies of congruent, concurrent, and predictive validity appear very promising, though limited in number. The validity of the test against criteria of academic achievement is particularly promising. This factor, coupled with its ease of use, makes the PMAT appealing, especially in settings where testing is done primarily for educational planning.

Other Intelligence Tests

As indicated previously, the number of tests available for measuring intelligence is far too great to provide a complete review in this context. Several additional tests, however, warrant at least brief mention. These tests fall itno several broad categories. Several intelligence tests were deleted from the detailed review because they failed to meet the selection criteria set forth, but which nevertheless appear to have some promise for use with the retarded. Mention should be made of several tests designed for evaluating intellectual behavior of very young children. Several special purpose tests also warrant brief consideration since they are used for many similar purposes even though they are not, strictly speaking, intelligence tests.

At least five additional general intelligence tests warrant brief consideration. Two tests, the Leiter International Performance Scale (Leiter, 1955) and the Kuhlman-Binet (Kuhlman, 1939), were not reviewed in detail because of the serious lack of data on reliability and validity. Nevertheless, both tests have been used to a considerable extent in the evaluation of retarded subjects with some promising results. Two other tests, the Kahn Intelligence Tests (Kahn, 1966) and the Slosson Intelligence Test for Children and Adults (Slosson, 1963) appear very promising in terms of initial investigations with normal populations. To date, however, these instruments have not been studied to any extent with retarded populations. Finally the Van Alstyne Picture Vocabulary Test (Van Alstyne, 1961) should be mentioned since the highly similar PPVT, QT, and FRPVT have been reviewed in detail. However, the narrow age range (2 to 7) over which it is normed, make it generally less useful than its competitors. In general, the quality and usefulness of these instruments have been less well documented than the tests which were reviewed in detail. Nevertheless, each exhibits some promising features and should be considered as possible supplements to better studied instruments.

The detailed review also omitted consideration of infant intelligence scales. This was in part an arbitrary decision. However, it should be noted that the utility of such tests is limited somewhat by the trend toward norming general intelligence tests to fairly low age levels. In addition, relatively little information is available dealing specifically with the use of these tests with retarded populations. For the examiner who is called upon frequently to evaluate very young children at least four tests should be mentioned. The Cattell Infant Intelligence Scale (Cattell, 1940), the Gesell Development Scales (Gesell, 1940), and the Minnesota Preschool Test (Goodenough, Maurer, and Van Waganan, 1940) are probably the best established instruments for use at early ages. The characteristics of these tests, including generally low reliability and validity, are fairly well documented and at least limited information is available on their use with retarded children. Bayley's Infant Scales of Motor and Mental Development

(1967) are extremely promising, but as yet too recent to have been well tested.

A fair number of tests which were not designed specifically as intelligence tests are either used to assess intellectual functioning as well as for other purposes or are used for the measurement of variables closely akin to intelligence. Tests in the first category for which substantial research with retarded populations is available include the Visual-Motor Gestalt Test (Bender, 1938), and the Benton Visual Retention Test (Benton, 1955). Within recent years there has been an increasing emphasis on the critical role of language and perception as determinants of intelligence. As a result, tests of these behaviors are frequently used in much the same way as intelligence tests, particularly in terms of prediction of academic ability. The Developmental Tests of Visual Perception (Frostig, Lefever, and Whittlesey, 1961) is probably the best example of such a perceptual test. The statistical characteristics of the test are reasonably well established and some information is available regarding the performance of retarded children on the test. It was not intended as a measure of intelligence, nor should it be used as such. Nevertheless, the information it provides may be an important supplement to IQ and MA data in many situations. A similar situation exists in the area of language development. Probably the most comprehensive instrument in this area is the Illinois Test of Psycholinguistic Abilities (Kirk, McCarthy, and Kirk, 1968). This test has been recently revised, but an earlier edition (McCarthy and Kirk, 1961) stimulated a great deal of research suggesting high reliability and reasonable validity for a number of purposes. Initial studies of the revised edition appear promising.

INTELLIGENCE TESTS: Summary

Extensive review of recent literature suggests that the evaluation of intellectual efficiency of the retarded is, as has been the case for a number of years, closely tied to the Stanford-Binet and the Wechsler scales. Though the number of investigations directly related to the validity and reliability of these scales with retarded populations is not extremely great, they continue to be the standard against which other tests are judged. There is ample evidence of excellent reliability and validity with the general population, and earlier criticisms (Baumeister, 1964; Himmelstein, 1968) of lack of specific reliability and validity studies with retarded populations has been somewhat attenuated by recent studies in these areas. Perhaps most critical, they are the only intelligence tests which have been validated to any substantial extent against relatively independent criteria.

The choice between the two instruments frequently reduces to a matter of individual choice. The Binet does appear to be somewhat more appropriate with severely impaired subjects and, until further information is available on the WPPSI, with subjects below about eight years of age. The Binet may also have a slight edge when the purpose of testing is strictly limited to the prediction of academic potential. Conversely, in some situations the availability of separate scores for Verbal and Performance scales and individual scores on subtests on the Wechsler scales may be advantageous. It should be noted, however, that research has not been strongly supportive of the Wechsler tests as instruments for differential diagnosis. There is also limited evidence that the WAIS may be superior to the Binet at estimating potential for employment. Overall, research continues to indicate consistently high correlations between the two tests, and essentially equal validity for most purposes for which the tests are used.

In earlier years the development of new intelligence tests appears to have been largely a result of differences in theories of what constituted intelligence and how it should be measured. The majority of more recently developed tests, and most of the instruments reviewed in this chapter, appear to result less from differences in theoretical position than from response to economy in testing. Most of these tests were developed to obtain estimates of intellectual efficiency from samples of behavior that can be obtained more quickly and objectively than is possible with the Binet and Wechsler scales. In this effort test authors have been eminently successful. Each of the tests reviewed in detail in this chapter can indeed be administered in substantially less time than either the Binet or Wechsler. In general, they are also more objective in administration and scoring, allowing less skilled, and therefore less expensive, examiners to use them reliably. Unfortunately, the extent to which these tests provide reliable and valid estimates of intelligence is not so clear cut.

Only in the case of the PPVT has there been a substantial amount of research specifically investigating the characteristics of the test with the retarded. The reports of reliability are generally quite supportive but studies of validity yield quite varied results. Despite a few quite negative reports, it seems fair to say that the congruent validity of the PPVT with the Binet and Wechsler has been adequately documented in terms of correlational studies. However, the lack of equivalence among scores derived from the three instruments is almost as well documented. This should present no major problem to the examiner who has studied the literature carefully enough to interpret PPVT scores in the light of this extensive literature. Thus, particularly in settings where economy is critical, the PPVT may indeed be a reasonable alternative to the longer tests. It should be kept clearly in mind, however, that the PPVT provides only a reasonable estimate of the score that might be expected were the Binet used instead. The evidence available at this writing provides essentially no support for the PPVT as a predictor of academic achievement or indeed most of the other relevant behaviors which intelligence tests are frequently expected to predict.

None of the other instruments reviewed have been sufficiently studied with retardates to warrant serious consideration as a substitute for the Binet or Wechsler with that population. Nevertheless, several appear quite promising in general, or have specific features to recommend them despite the limited literature available. A number of these tests, including the several picture vocabulary tests (FRPVT, QT, VAPVT), the Columbia, the Progressive Matrices, and figure drawing tests, provide the same advantages as the PPVT in terms of utility, though their reliability and validity, especially with the retarded, are less well established. Adequate study of these instruments might well demonstrate significant value for any of these tests. However, these tests also share one other important characteristic with the PPVT—each derives its estimate of intellectual performance from responses to a single type item. Considering the complexity of intelligence and the use to which we put intelligence tests, it may well be that no single type of behavior will ever prove to be a completely adequate predictor. Estimates based on sampling of a variety of behaviors may be inherently superior.

Both the Pictorial Test of Intelligence and the Primary Mental Ability Test do sample a reasonable range of behaviors, but have received only limited study with the retarded. Initial studies of both tests appear quite promising. They represent a reasonable compromise between the more traditional batteries and the very short tests in terms of utility vs. variety of performance required. To the extent that reliability and validity have been established, they appear satisfactory. Finally, despite the limited amount of data available, there have been some attempts to go beyond congruence with other intelligence tests in the study of their validity. It is reasonable to expect that tests should be validated against the criteria that they are developed to predict, rather than against other instruments purporting to measure essentially the same behavior. At least to the extent that intelligence tests are used to estimate potential, the PTI and PMAT appear fairly promising.

ADAPTIVE BEHAVIOR

The AAMD classification system (Heber, 1961) defines adaptive behavior as the *effectiveness of the individual in adapting to the natural and social demands of his environment*. The explanation of this definition suggests that this is reflected primarily in terms of maturation during the early years, academic performance during school years, and social and economic independence in adulthood. However, it is immediately apparent that a wide variety of behaviors could be involved in the estimation of adequacy of adaptive behavior, and consequently a wide variety of instruments may warrant consideration in this section. As an example, Swassing (1969) in reviewing special education projects being conducted under Federal support noted that adaptive behavior was considered in terms of perceptual abilities, motor performance, physical fitness, speech proficiency, and vocational competence, in addition to academic achievement, despite the fact that the projects were almost entirely involved with school age children.

Adaptiveness of behavior of retarded individuals assumes a direct relationship to what is viewed as normal behavior in a given setting. Thus, it is not unreasonable to consider that it is generally appropriate to use whatever instruments are available to measure various behaviors which are critical in a given situation. Nevertheless, the special needs for measurement of adaptive behavior among the retarded have led to some specific developments in this area. Two aspects of measurement in this area have stimulated sufficient interest to warrant detailed discussion: general tests of social competence and tests of achievement.

General Adaptive Behavior Scales

Several attempts have been made to develop general measures of adaptive behavior, or social competence as such scales are frequently identified. In contrast to most areas of measurement, few attempts have been made to develop instrumentation for direct measurement in this area. Typically, instrumentation for the evaluation of general social competence has focused on use of interview techniques with persons having close contact with the subject or rating scales used in connection with observation in a natural environment. Such scales typically consider such variables as physical and social independence, communication skills, vocational and prevocational skills, and socialization. Review of the literature on mental retardation and practices in programs for the retarded suggests that many attempts have been made to construct adaptive behavior scales with a heavy emphasis on appropriateness to local situations and needs. As a result, relatively few such scales have received broad acceptance. Limited general information is available on a number of instruments, but very few have been studied intensively. Increased interest in this area within the past few years promises considerable improvement in this situation. The recent publication of the Parsons Adaptive Behavior Checklist (Leland, 1969) makes available an additional instrument for measurement in this area. Though insufficient information is available to warrant detailed review, initial results with this instrument appear very promising.

Vineland Social Maturity Scale

The Vineland (Doll, 1953) is a questionnaire type instrument for the measurement of general social competence (adaptive behavior). The 117 item scale can be administered by direct observation and interrogation of the subject, or as is usually the case, through interviewing an informant who is familiar with the behavior of the subject. Items are ordered as to level of development so that only items over a critical range need be administered for any given subject. The scale includes items on self-help skills, self-direction, locomotion, occupation, communication, and social relations. Norms are provided for the conversion of raw scores to social age equivalents and instructions are given for deriving a ratio social quotient. Wolfensberger (1962) has provided norms for derivation of standard scores.

The Vineland was standardized on a sample of 620 caucasian, middle class subjects, ten male and ten female at each level 0 to 30 years. The extended manual (Doll, 1953) includes extensive information about the development of the Vineland including discussion related to reliability and validity. In general reliability estimates fall in the low 0.90s, but it is frequently difficult to determine whether the author is discussing interrater reliability or reliability of the scale itself. Validity is somewhat of a problem due to the difficulty of determining appropriate criteria. Social quotients have frequently been compared with IQ scores with coefficients running into the high 0.80s. Certainly the level of acceptance of the test and the extensive literature available argue for its quality though the actual data are frequently difficult to interpret.

The Vineland has been used extensively in the evaluation of retarded subjects, though references specifically directed to the characteristics of the test with this population are relatively limited. Beyond the literature cited in the manual only one major investigation of the Vineland was uncovered. Goulet and Barclay (1963) examined the Vineland as a predictor of mental age with a group of 164 retardates. Mental age scores were predicted significantly by SA (r = 0.78) though SA scores exceeded MA especially at higher levels of functioning. It was also noted that SA and MA were equally correlated with chronological age. Investigating stability of intellectual and adaptive behavior, Barclay, and Goulet (1965) found that adaptive behavior, as measured by the Vineland, improved more than intellectual performance over a period of eighteen months, but did not comment directly on the reliability of the scale. They did suggest that development of social behavior was less closely related to chronological age than is intellectual performance. Further follow-up of this group (Barclay, 1969) suggested relatively stable growth in terms of adaptive behavior over a period of thirty-six months, though the greater stability of intelligence test scores was again confirmed.

The Vineland is generally acceptable in terms of usability. The interview generally requires twenty to thirty minutes. Scoring is relatively objective, but considerable examiner skill is required to assure correct interpretation of questions by the informant, and because of the need for judgment of informant accuracy and honesty. Nevertheless, interrater reliability has been shown to be adequate. One recent study (Behrle, 1968), however, suggests that Vineland scores are susceptible to examiner bias. Silverstein (1963) found that the Vineland was among the most frequently used instruments used in the evaluation of the retarded in state institutions.

Historically, the Vineland has been the measure of social competence. Usability, reliability, and validity are well documented including studies with retarded populations. Though several newer scales have been developed for similar purposes, the Vineland continues to find broad use in evaluation of the retarded.

Cain-Levine Social Competency Scale

The Cain-Levine (Cain, Levine & Elzey, 1963) is an interview type scale designed to evaluate the social competence of trainable level retarded children. Ratings of social competence are obtained through a structured interview with an informant who has regular opportunity to observe the subject's typical behavior. The scale is made up of forty-four items measuring behavior in the areas of self-help, initiative, social skills, and communication. Each item is scored on a four to five point scale. The end points of each scale typically indicate that a given behavior is or is not within the repertoire of the subject, while intermediate points represent successive approximation to the independent performance of the behavior sampled by a given item. This scaling technique is purported by the test authors to be a major improvement over most other adaptive behavior scales which simply indicate the presence or absence of a given behavior.

The Cain-Levine was standardized on 176 trainable mentally retarded children ranging in age from 5–0 to 13–11 years. The final standardization sample was limited to children in public school programs and children identified through public schools but still in the home due to their younger ages. However, substantial numbers of institutionalized children were included at earlier stages in the development of the scale. Tables are provided for converting raw scores to percentile ranks for various age groups. Percentiles are provided for each subscale as well as the total scale.

Essentially all of the information regarding characteristics of the scale relate to the retarded. The test manual reports split-half estimates of test reliability by sex, age group, and subscale. Reliability of the total scale ranges from 0.75 (8–9 year old males) to 0.91 (5 year old females). Reliability estimates for the subscale fall mostly within the same range with the communication subscale consistently producing the highest correlations followed by Self-Help, Initiative, and Social Skills. Differences in reliability at various age levels appear to be inconsequential as do sex differences. Test-retest reliability was checked on a sample of thirty-five subjects (age unspecified) with a lapse of three weeks between administrations. The resulting reliability estimate for the total scale was 0.98 with subscale coefficients ranging from 0.88 to 0.97. These data, while certainly limited in extent, suggest reasonable reliability for the scale. However, additional, independent information on this point is clearly needed.

The authors initially attempted to validate their scale by comparing scores with a number of variables thought to be associated with social development: mental age, IQ, chronological age, school experience, number of siblings, family occupation and income, and parents' education. Correlations with CA were 0.45 for males and 0.47 for females. Mental age scores of males and females produced coefficients of 0.26, 0.29 respectively with the effect of CA partialed out. Correlations with other variables were even lower. However, significant increases in scores were observed across the 5 age groups included in the sample. Significant sex differences were also observed and a correlation factor built into the test norms. In a subsequent study (Levine, Elzey & Paulson, 1966) a group of 93 TMRs were evaluated with the scale. Subjects accepted into school (N–72), and those denied entrance (N–21) were compared. Scores of the two groups differed significantly on all subscales as well as the total scale. Correlations between Cain-Levine scores and school acceptability ranged from 0.43 to 0.60 for the subscales with a total scale validity estimate of 0.53. Though these initial estimates of validity of the scale are not impressive, further data are required before reaching any firm conclusions.

The Cain-Levine appears fairly promising from the point of view of usability. It appears to be equally usable as the better established Vineland, and the objectivity of the items may represent an improvement in terms of demands on interviewer sophistication. Efficiency of administration should also be relatively equal to the Vineland though data on this point are not available. The fact that the test was designed for and standardized on a very specific sample clearly represents a limitation in terms of general utility, but is of little significance in the present context.

In summary, the Cain-Levine appears to be a fairly promising scale for evaluating adaptive behavior among trainable retarded children. Reliability is reasonably good, and usability appears to be equal to other scales designed for the same purpose. Available data on validity are less promising. Overall, though the characteristics of the scale clearly require further investigation, such study and careful clinical use appear fully warranted.

San Francisco Vocational Competency Scale

The San Francisco Scale (Levine and Elzey, 1968a) was developed to assess the personal-social and vocational competence of dependent and semidependent retardates. It can reasonably be viewed as an upward extension of the Cain-Levine Social Competency Scale both in terms of the purpose and the structure of the scale. The scale is made up of thirty items tapping the areas of manual skills, cognitive skills, dependability, and social adjustment. Each item is rated on a 4 to 5 point scale on the basis of the effectiveness and independence of the subject's typical performance.

The San Francisco Scale was standardized on a representative sample of 582 retarded individuals in sheltered workshops. Significant differences were observed between the scores of male and female subjects so separate percentile norms are provided by sex.

Based on the standardization sample, a split-half reliability estimate of 0.95 was obtained. A test-retest study of fifty-four subjects randomly selected from the standardization sample yielded a coefficient of 0.85 for scores with an intertest interval of one month. This estimate may have been attenuated somewhat by the fact that informants were not held constant over the two ratings.

The test was validated against several variables thought to be related to vocational competency, including chronological age, mental age, IQ, school experience, and workshop experience. Low but significant correlations between San Francisco scores and IQ were obtained for both males (0.48) and females (0.38). Correlations with years of education were significant but very low, and other variables produced essentially zero correlations. A factor analysis was carried out to determine the possible value of using subscales on the instrument (Levine & Elzey, 1968b). Results indicated a very strong general factor and failure to identify a factor structure similar to the types of behavior sampled by the scale items.

Usability of the scale appears to be good, though the test is too recent to have achieved broad acceptance or to adequately determine its ease and efficiency of use. The potential value of this scale appears to be relatively high though insufficient data are available to justify firm conclusions.

ACHIEVEMENT TESTS

Undoubtedly, the most frequent demand for measurement of adaptive behavior comes in connection with school situations where the basic concern is with academic achievement. Indeed, many individuals who go unnoticed in other situations are identified as borderline or mildly retarded during their school years because of their inability to cope with the demands of academic learning. These mild and borderline retardates make up the large majority of the retarded population. Measurement of academic achievement is also particularly critical because of its influence on programming for the individual. Few areas of evaluation provide data which are amenable to such direct translation into treatment programs. Even in institutional settings where the proportion of moderately, severely, and profoundly retarded is high, the demand for evaluation of academic achievement remains. Silverstein (1963) found that one achievement test was among the ten most frequently used tests in institutions, and Swassing (1969) found a number of achievement measures being used in these settings.

The high demand for evaluation in the area of academic achievement is accompanied by a large variety of instruments designed for this purpose. These achievement tests vary greatly in many characteristics, some of which are particularly critical in assessment of retarded children. The majority of achievement tests are group administered paper and pencil tests. While conclusive data on the relative value of group and individual tests is lacking, there is relatively good agreement among professionals that group tests are less adequate in several respects. It is more difficult, for example, to ascertain the extent to which scores may be influenced by factors other than the subject's knowledge of the content being tested. Particularly with retarded subjects it is likely that obtained achievement scores may be depressed by lack of understanding of the expectations of the test. This situation may be further complicated by the poorer attention and slower pace frequently exhibited by retarded subjects. In many achievement tests the selection of an appropriate level for use with the retarded presents a further problem. Further, and probably most critical, available group achievement tests were largely designed for and standardized on a general population. In many situations, the goals of programs for retarded children are sufficiently different from general academic goals, to render the use of standardized achievement tests inappropriate for the retarded. There is usually little to be gained by testing behaviors which are not expected of retardates nor within their school experience, even if those behaviors do represent adaptive responses to the general academic setting.

Despite considerable concern over the appropriateness of standardized achievement tests with the retarded, they continue to be used widely with the retarded, especially in public school settings. Therefore, selection of appropriate instruments is critical. It is vital to select tests which minimize the extraneous sources of variance noted previously. In addition, available information on the use of a given test with retardates, adequate range of norms, and compatability with the overall testing program in a given setting, should be considered.

The shortcomings of standardized achievement tests as measures of achievement among the retarded has resulted in some efforts to develop more appropriate instruments. These attempts have taken two primary attacks: development of individually administered tests, and development of group tests specifically based on goals of educational programs for the retarded and standardized on a retarded population. One achievement test, the Wide Range Achievement Test has been designed for individual administration and has been used widely with the retarded. At this writing the Peabody Individual Achievement Test, a much more comprehensive instrument, is undergoing final standardization. No group test specifically designed for the retarded is generally available. However, the New York Achievement Tests have been made available by its authors on a limited basis. It is reviewed in detail here because of its uniqueness and apparently high potential for use with the retarded.

Wide Range Achievement Test

The WRAT (Jastak, 1946, 1964) is an individually administered test of achievement in reading, spelling and arithmetic from kindergarten through college level. The reading score is based on word recognition (letter recognition at the bottom of the scale). Words are listed in approximate order of difficulty and the examinee is asked to read through the list to a point where ten consecutive words are missed. The author contends that the word recognition task is the purest measure of reading ability since the subject cannot rely on context or general knowledge for clues for identification of the word. The spelling test is administered by reading the words and having the subject write each word. At the lowest level the test requires that the subject spell his name or simply write letters of the alphabet. The arithmetic is entirely computation, again arranged in approximate order of difficulty. The author defends the use of a purely computational test on the grounds that more involved tests of mathematical ability tend to be contaminated with other ability factors, particularly reading. Examination time tends to run from fifteen to thirty minutes, though group administration can be used for the spelling and arithmetic sections which may reduce total testing time considerably for a class. Raw scores can be converted directly to grade equivalent scores. These in turn can be converted to age equivalent and ratio IQ scores by means of tables.

The WRAT was standardized on approximately 4,000 students primarily in New York and Delaware. To control for the local nature of this sample, the author developed the norms so that WRAT scores would conform to the nationally standardized Stanford Achievement Test. Validity is reported as being checked by correlations with Stanford scores but coefficients are not presented. Test-retest reliability (reading, 0.95; arithmetic, 0.90; spelling, 0.88) are reported in the manual, these figures representing data on slightly over 100 cases in each instance.

A fairly substantial body of literature is available when one considers both the 1965 edition of the test and the earlier edition (Jastak, 1946). A recent study by Attwell, Jamison, and Fils

(1969) strongly supports the equivalency of the two forms. The obtained coefficients of congruent validity for the two editions were: reading, 0.97; spelling, 0.97; and arithmetic, 0.95. In light of these results, and the minimal modifications in the new edition, it does not seem to differentiate between the editions. These findings were also supported by Cochran and Pedrini (1969) who reported coefficients of congruence ranging from 0.89 to 0.92.

Only one study (Attwell, *et al,* 1969) was noted which directly addressed the question of the reliability of the WRAT with retardates. Test-retest scores over a period of one year produced reliability coefficients ranging from 0.93 to 0.97.

Studies of WRAT validity are more numerous. One study directly related to the validity of the WRAT (Lawson & Avile, 1962) demonstrated a correlation of 0.94 between reading scores on the WRAT and the Gray Oral Reading Paragraphs with a group of thirty adult retardates. A second study (Saxton, Blackman, and Tretakoff, 1963) compared the WRAT and the California Achievement Test performance of a group of 109 institutional retardates. Correlations of these test scores with Wechsler IQ scores suggested that the tests were equal in their relation to intelligence. Congruent validity coefficients for spelling, 0.81; arithmetic, 0.83; and reading, 0.86 were reported, but the WRAT yielded significantly higher scores on all subtests. It was also noted that teacher ratings of spelling performance correlated equally with the spelling subtests of the two instruments. Mueller (1965) obtained coefficients of congruent validity of 0.46 for reading and 0.70 for arithmetic between scores derived from the WRAT and the New York Achievement Test of 101 young EMR subjects. These data also produced significant correlations between WRAT spelling and arithmetic with age equivalent scores derived from the Binet. PMAT, Pictorial Test of Intelligence, and ITPA ranging from 0.46 to 0.77. However, agreement of reading scores with the ability scores was very low. Other studies have considered the WRAT in comparison with related, non-academic behavior. Attwell, et al (1969) in a study of 51 TMR subjects found that WRAT scores were significantly related to intelligence, ratings of speech quality, and test behavior.

Cochran and Pedrini (1969) reported comparisons between WRAT standard scores and IQ scores derived from the WAIS, Binet, and PPVT based on a sample of seventy-two adult, male retardates. Though several significant differences were observed between IQ and achievement scores, correlations were reasonably good. Coefficients of congruent validity ranged from 0.38 to 0.78. As might be expected from available data on intelligence tests, the highest correlations were obtained with Binet scores and Full Scale and Verbal IQ scores from the WISC. One study (Reger, 1966) reports no significant correlation between WRAT and WISC scores. However, it should be noted that this investigation of thirty-one mildly retarded children also produced curiously low correlations in a number of comparisons among subtests of the WISC.

In addition to the largely favorable data on statistical reliability and validity, the content validity is good and the rationale underlying the reading and arithmetic tests seem particularly appropriate for some purposes. It is the only individual achievement test which is generally available, the short administration time is appealing. Perhaps most important, it appears to have sufficient floor to be used in the evaluation of young EMR children. The WRAT has been used as a criterion of achievement in a number of studies of the validity of intelligence tests (Wolfensberger, 1962; Tobias & Gorelick, 1961), and it has received fairly broad acceptance, especially among teachers of the mentally retarded.

In summary, there is substantial evidence to support the use of the WRAT as a measure of academic achievement of the retarded. The test is readily usable by teachers, validity is well documented, and reliability, to the extent data are available, appears adequate.

New York Achievement Tests

The New York Achievement Tests (Wrightstone, *et al.,* 1959) are a battery of three tests, the Wide Range Test of Reading Achievement, the Wide Range Test of Mathematical Concepts, and the New York City Core Achievement Test. The Wide

Range Test of Reading Achievement is a group administered test of reading achievement providing one score for the measurement of reading skills through the fifth grade level. Skills measured include word recognition, word meanings, sentence comprehension, and paragraph comprehension. The test requires multiple choice responses to 123 items. The mathematics test is designed to measure proficiency with mathematics concepts as opposed to computational skills and includes such items as meaning of mathematical terms and symbols, money problems, telling time by clock and calendar, and miscellaneous practical problems in mathematics. The test is comprised of thirty-five multiple choice items. The New York City Core Achievement Test is designed to measure proficiency in those elements of a typical EMR curriculum other than reading and mathematics. The Core tests include primary and advanced questions regarding health, safety, personal care, knowledge of home and neighborhood, travel in the community, and practical purchasing. Each test has fifty-three choice, picture response items, and the advanced test also uses sixty verbal questions requiring a yes or no response. These tests were developed specifically to measure the acheievement of retarded children, based on achievement expectations associated with the New York City school program.

Though these tests have not been standardized in the strictest sense, information based on administration of each test to over one thousand mentally retarded subjects is available. Percentile norms based on rather small numbers of subjects are presented, but are listed as tentative. All reliability information reported for the tests is in terms of internal consistency estimates based on Froelich's approximation of a Kuder-Richardson formula and are reported for the reading test ranging from 0.95 to 0.96, for mathematics from 0.81 to 0.85, and for core from 0.79 to 0.84. Validity of the scale is discussed only in terms of face validity of the tests as supported by teachers and supervisors in New York's Bureau CRMD.

Since the New York tests are not generally available, independent investigation of test characteristics is quite limited. In one investigation (Mueller, 1965; Mueller, 1969) the Wide Range Test of Reading Achievement, Wide Range Test of Mathematical

Concepts, and New York Core Achievement Test, Primary Series were administered to a sample of eighty-nine young EMR children. Test-retest correlations with an interest interval of two years were reading, 0.81; mathematics, 0.89; and core, 0.85.

Several validity estimates were also derived from this investigation. Congruent validity with WRAT scores ranged from 0.46 to 0.83 with consistently higher estimates being derived from the second testing. A large number of comparisons between NYAT scores and various measures of intelligence were also obtained in this study. Though the magnitude of the obtained coefficients varied greatly (0.00 to 0.73) they were generally supportive of a valid relationship between intelligence and achievement as measured by the New York test.

This battery of tests appears quite promising in terms of possible utility. Group administration procedures and a relatively low number of items assures efficiency. The content of the tests is specifically related to usual expectations of EMR programs, and the wide range of each test provides further advantages over most standardized achievement tests. Unfortunately, a few items, especially on the Core tests, are quite specific to the New York City environment for which they were developed. This seriously impairs the usefulness of the norms for use in other locations, but substantial information can still be derived from the tests. Lack of commercial availability, of course, is the major detriment to wider use of these tests.

In summary, the New York tests represent an almost unique effort to develop quality instruments for measurement of academic achievement of the retarded. While data on reliability and validity are quite limited, what is available is consistently favorable. Lack of general availability is the only serious problem in terms of utility. Clearly, the tests are sufficiently promising to warrant further study and broader distribution.

ADAPTIVE BEHAVIOR: Summary

Measurement of adaptive behavior of the retarded presents particular problems because of the lack of generality in what constitutes adaptive behavior. Aadaptation involves the relationship of an individual's behavior to the demands and expectations of his environment, which in turn may vary greatly from one setting to another. Thus, the best instrument for assessing adaptive behavior is that which best samples whatever behavior is critical in a given situation.

Nevertheless, some more general instruments for assessment of adaptive behavior are available. The Vineland Social Maturity Scale is a well established test sampling a variety of behaviors which may be viewed as generally adaptive. The reliability, validity, and usability of the Vineland are well established, and it has been widely accepted for use with the retarded. Two newer scales, the Cain-Levine Social Competency Scale and the San Francisco Vocational Competency Scale, also appear promising as general measures of adaptive behavior. In combination they cover as wide an age range as the Vineland, are equally usable, and they provide for more sensitive evaluation of many similar behaviors. Reliability and validity are not well established at this writing, but the limited data available are supportive. An even newer instrument, the Parsons Adaptive Behavior Checklist, became available just at the time of this writing. Though the characteristics of this test have not been tested substantially, inspection of the checklist and standardization data suggest high promise.

Aside from general measurement of adaptive behavior, the most frequent need for measurement of a specific class of behavior is in the area of academic achievement. A number of standardized achievement tests are currently available, but data on the use of these tests with retarded populations are extremely sparse. In addition, the opinion has been widely expressed that such instruments are not appropriate for testing the retarded. One individually administered test, the Wide Range Achievement Test, has received wide acceptance in use with retarded populations. Information available regarding reliability, validity, and usability of the WRAT tends to justify its popularity. In addition, considerable interest has been expressed in the development of a group test designed specifically for use with the retarded. One battery of this nature, the New York Achievement Test, has been made available on a limited basis for experimental purposes.

Despite the number of at least marginally appropriate tests available currently, instruments for the measurement of achievement of the retarded remains a critical need in the field.

TRENDS IN ASSESSMENT

Despite substantial recent efforts to develop more efficient devices for the assessment of the retarded, the most apparent trend in the area is the continued use of traditional instruments. The plethora of new tests of intelligence has failed to substantially reduce the popularity of the Binet and Wechsler scales for measuring intellectual functioning of the retarded. Several other tests appear quite promising, especially in terms of increased efficiency, but only one of these tests, the Peabody Picture Vocabulary Test, has been studied intensively with retarded populations. Recent developments in the testing of adaptive behavior have been equally unimposing. The Vineland continues to be widely accepted as the prime general measure of social competence, and instruments for measurement of specific adaptive skills have received only limited attention. Though some new instruments are being developed, promising initial data have yet to be broadly verified. In short, fairly active research and development efforts related to assessment do not disguise a reasonably strong trend toward stability in assessment related to retarded populations.

Aside from an appearance of stability in this area, several developments show promise of having a major impact on assessment. Perhaps the most critical of these developments are the increasing interest in: more direct measurement of intelligence, factors in intelligence, diagnostic teaching, and functional analysis of behavior. Developments in these areas may lead to substantial changes in assessment procedures in the future.

Interest in more direct measurement of intelligence is not particularly new, but is receiving increasing attention in research and development efforts related to the retarded. This concept has been variously described as fluid vs. crystalized intelligence (Cattell, 1968), process vs. product oriented tests (Newland, 1963), and learning potential (Budoff, 1968). Basically these authors criticized traditional intelligence tests for an emphasis on items which sample behavior which results from learning, rather than attempting to sample learning ability more directly. The major advantage of this approach to testing is hypothesized to be that it is less dependent on the previous experience of the subject. Thus, a traditional test might identify subjects as retarded on the basis of their not having acquired certain behaviors sampled by the tests. A process oriented test would, theoretically at least, differentiate between subjects who were performing at such a level because of basic intellectual deficiencies, and those who simply had not had opportunity to acquire certain behaviors. This differentiation may prove to be quite important in view of recent findings regarding the effect of teacher expectancy on achievement and special class placement based on cultural rather than intellectual differences. Actually two tests which are highly process oriented have been available for some years, the IPAT Culture Fair Intelligence Test (Cattell, 1960) and the Leiter International Intelligence Scale (1955). Despite the fact that the availability of these tests has not created a noticeable change in assessment of the retarded, interest in this area is currently increasing. Recent investigations (Mueller, 1969; Wortman, 1968; Bonfield, 1968) suggest that direct measurement of learning ability shows promise in the prediction of achievement of retarded children. The work of Budoff (1969) further suggests that process testing may have important implications for curriculum planning for the retarded.

Measurement of specific aspects of intellectual performance is another area where a fairly well established interest appears to be increasing. The Primary Mental Abilities Test is perhaps the best established test of differential measurement of intellectual abilities and has been discussed previously. More recent interest has grown out of investigations of the structure of intellect. These developments can be contrasted with traditional intelligence testing which can be characterized by an emphasis on obtaining a single score to describe intellectual behavior, or at best describing a small number of facets of performance. The more traditional approach is well grounded in theory and research. There is ample evidence that a strong general factor underlies a great deal of human behavior, but there is mounting evidence that determination of general ability does not provide sufficient information to develop effective programs for the retarded. The retarded, as defined by general intelligence test scores, are clearly not a homogeneous group. The need to differentiate specific abilities is supported by several lines of research.

Baumeister and Bartlett (1962a, 1962b) have demonstrated a qualitative difference in the performance of retarded and normal subjects in terms of factor analysis of WISC scores. Such difference could have important implications for methods of teaching the retarded. Indeed, Budoff (1969) has demonstrated that curriculum can be effectively modified to make the most of specific abilities of retarded subjects. Differential ability testing is also critical as a means of better identifying specific deficiencies in learning ability which may be remedial. Work by Martin (1967) has clearly demonstrated that learning strategies (specific intellectual abilities) are amenable to training. In summary, there appears to be considerable evidence supporting the potential value of continued work in the measurement of specific intellectual abilities.

Considerable interest is currently being expressed in the use of diagnostic teaching. Though this movement has been most active in general education, it has potentially important implications for assessment among retarded populations. In the first place, proponents of diagnostic teaching place relatively little value on using general tests, such as intelligence tests, to differentiate groups of children, except for strictly instructional purposes. Thus, the identification of a given subject as *retarded* would be of little interest to the diagnostic teacher. Expansion of this movement would undoubtedly decrease the need for testing aimed at differentiating retarded and normal groups. Second, the value of traditional assessments procedures would be reduced by the very nature of the diagnostic teaching situation, which emphasizes use of instructional situations not only to remediate, but also to identify specific deficiencies in academic learning ability. Though broad acceptance of such a diagnostic approach to assessment is not extremely likely because of its efficiency, it does seem reasonable to expect that information of more direct relevance to the classroom will be demanded of assessment specialists in the future. It is even more apparent that there will be a decreasing demand for assessing subject characteristics which are only related to, rather than a part of, the instructional process.

Over the past few years proponents of the functional analysis and modification of behavior have made concerted efforts to carry their technology from the animal laboratory into the real world of modifying behavior in practical situations. Particular behavioral problems of retarded populations have come in for major attention in this connection. As with proponents of diagnostic teaching, behavior modifiers place little value on information aimed only at classification of groups. The *fact* that a subject is retarded is far less relevant than whether or not he exhibits a given behavior. Thus again, broad implementation of behavioral technology would significantly reduce the demand for psychoeducational assessment as we know it. In addition, the type of assessment which is required in connection with the application of behavioral principles is markedly different than much of what now comprises psychoeducational appraisal. Two major changes would seem likely to result from extension of behavior to special educational settings. First, limited sampling of a wide variety of behaviors would be replaced by much more intensive analysis of specific performances. Second, objectivity and usability would become increasingly important aspects in the evaluation of assesment techniques with correspondingly less concern for reliability, validity, and generability. Critical features of tests to be useful within this frame of reference include precise definition of what constitutes a criterion of behavior, objectivity and observability of that behavior, and feasibility of describing that behavior in terms of countable units.

Overall, these trends suggest two major movements in connection with assessment of mentally retarded subjects. First, increasing interest in measuring specific aspects of behavior is apparent with an associated diminuation of general tests of ability or attanment. Second, it is becoming increasingly important to measure behaviors directly involved in the education and training of the retarded rather than relying on inferences. Educators in particular are insisting on obtaining data which can be translated directly into programming for retarded children. Nevertheless, these trends, and the considerable research and development work in the field of assessment, do not mask the fact that traditional techniques and instruments continue to play a major role in the psychoeducational evaluation of the retarded.

REFERENCES

Allen, R. M., Haupt, T. D., and Jones, R. W.: A suggested use and non-use for the Peabody Picture Vocabulary Test with the retarded child. *Psychol Rep, 15:*421–422, 1964.

Ammons, R. B. and Ammons, Helen S.: *Full-Range Picture Vocabulary Test.* Missoula, Montana, Phychological Test Specialists, 1948.

Ammons, R. B. and Ammons, Helen S.: *Quick Test.* Missoula, Montana, Psychological Test Specialists, 1962.

Anastasi, Anne: *Psychological testing.* (2nd ed.) New York, Macmillan, 1961.

Attwell, A. A., Jamison, Coleen, and Fils, D. H.: Relationship between the WRAT, a behavior guide, and achievement with retarded adolescents. *Am J Ment Defic, 73:*879–882, 1969.

Barclay, A.: Longitudinal changes in intellectual and social development of non-institutionalized retardates. *Am J Ment Defic, 73:*831–835, 1969.

Barclay, A. and Goulet, L. R.: Short-term changes in intellectual and social maturity of young non-institutionalized retardates. *Am J Ment Defic, 70:* 257–261, 1965.

Baumeister, A. A.: Use of the WISC with mental retardates: A review. *Am J Ment Defic, 69:*183–194, 1964.

Baumeister, A. A. and Bartlett, C. J.: A comparison of the factor structure of normals and retardates on the WISC. *Am J Ment Defic, 66:*646, 1962 (a) .

Baumeister, A. A. and Bartlett, C. J.: Further factorial investigations of WISC performance of mental detectives. *Am J Ment Defic, 67:*257–261, 1962 (b) .

Behrle, F. J.: Examiner bias on the Vineland. *Training School Bulletin, 64:* 108–115, 1968.

Bender, Lauretta: *Visual Motor Gestalt Test.* New York, American Orthopsychiatric Association, 1938.

Benton, A. L.: *Revised Visual Retention Test.* New York, Psychological Corporation, 1955.

Bibb, J. J.: A study of the Quick Test as a screening instrument for educable mentally retarded children. *Dissertation Abstract, 25:*3386–3387, 1964.

Bligh, H. F.: Concurrent validity evidence on two intelligence measures for young children. In E. M. Huddleston (Ed.) , *The 16th Yearbook of the National Council on Measurement Used in Education.* New York, National Council on Measurement, 1959.

Blue, C. M.: PPVT temporal stability and alternate form reliability with the trainable mentally retarded. *Am J Ment Defic, 73:*745–748, 1969.

Bonfield, J. R.: *Predictors of achievement for educable mentally retarded children.* University Park, Pennsylvania, Pennsylvania State University, 1968.

Brown, L. F. and Rice, J. A.: Peabody Picture Vocabulary Test: validity for EMRs. *Am J Ment Defic, 71*:901–903, 1967.

Budoff, M.: *Social and Psychometric test data correlates of learning potential status.* Cambridge, Massachusetts: Cambridge Mental Health Center, 1968.

Budoff, M. and Meskin, Joan: An educational test of the learning potential hypothesis with adolescent mentally retarded special class children. U.S. Office of Education, Project No. 6–1184, 1969.

Budoff, M., and Purseglove, E. M.: PPVT performance of institutionalized mentally retarded adolescents. *Am J Ment Defic, 67*:756–760, 1963.

Burgemeister, Bessie B., Blum, H., and Lorge, I.: *Columbia Mental Maturity Scale,* Revised Edition. New York, Harcourt, Brace, World, 1959.

Burke, H. R.: Raven's Progressive Matrices: a review and critical evaluation. *J Genet Psychol, 93*:199–228, 1958.

Burnett, A.: Comparison of the Peabody Picture Vocabulary Test with the Wechsler-Bellevue and Stanford-Binet on educable mentally retarded children and adolescents. Owatonna, Minnesota, Owatonna State School, 1964.

Buros, O. K. (Ed.): *The Sixth mental measurement yearbook.* Highland Park, New Jersey, Gryphon Press, 1965.

Byrd, Coleen and Springfield, Lynn: A note on the Draw-A-Person Test with adolescent retardates. *Am J Ment Defic, 73*:578–579, 1969.

Cain, L. F., Levine, S., and Elzey, F. F.: *Cain-Levine Social Competency Scale.* Palo Alto, California, Consulting Psychologists Press, 1963.

Carr, D. L., Brown, L. F., and Rice, J. A.: PPVT in the assessment of language deficits. *Am J Ment Defic, 71*:772–775, 1967.

Cattell, Psyche: Measurement of intelligence of infants and young children. New York, Psychol. Corp., 1940.

Cattell, R. B.: A culture free intelligence test. *J Educ Psychol, 31*:161–179, 1940.

Cattell, R. B.: IPAT Culture Fair Intelligence Test Scales 1, 2, & 3. IPAT, Rev. 1960.

Cattell, R. B.: Theory of fluid and crystallized intelligence. *J Educ Psychol, 54*:1–22, 1963.

Cattell, R. B.: Are IQ tests intelligent? *Psychol Today,* 56–62, 1968.

Cochran, M. L. and Pedrini, D. T.: Concurrent validity of the 1965 WRAT with adult retardates. *Am J Ment Defic,* 1969.

Collman, R. D. and Newlyn, D.: Changes in Terman-Merrill IQ's of mentally retarded children. *Am J Ment Defic, 63*:307–311, 1958.

Cordell, J. F.: Note on the use of the Ammons Full-Range Picture Vocabulary Test with retarded children. *Psychol Rep,* 5:150, 1959.

Cronbach, L. J.: *Essentials of Psychological Testing* (2nd ed.). New York, Harper, 1960.

Dils, C. W.: Coolred Progressive Matrices as an indicator of brain damage. *J Clin Psychol*, 414–416, 1960.

Doll, E. A.: *Vineland Social Maturity Scale*. Minneapolis, Educational Test Bureau, 1953.

Dunn, L. M.: *Peabody Picture Vocabulary Test*. Minneapolis, American Guidance Service, 1959.

Dunn, L. M.: *Expanded manual for the Peabody Picture Vocabulary Test*. Minneapolis, American Guidance Service, 1965.

Dunn, L. M. and Harley, R. K.: Comparability of Peabody, Ammons, Van Alstyne, and Columbia test scores with cerebral palsied children. *Except Child, 26:*70–74, 1959.

Fine, M. J. and Tracy, D. B.: Performance of normal and EMR boys on the FRPV and GHDT. *Am J Ment Defic, 72:*648–652, 1968.

Fisher, G. M., Shotwell, Anna M., and York, Dorothy H.: Comparability of the Ammons Full-Range Picture Vocabulary Test with the WAIS in the assessment of intelligence of mental retardates. *Am J Ment Defic 64:* 995–999, 1960.

French, J. L.: *Pictorial Test of Intelligence*. Boston, Houghton Mifflin, 1963.

Frostig, Marianne, Lefever, D. W., and Whittlesey, J. R. B.: *Developmental Test of Visual Perception*. Palo Alto, California: Consulting Psychologists Press, 1961.

Gardner, Ann M. and Birnbrauer, J. S.: Note on possible form differences in the Peabody Picture Vocabulary Test. *Am J Ment Defic, 73:*86–87, 1968.

Gesell, A.: *Gesell Developmental Schedules*. New York, Psychological Corporation, 1940.

Goodenough, Florence L.: *Goodenough Intelligence Test*. New York, Harcourt, Brace, World, 1926.

Goodenough, Florence L.: *Goodenough Intelligence Test*. New York, Harcourt, Brace, World, 1963.

Goodenough, Florence L., Maurer, Katherine M. and Van Waganen, M. J.: *Minnesota Pre-School Scale*. Minneapolis, Education Test Bureau, 1940.

Goulet, L. R. and Barclay, A.: The Vineland Social Maturity Scale: utility in assessment of Binet MA, *Am J Ment Defic, 67:*916–921, 1963.

Green, M. W., and Ewert, J.: Normative data on Progressive Matrices (1947). *J Consult Psychol, 19:*139–142, 1955.

Hammill, D. and Irwin, O. C.: Peabody Picture Vocabulary Test as a measure of intelligence for mentally subnormal children, *Training Sch Bul, 62:* 126–131, 1965.

Hammill, D. C. and Irwin O. C.: Factors affecting equivalency of PPVT and RSB when used with mentally subnormal children, *Am J Ment Defic, 71:* 793–796, 1967.

Heber, R. (ed.): A manual on terminology and classification in mental retardation. *Am J Ment Defic Monogr Supple* (Rev.), 1961.

Himmelstein, P.: Use of the Stanford-Binet, Form LM, with retardates: A review of recent research, *Am J Ment Dec, 72:*691–699, 1968.

Ho, D. and White, Delilah T.: Use of the Full-Range Picture Vocabulary Test with the mentally retarded, *Am J Ment Defic, 67:*761–764, 1963.

Jastak, J.: *Wide Range Achievement Test.* New York, Psychological Corp., 1946.

Jastak, J.: *Wide Range Achievement Test.* New York, Psychological Corp., 1964.

Junkala, J. B.: Changes in PMA relationships in noninstitutionalized Mongoloids. *Am J Ment Defic, 71:*460–464, 1966.

Kahn, H.: Evidence for the long term reliability of the PPVT with adolescent and young adult retardates. *Am J Ment Defic 70:*895–898, 1966.

Kennedy, W. A., VanReit, V., and White, J. C.: *The standardization of the 1960 revision of the Stanford-Binet Intelligence Scale on Negro elementary school children in the southeastern United States.* Tallahassee, Florida State University, 1959.

Kicklighter, R.: *Comparison of PPVT and RSB test scores of educable mentally retarded children.* Atlanta: State Department of Education, 1964.

Kimbrell, D. L.: Comparison of Peabody, WISC, and Academic Achievement scores among educable mental defectives. *Psychol Rep, 7:*502, 1960.

Kirk, S. A., McCarthy, J. J., and Kirk, W. D.: *Illinois Test of Psycholinguistic Aibilities.* Urbana, University of Illinois Press, 1968.

Klauer, K. J.: Der Progressive-Matrices-Test be, Volks-und Hilfsschulkindern. Ein Beitrag zum Problem des anschaulichen Denkens und der Intelligenzdingnostic. *Heilpadagogische Forschung, 1:*13–37, 1964.

Koh, T. H. and Madow, A. A.: Relationship between PPVT and Stanford-Binet performance in institutionalized retardates. *Am J Ment Defic, 72:*108–113, 1967.

Kuhlmann, F.: *Tests of mental development.* Minneapolis, Educ. Test Bureau, 1939.

Lawson, J. R., and Avile, D.: Comparison of Wide Range Achievement Tests and Gray Oral Reading Paragraphs reading scores of mentally retarded adults. *Percept Mot Skills, 14:*474, 1962.

Leland, H.: *AAMP Adeptive Behavior Scale.* Washington, American Association of Mental Deficiency, 1969.

Leiter, R. G. and Arthur, Grace: *Leiter International Performance Scale.* Chicago, C. H. Stoelting, 1955.

Levine, S. and Elzey, F. F.: *San Francisco vocational competency scale.* New York, Psychological Corp., 1968 (a).

Levine, S. and Elzey, F. F.: Factor analysis at the San Francisco Social Competency Scale, *Am J Ment Defic, 73:*509–513 (b), 1968.

Levine, S., Elzey, F. F. and Paulson, F. L.: Social competency of school and non-school trainable mentally retarded. *Am J Ment Defic, 71:*12–116, 1966.

McArthur, C. R. and Wakefield, H. E.: Validation of the PPVT with the Stanford-Binet-LM and the WISC on educable mental retardates. *Am J Ment Defic, 73:*465–467, 1968.

Malpass, L. F., Brown, R., and Hake, D.: The utility of the Progressive

Matrices (1956 edition) with normal and retarded children. *J Clin Psychol, 16:*350, 1960.

Martin, A. W., and Wiechers, J. E.: Raven's Coloured Progressive Matrices and the Wechsler Intelligence Scale for Children. *J Consult Psychol, 18:* 143–144, 1954.

Martin, C. J.: *Associative learning strategies employed by deaf, blind, retarded and normal children.* Educational Research Series No. 38, Michigan State University, 1967.

McCarthy, J. J., and Kirk, S. A.: *The Illinois Test of Psycholinguistic Abilities.* Madison, Wisc., ITPA, Inc., 1961.

Mein, R.: Use of the Peabody Picture Vocabulary Test with severely subnormal patients. *Am J Ment Defic, 65:*482–485, 1962.

Mental Retardation Abstracts. Application of the Stanford-Binet and Wechsler Intelligence Scales with the mentally retarded (an annotated bibliography), *1:*177–184, 1964.

Methvin, Marilyn: Quick Test performance of mentally retarded individuals. *Am J Ment Defic, 68:*540–542, 1964.

Miller, M. B.: Psychometric and clinical studies in mental deficiency, 1954–59; a selective review and critique. *Am J Ment Defic, 65:*182–193, 1960.

Money, J. and Alexander, D.: Turner's syndrome: further demonstration of the presence of specific cognitional deficits. *J Med Genet, 3:*47–48, 1966.

Moss, J. W.: *An evaluation of the Peabody Picture Vocabulary Test with the PMA and 1937 Stanford-Binet.* University of Illinois, Institute for Research on Exceptional Children, 1962.

Mueller, M. W.: Comparison of the empirical validity of six tests of ability with educable mental retardates. *IMRID Behavioral Science Monograph.* 1965, No. 1.

Mueller, M. W.: Validity of six tests of ability with educable mental retardates. *J Sch Psychol, 6:*136–146, 1968.

Mueller, M. W.: Prediction of achievement of educable mentally retarded children. *Am J Ment Defic, 73:*590–596, 1969.

Newland, T. E.: Psychological assessment of exceptional children and youth. In W. M. Cruickshank (Ed.): *Psychology of exceptional children and youth* (2nd ed.). Englewood Cliffs, N.J., Prentice-Hall, 1969.

Ogden, D. P.: WISC IQ's for the mentally retarded. *J Consult Psychol, 24:* 187–188, 1960.

Pasewark, R. A., Sawyer, R. N., Smith, E., Wasserberger, M., Dell, D., Brito, H., and Lee, R.: Concurrent validity of the French Pictorial Test of Intelligence. *J Educ Res, 61:*179–183, 1967.

Raven, J. C.: *Progressive Matrices: A perceptual test of intelligence, 1938, Sets A, B, C, D, and E.* London, Lewis, 1938.

Raven, J. C.: *Progressive Matrices* (1947). London, H. K. Lewis and Groege G. Harrap, 1947.

Reger, R.: WISC, WRAT, and CMAS scores in retarded children. *Am J Ment Defic, 70:*717–721, 1966.

Rice, J. A. and Brown, L. F.: Validity of the Peabody Picture Vocabulary Test in a sample of low IQ children. *Am J Ment Defic, 21*:602–603, 1967.

Rohns, F. W., and Haworth, Mary R.: The 1960 Stanford-Binet, WISC, and Goodenough tests with mentally retarded children. *Am J Ment Defic, 66*:853–859, 1962.

Saltzman, S.: The influence of social and economic background on Stanford-Binet performance. *J Soc Psychol, 12*:71–81, 1940.

Saxton, G. H., Blackman, L. S., and Tretakoff, M. I.: Achievement measurement and academic grade placement in educable mental retardates. *Am J Ment Defic, 67*:748–750, 1963.

Schmidt, Bernardine G.: A description and evaluation of an experimental educational program for adolescent children classified as feeble-minded. In, Northwestern University, *Summary of Doctoral Dissertations*, 1945, *13*:59–64, 1946.

Science Research Associates, Inc. *Primary Mental Abilities technical report.* Chicago, Authors, 1965.

Shaw, D. J., Matthews, C. G. and Klue, H.: Equivalence of WISC and PPVT IQs. *Am J Ment Defic, 70*:601–604, 1966.

Shotwell, Anna M., O'Conner, Gail, Gabet, Yvonne, and Dingman, H. F.: Relation of the Peabody Picture Vocabulary Test IQ to the Stanford-Binet IQ. *Am J Ment Defic, 74*:39–42, 1969.

Silverstein, A. B.: Psychological testing practices in state institutions for the mentally retarded. *Am J Ment Defic, 68*:440–445, 1963.

Silverstein, A. B.: WPPSI IQs for the mentally retarded. *Am J Ment Defic, 73*:446, 1968.

Sloan, W. and Bensberg, G. J.: An exploratory study of the Full-Range Picture Vocabulary Test with mental defectives. *Am J Ment Defic, 58*:481–485, 1954.

Slosson, R. L.: *Slosson Intelligence Test.* Aurora, N.Y., Slosson Educational Publications, 1963.

Smith, B. S.: The relative merits of certain verbal and non-verbal tests at the second-grade level. *J Clin Psychol, 7*:53–54, 1961.

Stacey, C. L., and Carleton, F. O.: The relationship between Raven's Coloured Progressive Matrices and two tests of general intelligence. *J Clin Psychol, 11*:84–85, 1955.

Stacey, C. L., and Gill, M. R.: The relationship between Raven's Coloured Progressive Matrices and two tests of general intelligence for 172 subnormal adult subjects. *J Clin Psychol, 11*:86–87, 1955.

Stott, D. H.: Observations on retest discrepancy in mentally subnormal children. *Brit J Educ Psychol, 30*:211–219, 1960.

Swassing, R. H.: *A comparison list of instruments used in evaluating project effectiveness of Title VI-A (ESEA) and P.L. 89–313 activities.* U.S. Office of Education, Project No. 26–2176, 1969.

Taylor, J. B.: Use of human figure drawings with the upper mentally retarded. *Amer J Ment Defic, 71*:423–426, 1966.

Terman, L. H., and Merrill, Maud A.: *Stanford-Binet Intelligence Scale: Manual for the third revision, Form L-M.* Boston, Houghton Mifflin, 1960.

Thurstone, L. L. and Thurstone, Thelma G.: *Examiners manual, PMA, Primary Mental Abilities.* Chicago, Science Research Associates, 1962.

Tobias, J., and Gorelick, J.: The validity of the PPVT as a measure of intelligence of retarded adults. *Train Sch Bull, 58*:92–98, 1961.

Van Alstyne, Dorothy: Van Alstyne Picture Vocabulary Test, New York, Harcourt, Brace, World, 1961.

Wechsler, D.: *Wechsler Intelligence Scale for Children.* New York, Psychol. Corp., 1949.

Wechsler, D.: *Wechsler Adult Intelligence Scale.* New York, Psychological Corp., 1955.

Wechsler, D.: Wechsler Preschool and Primary Scale of Intelligence. New York, Psychol. Corp., 1962.

Weise, P.: Current uses of Binet and Wechsler tests of school psychologists in California. *Calif J Educ Res, 11*:73–78, 1960.

Wells, D. G., and Pedrini, D. T.: Relationship between the S-B, L-M, G-H, and PPVT with institutionalized retardates. *Am J Ment Defic, 72*:412–415, 1967.

Wolfensberger, W.: The correlation between PPVT and achievement scores among retardates: A further study. *Am J Ment Defic, 67*:450–451, 1962.

Wortman, R. A.: *Coaching and Teaching in retardates: The Raven Matrices as a learning situation.* U.S. Office of Education, Project No. 6–8441, 1968.

Wrightstone, J. W., Forlano, G., Lepkowski, J. R., Sontag, M., and Edelstein, J. D.: *A comparison of educational outcomes under single-track and two track plans for educable mentally retarded children.* U.S. Off. Educ. Coop. Res. Br., Contract No. 6908, Project No. 144, 1959.

CHAPTER V

BLIND AND PARTIALLY SIGHTED

Mary K. Bauman

INTRODUCTION

What is Blindness?

ALTHOUGH BLINDNESS USUALLY attracts both so much attention and so much sympathy that we guess it to have been one of the first of human ills to be recognized and one of the most frequently mentioned in history and literature, it is still difficult to describe or define.

To many lay people the word *blind* means a total lack of vision but *legal blindness* includes persons whose acuity varies from total blindness to the ability to see at twenty feet what persons of normal vision can see at two hundred feet. Indeed, an individual may be *legally blind* if he has quite good acuity but a field of vision so narrow that it subtends an angle no greater than 20°.

Such technical definitions are important chiefly to ophthalmologists and administrators of certain educational, rehabilitation, or welfare programs whose benefits are, by law, available only to persons whose vision has been declared, upon ophthalmological examination, to fall within the above limits; therefore, to fall within the limits of *legal blindness*. For many purposes, including assignment to low vision or sight-saving classes, children with much more than 20/200 acuity may fall within the definition of persons to be served by a special education program. Either the local school district, the county, or the state may define those to be served by a given program and frequently children with as much as 20/70 acuity may be included. This, of course, means that such children may see at twenty feet as much as normally seeing children discern at seventy feet. This amount of vision usually handicaps the child only when he needs to read from the board although he might have difficulty with small print notations in algebra or certain other especially demanding visual tasks.

The test administrator will find that his visually handicapped clients fall roughly into three groups although exact lines cannot always be drawn between these groups:

(1) Those for whom vision is of no practical use in a testing or working assignment: The totally blind obviously fall into this classification but also included are individuals who can differentiate between light and dark or even some who can distinguish shapes but can do so only when those shapes are held between the eyes and the source of light.

(2) Those for whom vision is of some assistance in handling large objects, locating test pieces in a work space, or following the hand movements of the examiner during a demonstration, but who cannot read even enlarged ink print really effectively: Such individuals often use a combination of vision and touch to work with formboards and other concrete tests and definitely have certain advantages over the client who must depend entirely upon touch. However, they are placed at a great disadvantage if required to try to read; they are slow at reading, usually have done so little of it that word recognition skills are inadequate, and they may tire quickly under the stress of reading.

(3) Those who read ink print efficiently although they may need large type, may hold the page very close to their eyes, or may use a magnifier or special visual aid.

Obviously the psychologist must choose, or adjust, his procedures in terms of the amount of useful vision the child brings to the task. When tests involve concrete or performance materials, the psychologist must be careful to use the normative group with vision similar to the client's if the test manual provides separate norms for the several vision groups. Unfortunately, as will be noted later, some tests do not provide norms for partially sighted groups in which case the test can be used only as a clinical instrument, interpreted on the basis of the psychologist's experience only.

While it is certainly useful if the psychologist can have a copy of the ophthalmological report, even this provides only a general notion of how much vision the child will bring to the testing situation. Children with the same acuity rating may differ greatly in the effective use of their remaining vision because of real differences in field of vision, in sharpness of image, and in the strain involved in reading, because the age at which vision was lost might affect ability to interpret slight cues, and because some children do learn to use remaining vision far more efficiently than others do. With children of some maturity the wisest procedure may be to allow the child himself to decide whether he prefers to read or to have test material read to him. It is also sensible to have the child demonstrate his skill by reading aloud briefly, since some children overstate their ability to handle ink print.

Incidence

No one knows exactly how many people in the United States fall within the limits of legal blindness but, for the year 1970, a considered estimate placed the number at about 450,000. However, it is probable that less than 10 percent of these are under twenty years of age and it is well known that at least 50 percent are over the age of sixty. Blindness is typically an ill of old age. It has been estimated that the number of school age children who may legally be defined as blind is no greater than 23,000.

With so small a population, rather few teachers have had significant experience in teaching children with severe visual handicaps and the teacher newly facing the responsibility for instructing such a child naturally turns to the psychologist for suggestions and guidelines. If he is slow, how much of his slowness is mental, how much visual? How can she best present materials so that this child can profit by them? Can he do the regular work if allowed extra time? To such practical questions the psychologist must address himself.

In localities where children with acuity as great as 20/70 are included in the special education population, the number of children involved is of course much greater. Frequently a child with this much vision attracts no attention if he learns normally but if he is a slow learner this slowness may be blamed upon poor vision. In such cases, the psychologist is called upon to determine whether educational methods should be adjusted to the limited vision, to mental dullness, or to both.

THE EVALUATION PROCESS

Problems in Test Administration

Newly confronted by the testing of a totally blind individual, the psychologist may be concerned about just what help to offer so that he may equalize the individual's opportunity for success on tests with the opportunities of sighted clients, yet not give so much help that test results are biased.

A rough but workable guide is to tell the blind person all information about the tests and testing situation that a sighted individual would get visually. Some of this information may seem obvious but, in order to be sure, review it as part of an orienting conversation. Unless the object of the test is to determine how well the individual can, by touch or other means, identify the material before him, the examiner may quietly describe the object, as, "Here are four blocks which are all alike. They have sides which are smooth and white, one side which is rough and black, and one side which is half smooth and white, half rough and black. Touch them so that you are familiar with them." If the client hesitates, the examiner may guide his hands and give ample time for the client to become acquainted with the blocks. The psychologist must, of course, be quite clear in his own mind about what he wants to learn from each test or task; he must tell the blind person everything about the material except what the test is testing so that he eliminates as nearly as possible the contamination of his results. If he does not describe the test materials well, he may later find that he was really testing tactual discrimination when he meant to test speed, or really testing orientation when he meant to test the ability to follow instructions.

Questionnaire types of tests, such as those of personality or interest, may be readily adapted for use with blind clients by reading them aloud, either in person or through tape recording. Such material can also be put into braille, but the psychologist may find that many of his clients do not read braille well enough to make this useful. Unless the client population is made up of rather successful students in the upper school grades or college, their braille reading may be slow and inaccurate so that use of recordings results in more accurate test results. Some tests, particularly achievement tests, are available in large type for the partially seeing.

If a test is read aloud to one testee, his answers can be given orally and recorded by the examiner. This procedure is quite efficient when a single decision is involved, such as a personality item to which a *True* or *False* reply is given. However, in the multiple choice type test, such as the Miller Analogies or certain tests of judgment, sales insight, etc., the blind person's score is likely to be lowered by the requirement that he hold in mind with considerable accuracy each of three to five alternative answers. If such tests are frequently to be presented orally, the possible answers should be provided in braille so that the client may refer to them as he decides upon his choice. In the case of the Miller Analogies Test both the test items and the answers are available in braille through The Psychological Corporation, leaving the examiner to act only as recorder.

While individual reading and oral answering of an inventory may be comfortable, it is time consuming for the examiner and deprives the testee of the privacy a sighted client has when he reads a test for himself and records his own answer. Both problems may be overcome by presenting the inventory items through a tape recording and finding an appropriate way for the client to indicate his response for himself. A variety of braille and large type answer sheets for this purpose are available from the American Printing House for the Blind and are relatively easy to score. For those clients who can read neither braille nor large type, responses may be indicated by having the client place tickets, one for each response, in different piles. (See Fig. V.1.)

These tickets may be small pieces of cardboard which have been prepared ahead of time by numbering as many as are required for the test to be given, placing them in order in a box, and having the client take them out one at a time and place them

Figure V.1. Multiple choice answer sheets in braille and large type.

to the right for True and to the left for False. Such cards can be used many times but have the disadvantage that they must be put back into numerical order following each use. Strips of numbered tickets (of the type used for selling chances or for admission to various events) may be readily purchased and prepared, prior to testing, in rolls containing the number of tickets needed for the test to be administered. In preparing the rolls, each tenth (or other designated) ticket should have a hole punched through it; the voice on the recorded test can state when the next ticket to be used should have a hole punched through it and the client can be instructed to let the test administrator know if he does not come to such a punched ticket when the recording says he should. In this way, there will be regular checks upon whether he is working with the correctly numbered portion of his roll of tickets and occasional errors can be quickly corrected. Without such check points, some clients lose their place in the roll of tickets and end with too many or too few, requiring the whole test to be done over. With such check points, even clients of rather limited ability can usually respond correctly to a tape recorded test. When the test has been completed, a secretary can readily record the responses, from the numbered tickets to the standard answer sheet, and the test can be scored.

Interpretation of Test Results

The psychologist usually expects to receive, with any test he purchases, not only information concerning the validity and reliability of that test but norms upon which he can rely. Assuming that one's client falls within the described normative group, the above data makes it possible to interpret the results of even an unfamiliar test with considerable confidence. However, the psychologist who works with blind children may find small comfort in such standard data.

If the test he uses was developed for blind children he will often find that the normative group was very small, the reliability and validity data weaker than he would like, and application of norms clouded by the fact that the term *blind* applies to children with such varied amounts and kinds of vision. It is not easy to find a large enough number of blind children to produce good norms. Too often the test developer takes the easy path to locating subjects by using chiefly or entirely children in residential schools since such schools usually have the only large groups of blind children to be found in one location. Until the past twenty, or perhaps thirty years, most blind children were educated in residential schools but it is now increasingly likely that capable children will be retained in their local schools so that the population of residential schools today tends to be highly selected.

The characteristics which are likely to lead children into residential schools today are their being multiple handicapped, coming from very deprived or neglecting homes, emotional and social rejection within the home and community, or coming from a rural setting where the school district cannot effectively cope with teaching one blind child in the regular class. In other words, test norms based, within recent years, upon children in residential schools may also be based upon children with many problems in addition to blindness.

On the other hand, if the psychologist uses tests designed for normally seeing children he must recognize that his seriously visually handicapped subjects may differ from the normative group not only in their poor vision but in other less obvious but significant ways.

For example, the blind child is often overprotected. Out of concern for his safety, out of pity, or merely out of a wish to be helpful, people around him may have done so much for the child that he has not had normal learning experiences. He may not learn to dress, or even to feed, himself at the normal age because his mother does it for him. He may not learn to distinguish one thing from another tactually, to put things together or to take things apart, may not learn to use scissors or how to strike a match; his concepts of material things and how they function are consequently limited although he may verbalize surprisingly well about them. He learns to say what others say about these objects without quite knowing what the words mean.

Exclusion, sometimes deliberate, sometimes unintentional, may also limit the blind child's experiences. From the early school grades through college, he may have been excluded from certain courses or extra-curricular activities. Often the reasons given for such exclusion are concern for his safety, the sincere belief that he could not understand or perform the activity, or the belief that he could have no use for such knowledge. Too often, under these socially acceptable reasons, there lies an unwillingness on the part of school staff to give the extra time and thought necessary to adapt the activity for the blind child or a fear of what seems to be an added responsibility for him. Regardless of the reasons given, the child has lacked learning opportunities.

Even with the best of intentions, the teacher may be unable to provide equal learning opportunities for the blind child because appropriate equipment is lacking. Particularly in the evaluation of achievement, the psychologist needs assurance that the student has had resources for learning which were suited to his visual condition. Have books in large print, braille, or recorded form been available to him? Did he have the same edition of the textbook that his class used so that he could really do each assignment along with them, with at least some description of any pictures, charts, graphs and tables provided in the regular print text? If books were recorded or brailled for him, were the books ready at the beginning of the term or did he receive them (as too often happens) only a month or two before the end of the school year? Does he have a good system for taking notes? Were classroom tests adapted for him or did teachers just give him passing grades because they could think of no way to test his knowledge?

Too often, the psychologist is in the difficult position of trying to determine whether he is testing the child or his environment. When there are failures, are these the failures of the student, or of his family, or of his school? Each test record must be interpreted on the basis of careful review of the client's history, and particularly of evidence relating to whether the client had truly equal opportunities for learning.

What Tests Shall I Use?

During the winter of 1966–67, Bauman attempted by questionnaire to reach every psychologist working with blind people in United States and Canada, asking what tests they used and how they felt about those tests (Bauman, 1968). Questionnaires were returned by at least one psychologist in each of forty-six states, the District of Columbia, and Canada, a total of 319 responses.

One of the most frequent comments made by the respondents was that they had very little experience in testing persons who are blind or seriously visually handicapped and the figures they sent in show this. Half of them see less than ten blind clients per year, three-quarters see less than twenty-five blind clients per year. When we consider the great variations among blind people, already discussed, this must mean that the majority of psychologists rarely see two blind clients who seem very similar and as a result they cannot build up that sense of professional confidence which comes from an accumulation of related experiences. In preparing for each new appointment with a blind client, the psychologist is likely to ask himself, "What tests should I use?"

The feelings of professional insecurity are not reduced by the fact that so many of the tests designed especially for use with the visually handicapped are recent, experimental, have poor norms, and have not been studied and validated with any but the original normative group. Inevitably, those who work with blind persons wish for better tests, better norms, and much more research both on the tests and on the psychological and social effects of visual loss.

If the psychologist feels that he knows little about blindness and less about the tests he must use, he is likely to be uncomfortable in relating to his client and apologetic in writing his report. If only to reduce that insecurity, he will do well to include in his test battery one or more tests with which he feels familiar and on which he knows quite well what to expect when using them with sighted persons. If he finds that his client can do well on these tests, despite limited vision, he will feel more sure that good scores on the unfamiliar tests of the battery really mean superior ability; if the client has great difficulty with the familiar tests, the psychologist will often quickly recognize that the difficulty is mental, not visual, because he has previously observed that type of error in sighted clients who were mentally dull. We evaluate all of our clients not only by the bare scores but by the quality, speed, and originality of their responses. Unless the test is highly visual in nature, those aspects of test response may still be clearly recognizable in the visually handicapped person.

If the test does not involve a time limit, even regular print material may be used with the many visually handicapped, or even legally blind, children who can still manage ink print held close to their eyes or with use of a magnifier. A recent study by Sykes (Sykes 1971) shows that:

> Both the legally blind students and the partially sighted students were able to comprehend standard print as effectively as they did large print, and they read standard print as quickly as they did large print. The legally blind students found standard print no more fatiguing to read than large print, although the partially sighted students experienced less visual fatigue when reading large print than standard print.

One must, of course, be sure that the student really can read ink print; it is one thing to discern the letters, another to read. A brief reading test, perhaps one of reading aloud, may be a good way to begin the evaluation session.

In the immediately following sections, we will discuss possible test batteries at the preschool, school, and vocational levels with brief comment on familiar tests which may be used with the visually handicapped almost without adaptation. This will be followed by more detailed discussion of those tests which are unique to psychological evaluation of the blind.

Evaluation at the Preschool Level

Many of the observations commonly used to indicate development in sighted children are equally valuable with the blind child, such as balancing the head without support, grasping an object brought into contact with the child's hands, rolling over, or response to a familiar person. Response to commands which do not require visual orientation and development of speech patterns should also appear at about the same ages as in sighted children if the young child has lived in a stimulating environment. However, if these basic developmental indices have not appeared at the expected time, one must closely question the parents to determine whether they have offered the stimulation needed for such development; in the blind child, such stimulation must often be deliberately and repeatedly brought to the child and neglecting or rejecting parents may have failed to bring this. In short, failure may reflect not the child but the environment.

As the child approaches nursery school age, one is concerned with his ability to respond to simple commands, his ability to communicate in speech and gesture, his willingness to answer simple questions, and his conformity within the interpersonal and inter-group settings. Because parents are uncertain what to expect of blind children and hesitate to discipline and train them, children sometimes approach nursery school almost uncontrolled and the psychologist is asked whether they can be handled in the nursery school group. If the child shows any sign of responding to the psychologist, doing briefly what is requested, sitting still long enough for a short work session, exploring materials offered, etc., a skilled teacher will usually fit him into the group without much difficulty. Give the child a chance!

Even before most standard verbal measures of intelligence apply, the child's response to formboards and chosen toys represents a rough ability measure. Norms have never been established for these, but pegboards, the Three Figure Formboard (circle, square and triangle) , and even the Seguin Formboard may be used quite effectively with blind children. With the child of partial vision they apply at about the same ages as with normally seeing children. So-called educational toys can often be used as informal tests and one learns much from simply observing whether the child plays constructively rather than just banging or throwing the toys. Curiosity, initiative in exploring, willingness to try to follow instructions and the actual ability to carry out commands, and quality and duration of attention can all be evaluated with such materials.

During these preschool years, one of our most dependable measures is the Maxfield-Buchholz Social Maturity Scale (discussed later) , an adaptation of the Vineland Social Maturity Scale for blind children. The Wechsler Preschool and Primary Scale may be used as a whole if the child's visual handicap is not severe, or the verbal sections only if the visual handicap is severe. However, even the verbal items often depend largely upon visual observation in a fairly rich environment and one should not be too discouraged if it does not yield very favorable results with the typical totally blind child.

As a specific aptitude test for learning braille, the Roughness Discrimination Test (discussed later) may be added to the battery for totally blind children about to enter school.

Evaluation from Six to Sixteen

During these school years concern is likely to center in those largely verbal learning abilities which are so essential to academic progress. As is true in most studies of normally sighted children, the best predictors of school progress are the verbal IQs resulting from the Wechsler Intelligence Scale for Children or an adaptation of the Binet (discussed later) . A great advantage of the WISC lies in the lack of need for adaptation and therefore the direct applicability of norms based on large numbers of children in well defined age groups. The fact that most psychologists working with school children know the WISC well and find much meaning in subtest values, quality of responses, etc., also adds to its value. The WISC is, according to Bauman's study, used with well over three thousand visually handicapped children each year and is regarded as adequate by about half of the psychologists who report its use.

The potential test battery for these school years is weakened by the lack of any really good performance test for children with vision too limited to handle the Performance Scale of the WISC. The Non-language Learning Test (discussed later) can be of some use and as children approach the age of 16, some of the performance tests discussed in the next section may be tried even though their norms do not go below 16. Bauman's study shows that some psychologists are using the Merrill-Palmer Scale, the Goodenough Drawing Test, the Raven Progressive Matrices, and a variety of formboards but, except for children with a good bit of vision, interpretation of these instruments must depend largely upon the experience of the psychologist rather than upon norms.

Because measurement of achievement is so important during these school years, several group tests of aptitude and achievement have been developed in a combination of braille, large print, and recorded form. As early as 1918 there were adaptations of such materials as the Gray Oral Reading Check Tests, the Metropolitan Achievement Tests, the Myers-Ruch High School Progress Test, and many editions of the Stanford Achievement Tests. Nolan gives an excellent discussion of the problems in adapting such standard tests to use with visually handicapped children and any psychologist or teacher who considers such an adaptation would be wise to read his comments. (Nolan, 1962).

A major investment of time, effort, and professional know-how has gone into adapting the Stanford Achievement Tests, Forms X and W, so that these can be used in braille or large print form with a high level of confidence. The only disadvantage is that the time required for their administration, especially in the braille edition, is far greater than the time required for the regular print versions with normally seeing children so that it is almost impossible to administer the two versions at the same time.

The Scholastic Aptitude Test of the College Entrance Examination Board has been put into braille and oral presentation form, with answers typed by the student. Widely used at the junior and senior high school levels, and required for admission by many colleges, these tests are distributed by CEEB under the same control applied for the sighted student and must be administered by approved persons and returned to CEEB for evaluation. The resulting scores are treated as the equivalent of scores resulting from the regular printed version of the test. Procedures for the administration of the SAT to blind students allow almost unlimited time and therefore permit each student to proceed at his own pace. There has been no clear study of the effect of this lack of time limit upon the predictive value of the test but one assumes that scores may be somewhat inflated by it.

Like the Stanford Achievement Tests, the Sequential Tests of Educational Progress (STEP) has been adapted for use with blind students by a careful and technically complex process and can be used with confidence. The catalogue of The American Printing House for the Blind also lists the availability of the Cooperative School and College Ability Tests (SCAT), the Diagnostic Reading Tests, and the Iowa Tests of Basic Skills. Although the Gray Standardized Oral Reading Paragraphs, one of the first tests to be brailled for blind children, is still available it does not seem to find much use. For children with partial vision, it is possible to use the regular print tests used with their classmates by allowing some extra time for the slower reading of the visually handicapped child.

In the same way, printed aptitude tests may be used with children of limited vision with only minor adjustments in procedure and timing. For verbally apt blind children, the mastery of a foreign language may hold special interest. Consequently Gardner modified the Modern Language Aptitude Test to evaluate which students would profit most by training in modern languages and perhaps find careers in translation (Gardner, 1965). However, both the learning and, more especially, the application of language aptitude in employment seem to require many elements not reached by a language aptitude test and this is now rarely used.

During the earlier school years, good personality measures are difficult to find for any child and especially so for the blind child. If the psychologist favors any particular questionnaire type inventory, he may read it to the child, often finding as much value in the child's comments and manner of response as in the score. The sentence completion type of material can, of course, also be read to the child. For the child with some remaining vision, projectives may be used even though the stimulus is in print form. In the teens, the Adolescent Emotional Factors Inventory (discussed later) provides the advantage of norms based on blind youth.

All of the above measures omit one very important aspect of the blind child's development, his social competency. To fill this gap, Bauman has in the process of development, and now available with tentative norms, the Overbrook Social Competency Scale (discussed later).

Vocationally Oriented Evaluation

When the student reaches age 16, the test battery may be enlarged with a variety of material for which norms begin with that age.

Most familiar among these is the Wechsler Adult Intelligence Scale which can be used in its entirety if the subject has enough vision to distinguish the Performance Scale materials, or merely as a Verbal Scale. As with the WISC, the WAIS Verbal Scale can be used without change even with the totally blind subject and there is no need to adjust time limits or norms. Little wonder, then, that Bauman's study shows that this test is administered to more than 4,500 blind persons each year. The older Wechsler-Bellevue II or even Wechsler-Bellevue I are still used by psychologists who are comfortable with them and evidently reluctant to change to newer and less familiar materials. This fact is a good illustration of the view that the psychologist should use the tests he feels most competent to interpret if they are at all applicable.

Developed especially for use with blind clients, and all with norms beginning at age 16, are the Haptic Intelligence Scale for the Adult Blind (HIS), the Stanford Kohs Block Design Test, the Vocational Intelligence Scale for the Adult Blind (VISAB), and the Tactual Reproduction Pegboard (TRP). All of these will be described in the next section of this chapter. Since all attempt to measure performance ability, the psychologist may choose from among them one, or at most two, to supplement and round out the information from the verbal intelligence scale.

The vocational future of visually handicapped students who are not college bound often depends very much upon how effectively they use their hands. Not only is sheer speed important, as it usually is to sighted workers, but tactual discrimination, orientation in the work space, and ability to follow patterns of movement smoothly, all play a large part in job success for the blind worker. Consequently dexterity tests were developed early for test batteries used with the blind and will be discussed in more detail later in this chapter.

As the blind child approaches graduation from school and competition for employment in a sighted world, social competency continues to be a matter of grave concern so that the Overbrook Social Competency Scale may still play a significant part in counseling.

With the need for making a vocational choice, interest becomes a center of attention. Almost any of the inventory type interest measures may be used by reading them to those clients who do not see enough to read for themselves. Three, the Kuder Preference Record, the California Occupational Interest Inventory (Lee-Thorpe), and the Strong Vocational Interest Blank, have seen wide and successful use, and need no adaptation except that the student be instructed to make his choices purely on the basis of liking for the item, not on the basis of whether, visually, he thinks it is possible for him. Bauman has just developed an interest inventory (discussed later) made up of items from the job descriptions of legally blind clients and with certain advantages in administration and interpretation.

Personality also plays an extremely important part in job adjustment. Again the psychologist may wish to use the personality inventories with which he is most familiar and one, the Minnesota Multiphasic Personality Inventory, has seen especially wide use. It requires no adaptation except oral presentation and often responses are indicated by cards or tickets, in the procedure previously described. The Emotional Factors Inventory (discussed later) was developed for use with blind persons and includes a scale of adjustment to blindness. Several short scales have been developed, such as the Jervis scale for adjustment and the Hardy scale for anxiety but they suffer from the fact that they seek to measure only one narrow aspect of personality, from limited normative groups, and from lack of enough reported use to place them beyond the experimental stages (Jervis 1960, Hardy 1968).

The psychologist who prefers projectives may use, without modification, verbal stimulus types of procedures, such as a sentence completion test, or may use ink blots, pictures, and other printed material with clients with partial vision. His interpretation of the protocols must, of course, take into consideration the effects of blindness but he must be equally careful not to dismiss every emotional reaction as merely the result of blindness. He will be most successful if he perceives his visually handicapped clients as total human beings, not as blind people. Most of his training in clinical psychology will apply just as much to his blind clients as to any others. There have been a number of efforts to develop projective materials especially for the blind, and these will be discussed later.

Tests Especially for the Visually Handicapped

Verbal Intelligence Measures

We have already noted that, with blind and visually handicapped subjects of all ages, much of the most widely used measure is the age-appropriate form of the *Wechsler*. Essentially no modification is required for its use even with totally blind persons. Where the instructions indicate that the arithmetic items should be read by the testee, these can be provided in braille or large type, but Hayes suggested that the items be read twice before timing was started, and experience shows that if this is done no print form of the item is needed (Hayes, 1941). A few Comprehension items may be slightly rephrased because the totally blind child would be unlikely to have the specified experience. For example, the WISC item, *What would you do if you were sent to buy a loaf of bread and the grocer said he did not have any more?* might be stated as, *What should a boy do if he were sent to buy a loaf of bread and the grocer said he did not have any more.* Experience shows, however, that even if the question is not rephrased few children feel limited by their blindness in making their answer.

Before the publication of the Wechsler scales, the *Interim Hayes-Binet* was widely used with blind children and it continues to see some use among psychologists long accustomed to it. Developed by Dr. Samuel P. Hayes, an early leader in psychological evaluation of blind children, this scale combines verbal items from Forms L and M of the Stanford Binet. Some of the content is still as appropriate as it was when Hayes published the form about thirty years ago, but other items seem sadly dated and awkward for use in today's world.

For the past several years, Carl Davis, Psychologist at Perkins School for the Blind, Watertown, Massachusetts, has been developing an adaptation of recent versions of the Binet, to be called the *Perkins Binet.* Although still predominantly a verbal scale, he has added performance items to give far better balance so that when this becomes available in the near future it should provide an excellent resource for evaluating both verbal and performance learning ability through a single measure.

Performance Measures of Intelligence

For many years, psychologists working with blind people bemoaned the lack of means for evaluating performance, or nonverbal, learning potential. If the client retained some useful vision, the Wechsler Performance Scales might be used but if the resulting Performance IQ was low, the psychologist could not be sure whether he was measuring lack of vision or lack of mental ability.

In an early effort to fill this gap, Bauman adapted the Dearborn Formboard, naming the adaptation the *Non-language Learning Test.* Bauman describes this as a clinical instrument, rather than a test, because she varies administration with the amount and nature of the client's vision and, to some extent, with guessed variations in the client's ability. The NLL has the advantage of being usable over a wide range of ages since a very few capable preschool children do it well, while it can be a challenge to the totally blind adult. It also has the advantage of enabling the psychologist to observe the reactions of the testee to a far greater extent than some tests permit, and the even greater advantage of showing the client's amount of learning in terms of his improvement from trial to trial. Through variations in the mode of presentation, the level of difficulty can be somewhat modified, and the task may be used both as a measure of problem solving and as a measure of learning. Observations are often more important than the speed score so that the meaning of the task rapidly gains depth as the psychologist gains experience with it. Administration is rather simple since the NLL is merely a formboard with four kinds of holes in it, two of each of four shapes. Certain blocks are removed and the remaining blocks so rearranged that the subject must make certain moves in order to get all the blocks back into the board.

Although Shurrager states in the manual that the *Haptic Intelligence Scale* was not intended as an adaptation of the WAIS Performance Scale, some subtests were clearly inspired by the WAIS and the normative group was carefully chosen to parallel that used for the WAIS (Shurrager, 1964). As is true for the WAIS, norms start with age 16. The test consists of six subtests:

Digit Symbol: A series of shapes are presented in raised form and numbered from one to six by raised dots. On a companion plate, the same six forms are presented in random order and the subject is asked to associate the proper number with each form. The more efficiently he learns to do this and moves correctly and speedily through the process of identifying each form by giving its associated number, the better his score is.

Block Design: Using the basic concept of the Kohs Block Design Test in tactual form, the testee is asked to copy a series of designs through various placements of four blocks.

Object Assembly: The parts of four objects, a doll, a block, a hand, and a ball, are presented in succession. Objects are to be assembled by putting the pieces together.

Object Completion: From sixteen familiar objects, such as a comb, an animal, a lock, and a telephone, one important part has been removed. The subject is asked to identify the missing part.

Pattern Board: In a 7½ inch square board are 25 holes, half an inch in diameter and arranged in rows of five, except that a fixed peg fills the center hole to serve as a reference point. Loose pegs may be inserted in the remaining holes to form increasingly complex patterns. The subject is asked to examine each pattern with his fingers, then the loose pegs are withdrawn and he reproduces the pattern.

Bead Arithmetic: The abacus is the basis of this test; five spokes are set in a frame, each with five large beads below the divider and two above. The subject is taught how to identify and read numbers of increasing complexity, how to set these up for himself, and how to add, and he is asked to perform each of these operations independently. Learning to use and understand the principles of an abacus forms the core of this test and its validity as a testing device is vitiated by previous training in abacus use.

Figure V.2 illustrates the above subtests.

The HIS was developed carefully under competent professional direction and much effort went into obtaining normative data in parallel with the norms of the WAIS. It was therefore hoped that the test might satisfy the expressed need of psychologists for a performance scale which could confidently be used with blind clients as the equivalent of the WAIS Performance Scale with sighted clients.

In fact, this has not worked out for at least some of the following reasons: the quite long time (one to two hours) usually required for administration, the fact that norms do not go below age 16, and the fact that norms are based entirely on subjects

Figure V.2. Haptic Intelligence Scale for Adult Blind (HISab). Subtests: 1, Digit Symbol; 2, Block Design; 3, Object Assembly; 4, Object Completion; 5, Pattern Board; 6, Bead Arithmetic.

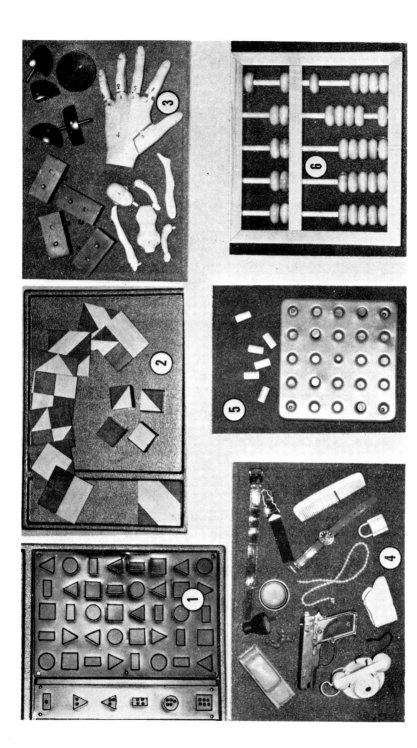

without useful vision. In addition, recent years have seen a rapid growth in the use of the abacus in teaching arithmetic to blind children and such teaching invalidates one subtest of the HIS. As a result, a test once greeted so eagerly has fallen into disuse except in those few settings where a psychologist works with a large number of totally blind persons. It is sincerely hoped that financial support may be found for the small amount of additional work necessary to overcome the defects in this basically excellent test.

The *Stanford Kohs Block Design Test* is an adaptation of an adaptation, as it were. Owaki, in Japan, put the Kohs Block Design Test into tactual form by covering blocks with cloth of different textures; these required such fine discriminations that the true intent of the test was defeated for most subjects, and the cloth covering soon became worn and dirty. Suinn and Dauterman made the blocks larger, with only two kinds of surface—smooth white and rough black—and used materials which could readily be kept clean and did not deteriorate with normal use (Suinn, Dauterman, 1966). With these blocks, the client is asked to copy patterns of increasing complexity, the score depending upon the speed and accuracy with which this is accomplished through a series of twenty patterns. (See Fig. V.3.)

Unlike the HIS, where six kinds of mental operations are involved, the Stanford Kohs has the disadvantage of depending entirely upon the subject's ability to distinguish and copy patterns and for a few otherwise very competent blind people this proves an impossible task. Since these people may, on other tests, demonstrate superior handling of concrete materials, it seems to be the test rather than the subject which has failed, and it certainly cannot be described as a complete measure of performance ability. Again, for some totally blind subjects, the test can be very time-consuming and fatiguing, and the fact that present norms do not go below age 16 is regrettable. Its advantages lie in the availability of norms for both totally blind and partially seeing subjects, the fact that the materials of the test are not cumbersome, the evidence that most clients are challenged and highly motivated by it, and the excellent opportunities provided for observation of just how each subject approaches his task. There is also some evi-

Figure V.3. The Stanford Kohs Block Design Test.

dence, not yet documented by a formal study, that reactions typical of organic brain damage may be detected, especially when the subject loses his concept of squareness, reverses patterns, etc.

The *Vocational Intelligence Scale for the Adult Blind* (VISAB) and the *Tactual Reproduction Pegboard* (TRP) were developed by Jones and Gruber as four doctoral candidates combined their efforts in a project directed by Tiffin (Tiffin, 1960). Subjects used to develop the norms for these two tests also participated in other published studies, including the development of The Sound Test which will be described below. Thus unusually detailed information is available on this normative group. Norms begin at age sixteen but are available for both totally blind and partially sighted. The VISAB asks the subject to determine which, in a group of raised figures, is least like the others. The TRP is a large pegboard divided by a bar down the middle. On one side the examiner sets up peg patterns of increasing complexity; on the other side the subject attempts to copy those patterns both quickly and accurately. Neither test has had great acceptance, in part because of limited evidence about their predictive value, in part because rather few copies of the tests were made and these have long since been distributed.

Measures of Discrimination, Orientation, and Dexterity

Reading readiness tests for sighted children usually evaluate the child's ability to discriminate differences and/or perceive similarities in pictures, in abstract symbols, and finally in letters and words. To read braille, discrimination by touch is required so that the ability to use the tactual receptors and the hands in a coordinated and orderly fashion becomes the foundation for successful braille reading.

The Roughness Discrimination Test was developed as a measure of these abilities. The test consists of cards on which two inch

Figure V.4. The Roughness Discrimination Test.

squares of sandpaper are mounted. On each card, three squares are identical in grit size while the fourth is of a different size. The child is asked to indicate which is different. The task has some of the appeal of a game for the preschooler and while attention probably does affect its results the authors feel that same factor of attention also affects learning to read; the indirect measurement of attention during this task may therefore increase the validity of the test. (See Fig. V.4.)

Nolan and Morris report that, for first grade students tested at the beginning of the school year, the RDT correctly predicted the child's placement in the upper or lower half of his reading group at the end of the year, 70 percent of the time when reading errors formed the criterion, and 75 percent of the time when reading speed was the criterion (Nolan, Morris, 1965). If both IQ and RDT scores are used, prediction is considerably increased since IQ brings into the equation the child's ability to attach meaning to a symbol, as well as to discriminate tactually.

Even in work at higher status levels, the blind person must often depend more upon his hands than the sighted worker does. A combination of orientation within the work space, quick tactual discrimination of materials, and smooth, dextrous manipulation of those materials enhances success in many jobs even when they do not seem to be primarily manual in nature. Consequently, measures of manual dexterity play a larger part in psychological studies of blind clients than in similar studies of sighted persons. In addition to the direct value of the scores, these tests provide an opportunity for observing the client in action, doing rather than verbalizing. His ability to relate to the material placed before him and to follow patterns of movement, his patience under frustration, his attention, energy level, and motivation, are all on display. Without such action tests, the psychologist might miss some important facets of the client's total reaction pattern.

When used for these purposes, dexterity tests may appropriately be used with children as young as nine or ten, even though norms are lacking for these age levels and prediction of success in manual work is scarcely the issue. Any manipulative task with which the psychologist is quite familiar may help him toward a better understanding of how a given client functions. On five tests, norms are available on goodly numbers of blind and partially sighted subjects subdivided in terms of sex and age groups (Bauman, 1968). These five tests are the two parts of the *Minnesota Rate of Manipulation*, the two parts of the *Penn Bi-Manual Worksample*, and the screw driver section of the Crawford *Small Parts Dexterity Test*. Since all are available from well known test distributors and may be familiar because of their use both in rehabilitation and in industry, they will not be described here. The unique aspect of these tests, in relation to blindness, is the manner of administration, the number of trials allowed, and of course the special norms. All these procedures are described in detail by Bauman and should be studied carefully before evaluating a blind client with these materials (Bauman, 1968).

Measures of Social Competency

Few would argue that the correlation between intellectual ability and social competency is high even among sighted youth but there is reason to believe that among visually handicapped young people the correlation is even lower. The fact that the totally blind child cannot learn by simply watching what others do, the fact that his life experience may be relatively limited especially in the early years, and the fact that it is often easy for him to allow others to do things for him, all tend to reduce both his social skills and even the skills of independent daily living. Yet in casual contacts with the public, with fellow students and with fellow workers, such skills may be the first, if not the only, qualities observed.

In part for this reason, in part because very young children rarely respond well to formal tests, a scale of social development at the preschool level was devised by Maxfield, refined several times, and reached its final form in the Maxfield-Buchholz *Social Maturity Scale for Blind Preschool Children*.

At the 0–1 age level, items are largely physical, such as balancing the head, rolling over, reaching for objects, pulling self to standing position with help, and grasping with thumb and finger. At higher age levels, items concerning dressing, self care, eating habits, play, and adjustment to group situations, are included. Although the scale stops at age 6–0, it has long provided an extremely valuable resource, the more needed because of the unsatisfactory nature of verbal or performance testing materials at the preschool level.

Recently Bauman has extended the values of a social competency measure to the young adult level through the *Overbrook Social Competency Scale*. Although present norms are tentative and the author regards the scale as needing further revision, she is willing to share it with experienced workers who may wish to have supplemental information on those aspects of individual development which are related to independence in daily living, interpersonal skills, mobility, and many aspects of group participation and leadership.

For both the Maxfield and Overbrook scales, administration is through an interview, usually not with the subject himself but with a parent, residence supervisor (in a residential school) or similar person who can accurately describe the typical behavior of the child or adolescent. Both scales may be used as guides for training and counseling toward improved skills; their scores should be regarded as a foundation for growth toward better adjustment rather than as a criticism of present adjustment. An additional advantage, particularly in the evaluation of very young children, is that results are based on the child's reported typical behavior, whereas his response to tests may easily be affected by his health and energy on the day of examination, his fright at being taken to an unfamiliar place for testing, the fatigue and excitement of the trip, etc.

Measures of Personality

In personality evaluation, perhaps more than in any other aspect of psychological testing, the familiarity of the psychologist with his instrument is extremely important. Consequently, many psychologists quite correctly prefer personality measures which they know well from long use with sighted subjects and they apply them rather effectively with their blind clients.

Two full scales and several short measures of single traits have been developed especially for use with blind and visually handicapped persons. Bauman has developed an *Emotional Factors Inventory* (Bauman, 1968) and, more recently, an *Adolescent Emo-*

tional Factors Inventory (Bauman, Platt, Strauss, 1963), whose items are largely based upon adjustment behavior as described by visually handicapped persons. Some of this behavior is common to all people, with or without good vision, so that some items might be found in any personality questionnaire; other items, however, especially relate to the limitations and frustrations resulting from lack of vision.

It is strongly recommended that these measures be administered either through large print (for the individual who can read this) or through tape recording with one of the answer procedures described earlier in this chapter. This opportunity for privacy in making his responses could be important to the blind person and probably improves the predictive value of the results.

Both EFI and AEFI result in scores on a series of sub-scales: sensitivity or the broad tendency to become emotional, somatic symptoms of inner tension, social competency or confidence in social contacts, attitudes of distrust or mildly paranoid tendencies, feelings of inadequacy or doubt of one's ability to cope, depression or lack of the morale and positive orientation so important to accomplishment, and attitudes regarding blindness. The AEFI also includes measures of the young person's relationship to family, peers of the opposite sex, and school. Both questionnaires include a validation scale. Separate norms are provided for each sex and are based on considerable numbers of legally blind subjects.

The psychologist who is most comfortable with projective procedures naturally wishes to use them with his blind clients and, as noted earlier, may easily do so if the subject has a little vision or if he uses a verbal stem, as in the various sentence completion procedures. Since it is relatively easy to produce both auditory and tactual stimuli, a number of these have been developed for use with totally blind clients but few have had enough study and application to be described as beyond the experimental stage. *The Sound Test* (Palecios, 1964) was part of the test development project under Tiffin and can therefore offer some fairly solid evidence of what it measures (Tiffin, 1960). This evidence is based on persons over sixteen years of age with a rather heavy loading of persons in sheltered employment, but the procedure does show promise. On the test record are a series of stimuli, some merely sounds such as footsteps, water running, the sound of a splash, etc., many combining such sounds with brief verbal interchanges. In response to each stimulus the subject is asked to tell a story. Thus the test follows the general procedure of the Thematic Apperception Test with auditory rather than visual stimuli.

Measures of Interest

Any interest inventory may be used with visually handicapped clients if they are instructed to make their choices on the assumption that they have ample vision to handle all the activities listed. Most visually handicapped persons seem able to do this, but at times clients openly object that they cannot see well enough to do most of the things listed, or their occasional comments betray the fact that they have been thinking in terms of vision more than in terms of true interest.

To meet this bias, Bauman has close to publication the *PRG Interest Inventory*, based entirely on content of jobs done, or hobbies chosen, by blind people. The administration procedure is very simple, can be handled by tape recording, and does not require a lot of time. Included is a simple calculation by which to compensate for the tendency of some clients to say they like almost everything, or almost nothing—tendencies which throw valuable light upon their personalities but confound the application of norms in most tests.

In trying to interpret the results of interest measures using regular sighted norms, the psychologist should beware of the marked tendency, among visually handicapped persons, to make many choices in the social service area and, to slightly less extent, in music. The strong social service leaning seems to result from the fact that blindness has often enforced dependence upon others and the individual would both like to repay this and might find ego satisfaction in playing the role of the helper; or perhaps he is merely curious about other people who suffer misfortune. The interest in music arises in part from the fact that the blind person, of necessity, turns to sound as a source of pleasure and perhaps in part from extra emphasis upon music in some schools for the blind. Without support of real talent, this interest in music must be regarded as avocational.

Suppliers of Tests

American Foundation for the Blind, 15 W. 16th Street, New York, N. Y.

Maxfield-Buchholz Social Maturity Scale for Blind Preschool Children

American Printing House for the Blind, 1839 Frankfort Avenue, Louisville, Ky.

Roughness Discrimination Test

Stanford Achievement Test—Braille or large print

Sequential Tests of Educational Progress—Braille or large print

School and College Ability Tests—Braille or large print

Nathan P. Bauman, 400 Orchard Lane, Fort Washington, Pa. 19034

Stanford Kohs Block Design Test

Educational Testing Bureau, 720 Washington Ave., Minneapolis, Minn.

Minnesota Rate of Manipulation

Penn Bi-Manual Worksample

Educational Testing Service, Princeton, N. J.

Scholastic Aptitude Test—Braille or large print

Perkins School for the Blind, 175 N. Beacon St., Watertown, Mass. 02172

Hayes Interim Binet

Perkins Binet

Personnel Research and Guidance Inc., 1604 Spruce St., Philadelphia, Pa. 19103

Non-language Learning Test

Overbrook Social Competency Scale

Emotional Factors Inventory

Adolescent Emotional Factors Inventory

PRG Interest Inventory for Blind

Psychological Corporation, 304 E. 45th St., New York, N. Y. 10017

Various forms of Wechsler Scales

Modern Language Aptitude Test

Crawford Small Parts Dexterity Test

Minnesota Multiphasic Personality Inventory

Psychology Research, Box 14, Technology Center, Chicago, Ill.
60616
Haptic Intelligence Scale for the Adult Blind
Dr. Robert J. Teare, 185 Kings Rd., Athens, Georgia 30601
Vocational Intelligence Scale for the Adult Blind
Tactual Reproduction Pegboard
The Sound Test

REFERENCES

Bauman, Mary K.: *A Report and a Reprint: Tests Used in the Psychological Evaluation of Blind and Visually Handicapped Persons* and *A Manual of Norms for Tests Used in Counseling Blind Persons*. Washington, American Association of Workers for the Blind, Inc., 1968.

Sykes, Kim C.: A comparison of the effectiveness of standard print and large print in facilitating the reading skills of visually impaired students. *Educ Visually Handicapped, 4:*97–105, 1971.

Nolan, C. Y.: Evaluating the scholastic achievement of visually handicapped children. *Except Child, 28:*493–496, 1962.

Gardner, R. C.: A language aptitude test for blind students. *J Appl Psychol, 49:*135–141, 1965.

Jervis, F. M.: A comparison of self-concepts of blind and sighted children, in *Guidance Programs for Blind Children*. Watertown, Mass., Perkins School Publication No. 20, 1960.

Hardy, R. E.: A study of manifest anxiety among blind residential school students. *New Outlook for the Blind, 62:*173–180, 1968.

Hayes, S. P.: *Contributions to a Psychology of Blindness*. New York, American Foundation for the Blind, 1941.

Shurrager, Harriett C. and Shurrager, P. S.: *HISAB Manual: Haptic Intelligence Scale for Adult Blind*. Chicago, Ill., Psychology Research, 1964.

Suinn, R. M. and Dauterman, W. L.: *Manual for the Stanford-Kohs Block Design Test for the Blind*. Washington, Vocational Rehabilitation Administration, U. S. Dept. of Health, Education, & Welfare, 1966.

Tiffin, J. (Project Director): *An Investigation of Vocational Success with the Blind*. Lafayette, Ind., Purdue Research Foundation, Purdue University, 1960.

Nolan, C. Y. and Morris, June E.: *Roughness Discrimination Test Manual*. Louisville, Ky., American Printing House for the Blind, 1965.

Maxfield, Kathryn E. and Buchholz, Sandra.: *A Social Maturity Scale for Blind Preschool Children*. New York, American Foundation for the Blind, Inc., 1957.

Bauman, Mary, Platt, H., and Strauss, Susan: A measure of personality for blind adolescents. *Inter J Educ of the Blind, 13:*1–6, 1963.

Palacios, May H.: *The Sound Test: An Auditory Technique*. Marion, Ind., Author, 1964.

CHAPTER VI

DEAF AND HARD OF HEARING

McCay Vernon

Description of the Handicap

ROUTINE PSYCHOLOGICAL procedures are not appropriate for deaf children because of the marked communication disability created by profound hearing loss. It is important, therefore, that the three major aspects of this disability and its ramifications be delineated.

The first aspect of the communication barrier is that being unable to hear speech, the deaf person must depend upon lipreading to comprehend what others say. Unfortunately, lipreading is by no means the magic route to understanding that hearing persons often assume it to be. Over half the sounds in the English language are not visible on the lips or if visible, they are identical in appearance to other sounds. Additional complicating factors such as mustaches, protruding teeth, bad lighting, head movements, etc., all contribute to the fact that the deaf youth, if forced to depend solely upon lipreading, will generally not understand much of what is said (Rose, 1970). This disability obviously limits potential value of certain psychological tests and procedures.

A second aspect of the deaf youth's problem in communication is his own speech. Not being able to hear how he articulates, he cannot accurately monitor his pronunciation, pitch, or volume. In the case of the child deafened early in life, he not only has the problem of monitoring his speech, but he must cope with the fact that he has never heard the sounds of English and knows about them only as he has visually perceived them on the lips of others. Perhaps the immense task such an individual faces in maintaining or developing intelligible speech is best understood by those who are not deaf if they place themselves in the imaginary position of trying to learn to speak a foreign language if placed in a soundproof room and outfitted with ear plugs that prevented them from hearing both themselves and their teachers. The problem faced in learning to speak the foreign language and the level of clarity acquired illustrate in a small way, the problems in speech development of youth deafened before they learned to talk. Those deafened after having acquired speech or those with usable hearing, face a less awesome but still difficult task in acquiring or maintaining intelligible speech (Davis and Silverman, 1970).

The final, least recognized, but most important aspect of the deaf youth's communication barrier is his level of language development. Once again, the full ramifications of this problem are most readily understood if illustrated by analogy. The youth suffering an early and profound hearing loss has the same overwhelming task in learning English that a hearing child would have in learning Russian if he were required to do it from the confines of a soundproof, glass-enclosed room with the instructor on the outside. In order to complete the analogy, the instructor would not be able to use English as a frame of reference for teaching Russian because the deaf youth has no language which is used as a basis in learning English. A full perception of this analogy gives one some empathy with the language disability that results from deafness. It makes understandable the fact that the deaf child generally starts school with little or no vocabulary or grasp of the syntax of English. By contrast, the average hearing first grader knows approximately 5,000 to 26,000 words and enough grammar to use these in sentences. This language deficiency with which the deaf child begins his education is rarely if ever overcome because, while his hearing counterpart is being bombarded by language twelve to fourteen hours daily through his ears, the deaf youngster only has an hour or so a day when he is actually exposed to language in a form he is able to perceive. Even then exposure is often through the broken or distorted

pattern it is possible to grasp through lipreading (Scouten, 1969).
The reason for extensively discussing the significance of the
communication problem caused by deafness is that it is this
problem that makes the proper psychological evaluation of deaf
children difficult and specialized procedure (Levine, 1960). When
it is realized that conventional psychological evaluation consists
of interviewing or the use of psychometric instruments involving
sophisticated levels of language development, it becomes readily
apparent that the deaf youth's language deficiency and his
limitation in oral communication make these conventional approaches inappropriate for and unfair (Vernon, 1967). Instead
of measuring his intelligence, personality, and vocational aptitudes, they would simply reflect his commnuication disability.
There is ample proof of this evaluative injustice in cases of deaf
individuals hospitalized as mental defectives on the basis of
IQ tests involving language. Later, on non-language IQ tests,
these same individuals were found to be above average in intelligence and to have the ability to function adequately in
public school programs for the deaf (Vernon and Brown, 1964).
By the same token the primitive language of a semi-literate deaf
child has been known to mimic that of the psychotic mental
patient contributing to a misdiagnosis of schizophrenia.

Classification

Hearing represents a continuum varying from the very acute
auditory perception of the gifted musical conductor who can
detect one out of tune violin in an orchestra of 100 pieces to the
total deafness of the individual whose only awareness of sound
is his tactile perception of strong vibrations. In addition to degree
of hearing loss, factors such as site of auditory lesion, age at
onset of hearing loss, cause of deafness, response to hearing aids,
and speech discrimination ability enter into the problem of
determining who should be classified as deaf and who as hard
of hearing. *The determining factor from the point of view of
psychological evaluation is the extent to which communication
has been effected.* For the purpose of psychological evaluation
procedures, the following general groupings are suggested for
determination of whether regular psychological procedures

should be used or whether the special evaluation designed for those with hearing loss would be in order.

The first of these groups, that consisting of children with a hearing loss of less than 15 db. in the speech range (ISO 1964) should certainly be given the same set of standard psychological tests and interviews that are administered to the non-deaf. In group testing situations care should be taken to seat these individuals towards the front of the room near the examiner. Other than this, they need no special consideration in psychological evaluations.

The second group, those with a hearing loss of 75 db. (ISO 1964), or more in the speech range, should be evaluated using procedures devised for children who are deaf or have profound hearing losses, procedures which will be outlined later in the chapter.

The middle group, those whose loss is between 20 and 70 db. (ISO 1964), represents a less clearly defined category from the viewpoint of psychological evaluation. Usually within this grouping some will have a communication problem severe enough to require special procedures. Others will have communication skills comparable to those of hearing people. Thus, some would best be evaluated using techniques devised for deaf children while a certain percent would be appropriately tested with conventional instruments.

Ideally, audiological psychological evaluations including speech discrimination tests, pure tone hearing measurement, case history data, and educational testing should be used in making a final decision on whether or not an applicant should be screened by routine procedures or by those designed for individuals with profound hearing losses. However, this may not be practical. If not, the child should be given parts of both types of evaluations. Large differences between scores on verbal or compared to non-verbal tests, in the presence of a hearing loss of 25 decibels or greater, would suggest that the applicant's hearing loss has a significant effect on his communication skills and that he should be evaluated on the basis of his performance on psychological procedures designed for those with profound hearing losses.

It should be noted that in cases where hearing loss occurred after three and a half years of age or when scores on the psychological evaluations for profoundly deaf youth are exceptionally high, the regular evaluation for the normal hearing should also be given. It may be that in certain cases the hearing impaired applicant has overcome the communication problem usually found among deaf youth and should, therefore, be screened by regular procedures.

Psychological Evaluation of Children with Profound Hearing Loss

The rationale for special psychological evaluation procedures for applicants with profound hearing loss has been established earlier in the chapter. Recommendations will now be made regarding the instruments and techniques which should comprise the special evaluation.

Intelligence Testing

BASIC CONSIDERATIONS IN THE INTELLIGENCE Testing of Deaf and Hard of Hearing Children. A clear understanding of the following factors should precede any efforts to test or interpret test findings with deaf children:

1. To be valid as a measure of the intelligence of a deaf youngster an IQ test must be a non-verbal performance-type instrument (Burchard and Myklebust, 1942; Lane and Schneider, 1941). Verbal tests with deaf children are almost always inappropriate. They measure language deficiency due to hearing loss rather than intelligence (Brill, 1962; Heider, 1940; Levine, 1960; Myklebust, 1962; Myklebust, 1954). An example of the tragic consequence of incorrect choice of tests is a student presently at the California School for the Deaf in Riverside who was given a Stanford Binet (verbal test) and received an IQ of 29 which led to her commitment to a hospital for the mentally retarded where she remained five years. Upon re-evaluation, using a performance IQ test, this girl was found to have an IQ of 113 which led to her dismissal from the hospital and her enrollment in a school for the deaf. In the California School for the Deaf at Riverside alone there are three deaf children previously mis-

diagnosed as mentally deficient who have been given performance tests yielding scores indicative of favorable academic potential, a finding subsequently demonstrated in the classroom.

It should be noted that all non-verbal tests are certainly not appropriate for use with deaf children. One main reason is that while many have non-language items they may nevertheless require verbal directions (Heider, 1940; Lane and Schneider, 1941; Myklebust, 1962; Wechsler, 1955; Zeckel, 1942; Zeckel and Kalb, 1939).

Hard of hearing children may give the impression of being able to understand verbal tests, but this is often an artifact (Levine, 1960; Myklebust, 1962; Myklebust, 1954). In testing such children it is essential to begin with a performance measure and then, if desired, to try a verbal instrument. In cases where the score yielded by the former is appreciably higher, the probability is that it is more valid, and further, that the lower score on the test involving language is due to the subject's hearing impairment and does not constitute a true measure of intelligence.

2. Even more than with hearing subjects, scores on preschool and early school deaf and hard of hearing children tend to be extremely unreliable (Heider, 1940; Hiskey, 1955). For this reason, low scores in particular should be viewed as questionable in the absence of other supporting data.

3. There is far more danger that a low IQ score is wrong than that a high one is inaccurate (Heider, 1940; Myklebust, 1954; Wechsler, 1967). This is due to the many factors that can lead to a child's not performing to capacity; whereas, in contrast, there are almost no conditions that can lead to performance above capacity.

4. Tests given to deaf children by psychologists not experienced with the deaf or hard of hearing are subject to appreciably greater error than is the case when the service is rendered by one familiar with deaf youngsters. The atypical attentive set of the hearing impaired child to testing which has been frequently cited in the literature is felt to be one of the reasons for this (Hiskey, 1955; Myklebust, 1954; Zeckel, 1942).

5. It must be noted that the performance part of many conventional intelligence tests is only half, or less, of the test.

Therefore, to approach the validity of a full IQ test with a deaf child it is necessary to give at least two performance scales.

6. Intelligence tests for young deaf or hard of hearing children (age 12 or below) that emphasize time are not as valid in most cases as are other tests which do not stress time (Hiskey, 1955; Lane and Schneider, 1941). This is because these children often react to the factor of timing by either working in great haste and ignoring accuracy or else disregarding the time factor completely. In either case, the result is not necessarily a reflection of intelligence.

7. Group testing of Deaf and Hard of Hearing children is a highly questionable procedure that, at best, is of use only as a gross screening device. (Hiskey, 1955; Lane and Schneider, 1941; Levine, 1960; Myklebust, 1962).

Table VI.1, Evaluation of Some Intelligence Tests Most Commonly Used With Deaf and Hard of Hearing Children, has been included here to evaluate these tests in a concise manner conducive to easy referral. In fairness to both the tests and the reader, it should be stated that these evaluations are based on the experience of the author and the limited literature relevant to this area. For this reason, they are to a degree subjective and open to question. However, the tests described enjoy a wide acceptance and application by psychological personnel in schools and agencies working with hearing-impaired children (Brill, 1962; Levine, 1960; Myklebust, 1962; Myklebust, 1954; Myklebust, 1960).

Personality Testing

General Considerations to Be Made in the Personality Testing of Deaf and Hard of Hearing. As in the case of intelligence testing it is important in the personality measurement of hearing-impaired children to take into consideration certain basic factors prior to evaluating specific tests. These factors are:

1. Personality evaluation is a far more complex task than is IQ testing, especially with deaf children. Because of this, test findings should be interpreted in light of case history data and personal experience with the child. In fact, it behooves educators of the deaf with long experience in the field to view with

skepticism results reported by examiners who are unfamiliar with deaf children when these findings sharply contradict their own impressions of youngsters they know well.

2. Because of communication problems inherent in severe hearing loss, personality tests are more difficult to use with deaf subjects than with the general population (Graham and Kendall, 1960; Levine, 1960; Myklebust, 1962; Myklebust, 1954; Zeckel, 1942). Not only do these tests depend on extensive verbal interchange or reading skill, but they also presuppose a rapport and confidence on the part of the subject that is difficult to achieve when the person examined cannot understand what is being said or written. Paper and pencil personality measures are perhaps suitable for hearing-impaired children with well developed expressive and receptive language ability, but such youngsters are rare, and even with them the problems of test administrators and interpretation make the meaningfulness of results highly fallible (Graham and Kendall, 1960; Levine, 1960; Myklebust, 1962; Myklebust, 1954). The need for fluency in manual communication by the examiner is especially evident in the area of projective testing.

3. There is some question as to whether the norms for the personality structure of hearing people are appropriate for deaf and hard of hearing subjects (Zeckel, 1942). Conceivably, deafness alters the perceived environment sufficiently to bring about an essentially different organization of personality in which normality would then differ from what it is in the case of a person with normal hearing (Bender, 1938; Hathaway and Mc-Kinley, 1951; Myklebust, 1954; Zeckel, 1942). Although this is presently an unresolved problem, it is one that is frequently raised by scholars in the field of deafness and should be considered in any discussion of the personality of those with severe hearing loss.

4. The use of interpreters who express the psychologist's directions in fingerspelling and sign language is a questionable procedure. What is required is an interpreter, fluent not only in manual communication, but also in psychology and testing (Zeckel and Kalb, 1939). Obviously such an individual would be doing the examining himself and not interpreting it for

Table VI.1. Evaluation of Some of the Intelligence Tests Most Commonly Used with Deaf and Hard of Hearing Children

Test	Appropriate Age Range Covered by the Test	Evaluation of the Test
1. Wechsler Performance Scale for Children (1949)	9 years–16 years	The Wechsler Performance Scale is at present the best test for deaf children ages 9–16. It yields a relatively valid IQ score, and offers opportunities for qualitative interpretations of factors such as brain injury or emotional disturbance (Wechsler, 1955, pp. 80–81). It has good interest appeal and is relatively easy to administer and reasonable in cost.
2. Wechsler Performance Scale for Adults (1955)	16 years–70 years	The rating of the Wechsler Performance Scale for Adults is the same as the rating on the Wechsler Performance Scale for children.
3. Wechsler Preschool and Primary Scale of Intelligence Performance subtests (Wexler, 1967)	3 years, 11 months to 6 years, 8 months	This scale is not as good for use with deaf and hard of hearing children as the other Wechsler Scales. Picture Completion and Mazes are difficult to explain non-verbally. Other performance subtests are excellent. Standardization seems a little high.
4. Leiter International Performance Scale (1948 revision)	4 years–12 years (also suitable for older mentally retarded deaf subjects)	This test has good interest appeal. It can be used to evaluate relatively disturbed deaf children who could not otherwise be tested. This test is expensive and lacking somewhat in validation. In general, however, it is an excellent test for young deaf children. Timing is a minor factor in this test. One disadvantage is in the interpretation of the IQ scores because the mean of the test is 95 and the standard deviation is 20. This means that the absolute normal score on this test is 95 instead of 100 as on other intelligence tests. Scores

of, for example, 60, therefore, do not indicate mental deficiency but correspond more to about a 70 on a test such as the Wechsler or Binet. Great care must be taken in interpreting Leiter IQ scores for these reasons.

Test	Age Range	Description
5. Progressive Matrices (Raven, 1948)	9 years–adulthood	Raven's Progressive Matrices are good as a second test to substantiate another more comprehensive intelligence test. The advantage of the Matrices is that it is extremely easy to administer and score, taking relatively little of the examiner's time and is very inexpensive. It yields invalid test scores of impulsive deaf children, who tend to respond randomly rather than with accuracy and care. For this reason, the examiner should observe the child carefully to assure that he is really trying.
6. Ontario School Ability Examination (Amoss, 1949)	4 years–10 years	This is a reasonably good test for deaf children within these age ranges.
7. Nebraska Test of Learning Aptitude (Heider, 1940; Hiskey, 1955)	4 years–12 years	A test comparable in value to the Ontario, and standardized for both hearing and deaf children.
8. Chicago Non-Verbal Examination (Brown, et al., 1947)	7 years–12 years	This test rates fair if given as an individual test; very poor if given as a group test. The scoring is tedious and reliability is rather low.
9. Grace Arthur Performance Scale (Arthur, 1947)	4.5 years–15.5 years	This is a test that is poor to fair due to the fact that timing is heavily emphasized, norms are not adequate, and directions are somewhat unsatisfactory. This test is especially unsatisfactory for

Table VI.1—Evaluation of some of the Intelligence Tests Most Commonly Used with Deaf and Hard of Hearing Children—Continued

Test	Appropriate Age Range Covered by the Test	Evaluation of the Test
		emotionally disturbed children who are also deaf. With this type subject this test will sometimes yield a score indicating extreme retardation when the difficulty is actually one of maladjustment. It is also poor for young deaf children who are of below average intelligence because they often respond randomly instead of rationally.
10. Merrill-Palmer Scale of Mental Tests (Sutsman, 1931)	2 years–4 years	The Merrill-Palmer is a fair test for young deaf children, but it must be adapted in order to be used and would require a skilled examiner with a thorough knowledge of deaf children.
11. Goodenough Draw-A-Man Test (1926)	8.5 years–11 years	Directions are very difficult to give young children in a standardized manner. Scoring is less objective than would be desired, so this test is relatively unreliable. It does, however, have some projective value in terms of personality assessment.
12. Randalls Island Performance Tests (1932)	2 years–5 years	This is one of the few non-verbal instruments available for measuring preschool children. It consists of a wide range of performance and manipulative tasks which, used by a competent examiner, provide diagnostic and insightful information. This test is relatively expensive, but valuable.
13. Dr. Alathena Smith's Test for Preschool Deaf Children (Smith, 1967)	Preschool: 2 years–4 years	This test is not officially on the market but the dissertation which contains the necessary information can be obtained from Dr. Smith at the Tracy Clinic. The test materials are available in most psychologists' offices and Dr. Smith gets excellent results with the test.

It is the only intelligence test for deaf or hard of hearing children in this age range which is well standardized on a large sample.

Test	Appropriate Age Range Covered by the Test	Evaluation of the Test
14. Vineland Social Maturity Scale	1 year–25 years	This is a questionable test for deaf and hard of hearing children generally, but can be used for very, very difficult to test emotionally disturbed youngsters. It is given by asking the parents questions on the development of their child. The norms of this test have to be adapted for the hard of hearing because many of the questions involved such things as onset of speech, length of sentences, vocabulary, etc. This test is inexpensive and can be given to otherwise untestable children.

Table VI.2. Personality Tests Used With Deaf and Hard of Hearing Children

Test	Appropriate Age Range Covered by the Test	Evaluation of the Test
1. Draw-A-Person (Machover, 1949)	9 years–adulthood	This is a good screening device for detecting very severe emotional problems. It is relatively non-verbal and is probably the most practical projective personality test for deaf children. Its interpretation is very subjective and in the hands of a poor psychologist it can result in rather extreme diagnostic statements about deaf children.
2. Thematic Apperception Test (TAT) or Children's Apperception Test (CAT) (Stein, 1955)	Can be used with deaf subjects of school age through adulthood who can communicate very well in written language	This is a test of great potential, if the psychologist giving it and the deaf subject taking it can both communicate with fluency in manual communication. It is of very limited value otherwise unless the deaf subject has an exceptional command of the English language. This test could be given through an interpreter by an ex-

Table VI.2—Personality Tests Used With Deaf and Hard of Hearing Children—Continued

Test	Appropriate Age Range Covered by the Test	Evaluation of the Test
3. Rorschach Ink Blot Test (Rorschach, 1942)	Can be given to deaf subjects as soon as they are able to communicate fluently manually or if they can communicate with exceptional skill orally.	ceptionally perceptive psychologist, although it is more desirable if the psychologist can do his own communicating. In order for the Rorschach to be used it is almost absolutely necessary that the psychologist giving it and the deaf subject taking it be fluent in manual communication. Even under these circumstances it is debatable if it yields much of value unless the subject is of above average intelligence. It would be possible with a very bright deaf subject, who had a remarkable proficiency in English, to give a Rorschach through writing, but this would not be very satisfactory.
4. H.T.P. Technique (Buck, 1949)	School age through adulthood	This is a procedure similar to the Draw-A-Person test. It requires little verbal communication and affords the competent clinician some valuable insight into basic personality dynamics of the subject.
5. Rotter Incomplete Sentences Blank (Rotter and Rafferty, 1950)	At least fifth grade reading level	Useful with subjects who understand the vocabulary of the test. Many hard of hearing youth do not. Some experienced examiners substitute simple terms for some of the complex ones on the test.
6. Make-A-Picture-Story Test (MAPS) (Schneidman, 1952)	About same as TAT and CAT above except that it is somewhat less verbal	Basically the same as the CAT or TAT except that there are actual figures and a stage which can be moved about and grouped in ways that are indicative of social and personality dynamics.

another. Therefore, results reported where an interpreter is involved are not likely to meet high standards of validity.

EVALUATION OF PERSONALITY TESTS COMMONLY USED WITH DEAF AND HARD OF HEARING CHILDREN. Because of the difficulties that have been pointed out above, few personality tests have had wide application with deaf or hard of hearing children. Four of the more commonly and successfully used are evaluated in Table VI.2.

Screening Tests for Brain Injury

Because of the high incidence of brain injury among deaf children, especially those whom a teacher is likely to refer for psychological evaluation, it is appropriate to discuss some tests used to diagnose and measure this condition (Vernon, 1961). A thorough assessment of neurological impairment would generally include one or more of these psychological instruments plus neurological and audiological techniques of diagnosis (Vernon, 1961). A brief discussion of some tests and items from tests that are useful for detecting brain injury follows.

1. Bender-Gestalt (Bender, 1938). This is probably the most widely used screening instrument for the detection of gross neurological impairment. Standardization of norms is being continued; interpretation requires extensive training and experience. However, the Bender is a valuable part of a test battery for deaf subjects (Myklebust, 1962).

2. Wechsler Performance Scale (Wechsler, 1949; Wechsler, 1955). Quantitative pattern analysis of these scales is of controversial validity as a diagnostic tool for neurological dysfunction. There is a fairly general agreement, however, that in the hands of a capable clinical psychologist, a partial qualitative type of diagnosis is possible (Levine, 1960; Myklebust, 1954).

3. Memory For Designs Test (Graham and Kendall, 1960). A relatively new test, this appears to have considerable value. Its precise scoring technique controls for variation in age, intelligence, and vocabulary level.

4. Ellis Visual Designs Test (Strauss and Kephart, 1955). This test appears to have definite possibilities, but lacks validation (Levine, 1960).

5. Strauss-Werner Marble Board Test (Strauss and Kephart, 1955). This test is potentially excellent, but it is very hard to get. Scoring instructions are inadequate (Levine, 1960).

6. Hiskey Blocks (Heider, 1940). This test requires a great deal of visualization and abstract ability and is of value for this reason (Heider, 1940; Myklebust, 1954).

7. Rorschach (1942). The use of this test requires not only competency in administering the test, but also a fluency in the use of manual communication employed by the deaf. Results reported where these conditions are not met are of highly dubious validity.

8. Kohs Blocks (Kohs, 1923). These are similar to the block design subtest of the Wechsler Scales, but are more expensive. A qualitative diagnosis is possible, but norms are lacking for organic involvement.

9. The Diamond Drawing from the Stanford Binet (Terman and Merrill, 1937). This test has good validity, is generally available, and can be easily administered.

10. Various measures of motor ability and development. Among these would be the railwalking test, tests of laterality, and certain items on the Vineland Social Maturity Scale that pertain to motor development.

Suggested Test Batteries for Deaf and Hard of Hearing School-Age Children

Because an adequate psychological assessment should properly be based on a series of tests rather than a single instrument, the following test batteries are suggested for the various age groups of a school population:

1. Preschool. Measurement of intelligence should be based on at least two of the following IQ tests: the Leiter International Performance Scale, the Merrill-Palmer Scale of Mental Tests, or the Randalls Island Performance Tests.

There are no suitable personality tests or tests for brain injury for deaf preschool children. Clinical judgment, medical, audiological, and case history data must be depended on exclusively for evaluation in these areas.

2. Beginning School Age Through Age Nine. IQ tests should

include at least two of the following: the Leiter International Performance Scale, WISC or WPPSI Performance Items, Nebraska Test of Learning Aptitude, Ontario Test of School Ability, Goodenough Draw-A-Man Test, Smith Test, or Progressive Matrices. Human figure drawing interpretation and Bender-Gestalt responses should be used to screen for personality deviations and organic brain damage.

3. Ages Nine Through Fifteen. The most appropriate measure of intelligence for this age range is the WISC Performance Scale. It can best be supplemented with Progressive Matrices, the Chicago Non-Verbal Test, or the Leiter International Performance Scale. Human figure drawings and the Bender-Gestalt become increasingly valid measures in this age range and are the best screening techniques for personality disturbance and brain damage.

4. Age Sixteen Through School Graduation. The WAIS Performance Scale stands out as the superior measure of intelligence for this age range. The second measure for intelligence found most valid is the Progressive Matrices. To the Bender-Gestalt and Draw-A-Person Test can be added or substituted the Memory-For-Designs Test as a screening measure for organic brain damage. Vocational tests should be added at this age. Their selection is a highly individual matter depending on the subject and available vocational educational facilities. For discussion of these tests, Helmer Myklebust's article is most helpful (1962).

Educational Achievement Measurement

A full evaluation should include not just the psychological measure just described but also an assessment of educational level. A major reason for this is the prevalence of academic difficulty among deaf and hard of hearing youngsters. The most appropriate tests for obtaining this information are the Metropolitan or the Stanford. The former has norms for hearing and deaf subjects. Both tests are easy to administer, but the examiner must make certain that the child understands and successfully completes the sample items for each subtest. Another crucial point in using these or any achievement tests is to choose a battery that is at a level appropriate to the person being tested.

In interpreting results of achievement testing it is important to keep in mind not only the average achievement levels for the normally hearing but also those for the deaf and more severely hard of hearing. These are as follows: only about five percent of graduates from day and residential schools for the deaf attain a tenth grade level in educational achievement, 41 percent seventh or eighth grade, 27 percent fifth or sixth grade, and approximately 30 percent are functionally illiterate by present governmental standards (McClure, 1966).

Evaluation of Communication Skills

It is in the realm of communication that hearing loss presents its major handicap. For this reason, it is important that an evaluation include an assessment of communication skills.

There are three aspects of communication which should be appraised in the deaf or hard of hearing child. First is the ability to read and write because those are primary determinants of educational and vocational potential. Educational tests will provide reading levels. Sentence completion or several of the verbal subtests of the Wechsler, in addition to their clinical data, will yield a reasonably accurate picture of writing skills.

Speech and speechreading are the other key parts of communication to be evaluated. These skills may have considerable potential to deaf or the hard of hearing child at school and later in the world of work. Psychologists have little difficulty in assessing in practical lay terms the intelligibility and pleasantness of the speech. These should be noted in the child's report.

Speechreading skill is a more complex function to measure. Audiological specialists are needed to do this thoroughly. However, it is important for the psychologist to report the extent to which the youngster is able to understand conversation in a one-to-one situation. It is also helpful if note can be made of the relative degree to which the youngster depends upon visual clues (speechreading) as contrasted to using his residual hearing. From such information, the child's ability to communicate in groups can be estimated. One way for the psychologist to get this information is to cover his mouth or ask the child to turn his back during conversation.

The audiologist is the final authority in the area of communication. The psychologist functions only as a lay observer. In so doing, he must be particularly careful to indicate in his report whether or not his observations were in a relatively quiet one-to-one situation or whether he also assessed communication skills in other settings. The youth's capacities in a group situation such as a classroom, job, or social setting may be totally different from those in a one-to-one relationship. Generally they are far less effective.

Some hard of hearing children know fingerspelling and/or the language of signs. As these skills can be valuable assets in many situations the examiner should inquire about them. One final point must be made clear in evaluating communication skills. Psychologists familiar with manual communication are quickly able to determine the child's fluency. Many extremely bright and capable hard of hearing youth lack the ability to speak and lipread fluently. It is of critical importance that the psychologist not confuse difficulty in communication with lack of intelligence. It is also possible that a congenitally hard of hearing person may have a very high IQ yet have written language that is not sophisticated grammatically. The psychologist must be keenly aware of these factors if they are to be fair and helpful to a hard of hearing youngster.

Aptitude and Interest Testing

A basic part of a complete psychological evaluation for older youth is aptitude testing, i. e., finding out the particular abilities that a person may have. As there are hundreds of tests for this on the market it is not feasible to list or discuss them individually. Both Levine (1971) and Myklebust (1962) surveyed this area relative to the hearing impaired with excellence and completeness. However, certain information about the following three general areas of aptitude is often of great value because these kinds of abilities are directly related to the types of work the more communication limited hard of hearing adults do.

1. Manual dexterity
2. Mechanical aptitudes
3. Spatial relations

It is important in selecting from the many measures of aptitude available to choose some tests which are not primarily dependent on language for either their directions or administration.

Interest tests are almost without exception highly verbal. Thus, they can generally not be used effectively with all hard of hearing persons. There are pictorial tests designed for use with those who are deaf, but they are narrow in scope and offer limited data to a psychological evaluation. It can be stated categorically that interest tests rarely are of value unless reading skills are high and even then results may be questionable.

It would be inappropriate to discuss tests without mention of the General Aptitude Test Battery (GATB). As now constructed this test discriminates against a language impaired person. With the exception of certain parts, it yields more misinformation than help regarding these people. Fortunately, an adaptation of the GATB for use with the hearing impaired is now being undertaken through the auspices of the Rehabilitation Services Administration.

Case History Data

The past is still the one best predictor of the future. This was mentioned earlier but is of sufficient importance to elaborate at this point. Complete background information on a child, especially if he is deaf or hard of hearing and may not be accurately evaluated with regular psychological procedures, is an absolute necessity. Illustrative of this is that the best psychiatric and psychological evaluations are often based 75 percent on background information. A parental interview is often of value and will help the psychologist gain insight into the child's acceptance of his handicap as well as the parental attitude towards the child.

Audiological Reports, Physical Examinations, and Medical History

The findings of the audiologist and the speech therapist are basic to a meaningful evaluation of a deaf or hard of hearing child. They address themselves directly to an important part of what is generally integral to the child's problem. Audiology and speech pathology are complex fields involving evaluative procedures far beyond the scope of this chapter. It will suffice to say data from these specialists should be obtained on all deaf and hard of hearing children.

It is often extremely beneficial to a psychologist if he can obtain some data on a hard of hearing child's physical condition and medical history. Especially useful is data about etiology of hearing loss. As noted before many of the causes of impaired hearing also result in brain damage, learning disability, visual problems, seizures, mental retardation, aphasia, motor deficiency, orthopedic difficulties, cardiac anomalies, and behavior disturbances (Vernon, 1967, a, b, c, d, e, and 1968). These conditions are obviously highly relevant to a child's functioning and to a meaningful psychological evaluation. Often they are best understood if medical data is available.

By interrelating IQ, educational, and other facts about a deaf or hard of hearing child it is possible to derive a picture which reveals the role played by his hearing loss. If the youth's profile is similar to that of the normally hearing, his loss and the way it has been coped with is not particularly disabling. By contrast, if the profile is similar to that of a deaf child then the loss has had major effects on communication, language development, and education. Appropriate planning for the two kinds of children vary drastically. What would be constructive for one would in certain cases be devastating for the other. An evaluation which does not fully address itself to this issue has failed to serve one of its major functions. The issue cannot be handled without comprehensive information. Short cuts will not suffice and hasty inadequately done evaluations are actually unethical and wasteful of human resources.

Summary

Some general principles of psychological evaluation with deaf and hard of hearing children have been discussed, principles which attempt to adjust evaluation procedures to the role hearing loss plays in psychological functioning. Major areas of information required for evaluation have been delineated. Attention has also been given to the problem of differential diagnosis and some practical aspects of school psychology.

Throughout the chapter emphasis has been placed on the crucial necessity to understand the function hearing loss plays in language development and communication. A full grasp of this and its relationship to psychological evaluation procedures and the interpretation of their results is the substance of meaningful psychodiagnostics with the hard of hearing and the deaf.

REFERENCES

Amoss, H.: *Ontario School Ability Examination.* Toronto, Ryerson, 1949.

Arthur, G.: *A Point Scale of Performance Tests,* Rev. Form II. New York, Psychological Corporation, 1947.

Bender, Lauretta: *A Visual Motor Gestalt Test and Its Clinical Use.* The American Orthopsychiatric Association, New York, 1938.

Brill, R. G.: The Relationship of Wechsler IQ's To Academic Achievement Among Deaf Students. *Except Child, 28:*315–321, 1962.

Brown, A., Stein, D., and Ruhrer, R.: *Chicago Non-Verbal Examination.* Psychological Corp., 1947.

Buck, J.: The H.T.P. Technique, A Qualitative and Quantitative Scoring Manual. *J Clin Psychol,* Vol. IV, 1948, and Vol. V, 1949.

Burchard, E. M., and Myklebust, H. R. A Comparison of Congenital and Adventitious Deafness with Respect to its Effect on Intelligence, Personality, and Social Maturity, (Part I, Intelligence). *Ann Deaf, 87:*241–250, 1942.

Davis, H. (ed.), and Silverman, D. R. (Co. ed.) : *Hearing and Deafness,* 3rd ed. New York, Holt, Rinehart and Winston, 1970.

Goodenough, Florence: *Measurement of Intelligence by Drawings,* Chicago, World Book Co., 1926.

Graham, Frances K. and Kendall, Barbara S.: *Memory-For-Designs Test: Revised General Manual.* Perceptual Motor Skills Monograph Supplement 2–VII, 1960.

Hathaway, S. and McKinley, J.: *Minnesota Multiphasic Personality Inventory Manual* (Rev.) . New York, Psychological Corp., 1951.

Heider, G. M.: The Thinking of the Deaf Child. *Volta Rev, 42:*774–776, 804–808; 1940. (A review from an article in French by R. Pellet) .

Hiskey, M. S.: *Nebraska Test of Learning Aptitude for Young Deaf Children.* Lincoln, Univ. Nebraska, 1955.

Kohs, S.: *The Block Designs Test.* Chicago, Stoelting, 1923.

Lane, Helen S. and Schneider, J. L.: A Performance Test for School Age Deaf Children. *Am Ann Deaf, 86:*441, 1941.

Leiter, R.: *The Leiter International Performance Scale.* Chicago, Stoelting, 1948.

Levine, E. S.: Mental Assessment of the Deaf Child. *Volta Review, 73:*80–105, 1971.

Levine, Edna: *Psychology of Deafness.* New York, Columbia Univ. Press, 1960.

McClure, W. J.: Current Problems and Trends in the Education of the Deaf. *Deaf Am, 18:*8–14, 1966.

Machover, Karen: *Personality Projection in the Drawing of the Human Figure.* Springfield, Thomas, 1949.

Myklebust, H. R.: *Auditory Disorders in Children.* A Manual for Differential Diagnosis. New York, Grune Stratton, 1954.

Myklebust, H.: Guidance and counseling for the Deaf. *Am Ann Deaf, 370–*415, 1962.

The Randalls Island Performance Series, (Manual). Chicago, Stoelting, 1932.

Raven, J.: *Progressive Matrices.* New York, Psychological Corp., 1948.

Rorschach, H.: *Psychodiagnostics.* Berne, Switzerland: Hans Huber, 1942.

Rose, D.: *Audiological Assessment.* New York, Prentice Hall, 1971.

Ratter, J. B. and Rafferty, J. E.: *The Ratter Incomplete Sentence Blank.* New York, Psychological Corp., 1950.

Schneidman, E. S.: *Make a Picture Story* (MAPS) Manual. Teachers College: New York, Bur. Publ., 1948.

Scouten, E. L.: The Prelingually Deaf Child and His Oral Education in New Perspective. *Am Ann Deaf, 114:*770–776, 1969.

Smith, Alathena J.: Psychological Testing of the Preschool Deaf Child—A Challenge for Changing Times. *Proceedings of International Conference on Oral Education of the Deaf, 1:*162–181, 1967.

Stein, M. L.: *The Thermatic Apperception Test.* Cambridge, Addison-Wesley Pub.

Strauss, A. and Kephart, N.: *Psychopathology and Education of the Brain Injured Child.* New York, Grune and Stratton, 1955.

Sutsman, Rachel: *Mental Measurement of Pre-School Children.* New York, World Book Co., 1931.

Terman, L. M. and Merrill, M. D.: *Measuring Intelligence.* New York, Houghton Mifflin, 1937.

Vernon, M.: The Brain Injured (neurologically impaired) Child. A Discussion of the Significance of the Problem, its Symptoms and Causes in Deaf Children. *Am Ann Deaf, 106:*239–250, 1961.

Vernon, M.: Characteristics Associated with Post Rubella Deaf Children. *Volta Rev, 69:*176–185, 1967 (a).

Vernon, M.: Counseling the Deaf Client. *J Rehab Deaf, 1:*3–16, 1967 (b).

Vernon, M.: Meningitis and Deafness. *Laryngoscope, 77:*1856–1874, 1967 (c).

Vernon, M.: Multiply handicapped Deaf Children—The Causes, Manifestations, and Significances of the Problem. *Proceedings of International Conference on Oral Education of the Deaf, 2:*2136–2161, 1967 (d).

Vernon, M.: Prematurity and Deafness: The Magnitude and nature of the problem among Deaf Children. *Exceptional Children, 38:*289–298, 1962.

Vernon, M. and Brown, D. W.: A Guide to Psychological Tests and Testing procedures in the Evaluation of Deaf and Hard-of-Hearing Children. *J Speech Hear Disord, 29:*414–423, 1964.

Vernon, M.: Rh Factor and Deafness: The Problem, its Psychological, Physical and Educational Manifestations. *Except Child, 38:*5–12, 1967 (e).

Vernon, M.: Rubella: An Introduction. *National Hear. Aid,* 22:4, 22, 1968.

Vernon, M.: Tuberculosis, Meningitis and Deafness. *J Speech Hear Disord, 32:*177–181, 1967.

Wechsler, D.: *Wechsler Adult Intelligence Scale.* New York, Psychological Corp., 1955.

Wechsler, D.: *Wechsler Intelligence Scale for Children.* New York, Psychological Corp., 1949.

Wechsler, D.: *Wechsler Preschool and Primary Scale of Intelligence.* New York, Psychological Corp., 1967.

Zeckel, A. and Kalb, J. L.: A Comparative Test of Groups of Children Born Deaf and of Good Hearing by Means of the Porteous Test. *Am Ann Deaf, 84:*114–123, 1939.

Zeckel, A.: Research Possibilities with the Deaf, *Am Ann Deaf, 87:*173–191, 1942.

CHAPTER VII

PHYSICALLY AND NEUROLOGICALLY IMPAIRED

SAM D. CLEMENTS AND TOM J. HICKS

THE VARIETY OF exceptional children who could be included within the category of *physically and neurologically impaired* may well be limited by the single factor of tradition. For in the broad sense, the vast majority of conditions which produce exceptionality in the human organism are inherent in general physical and neurological status.

A review of commonly used textbooks designed to acquaint the student with the spectrum of children who are exceptional because of physical and neurologic impairment emphasizes the prevailing custom of categorizing by means of medical diagnosis. Thus, sections of a typical book are devoted to the cerebral palsies, the epilepsies, cardiac conditions, etc. The psychoeducational diagnostician should indeed be familiar with the array of conditions which effect children and the special language which accompanies such specific medical entities, since within this realm of exceptionality, he will, in most instances be in communication with physicians and other health-related professionals.

For the purposes of this chapter, all categories within the broad heading of physically and neurologically impaired will be treated as related conditions. This relationship is based on the proposition that any condition which alters physical integrity, body homeostasis, or central nervous system functioning, can manifest in a wide variety of learning and behavioral symptoms. The nature and extent of these deviations depend upon such factors as the particular anomaly, the specific disease process, and the cause, loci of assault, developmental stage of embryo, fetus, or child, and diffuseness or discreteness of the damage to the central nervous system. The disorders of learning and behavior which attend such impairment commonly result in the referral of the individual child for psychoeducational evaluation.

Many difficulties are encountered when an attempt is made to produce a classification model for these handicaps, since concomitant conditions are frequently found within the single child. A somewhat traditional method of grouping the physical and neurological impairments which affect children is as follows:

1. MUSCULAR AND/OR SKELETAL IMPAIRMENTS
    A. Impaired ambulation (scissored gain, clubfoot, etc.)
    B. Impaired hand use (underdeveloped appendages, absence of digits, etc.)
    C. Speech (cleft palate, tongue, etc.)
2. CHRONIC OR SPECIAL HEALTH PROBLEMS
    A. Arthritis.
    B. Cardiac conditions.
    C. Diabetes
    D. Hemophilia.
    E. Muscular dystrophy.
    F. Osteomyelitis.
    G. Severe allergies.
    H. Tuberculosis.
    I. Other debilitating conditions.
3. CENTRAL NERVOUS SYSTEM IMPAIRMENTS
    A. The cerebral palsies.
    B. The epilepsies.
    C. Traumatic brain damage.
    D. Post-encephalitis.
    E. Poliomyelitis.
    F. Other crippling conditions.
    G. Autism and other childhood psychoses.
4. MINIMAL BRAIN DYSFUNCTIONS INCLUDING SPECIFIC LEARNING DISABILITIES
    A. Perceptual deficits.

B. Cognitive deficits.

C. Motor integration deficits.

D. Hyperkinetic syndrome.

5. SEVERE DEPRIVATIONS WHICH INFLUENCE LEARNING AND BEHAVIOR

A. Nutritional.

B. Physical.

C. Cultural.

D. Interpersonal.

The following is an example of a highly specialized, therefore limited, classification based on the concept of a *continuum of impairment* within the central nervous system:

SYMPTOMS ASSOCIATED WITH BRAIN DYSFUNCTION	
MAJOR IMPAIRMENT(S)	MINIMAL IMPAIRMENT(S)
1. The epilepsies.	1. Electroencephalographic abnormalities without actual seizures, or possibly subclinical seizures, which may be associated with fluctuations in behavior or specific intellectual function.
2. The mental subnormalities.	2. Specific and circumscribed perceptual, cognitive, and memory deficits.
3. The cerebral palsies.	3. Impairment of fine or gross movement or coordination.
4. Blindness, deafness, and the severe aphasias.	4. Central processing dysfunctions of vision, audition, haptics, and language.
5. Autism, childhood psychosis, and other gross disorders of aberrant behavior.	5. Deviations in attention, affect, motor activity level, and impulse control.

The etiologies of all the above conditions are considered as due to organicity variables which include genetic variations, biochemical irregularities, perinatal brain insults, or the result of disease or injury sustained during the periods critical for the normal development and maturation of the central nervous system. Any physical impairment and/or disorganization of brain function due to these events places numerous hardships on the developing child and his family.

Regardless of the primary medical diagnosis, the psycho-educational diagnosis is unique since it forms the basis for the educational and behavioral management of the child.

Professional misunderstanding is possible if one fails to recognize that differences exist in the objectives of a medical diagnosis as opposed to a psychoeducational diagnosis. The major objective of the medical diagnosis is to demonstrate the existence of any causative factors of disease or injury capable of amelioration or prevention. The psychoeducational diagnosis involves the assessment of performance and capabilities. Its objective is to make possible the establishment of appropriate habilitative programs of education and management.

Commonly, but not necessarily, the request for a psychoeducational diagnosis will follow the medical one. For the psychoeducational specialist, the primary medical diagnosis should communicate certain aspects of the cause of the child's exceptionality, circumscribe probable areas of deficit or diminished skill, relate the need for special environmental considerations, and establish her role in the processes of diagnosis and treatment planning at any given time.

For some handicapping conditions, medical surveillance must be primary in order to assure continuance of life for the child. In such instances, educational and behavioral goals may, of necessity, become limited and secondary. However, many physical and neurologic events which produce exceptionality in children will have ceased in activity at the point when a psychoeducational diagnosis is requested. In such instances, the medical aspects may be static, and remedy for the child will no longer rest on a traditional medical cure of a specific condition. Rather, the concern focuses on achieving optimal levels of functioning in everyday life situations in accordance with the child's present condition and capacity. The chief ally may then become the plasticity of the child's central nervous system which may allow compensation for loss of certain functions, either in the natural course of development and integration, or by means of special education and training. The results of the psychoeducational diagnosis should produce information which would permit the initiation of a personalized program matched with more precision to the child's unique profile of individual differences.

Psychoeducational Evaluation

The prime referent in the evaluation of a child with physical and/or neurologic impairment is the individual himself. The assessment technique should not be the referent since it is but a behavior sampling tool. It is the concept of an impaired child in the context of a non-handicapped world which should be considered. The comparison of individual strengths and weaknesses should be made with the normal population. Normative data from a selected group of handicapped children would have little application for the population as a whole. Despite the fact that a child is physically impaired or otherwise handicapped, the same evaluative instruments and techniques should be used as with those who are not handicapped. The psychoeducational diagnosis is, in the main, an inventory of individual differences of the particular child, with special concern for those areas of personal performance by which children in our culture are generally judged. A prominent feature is the isolation of those areas of impaired functioning which can be relieved, remediated, or restored. Diagnosis is also a decision-making process which involves the selection of specific ameliorative methods and program objectives which should include occupational expectancies.

The psychoeducational diagnostician will be called upon to play a variety of roles, some of which are difficult to isolate as specifics since they will vary from work-setting to work-setting. Her employment affiliation may be with a public school, a private school, a public or private community agency, a state agency or institution, or in some instances as a private practicioner. She may work in relative professional isolation or as a member of a diagnostic team which might include any number of specialists from allied disciplines. In any event, the contributions of the psychoeducational diagnostician will require competency in at least four areas which are basic to the diagnostic process:

1. Observational Skills—The ability to systematically analyze the general and test behavior of the child.
2. Assessment Skills—The ability to properly select and admin-

ister a wide range of formal and informal structured procedures designed to methodically measure the child's strengths and weaknesses in cognitive, perceptual, motor, and social skills.

3. Interpretive Skills—The ability to evaluate the significance of the observational and assessment data and translate them into utilizable habilitative procedures. This should include, when applicable, the integration of supportive assessment information from physician, psychologist, social worker, physical therapist, etc., into the planning and implementation processes.

4. Implementation Skills—The ability to transform the results of the diagnostic process into specific recommendations to to be implemented by specific available resources.

In this regard, it should be underscored that a psychoeducational diagnosis at the highest level of sophistication can become but an empty and isolated activity unless a network of required services for the affected child and his family are conveniently accessible, comprehensive, and continuing.

The Assessment Procedure

Procedural problems may arise when an examiner attempts to administer assessment techniques to a severely involved handicapped child. These difficulties may be due to such factors as an inexperienced examiner; inappropriate test material; poor physical facilities; or a lack of understandng of the symptoms of the child's condition which may limit communication. Some children will have no handicapping involvement in the upper portions of their bodies; therefore, no difficulty may arise in test administration. In such cases, the only special provision necessary may be a lap board which fits over a wheelchair in order to facilitate work which requires near-point vision or the manipulation of objects by hand.

A too liberal interpretation of scores given the child not only contributes to an invalidation of the standardized norms, and may therefore preclude the original intent of the test, but may also result in a misdiagnosis.

Slight alterations in the routine of test administration is generally accepted by clinicians. The examiner may choose to begin the assessment session with performance items as an aid in the establishment of general rapport, rather than begin with direct questioning of the child or the presentation of items which involve verbal problem solving.

The omission of certain test items is not an infrequent practice among those who work closely with physically impaired children. Test items which require deftness in object manipulation or drawing may of necessity have to be excluded for children with severe involvement of the upper extremities.

In a procedural adaptation of a test, the examiner must leave the content intact, but may alter the technique of presentation. A variation in manner of response may be permitted a child with severe speech involvement.

It is sometimes advisable to have a third person who is well known to the child available in the testing room. The purpose is not only for the degree of comfort it may provide the child, but also for assistance and information which may be helpful to the examiner.

Any unusual alteration in procedure should be properly noted in the test report.

Children with physical and neurologic impairment tend to fatigue quickly under conditions of sustained effort. To assure top performance, the diagnostic evaluation may be more productive and better reflect the child's potential if given in several shorter sessions spaced over several days. This is not always possible, of course, but should be well considered.

Psychoeducational Diagnosis

Physical and neurologic impairments common to the human organism may affect the learning, thinking, or cognitive functions of the central nervous system in a variety of ways. All information processing functions in all learning and communication channels may be affected to a mild or severe degree; no functions may be affected to any significant degree; or specific functions only may be affected to some degree.

The usefulness of the psychoeducational diagnosis is measured by the proficiency with which it can be translated into treatment, training, or teaching strategies designed for the individual child. Therefore, it must be sensitive and specific to the major information processing systems. In this regard, we can conceptualize the child as a unit who has the capacity to receive, transform, and transmit information. Since physical and neurologic impairments may affect some or all of the child's activities, it is most likely that their nature and degree will be reflected by the profile of his test scores.

An understanding of the information-processing systems is basic to and essential for appreciation of psychoeducational diagnosis. The following diagram is an oversimplification of a highly complex and incompletely understood system of processing of information within the central nervous system.

Dysfunctions can occur in one or more of the three essential information processing areas of reception, transformation, or transmission of sensory data (input, analysis and synthesis, output) ; and in one or more of the three major information process-

Table VIII.1. Information-Processing System

RECEIVING OF SENSORY DATA INTO THE CENTRAL NERVOUS SYSTEM (Input)	TRANSFORMING OF SENSORY DATA WITHIN THE CENTRAL NERVOUS SYSTEM (Analysis and Synthesis)	TRANSMITTING OF SENSORY DATA FROM THE CENTRAL NERVOUS SYSTEM (Output)

1. Olfactory (smelling).
2. Gustatory (tasting).
3. Tactile (touching).
4. Kinesthetic (moving).
5. Auditory (hearing).
6. Visual (seeing).
	1. Arousal of CNS for readiness to receive data and determination of significance.
	2. Association of data with past experiences.
	3. Processing of data for meaning:
	  a. Scanning for possible interpretations.
	  b. Discarding irrelevant elements.
	  c. Retaining relevant elements for imposition of meaning.
	  d. Organizing relevant elements for meaning.
	4. Decision-making based on extracted meaning:
	  a. Immediate expression.
	  b. Storage for future use.
		1. Vocal activities (forms of oral language).
		2. Other motor activities (forms of non-oral language):
		  a. Gesturing.
		  b. Reading.
		  c. Drawing.
		  d. Writing.
		  e. Spelling.
		  f. Mathematics.
		  g. Art, music, etc.
		  h. Other

FEEDBACK

ing channels, auditory, visual, or motor (tactile and kinesthetic). The psychoeducational diagnostician must be knowledgeable with regard to the information processing systems and the variety of dysfunctions which can eventuate therein, since differential diagnosis of the individual child is founded upon them.

Assessment Techniques

The number and kind of assessment techniques available for psychoeducational diagnosis are many and varied. Some are shared among various disciplines, particularly psychology, education, pediatrics, and the language specialties.

The search for an assessment packet specific to children with physical and neurologic impairment will be unproductive, since the diversity of learning and behavior symptoms may manifest differently in different children and at different ages. The selection of useful and appropriate tests is determined through a reasoning process on the part of the diagnostician, taking into account such factors as the kind of physical or neurologic impairment, the degree of impairment, the age of the child, chief concerns, major symptoms, data from other sources, objectives of the diagnosis, availability of recommended services, and placement possibilities.

1. *Developmental Screening Methods*

The importance of detecting any developmental deviation during infancy and early childhood cannot be overstressed, since punctual diagnosis decreases the chance that a more severe condition will develop and increases the opportunity for successful corrective treatment. In this regard, several infant and early childhood assessment procedures are available to the clinician. Their primary usefulness is to assist in the early detection or substantiation of serious developmental delays which may require further investigation, the initiation of ameliorative treatment, and/or serial evaluations. Most of these methods do not yield a definitive measurement, e.g., a mental age or intelligence quotient, but rather alert the diagnostician to the existence of developmental deviations which may be due to physical or neurologic impairment. The following developmental screening techniques are among the most commonly used:

Bayley Scales of Infant Development—Mental and motor scales for the assessment of early mental and psychomotor development of infants and young children. For ages 2 months to 2.6 years.

Denver Developmental Screening Test—Assesses development in the four areas of gross motor, fine motor, language, and personal-social. For ages 2 weeks to 6.4 years.

Developmental Screening Inventory for Infants—Assesses development in the five areas of gross motor, fine motor, adaptive, language, and personal-social. For ages 4 weeks to 18 months.

Gesell Developmental Schedules—Assesses development in the four areas of motor, adaptive, language, and personal-social. For ages 4 weeks to 4 years.

Cattell Infant Intelligence Scale—A modified downward extension of the Stanford-Binet Intelligence Scale. For ages 3 months to 30 months.

2. *Measures of Global Intelligence*

The usual entry into psychoeducational diagnosis of a child is through the use of an individual test of intellectual functioning. To date, there is no widely accepted better method of estimating learning, academic, and vocational potential. Such instruments are designed to sample a variety of the information processing activities of the child even though they may be primarily measuring previous learning rates which have influenced current functioning levels. The most commonly used measures of global intellectual functioning are:

Stanford-Binet Intelligence Scale—(Combined L and M Form). Individually administered test of intelligence for ages 2 through 18 years.

Wechsler Preschool and Primary Scale of Intelligence (WPP-SI)—Individually administered test of intelligence for ages 4.0 to 6.6 years which provides separate scales for verbal and performance tasks.

Wechsler Intelligence Scale for Children (WISC)—Individually administered test of intelligence for ages 5.0 to 15.11 years which provides separate scales for verbal and performance tasks.

3. *Global Academic-related Measures*

The following assessment techniques are designed to measure a variety of academic readiness skills. They are valuable in isolating deficit areas which will require corrective attention.

Language and Learning Disorders of the Pre-academic Child— This book by Tina Bangs (Appleton-Century-Crofts, New York) includes assessment tools for language skills, avenues of learning, and pre-academic curriculum guides for ages 6 months through kindergarten.

*The Pre-School Inventory—*A series of tasks which measure achievement in the four areas of personal-social responsiveness, associative vocabulary, numerical concept activation, and sensory concept activation. For use with ages 3 years to 6 years.

*The Meeting Street School Screening Test—*An individually administered series of tests for the early identification of children with learning disabilities, including a behavior rating scale. For use with children ages 5.0 to 7.5 years.

*Predicting Reading Failure—*This book by de Hirsch, Jansky, and Langford (Harper and Row, New York) includes a series of ten tests which constitute The Predictive Index for identifying kindergarten age children with a high potential for reading disability.

*School Readiness—*This book by Ilg and Ames (Harper and Row, New York) contains a series of techniques for assessing developmental levels of children within the age range of 5 to 10 years.

4. *Measures of Visual-Motor Skills*

*Frostig Developmental Tests of Visual Perception—*Provides a perceptual quotient determined from the child's performance on subtests which include eye-hand coordination, figure-ground discrimination, form constancy, position in space, and spatial relationships. For use with children ages 3 to 10 years.

*Berry-Buktenica Visual-Motor Integration Test—*Provides an estimate of visual perceptual functioning through the copying of geometric forms. For use within the age range of 2 to 15 years.

*Bender Visual Motor Gestalt Test—*Provides an estimate of

maturational level of visual-motor development in preschool and school age children.

Lincoln-Oseretsky Motor Development Scale—Test consists of 36 tasks which measure general motor proficiency of children. For use with ages 6 to 14 years.

Ayres Space Test—A performance test which measures visual perceptual speed, spatial ability, and position in space. For use with ages 3 to 10 years.

Purdue Perceptual-Motor Survey—This book by Roach and Kephart (Charles E. Merrill, Columbus, Ohio) provides a variety of assessment techniques for indicating the level of perceptual-motor development in children.

5. *Measures of Language Skills*

Illinois Test of Psycholinguistic Abilities (IPTA)—Evaluates abilities along the three dimensions of communication channels (audio-vocal and visuo-motor), psycholinguistic processes (receptive, organization, and expressive), and levels of organization (automatic and representational). For use with ages 2 to 10 years.

Wepman Auditory Discrimination Test—Assesses auditory discrimination ability of children within the age range of 5 to 8 years.

The above list of assessment techniques is not meant to be as comprehensive or exhaustive as will be required by the psychoeducational diagnostician. Omitted were a large number of tests which measure such specific skills as reading, mathematics, writing, spelling, social competence, vocational proficiencies, etc. The nature of each referral will determine the diagnostic questions to be answered. The diagnostic questions will determine the assessment techniques to be used.

MINIMAL BRAIN DYSFUNCTION

In recent years, a new category of exceptional children has come to the attention of psychoeducational diagnosticians. In the opinion of most child specialists, this group constitutes the largest of the exceptionalities. It is composed of children who are compromised in learning and behavior as a result of milder forms of central nervous system dysfunction and/or developmental deviation. The term *minimal brain dysfunctions* is used as the medical designation for this heterogeneous grouping. The overlapping and complementary term *specific learning disabilities* which refers to one of the major manifestations of the condition, is the one preferred by educators and others in the educational management of such children.

A formal definition for minimal brain dysfunction appears in the report of Task Force One of the government sponsored National Project on Minimal Brain Dysfunction (Learning Disabilities) in Children, and is as follows:

> The term minimal brain dysfunction refers to children of near average, average, or above average general intelligence with certain learning and/or behavioral disabilities ranging from mild to severe, which are associated with deviations of function of the central nervous system. These deviations may manifest themselves by various combinations of impairment in perception, conceptualization, language, memory, and control of attention, impulse, or motor function. These aberrations may arise from genetic variations, biochemical irregularities, perinatal brain insults or other illnesses or injuries sustained during the years which are critical for the development and maturation of the central nervous system, or from unknown causes. The definition also allows for the possibility that early severe deprivations could result in central nervous system alterations which may be permanent. During the school years, a variety of learning disabilities is the most prominent manifestation of the condition.

The following companion definition for specific learning disabilities was developed by the National Advisory Committee of the Bureau of Education for the Handicapped of the U. S. Office of Education:

> Children with specific learning disabilities means those children who have a disorder in one or more of the basic psychological processes involved in understanding or using language, spoken or written, which disorder may manifest itself in imperfect ability to listen, think, speak, read,

write, spell or do mathematical calculations. Such disorders include such conditions as perceptual handicaps, brain injury, minimal brain dysfunction, dyslexia, and developmental aphasia. Such term does not include children who have learning problems which are primarily the result of visual, hearing, or motor handicaps, of mental retardation, of emotional disturbance, or of environmental disadvantage.

The following clinical signs and symptoms, or more correctly, certain combinations thereof, are descriptive of children with minimal brain dysfunction. They seldom however, obtain *in toto* for the individual child:

1. Specific disabilities in learning.
2. Aberrations in motor activity level.
   a. Hyperactivity.
   b. Hypoactivity.
3. Deficits in coordination and other soft neurologic signs.
4. Deficits in perception involving one or several of the sensory channels.
5. Deficits in receptive, integrative, and/or expressive language.
6. Lability of emotions.
7. Impulsivity.
8. Defects of attention.
9. Defects of memory.
10. Defects in abstractive ability.

Forerunners to these characteristics of minimal brain dysfunction and/or specific learning disabilities as they appear in the child of elementary school age, are a number of earlier behavioral manifestations. Among these are slow maturation or integration of developmental motor milestones. Excessive motor activity of an unfocused nature is another; and less frequently, a significantly diminished level of motor activity. An especially prominent indicator, and one which is frequently noted by parents, is delayed or atypical language development.

Definitive diagnosis of the child with minimal brain dysfunction or the prediction of a specific learning disability prior to the age of three years, is generally unreliable in our present state of knowledge. In skilled and experienced hands, the currently available standardized developmental assessment techniques have been found to correlate well with intellectual functioning levels and certain areas of deficit and diminished skill obtained later by use of established psychoeducational appraisal methods. Clinical research allows the speculation that failures specific to the development and use of language will identify a large number of children who will eventually fit the definition for specific learning disabilities.

The various types or subcategories of minimal brain dysfunction become more clearly distinguishable in children of elementary school age.

At present, it is possible to distinguish eleven types which may appear in relatively pure form and for which distinct prescriptions for teaching, remediation, and management will be required. The so-called *pure* entities constitute a small percent, perhaps 15 percent or less of all cases of minimal brain dysfunction. The vast majority, or 85 percent of children with minimal brain dysfunction fall into a twelfth group which have a mixed assortment of symptoms, usually three or more.

1. The Hyperactive Type.

In this subgroup, estimated at 2 percent of children with minimal brain dysfunction, the activity level and pattern is like that described for children with a known history of brain damage. However, in many of these cases, no such history can be established with any certainty, and the hyperactivity appears in an almost pure form without any specific disability in learning. The high degree of excessive, unfocused, and disruptive motor activity, quite beyond the control of the child, poses a very real problem in home, school, and social management. In fact, the high visibility of hyperactivity has led to an overemphasis on this symptom as the major characteristic of children with minimal brain dysfunction or specific learning disabilities. This is not true. The relatively pure type of hyperactivity is most clearly discerned when the child is of superior intelligence. It becomes evident that he has the mental ability to perceive and learn in a structured one-to-one situation and that his poor school performance is more related to his extreme drivenness which forces movement and attention from one thing to another.

2. The Hypoactive Type.

This subcategory is also rare, affecting perhaps only 2 percent of the population of children with minimal brain dysfunction. Such youngsters are consistently described from infancy as slow-responding and as displaying a low level of motor activity. Delayed or impaired language development is common in this group and appears as a precursor to later severe reading disability. A school-age description of children in this group will include remarks relating to their slowness in mental processing, movement, and expressive language. They are also characterized as personable, cooperative, work oriented, and even tempered. They are usually well coordinated and achieve high scores on performance type tests.

Note: The numbered entities from 3 through 8 form a series which can be subsumed under the heading of *Developmental Deficits in Symbol Functions,* which is a group of subcategories within the larger array of minimal brain dysfunction and refers to a small number of children whose major and even only significant deficit lies within a highly specific language or symbol function. These are children in whom the area of disability is almost solitary, and may range in different cases from very slight to profound. There is research evidence which indicates genetic factors as probable etiologies of these conditions.

3. Specific Developmental Dyslexia.
4. Specific Developmental Dyscalculia.
5. Specific Developmental Dysorthography.
6. Specific Developmental Dysgraphia.
7. The Developmental Dysphasias.

These disorders involve deficits in receptive, integrative, and/or expressive language and range from mild to severe.

8. Specific Developmental Deficits in Abstraction.
9. Developmental Dyskinesia.

Another small group of children display impairments in fine and/or gross coordination, but hyperactivity and disabilities in learning are not companion symptoms. When dyskinesia is the solitary manifestation, the child is rarely referred for diagnosis. He must often simply endure the annoyance of being chided for his clumsiness and dyscoordination.

10. Subclinical or Minimal Cerebral Palsy.

The children who comprise this group will more often have a history of a difficult pregnancy or delivery. It is a varied group, some with almost pure motor signs, some of them hard, such as altered deep tendon reflexes, dysarthric speech; and some of them soft, such as poor stance persistence and confusion in directionality and orientation in space; others will have clear deficiencies in one or more cognitive functions, such as impaired abstractive ability.

11. Specific Attention Defect.

In the small number of children involved, learning efficiency is impaired by a flaw in *scan* memory. A rapid fatigue of those central nervous system circuits which underlie the maintenance of attention may be at fault in this condition. Fidgetiness is also usually present in these children.

12. Mixed Minimal Brain Dysfunctions.

By far the most common condition within the category of minimal brain dysfunction is referred to simply as *mixed*. Such children, who make up an estimated 85 percent of the group, exhibit to varying degrees many of the signs and symptoms which are included in the group as a whole. Each child, however, is an individual composite unto himself. He has three or more signs, rather than one solitary or relatively pure symptom. The most common mixed type which may come to the attention of the psycho-educational diagnostician, will have a language deficit manifesting as moderate reading disability, short attention span, and mild to moderate hyperactivity. The child typical of this largest of subcategories within the diagnostic category of minimal brain dysfunction is restless, distractible, moderately hyperactive, but often demonstrating the ability to settle down in a one-to-one situation which is relatively free of extraneous stimuli. He shows deficits in language and symbol function which results in various combinations of disabilities in learning. His span of attention is short when compared with his age group; and he exhibits deficits in integrative acts of the motor system.

Essentially it is for this group, and especially those with reading disability as a major symptom, that the development of the newest category of exceptional children, i.e., children with specific learning disabilities due to minimal brain dysfunction came into existence.

Adequate diagnosis and treatment of children with minimal brain dysfunctions and specific learning disabilities require the joint participation of educational, health related, and medical services in case finding, evaluation, and habilitative management. Psychoeducational services will, in most instances, carry the major responsibility for improving skills of learning and communication, and in modifying general behavior.

The conditions termed minimal brain dysfunction can compromise the life achievement and adjustment of affected individuals. Even though our understanding of these central nervous system impairments are imperfect, anyone concerned with the provision and improvement of services to exceptional children and their parents should be committed to make optimum use of all knowledge currently available to intervene in these complicated conditions.

REFERENCES

Advanced Institute for Leadership Personnel in Learning Disabilities, Final Report. Bureau of Education for the Handicapped, U.S. Office of Education, 1970.

Ayres, A. Jean: Ayers Space Test. Western Psychological Services, Los Angeles, California.

Barsch, Ray A.: *Achieving Perceptual-Motor Efficiency*. Special Child Publications, Seattle, 1967.

Bayley, Nancy: Bayley Scales of Infant Development. The Psychological Corporation, New York.

Berry-Buktenica Visual-Motor Integration Test. Follett Publishing Company, Chicago.

Buktenica, Norman A.: *Visual Learning*. Dimensions Publishing Company, San Rafael, California, 1968.

Catell: Cattell Infant Intelligence Scale, Psyche. The Psychological Corporation, New York.

Caldwell, Bettye M.: Pre-School Inventory. Educational Testing Service, Princeton, New Jersey.

Chalfant, James C., and Scheffelin, Margaret A.: *Central Processing Dysfunctions in Children: A Review of Research.* NINDS Monograph No. 9. Task Force III of National Project on Minimal Brain Dysfunctions (Learning Disabilities) in Children, H.E.W. Superintendent of Documents, U.S Government Printing Office, Washington, D.C., 1969.

Clements, Sam D.: *Minimal Brain Dysfunctions in Children: Terminology and Identification.* NINDB Monograph No. 3. Task Force I of National Project on Minimal Brain Dysfunctions (Learning Disabilities) in Children, H.E.W. Superintendent of Documents, Government Printing Office, Washington, D.C., 1966.

Clements, Sam D., and Peters, John E.: Minimal Brain Dysfunctions in the School-age Child. *Arch Gen Psychiatry,* 6:185–197, 1962.

Cruickshank, William M. (Ed.) : *Psychology of Exceptional Children and Youth.* Prentice-Hall, Englewood Cliffs, New Jersey, 1963.

Cruickshank, William M., Bice, Harry V., Wallen, Norman E.: *Perception and Cerebral Palsy.* Syracuse University Press, New York, 1957.

William K. Frankenburg and Josiah B. Dobbs: Denver Developmental Screening Test. *J Ped,* 71:181–191, 1967.

Dunn, Lloyd M. (Ed.) : *Exceptional Children in the Schools.* Holt, Rhinehart and Winston, Inc., New York, 1963.

Frostig, Marianne (in association with Phyllis Maslow) : *Movement Education: Theory and Practice.* Follett Educational Corporation, Chicago, 1970.

Frostig Developmental Tests of Visual Perception, Consulting Psychologists Press, Palo Alto, California.

Gesell, Arnold and Amatruda, Catherine S.: *Developmental Diagnosis.* Hoeber Medical Division, Harper and Row, New York, 1964.

Hainsworth, Peter K., and Siqueland, Marian L.: Meeting Street School Screening Test. Crippled Children and Adults of Rhode Island, Inc., Providence, 1969.

Johnson, Doris J. and Myklebust, Helmer R.: *Learning Disabilities Educational Principles and Practices.* Grune and Stratton, New York, 1967.

Kirk, S. A. and McCarthy J.: Illinois Test of Psycholinguistic Abilities. University of Illinois Press, Urbana.

Kirk, Samuel A.: *Educating Exceptional Children.* Houghton Mifflin Company, Boston, 1962.

Knobloch Hilda, Pasamanick, Benjamin and Sherard, Earl S.: Developmental Screening Inventory for Infants. Supplement to *J Am Acad Ped,* 38:Part II, 1966.

Lincoln-Oseretsky Motor Development Scale. Western Psychological Services, Los Angeles, California.

Magary, James F., Eichorn, John R.: *The Exceptional Child: A Book of Readings.* Holt, Rinehard, and Winston, Inc., New York, 1960.

Magnifico, L. X.: *Education for the Exceptional Child.* Longmans, Green and Company, New York, 1958.

Minimal Brain Dysfunction in Children—Educational, Medical, and Health-Related Services. N&SDCP Monograph. Task Force II of National Project on Minimal Brain Dysfunctions (Learning Disabilities) in Children, H.E.W., Superintendent of Documents, Government Printing Office, Washington, D.C., 1969.

O'Donnell, Patrick A.: *Motor and Haptic Learning.* Dimensions Publishing Company, San Rafael, California, 1969.

Shaw, Charles R., and Lucas, Alexander R.: *The Psychiatric Disorders of Children.* Appleton-Century-Crofts, New York, 1970.

Smith, Robert M.: *Teacher Diagnosis of Educational Difficulties.* Charles E. Merrill Publishing Company, Columbus, Ohio, 1969.

Tarnopol, Lester (Ed.) : *Learning Disabilities—Introduction to Educational and Medical Management.* Charles C. Thomas, Publisher, Springfield, Illinois, 1969.

Telford, Charles W., and Sawrey, James M.: *The Exceptional Individual: Psychological and Educational Aspects.* Prentice-Hall, Inc., Englewood Cliffs, New Jersey, 1967.

Wepman, Joseph M.: Wepman Auditory Discrimination Test. Western Psychological Services, Los Angeles, California.

Wood, Nancy E.: *Verbal Learning.* Dimensions Publishing Company, San Rafael, California, 1969.

Zigmond, Naomi K., and Cicci, Regina: *Auditory Learning.* Dimensions Publishing Company, San Rafael, California, 1968.

CHAPTER VIII

SOCIALLY AND EMOTIONALLY HANDICAPPED

Calvin O. Dyer

Description of Handicap

Concepts

CONCEPTS OF EMOTIONAL and social handicap in children have connotations which defy consistency of definition. Not that there is a lack of essence for the disturbances, but more because there is lack of agreement in the ground rules for definition. Bases for such ground rules must consider from what vantage, direction, or level of focus one uses in describing personality and behavior. Definitions may swing from one focus to another without explicitly stating these rules. Each person professionally involved with children has unique interests and experiences resulting in different concerns and semantics for the handicapped. Teachers must deal with overt behavior when working with groups of students, others may deal with covert behavior, and some focus on minute observable acts of the child and count his interactions with the environment. Each sees a different person when looking at the same human object.

In addition, the concepts of emotional and social disturbance vary along multiple dimensions; they may be specific to a particular disturbance or attempt to be exhaustive, to describe severity of the disorder or its incidence, to consider whether the handicap is primarily acute or chronic, a single or multiple problem, primarily a biological or a social problem, etc.

One dimension which is particularly helpful in gaining an overview of study in the area is to look at the bases for defining mental illness in contrast to the content of what it is. Scott (1958) made an extensive search in the psychiatric and psychological literature with respect to varying definitions which were reported for mental illness. He reviewed these definitions and categorized them into six groups of operations which are involved in the definitions of normal and abnormal. These groupings are briefed as follows:

1. Mental illness may be defined as exposure to psychiatric treatment. Definitions within this category include as abnormal only the *takers* of psychiatric treatment, voluntary or not. Note that this view restricts the incidence of those who are called mentally ill as a function of the number of resources available.

2. Mental illness is equivalent to maladjustment. This definition is relative inasmuch as it depends upon differing expectancies of persons or subcultures within our society regarding what is considered maladjusted.

3. Mental illness is defined by psychiatric diagnosis. When this procedure is used for defining mental illness, only a limited set of persons may provide this function, and their sampling of behavior is limited to those who appear before them. As a result some subcultures or minority groups are eliminated from the samples from which normative statements are developed. In addition, not only is there lack of agreement upon bases of classification, but the ultimate consequences of the diagnosis, including the social responsibility, extends beyond the professional realm of those making the diagnosis.

4. Mental illness is subjectively defined. A person is ill only if he sees himself as mentally ill. This is the most relative of the operational definitions inasmuch as the criteria depends upon unique experiences and attitudes of each person.

5. Mental illness is defined by objective psychological tests. Although the methodology and instruments used in psychometric activities may be exemplary because of their precision, there is a circularity in using tests for defining mental illness which makes this definition objectionable. The objection is that the tests are

constructed to measure criteria which themselves are selected on the basis of other definitions of mental illness.

6. Mental health is defined as *positive striving*. In this set of definitions the emphasis is on what determines positive health rather than what is abnormal. One spokesman for this approach suggests mental health involves the process of coping in order to obtain end goals of adaptation and self fulfillment (cf. Johoda, 1958). Shoben (1957) says behavior is positive and integrative to the extent that it reflects the unique human attributes which include an ability to delay gratification, a social pattern of interdependency, and a capacity for civilization with a striving to act in accord with principles conceived of in that civilizaton. The concept of *degrees of freedom* indicating the quantity of available reactions to frustrations (Klein, 1960; Kubie, 1959; Smith 1959; etc.), as well as Murphy's (1962) concept of the development of coping skills, are also examples of goals within the positive striving definitions of mental health.

Although this particular definition implies values not necessarily universal to all cultures, it has certain relevance to education. It bridges the gap between focusing on pathology in one person with the contrasting focus of public schools toward normality and positive health for all children. It permits the skills and armamentarium of clinical workers to be brought to bear upon the problems of all children and the curricula of the public schools. The positive striving definition may be viewed as an integral part of what Hobbs (1964) describes as the third mental health revolution. The first revolution beginning with humane treatment of the insane, the second beginning with the analysis of the dynamics of conscious and unconscious behavior in man, and third revolution being the introduction of public health concepts into the mental health field.

Given these above bases for definitions of mental illness, any of the concepts for emotional and social disturbances used hereafter may use as a basis one of these operational definitions. The tack one takes is dependent upon the focus of concern one has, together with the orientation of the specialist. As later indicated, formal systems of classification for emotionally disturbed children usually employ the psychiatric definition basis, while some of the more informal and contemporary classification approaches tend to adopt the position striving basis for defining mental health.

Prevalence of Emotional Disturbance in Public Schools

Using the broadest definition of emotional disturbance, that of bad or strange behavior which teachers will report upon request, a comprehensive review of studies between 1925–1967 was made by Glidewell and Swallow (1968) for the Joint Commission on the Mental Health of Children. The data from these studies suggest there are at least mild subclinical problems of maladjustment in 30 percent of elementary school children. Approximately 10 percent have problems severe enough to justify clinical attention. Only about 4 percent are referred to clinical facilities if they are available. Although age differences in maladjustment are not great, there is some increase in antisocial behavior as adolescence is approached. Boys show maladjustment three times as frequently as girls. Regarding social class, the lower class tends to show a somewhat higher rate, especially among boys. Studies have not yet adequately investigated racial differences for maladjustment, although one study indicated negligible differences.

Of the types of maladjustment reviewed by Glidewell and Swallow (1968), intra-personal distress and tension was found in 5 percent to 25 percent of children with small and irregular sex differences and no clear social class differences. Interpersonal ineptitude was found in 10 percent to 30 percent of children and was more prevalent in boys. Among boys this ineptitude tended to be manifest by inappropriate aggression, and among the girls by inappropriate withdrawal. Antisocial behavior was found in 1 percent to 30 percent of children. There was a greater prevalence of this antisocial behavior in the lower social class. Developmental problems of maladjustment were reported to occur in varying rates depending upon the problem, and were more prevalent among boys in the upper-lower social class, including more nearly stable, low income families.

A perusal of this document by Glidewell and Swallow (1968) indicates the tremendous complexity of the task of determining incidence of emotional and social disturbances partly because of the differing definitions and criteria, the problems of research methodology, and the difficulty of obtaining samples for study. It is no wonder the results are still somewhat equivocal across variables such as race and social class. Further reviews of concepts and issues in emotional disturbance which have resulted in educational research activity over the past decade occur in Quay (1969), Balow (1966), and Morse and Dyer (1963).

Classification Systems for Emotional Disturbance

Certainly it is invalid to define emotional disturbances in children as a single diagnostic entity. The abnormal behaviors observed may change over time, and may involve many psychological phenomena. For each child they may be elicited by different circumstances and cues, and their outcomes may differ depending upon the childrens' interactions with other individuals and the environment. Thus, there is risk in attempting any classification system. Attempts at classification do occur, however, because they serve to communicate concepts and ideas among professionals and provide data for studies of incidence and the development of programs of treatment. Their form varies from formal, systematically determined taxonomies, to informal categories and colloquial statements of lay persons. Sometimes a tongue-in-cheek system may serve to show the folly of attempts to classify. One example is Fry's (1968) *Do It Yourself Terminology Generator* from which up to one thousand permutations may be generated by combining three words, each respectively coming from three lists named *qualifier, area of involvement*, and *problem*. The classifications systems vary also as to whether they are oriented to etiology and underlying psychological dynamics, or on the other hand are oriented to phenotypic descriptions and educational recommendations.

TAXONOMY OF THE AMERICAN PSYCHIATRIC ASSOCIATION. The formal system endorsed by the American Psychiatric Association (1968) for classifying psychiatric problems is recorded in the *Statistical Manual of Mental Disease*. This classification system is to some extent peripheral to the aims of psychoeducational assessment, but its ultimate coverage of serious psychiatric disorders within the broader realm of emotional disturbance makes it a necessity to use at times in the profession. Its historical precedent and comprehensiveness also favor its use. It would be well if all psychoeducational problems could be so comprehensively categorized as in this system, despite the intense interprofessional disagreement which still occurs around it.

The manual states that the taxonomy attempts to provide for the broadest possible use by professionals in treatment settings as well as in courts and industrial health services. The most recent revision is a deliberate attempt to be international in scope. Its objective is to facilitate maximum communication across these broad areas of professions and countries and to stabilize nomenclature in textbooks and professional literature. Because of these broad purposes, the manual indicates that it cannot be completely adequate for particular situations where a less comprehensive objective occurs.

Reproduced below are the ten major subdivisions of diagnostic nomenclature in this system. Although the outline below is very rudimentary, the manual further subdivides these ten into several levels. Further specifications of the disorders and additional qualifying phrases are also included in the manual.

    I Mental Retardation
    II Organic Brain Syndrome
    III Psychoses
    IV Neuroses
    V Personality Disorders
    VI Psychophysiologic Disorders
    VII Special Symptoms
    VIII Transient Situational Disturbances
    IX Behavior Disorders of Childhood and Adolescence
    X Conditions Without Manifest Psychiatric Disorder and Non Specific Conditions

As one looks into the manual at the categories which show most relevance to problems of children, the least serious problems are described in categories VII (Special Symptoms) and VIII (Transient Situational Disorders). Within the Special Symptoms category, for example, are speech disturbances, specific learning disabilities, and ticks, etc. In the category of Transient Situational Disturbances are problems described as adjustment reactions of infancy through adolescence, etc. In this category are disorders which seem to be acute reactions to overwhelming developmental stress, but which are transient and do not appear to have other underlying disorders.

More serious problems are described in category IX (Behavior Disorders of Childhood and Adolescence). These disorders are more stable, internalized, and resistant to treatment. Among them are reactions which are subcategorized as hyperkinetic, withdrawing, overanxious, runaway, unsocialized aggressive, and group delinquent reactions. Differentiation is principally on the basis of manifestations of the problem.

The most serious problems are described in categories V (Personality Disorder), IV (Neuroses), and III (Psychoses). These are more rare problems among children for at least two reasons. The disorder becomes stable and resistant to change only after sufficient time elapses and the intensity of conditions surrounding it continue. Also the development of personality in children tends to be undifferentiated and altering, thus making it difficult to observe or agree on what may be a rather permanent manifestation of a disorder.

Although the APA (1968) nomenclature is detailed and exhaustive, it of course does not provide a background discussion of personality development and the course which psychopathology takes. For such discussions, which parallel to some extent the APA nomenclature, one can refer to the texts on child psychopathology of Pearson (1949), Chess (1959), Finch (1960), as well as the writings of Kanner (1944) on autism. An excellent introductory text of behavior disorders in children is also that of Kessler (1966). Each of these provides descriptions of behavior problems of children and case studies which are categorized into systems slightly different from the APA nomenclature as based on their psychiatric and clinical psychology experience.

Discussions on the state of affairs in criticizing and developing formal classification systems for mental illness may be found in Brill (1965), Hoch and Zubin (1961), Katz, Cole and Barton (1968), Sharma (1970). Other reviews are found in Kessler (1966), Ullman and Krassner (1969), and Megargee (1966).

PHENOTYPIC CLASSIFICATIONS. Other approaches to classifying emotionally disturbed children focus on the behavior as it is manifest in the setting. Ross (1959) categorizes the various behaviors which bring children to the attention of child clinical psychologists. These categories are admittedly superficial, and he suggests resorting to them merely because they seem to furnish a convenient device by which to arrange the material and communicate to others the types of problems which occur. They do not explain or describe etiology nor severity of problems. One group includes the children who manifest aggressive behavior. They are physically assaultive, verbally abusive, generally hostile, and may be destructive. They may be overtly antisocial, and their behavior may include lying, stealing, temper outbursts, sulking, and pouting. They also may be considered predelinquent or delinquent depending upon their antisocial acts.

A second group includes children who manifest withdrawn behavior and possibly other physical symptoms. This group includes tense children whose emotional instability is marked by anxiety which may or may not be accompanied by physical symptoms of speech disorders, eating, sleeping, and elimination problems, as well as other mannerisms such as tics, thumb sucking, nail biting, or excessive masturbation. They might also display overdependence and school phobia. They may be shy, passive, fearful, cry easily, and tend not to be able to relate to peers as well as they can with adults.

An additional category includes children manifesting bizarre behavior. A list of bizarre behaviors is difficult to compile inasmuch as it can take so many forms. Included might be vacant staring, inability to communicate with other people, repetitive meaningless rituals, incongruous sex activity, hair pulling, unusual preoccupation with objects, etc.

A fourth category is children manifesting learning difficulties. Among some of these children lack of academic achievement might be explained primarily to be some degree of mental retardation or neurological disorder. Among others there might be functional difficulties primarily the result of emotional disorder. The two groups comprising this category overlap to a great extent since emotional problems can easily result from the stress and failure experiences associated with mental retardation and neurological disorders. Children of this category need specialized educational instruction even though the emotional components of the problem manifest themselves in such a way that they might also be categorized in the aggressive, withdrawn, or bizarre behavior groups. A circularity also occurs in these conditions in which these emotional components may appear as reactions to the academic difficulties in addition to being primary explanations for the lack of achievement.

Attempts by others at phenotypic descriptions of behavior problems are based on factor analyses of data which come from extensive check lists of observed behavior. Reports of several independent classification studies are made by Achenbach (1966) ; Pimm, Quay, and Werry (1967) ; Dreger (1968) ; and Quay, Morse, and Culter (1966).

For the interested reader an extensive review of etiology and treatment of phobias of childhood is presented by Berecz (1968), and of autism by Ward (1970).

PSYCHOEDUCATIONAL CLASSIFICATIONS. "The tendency . . . to disengage the diagnostic processes from the on-going educational remediation constitutes one of the basic professional problems we face." (Morse, 1966). Although only beginnings, excellent attempts are being made to resolve this problem. The following reviews demonstrate informal classifications which attempt to relate the behaviors observed with educational conditions appropriate to each.

Ross (1967) proposes a classification system which encompasses all learning disabilities and subsumes behavior disorders under the overall area. His rationale is noteworthy since it recognizes the inadequacy of the present status of classifying behavioral disorders. He suggests educators speak of learning problems rather than behavior disorders, and therefore may use language of an educator rather than a psychiatrist. Furthermore, the diagnosis is useless if not suggestive of remediation. The function of his system is to lead to a thorough evaluation of the learner regarding strengths and weaknesses and educational implications. The aim of the taxonomy is to be a meaningful and helpful communication system among teachers and other personnel. The diagnosis and remediation of any given student should be communicated in specific terms, i.e., descriptions of what the student can do,

Table VIII.1. Learning Difficulties; from Ross (1967).

Learning Dysfunctions		Learning Disorders		Learning Disabilities	
Without secondary reactions	With secondary reactions	Primary	Secondary	Chronic	Reactive
Special education	Special education plus therapy	Therapy plus remedial education	Problem-focused intervention	Therapeutic education	Therapy (plus tutoring)

what he cannot do, and the conditions under which each might occur.

In Ross' system (1967), children may be said to have learning difficulties if their academic achievement is lower than intellectual ability. These difficulties may fall into three major categories, each of which may be subdivided further. Throughout the system diagnosis and remediation are inseparable, as noted in Table VIII.1.

The category of Learning Dysfunctions includes children who manifest perceptual disorders which interfere with their school performance without significantly disrupting their overall intellectual abilities. The two subdivisions of this category distinguish between children who do not, from those who do, develop psychological reactions which further complicate their difficulties as a frequent exposure to peer competition or pressures from significant adults. For the children without secondary reactions, questions of etiology are not of the essence. Ross reviews approaches toward treatment that are appropriate. Among children with secondary psychological reactions, the reactions may take the form of the whole gamut of aggressive, withdrawn, or bizarre behavior characteristically described for children with emotional disturbance. Questions of etiology are important in this instance. Formulations of the treatment program must include attention both to habilitative treatment of academic work as well as rehabilitative therapy. The goal is to break the self-defeating cycle in which the secondary reactions further lower the academic work.

The second major category in the system describes Learning Disorders as inhibitions to learning from neurotic disorders. An important distinction for this category is a subdivision based on whether the learning difficulty is primary or secondary. Schoolwork is aversive to those with Primary Learning Disorders and their escape or avoidance occurs in and out of school setting. Treatment approaches are described which emphasize goals of strengthening learning-appropriate responses, weakening incompatible behavior, and also include remedial education. For children with Secondary Learning Disorders, their fear and avoidance is not directed toward acquiring academic skills but rather against the conditions surrounding it. Children with school phobia are included here. Treatment suggestions are made which are appropriate for desensitizing the children from the conditions and areas of conflict.

The third major category, labeled Learning Disabilities, includes children whose schoolwork is affected by psychological disorders not primarily related to learning, school, or teachers. This category may be subdivided into children with Chronic Learning Disabilities whose psychological problems are long term and pervasive, such as in autism and schizo-phrenia. The other subdivision is Reactive Learning Disabilities, which includes children who are reacting to crisis or trauma which distracts them or interferes with utilizing their cognitive processes in building new learnings or recalling old learning. Children with anxiety about separating from mother, or passivity in school as an attack on parents would be included in this subdivision. While treatment approaches for both these subdivisions are different, both emphasize goals for basic behavioral change, with educational tutoring being secondary. The value of this diagnostic framework should become obvious as one reads Ross' (1967) presentation. It can serve to organize and delineate responsibilities among various professionals, to emphasize the close coordination of school personnel with clinical specialists, and to provide a better overview and basis for selecting optimal treatment from among the specific approaches reviewed in each subdivision.

An alternative classification system proposed by Bateman (1964) is an attempt more at graphic overview than to be functional for individual program planning. She proposes a three dimensional view of learning disorders: (a) one dimension is a statement of type of problem, such as reading, or academic subjects, verbal communication, or visuomotor difficulties; (b) another dimension is orientation to either etiology, diagnosis, or remediation; (c) the third dimension is professional stance such as educational, psychological, or medical. Bateman states that while the overview is comprehensive and does provide one way of organizing a particularly sprawling area of special education, "it is necessarily superficial and provides little information in depth."

One additional classification system is a unique strategy proposed by Hewett (1968) of assigning emotionally disturbed children into categories along a developmental sequence toward educational goals. This approach to a classification system leads as directly as any others described in the literature into specific individual treatment programs. Table VIII.2 and VIII.3 illustrate the hierarchy of educational objectives, the levels of functioning at which children may be categorized, and implications for school practices and management.

Overview of Assessment

Concepts of emotional and social handicap together with goals

Table VIII.2. Summary of the Development Sequence of Educational Goals.

Level	Attention	Response	Order	Exploratory	Social	Mastery	Achievement
Child's Problem	Inattention due to withdrawal or resistance	Lack of involvement and unwillingness to respond in learning	Inability to follow directions	Incomplete or inaccurate knowledge of environment	Failure to value social approval or disapproval	Deficits in basic adaptive and school skills not in keeping with IQ	Lack of self motivation for learning
Educational Task	Get child to pay attention to teacher and task	Get child to respond to tasks he likes and which offer promise of success	Get child to complete tasks with specific starting points and steps leading to a conclusion	Increase child's efficiency as an explorer and get him involved in multisensory exploration of his environment	Get child to work for teacher and peer group approval and to avoid their disapproval	Remediation of basic skill deficiencies	Development of interest in acquiring knowledge
Learner Reward	Provided by tangible rewards (e.g., food, money, tokens)	Provided by gaining social attention	Provided through task completion	Provided by sensory stimulation	Provided by social approval	Provided through task accuracy	Provided through intellectual task success
Teacher Structure	Minimal	Still limited	Emphasized	Emphasized	Based on standards of social appropriateness	Based on curriculum assignments	Minimal

Table VIII.3. Composite Developmental Sequence Form.

STUDENT ASSESSMENT ACCORDING TO A DEVELOPMENTAL SEQUENCE OF
EDUCATIONAL GOALS

Frank M. Hewett, Ph.D.
University of California, Los Angeles

Assessment dates   Type of situation in which
                          child observed

3. _____ _____
2. _____ _____
1. _____ _____

Student _____
Birthdate _____
Grade _____
Teacher _____

STRUCTURE (Degree of teacher control)

A C H I E V E — M A S T E R Y — S O C I A L — E X P L O R A T O R Y — O R D E R — R E S P O N S E — A T T E N T I O N

	TASK					REWARD
ACHIEVE						Not rewarded by acquiring knowledge and skill — g.
MASTERY					Func- 21. tioning in self-care and intellectual skills be- low capacity	Not re- f. warded by doing learn- ing tasks correctly
SOCIAL			Does 19. not gain approval from others	Overly 20. dependent on others' attention or praise	Not e. rewarded by approval and avoidance of disapproval
EXPLORATORY		Does not 16. adequately explore environment	Depend- 17. ent on others for inter- ests and activities	Motor, 18. physical sensory, per- ceptual, or intellectual deficits	Not d. rewarded by multisensory experiences in learning
ORDER	Does not 12. follow directions	Uncon- 13. trolled in learning	Disruptive 14. in group	Does 15. not finish learning tasks	Not c. rewarded by finishing learning tasks
RESPONSE	Does 7. not respond to learning tasks	Perform- 8. ance level constricted	Exhibits 9. narrow range of learning interests	Withdraws 10. from teacher and peers	Cannot 11. function in regular classroom	Not b. rewarded by social attention
ATTENTION	Does 1. not pay attention to learning tasks	Prefers 2. fantasy to reality	Repeti- 3. tive beha- vior inter- feres with learning	Beliefs 4. and interests inappro- priate	Does 5. not pay attention to teacher	Does 6. not profit from instruction	Not a. rewarded by tangible re- ward ($, food) in learning

TASK   REWARD

of assessment are not independent of general personality theory. Thus, not only is there a large set of alternatives opened up for defining the concept, but also there are alternative assessment approaches which are favored by particular personality theories depending on what they say about motivation, anxiety, inter- action with others, adaptive behavior, etc.

Bases of Assessment from Personality Theory

Personality theories differ in what data is selected and in what implications for change which might occur in persons. Some definitions of personality lend little to our understanding of origin and prognosis of personality change, as for example those definitions which view personality as the sum of independent traits. (Horrocks, 1964). On the other hand, those definitions dealing with the interrelationships of inner psychological processes, or those stressing vertical organization through development are more useful in describing multiply determined problems and offering implications for change. Furthermore, those definitions which view the individual interacting and coping with his environment and culture do not restrict themselves to pathological behavior and may even offer a basis for value statements and guidelines for positive growth in mental health.

Horrocks (1964) reviews particular personality theories showing their consistency with particular assessment approaches. The organismic views of Goldstein and Meyer, for example, are nomothetic approaches and might utilize objective examinations in order to observe how the person copes with everyday life problems. The views of Allport and Stern are idiographic approaches and would use more subjective means of gathering information, since the criteria are derived from within the subject's own behavior. Murray's biosocial theory would utilize observation and perhaps projective devices in assessing the learning and strength of social motives. Maslow, Rogers, and Lecky's theories might require more of a study of interpersonal interactions with the individual in an attempt to assess his growth.

Gestalt and field theorists would tend to focus on perceptions subjectively obtained in order to determine degree of differentiation in elements in the life space. Psychoanalytic views utilize self report techniques, extensive use of individually administered psychometric instruments, and also observe interactions within the interviews. The neo-freudians with their emphasis on sociocultural events tend to capitalize more on normative data of subcultures. The elementaristic theories of personality such as those of Cattell, Guilford, Eysenck, and Thurstone lean heavily on group administered psychometric instruments. Among this latter grouping the instruments reach the highest degree of sophistication for assessment through statistical procedures of factor analysis. This peak of sophistication is not without its consequences, however, since the focus in this group has been more on cognitive rather than affective factors. This plight in contemporary assessment is noted by Sears (1969) in the statement, "I suspect we are at one end of a pendulum swinging away from libido towards cognition."

Functions of Assessment

The best use of the word *diagnosis*, Ross (1959) alludes, is an activity more properly called *assessment*. Assessment implies appraising or evaluating rather than categorizing or labeling, and includes obtaining and integrating data from multiple sources. The word assessment is not fixed and invariate, however. Ross (1959) relates the chronology of such words was first *psychometrics*, the *tests*, then *examination*, then *"assessment"*. He proposes further that perhaps the word *survey* with its various grammatical forms is the most appropriate word. It is defined as an act of critical inspection, to provide exact information with respect to certain conditions and prevalences; a comprehensive view; the finding and describing of contours, dimensions, and positions.

Whatever the words used for the activity, the functions should include any of the following: assessment may be for relatively static purposes of record keeping, or for communicating concepts about syndromes and patterns; or assessment may be for more active purposes of specifying baseline abilities and achievement, or for diagnosing particular areas for needed treatment as based on external norms; assessment may be also for evaluating change resulting from treatment procedures as based on criteria appropriate for the individual.

One key to appropriate assessment is that it will lead to decisions about what will be done with the individuals assessed. Results of assessment may lead to selection of children for special treatment, or may lead to classification of all children into appropriate differential programs.

Why and When to Test

Assessment of decision variables are still not enough, however.

The procedures of assessment must be incorporated into a broader model which takes into account the nature of the treatment options as well as the nature of the individuals placed. Morse (1966) reminds us that "the selective factor used for putting certain children together may not be the factor most operative when they are together,"—a situation that is repeated over and over again in the schools when children are grouped together for various special education purposes.

These general directions for assessment mentioned above reflect public school needs for testing, but there is also a theoretical basis for them from new developments relating to test theory. These new developments show an increased concern for the social context of psychological testing. Different situations make different demands on test instruments and the information obtained from different tests may be utilized more or less depending upon these situations and the decisions to be made.

One early point of view which suggests a new direction is Cronbach's (1957) statement of the need for two separate approaches in psychology to converge, the one approach being correlational research, with its emphasis on individual differences, and the other being experimental research with its emphasis on treatment effects. The results of such a convergence would provide more of a study for predicting the interaction of different individuals with different treatments. In a presidential address to the American Psychological Association at which he presented these views, Cronbach argues that neither of these approaches alone is satisfactory in its contribution. The experimental approach is characterized by submitting a treatment to many individuals to see how they vary in reaction to the treatment. The focus in this instance is on individuals, and any differences in treatments would introduce measurement error for this approach. The optimal contribution would come from having the two approaches converge so that difference among individuals as well as among treatments are simultaneously considered. The optimal effect would be that one can select persons who will profit most by particular treatments. This brief paragraph is a remarkable understatement of Cronbach's notions and their implications. Cronbach's views were both serious indictments of the limitations of these methodological approaches and a stimulus for new directions in multivariate research.

An additional landmark in these new developments is the lateral movement of decision theory into application in the field of testing and personnel decisions. In an original monograph, and then in a later elaboration, Cronbach and Gleser (1957, 1965), restate the historical concerns in testing which are primarily to study the accuracy of estimation on a continuous scale. They suggest, however, that a theory of testing should consider how tests can best serve in making decisions. Estimating and forcasting from test scores still is important, but the value of a test depends on many qualities in addition to its accuracy. "Especially to be considered are the relevance of the measurement to the particular decisions being made, and the loss resulting from an erroneous decision. Recommendations regarding the design, selection, and interpretation of a test must take into account the characteristics of the decisions for which the test will be used, since the test that is maximally effective for one decision will not necessarily be most effective elsewhere . . . An appropriate test theory can evolve from a general and systematic examination of the design problems for which tests are used and of the demands these problems place upon the test."

Their propositions extend into the testing and personnel decisions area to begin to fill a need as stated by a leading decision theory contributor that, ". . . . decision theory to date has been too much concerned with the mathematical foundations of the subject and less with its immediate application", (Girschick, 1954).

Their monograph describes formal characteristics that are significant for decision theory in order to encompass in some manner all the various decisions for which tests are used. Each of these has important implications for use in testing, some of which are summarized below.

1. *Institutional vs. Individual Decisions.* In the institutional decision the decision maker is trying to maximize the benefit from a whole series of similar decisions. He seeks a policy which will work *best* on the average over many decisions in the long run. He may consider individuals or groups, but he endorses a constant

philosophy or value system. In the individual decision, however, the best course of action depends on the uniqueness of the individual and varies among individuals depending on their differing needs and values.

Although test theory is most relevant to institutional decisions, the distinction above is important since many occur only once. Poor choices for the individual, such as in a curriculum or school placement may handicap him at the outset and continue to do so long after his curriculum is later altered.

2. *The Principle of Maximization.* The most generally useful strategy for institutional decisions is to maximize the average gain over many similar decisions. In order to maximize expectations from a decision, however, the decision maker must have a firm basis for these expectations. This assumes a prior knowledge, an assumption which is not always possible with certain tests and individuals. In such a case the *minimax principle* from game theory is possibly the better strategy. The minimax principle is described as . . . selecting the course of action which will yield the least loss when one's opponent makes the least favorable response.

An additional assumption must be considered in order to define and maximize the expected payoff of a decision. The scale of utility describing the possible outcomes may be a cardinal scale, expressing equal units of satisfaction, or it may be an ordinal scale merely ranking the possible outcomes—by preference. Although the ordinal scale is based on the weaker assumption, many decisions can only be appropriately made on this basis.

3. *Classification, Placement, and Selection.* The purpose for making decisions about persons is to determine what is to be done for them, a treatment. The information obtained from testing may be quantitative or qualitative, and can be described along one dimension or several in order to classify them. A special case of classification is when the data are reduced to one composite scale, in which case a *placement* is made. If some persons may be eliminated from consideration for a possible treatment, a *selection* is made.

Critical to making classifications is a consideration of the constraints upon the decisions. There may be limitations of treatments available for each person, and there may be limitations of persons for each treatment.

4. *Sequential and Single—Stage Strategies.* Decisions may be made on the basis of a single battery of tests administered to all persons, which is described as a single-stage decision procedure. Decisions also may be approached sequentially, in which case the decisions form a long change in a sequence of gathering information and assigning a temporary treatment until new information is obtained for further assignment. A decision making procedure that permits information at one point to determine what information will be gathered next is a sequential strategy. Necessarily the individual never leaves the hands of the decision maker unless he is assigned to no further treatment.

In addition to the types of decision and formal characteristics of decision making summarized above, additional concepts are described by Cronbach and Gleser (1965) which deal with characteristics of use and effort put into testing. For example, an analysis of the utility of a particular test should consider whether the objective is to estimate a single variable or to explore many separate variables. The language of communication theory is used to describe the dilemma which occurs in considering the testing objective. A *narrowband* test provides dependable information directed at one variable. The *wideband* test provides more information to cover more variables, but the fidelity or dependability of the information is less.

It should be noted that this approach challenges the decision maker to make more explicit his value system and objectives. *Outcomes* must be considered which consist of all the consequences of a particular decision. Each outcome then being evaluated on a scale is referred to as the *payoff*. The cost of a test or procedure for gathering information may be expressed in *utility* units. These concepts lend themselves to mathematical formulations appropriate for a theoretical base, but the application of several of the proposals are apparent without bringing in the mathematics. One especially pertinent section which will give the interested reader a view of perhaps the most dramatic application is the discussion of the value of wideband procedures. The context used for discussion is that of counseling and guidance and the usefulness of low validity and low reliability tests such as projective techniques, item patterns of success and failure, and the interview. The main contributions of these proposals are important to helping develop procedures for optimal professional objectives, and which will utilize professional personnel more appropriately, be financially justifiable and administratively efficient.

One set of writings which recognizes the importance of considering the broader context of psychological testing is that of Levine (1968) in a chapter, *Why and When to Test: The Social Context of Psychological Testing.* He attempts to analyze and clarify some of the more typical situations in which testing has been applied. Five institutional settings are described in which psychological tests are used, one of them being the educational setting. He makes suggestions defining the uniqueness of each of these settings and the questions and decisions imposed. This chapter is an important contribution for practitioners, since such material is not often included in available texts.

Testing Orientations

An additional variety of concepts exist in testing which help orient and focus the testing procedures. An understanding of the concepts is necessary in order to appreciate the breadth and full value of contributions which tests may make.

The distinction of *maximum performance* testing versus *typical performance* testing of Cronbach (1960) recognizes the assumptions that in the former the individual is highly motivated and the test is measuring the limits of repertoire possible for the individual, as in intelligence testing. In typical performance testing, however, the assumption is that the testing is oriented to assess performance under typical motivation without concern for measuring the limits in the repertoire. Typical performance testing is exemplified by tests of personality. It may be noted that the clinical use of intelligence tests frequently assumes a typical performance testing approach since observations of style of problem solving and of interactions within the interview are made. Assumptions of maximum performance testing do not necessarily hold with intelligence tests which are not appropriate for some subcultures of individuals. The lesson to be learned is that rather than the kits themselves, one's use of the test instruments as well as the type of subject interviewed determine what type of performance is assessed. Another distinction is the *idiographic* versus *nomothetic* approach which has served as a center of controversy for a number of years. The nomothetic view is that psychological laws may have a generalizing capacity and an individual may be understood in terms of these laws. A common application of this view is normative testing in which individuals are compared on one or more dimensions against the norm of the populations. The idiographic view is that man is a unique individual structure and psychological laws may pertain uniquely to him (Maher, 1966). The same circumstances do not have the same meaning for all persons, nor do norms of people represent the same causation or manifest trends (Allport, 1944). Standardized tests based on this view are constructed to be *ipsative* or demonstrate a person's performance on each dimension without relation to population norms. While the concepts nomothetic versus idiographic refer to views of psychological laws pertaining to man, another set of concepts, that of *actuarial* versus *clinical* prediction, pertain to the procedures used in analyzing and interpreting the data. Without elaborating on these dimensions and the considerable professional writing devoted to them, the stance which seems optimally useful is to capitalize on aspects of each of the poles of these views. Case studies should be devoted to study relative strengths and weaknesses within the individual, but also to study where the individual stands in reference to others. The *Guidelines for Testing Minority Group Children* (SPSSI, 1964) recognizes the issues and emphasizes the alternate functions of testing on the one hand for unique treatment and on the other hand for class placement. There are times when one should *search* for uniqueness and to organize information on clinically intuitive bases before processing data on actuarial bases and *justifying* placement into classes. Tyler (1959) suggests the concern is how in the profession we can modify the system ". . . so that the uniqueness of the individual is really taken into account." She maintains further that the proper modification will be broad enough to ". . . recognize significant patterns of choices that have been made at previous stages of life." She proposes these choice patterns be the object of assessment, rather than dimensions, and that the scale be nominal rather than ordinal or interval. The personal constructs theory of Kelly (1955), also exemplifies the stance taken here, in which he proposes that one can assess with statistical means the unique character and pattern of constructs which are the organizing and motivating foci for each individual. An additional issue which has relevance to recent approaches to remediation and instructional technology, is *norm reference* versus *criterion reference* testing as posed by Glasser (1963). Norm reference testing utilizes actuarial data from samples of the population under study and provides a standard to which an individual's performance may be compared. The individual's performance is discriminated along a continuum representing the population. Selection and classification of individuals for various treatment programs are the usual purposes for this type of testing. Criterion reference testing measures the actual level of performance leading to the criterion, but does not discriminate among individuals. The criterion is some objective for accomplishment or material for mastery. The testing is thus a measure of degree of mastery. The criterion reference perspective in testing is utilized in such approaches as programmed instruction, self pacing curriculum programs, and operant techniques in classroom instruction and management where baseline data, progress level reports, and mastery tests are useful. In criterion reference testing the usual statistical procedures for reliability and validity are in some ways different from norm reference testing. A consideration of these differences is stated by Popham and Husek (1971).

Professionalism and Ethics

An important aspect of the specialist's role in making psychological evaluations in a school setting is his conduct and personal bearing in making contacts with personnel, as well as his perceptions of responsibility in his role. A concern for professionalism and ethics should be critical to his evaluation of this role. There is much overlap between these two concepts, and what may appear at first to be questions of ethics may just as appropriately be questions regarding clarity of role and competence in it. For example, on occasion a school psychologist is explicitly asked to administer a specifically named test and arrive at a written diagnosis. Perhaps the actual case needs no more than expert observation in a natural setting and the accumulation of anecdotal data in order to arrive at recommendations for a school program. The ethical question of just how justifiable it is to begin the circle of *labeling* by written diagnosis, or who outside the discipline should dictate the tools of the trade to someone inside the discipline, can be resolved by the specialist holding a broader view to his activities and attempting to educate persons referring the case to his broader role.

Several readings should be noted which form the basis in ethics for persons practicing psychology. Ethical standards for the American Psychological Association are periodically printed in the *American Psychologist* (APA, 1963). Special sections in these standards relevant for professionals engaged in administering, interpreting and communicating psychological test information. Because these standards are broad enough to be subject to somewhat differing interpretations in various situations, they are sometimes seen merely as lower bounds of professional initiative and activity. Examples of interpretations from these standards are given in an additional publication by the American Psychological Association. Case studies of psychologists in public practice are described, demonstrating possible violations of ethics, together with the appropriate basis of interpretation from the ethical standards (APA, 1967).

Two additional readings focus on psychological practice in the fluid context of our social setting. Golann (1969) reviews emerging areas of ethical concern which cluster about recent movements in community psychology, innovations in psychotherapy, and practices in psychological research with human subject. The issues he describes were framed from survey data obtained by the Ethical Standards Committee. These issues are complex and often portentous. One set of issues questions whether there should be endorsement of nude marathons and other innovations in group techniques. Another set describes needs for guidelines in determining the extent to which community oriented attempts should be permitted to conflict with human rights to privacy and informed consent, and to conflict also, with differing values in programs of social change. Questions in addition were raised regarding the degree to which a psychologist should become involved with research projects and program evaluations which are inadequately conceived and which have possible consequences of misleading conclusions, inappropriate treatment, and waste of public funds. An alarming by-product of Golann's (1969) review was the wide indifference to problems of ethical standards as interpreted in the generally low rate of returns of questionnaires, and the high proportion of satisfaction with the present standards by those who did respond. He suggests with all the more concern that ethics education must receive a high priority in graduate training programs.

A provocative viewpoint of ethics in clinical psychology is given in a chapter by Hobbs (1965). Ethics has a new place in the concern of the professional person. The view that science is ethically neutral is considered aseptic and no longer appropriate. Ethical standards should be expressed in more than *ad hoc* admonitions: they should reflect mature consideration of assumptions underlying psychological interpretations. Hobbs lists possible underlying bases for deriving ethical standards, some of which he points out are inappropriate. He views ethics in psychology as taking on a much more dynamic perspective than other professions, including medicine. The unique importance of ethics in clinical psychology, as distinct from medicine, is that it is more than a guide to conduct and a protection of the client but is the very essence of the treatment itself: "The clinical relationship is in its essence an ethical enterprise." The conduct of the psychologist must be ethical to be effective since it provides the client with a concrete experience of an intrinsically mortal relationship with another human being. Of three levels of ethics described by Hobbs, too often professionals endorse only the lower levels called *courtesy* and *good practice,* without possibly recognizing a further level of *clear, moral responsibility.* Endorsing this higher level of clear, moral responsibility dictates areas for which there should be professional concern, and should result in initiative being taken in areas ordinarily left static. To Hobbs, a psychologist must continually re-examine his models in the light of the demands his responsibilities make upon him. Szasz's thesis (1960), for example, demands attention to redefining what is the appropriate and relevant criterion of mental illness. It suggests that regarding the concept *deviation from the norm,* psychosocial, ethical, and legal factors should be considered in defining that norm rather than merely medical or biological. A fresh look at illnesses should remove them from the category of *illness* and regard them, rather, as the ". . . expression of man's struggle with the problem of *how* he should live".

With an expanded view of the role of ethics, some of the areas of professional concern in the school may take on new interpretations and provoke answers different from the usual. In the writer's experience are questions regarding confidentiality of communications, the handling of role definitions of various disciplines in the setting, and where to place the emphasis in making recommendations and bringing about change. In the first category, the typical questions are the following: who should give permission to begin a case study and to administer a test to a child and an adolescent? To whom should the results be reported, including in this question the options of school personnel, the parents, the child under study, etc? Should one volunteer information to parents or school personnel received in interviewing regarding situations involving, for example, the use of drugs, promiscuous behavior, or unlawful acts? Regarding role definitions, typical questions are: who should initiate steps for treatment recommendations in the absence of particular specialists in the institution, or when it is clear that mere logistical or administrative hurdles might severely delay treatment if the recommendations are left to the usual procedures? How can one initiate coordination of various personnel such as administrator, counselor, social worker, etc, with a teacher and school psychologist? How does one deal with *politically active* interprofessional and interpersonal situations within a system which help trigger problems with certain children under evaluation?

In the third category mentioned, a stronger professional ethic may also help answer the question of where to place emphasis. Should broad and early intervention approaches be recommended and initiated which may detract from one's time and emphasis on treatment of children with more severe learning and emotional problems? How much should one cater to *institutional* and sometimes archaic programs, when more innovative approaches show promise? Should one emphasize individual case work or tend more to consultation and inservice training of other personnel? How much investment of energy should one give to promoting within the system a *problem solving* attitude toward classroom instruction and management of individual children, and to further promote research activity as a pragmatic functional activity? In consultation should one use the approach of maximizing contrast and confront the institution with radical recommendations? Or should one adopt the stance of minimizing contrast in order to reduce threat to change and hoping to involve personnel more broadly in the recommendations? The means may be different, but the ends appear to be the same. Important events have occurred in recent years regarding unionization of school personnel. Where does the school psychologist fit in regarding professional identity? To what bargaining agency, if any, does he identify? In some states he has only one or two options, his services and functions being included within the *community of interests* only of teachers, or perhaps administrator. Should he in these instances work against the grain in seeking special identity, or should he work assiduously within the larger group to get appropriate provisions included within his own contract?

An added challenge, perhaps as broad as any mentioned, is for the school psychologist to adopt a perspective to evaluate the direction and impact of his own work in the system. A particularly focused example of this need is the implication by Trippe (1967) that diagnosticians' behaviors may be shaped by politics and rich parents. Evidence by White and Charry (1966) of school disorders and social class, indicated that among certain syndromes of behavior there was a greater incidence of the label *cultural deprivation* among the lower class, and *neurological problem* among the higher social classes. A favored label seemed to be independent of the objective syndromes observed. Related is the concept of *action selectivity* observed in this study, a kind of *chasing their own tails* by psychologists, as Trippe (1967) calls it, in which there is a tendency for their early and sometimes premature decisions to influence their later conclusions and decisions.

Nor all of the ethical issues and questions raised are as unflattering as the latter above, nor are they unresolvable. A new and socially significant vantage occurs for the development of the profession by subsuming professional role and moral responsibility both under the rubric of ethics.

The Individual Evaluation

Defining and Organizing Steps in the Case Evaluation

Although the procedures in a case study appear to be straight forward and simple, there are several important aspects which are best considered sequential steps in the evaluation. The first is a recognition of what is the referral question. In some cases the referral question might be an arbitrary question merely to initiate administrative or referral procedures, and not completely relevant. The question might be an ambiguous, global, statement of a problem which is based on someone's hunch a child needs help. Whatever the initial question, however, there is often a larger set of questions that occur later when the complexities of the situation are considered, and it would be short sighted to pay attention only to the referral question. Sometimes even the referral question is not explicit, as in the following case. A school principal referred a child's name to the school psychologist without explanation about the case. After genuinely welcoming the specialist and introducing him to the teacher of the child, the principal politely withdrew. The teacher's first reaction was a question, "Now what can I do for you?" Obviously information is missing and the case is undefined, and a question exists regarding who is helping whom.

A second step is to determine what is the case. Most often in the case study approach the child is the object of study, but in school settings, sometimes the child interacting with a teacher becomes the case, or the child interacting with one of the parents. An entire classroom—teacher group may also be the focus of study. Recent research recognizes the importance of studying what dyadic unit is the most salient for optimal treatment (Bierman, 1969). As one searches, therefore, beyond the initial referral question to defining the broadest context of the case, the so-called *real questions* may be stated. These questions should be explicit, and the goal is to find answers which might be implemented in some kind of program or treatment. The word *treatment* is conceived broadly as including not only counseling or therapy, but also school curriculum and management practices, administrative procedures or tutorial activities.

The third step is to consider what are the best approaches and sources of data for which answers to these broader sets of questions can be obtained. It should be noted that very frequently objective individual tests are not at all indicated, but that the answers to these questions can be obtained by further observation, obtaining anecdotal records, or by integrating a mass of information which has been accumulated in the past. Perhaps answers can be obtained best by consultation and discussion with personnel involved in the case. Valid arguments for the importance of direct and systematic observation in the natural setting are presented by Brison (1967) and Weiner (1967). Aside from selecting best sources of information, how will the information be used? Breger (1968) reviews evidence suggesting it makes little sense to perpetuate the role of clinical testing in psychology when no treatment options are available. It is wasteful and may even be harmful if testing is conducted separate from treatment. His essay is a charge to take an honest look at testing in clinical practice in psychology; in most instances differential treatment does not follow differential categories from testing.

As data are gathered and integrated, the next step is a formulation of diagnostic statements and possible procedures for treatment. The words *diagnostic* and *treatment* should not imply static conditions; rather, a characteristic of this step should be that the problem is considered fluid, and procedures be recommended which are relevant and feasible for the setting. Statements of the problem and suggestions for help might be altered over time. The whole sequence may be analogous to hypothesis testing, in which one poses possible explanations and practices for change, to be confirmed by successive trial and check activities. Morse (1966) states, ". . . no diagnosis should stand as an arbitrary solution. It is the best hunch, with varying certainty, leading to possible remedial procedures." and, ". . . re-evaluation starts the very moment when actual work with the child begins."

The next step is to communicate the formulations to persons who can implement them. This step may perhaps dominate the others inasmuch as it is the step leading to change for the child and recognizes the necessity for continued monitoring of progress in the treatment program. A written report including a list of recommendations should rarely be considered the end goal, and usually satisfies merely the minimum in a sterile set of administrative procedures. Communicating to other personnel the results of a case study is one of the most important challenges for the specialist, requiring skill and experience in consultation. A number of approaches may be utilized depending on the situation and experience of the specialist. Minimally, information-giving conversations may be held with teachers, other school personnel, and parents. More often the consultation may utilize joint planning sessions with the school personnel. Perhaps inservice training may be necessary, or sequential trial-and-check activities with the child by specialist and personnel working together as peers may help implement a treatment program.

Some professional issues regarding role and function tend to be resolved naturally by the emphasis in this set of procedures. In summary: (a) testing is functional rather than an inevitable ritual; i.e., in some situations testing would not at all be considered necessary; when necessary, testing is selective inasmuch as the type of test given is directly related to the specific questions asked; blind testing, or testing without prior information about the case, would seldom occur; (b) the specialist must educate himself to the context; i.e., it is necessary for him to consider what treatment options are available and feasible given the particular personnel and their skills; he must know the *political-sociological* parameters which overlay the setting; (c) the specialist engages in an active and extending role of consultation; he functions in the area of his own expertise and defers when necessary to other personnel as peers in a joint consultation relationship; he searches for relevant psychoeducational practices rather than isolating his recommendations to psychological goals; he is oriented both to working *within the system* but at the same time to function in whatever realm which may facilitate necessary change in the system.

Conditions Affecting Assessment

PHYSICAL CONDITIONS. One can describe the ideal physical arrangements for individual evaluations, but in doing so, the object of stating the ideal is not that it is necessary but rather that it is an objective toward which one moves—but possibly never attains. The ideal is sometimes even more remote when less than perfect conditions are compounded with aggressiveness and hyperactivity of some children. The physical setting for an individual evaluation should be a small comfortable non-distracting private room with adequate ventilation and light as well as chairs and tables of appropriate height. Evaluations made in public schools are many times far from the ideal. With personal tolerance and adaptiveness, however, one can nevertheless get information. The burden of making valid interpretations is increased, however, as the distance from the ideal conditions increases. It is not infrequent to find individual examinations going on at one end of a gymnasium not in use, or in a multi-purpose room with external distractions of lunch in preparation, or in a stock room of books and supplies. Compromises even occur with personnel dropping in the room unannounced to pick up materials or leave notes.

The examinee should be able to sit squarely at a table appropriate for his height and be able to touch his feet to the floor and have his knees uncrowded. This may mean the examiner alters his normal position of sitting behind the desk in favor of the examinee's sitting at the desk. In this case, the examiner may sit at right angle to the subject in order to present materials. All materials and tasks presented to the child should be easily available to him as he sits squarely at the desk or table. All test materials, in addition, should be off the table or desk until presented as test items. A supplementary table or chair is usually essential for this material. The manual of instructions may be placed vertically on the table with use of a metal bookholder. The record blank is most easily handled with the use of a clipboard and should be kept off the table. The use of a manual, record blank, and stopwatch should be manipulated naturally but as unobtrusively as possible.

Active children and management problem children not infrequently pose serious problems for the examiner by their getting out of their seats and sometimes getting into the equipment. How one reacts in these situations can only be answered in the specific settings except that the examiner should maintain both enough structure and control to permit testing to proceed in as standard a manner as is possible, but at the same time not to lose sight of the possible interpretations from such data regarding the child's active manipulation of the interaction and the material. Compromises in obtaining maximum performance testing do occur when the examiner is observing the limits of this active behavior, but when sufficient data is obtained for interpretation of this type of behavior then it is pointless to permit continued and excessive disruptions of standard testing conditions. The subject who gets out of his seat and tends to play with the materials of the testing kit is not the only management problem occurring for the examiner. The nature of the emotional disorder in the person being referred for evaluation suggests that the child has already had unfortunate school and personal experiences and these will manifest themselves in the social interaction setting. The child may come to the interview and react with shyness and passive resistance, or he may be highly distractable and not respond to the tasks except by getting up and walking around, or talking about the activities inappropriately. Other forms of resisting the testing may occur more actively in the form of physical resistance, flight from the room, or verbally protesting or crying. Attempts by the examiner to counter these forms of resistance to testing may be varied. Aside from his verbal skills in such interactions, the examiner may attempt several other age-old activities to resolve these forms of resistance. Permitting a period of free play or providing small privileges contingent upon completing specific tasks, taking the subject around the area while engaging him in natural conversation may help. Sometimes it is appropriate to invite the mother or teacher to sit in the room behind the child, or leave the door slightly open so that the child can visually recognize a familiar setting. Another method is *the challenge approach* inferred in such comments as, "I'll bet you can't do this . . .", or the projection method of asking the child to talk through the dolls or the telephone, etc. (Stutsman, 1948; Symmes, 1933). There are some circumstances when physical restraint, if accompanied by genuine positive support for the child, may be appropriate, as for example in attempting to obtain maximum performance data from otherwise distracted and hyperactive behavior. These approaches are many and varied, and limited only by the experience and resourcefulness of the examiner with behaviors in such children. They will not always succeed, and in some cases are definitely inappropriate for the type of information one wishes to obtain.

Preparation of the examinee is an important consideration to success of the evaluation procedures. The presence of an unfamiliar adult in a classroom or the child's introduction to an unfamiliar examiner poses a problem to many children. That *time has a tranquilizing effect* regarding the influence of observers of children in classrooms is one advantage. The child cannot stop for long in being himself, and perhaps the observer's role, and that of the examiner also, is to fade into the background and be a somewhat neutral bystander. At the same time the examiner should be active enough to use peripheral vision in observing, and show openness and candor in answering questions when necessary. Partly related to time as an element of preparation, is familiarity of the subject with the examiner. For good reason, Landreth (1961) in her article *Playing Games* suggests that any person in doing work with children spend time observing them in their regular setting before taking them into a private interviewing session. Once in the interview, moreover, an orientation or set of mind for younger children that is often helpful is that of playing games.

Considerable evidence has been accumulated in the past that a fundamental requirement of test administration is advanced preparation and uniform testing conditions (Anastasi, 1968). Lack of uniformity in speed of language, in timing, in wording of directions, and modification of directions all affect performance on tests. Even desks as contrasted with arm-tablets have made a difference (Linquist, 1951). Specific activities which the examinee has engaged in preceding the test, as well as broad and pervasive experiences of the examinee have also been shown to affect performance. Emotionally gratifying experiences can facilitate performance (McCarthy, 1944; Reichenberg and Hackett, 1953), as well as socialization with adults and time in school activities for kindergarten children (McHugh, 1943). Test anxiety and expectation of failure have varied effects, but result in lowered test performance in some situations (Katz, Epps and Axelson, 1964; Katz, Roberts and Robertson, 1965). An important study by Hutt (1947) suggested that poorly adjusted children were more susceptible than adjusted children to failure experiences within subtests of the Stanford-Binet Intelligence Scale. Their performance was facilitated when the presentation of items was modified so that success items immediately followed failure items. There is sufficient evidence to indicate that motivation is selective and variable among children with adjustment problems, preschool children, ethnic minorities, delinquents, etc. For these groups, incentive for testing is not at all necessarily representative of the standardization population for the test used. In dealing with a child from a minority group defined along any dimension one should not assume motivation is optimal. The burden of proof rests with the examiner to determine the degree to which the subject was approaching maximum performance.

Although evidence exists that simple incentives do not readily alter test scores, the degree of involvement of the subject to do well does. When children learn patterns of wanting to do well on individual performance tasks for the praise, special opportunities, and attention provided by adult authorities, these patterns can have a profound effect upon their involvement and skill in taking tests. For children who learn patterns of performance which do not include academic tasks, and who depend for approval more on peers and less on adult authorities, their test taking may be more careless and unmotivated. Any obtained score on a test may most appropriately be conceived as a reflection both of a measure of what is in the repertoire of the subject, and also a measure of his incentive to demonstrate performance by giving responses (Liverant, 1960). Preparing an individual for testing by stating the purposes and giving information about test materials is increasingly being recognized as an important aspect of increasing the subject's involvement. Brochures and sample test materials being published for secondary school and college testing programs help serve this purpose. There is a unique line of research by Frank and others (Frank, 1965) accumulating evidence of the interaction between what a person expects from treatment and his success in treatment. Telling individuals what activities and interpersonal feelings will occur in therapy tended to result in more favorable responses to therapy. An open and provacative area for study is whether this interaction effect may be generalized also into testing activities and in work with children as a means of increasing involvement.

Observations of general behavior and test performance should be recorded during the evaluation. Inexperienced examiners most often err in the direction of taking too few notes and should thus overcompensate by copious recordings of observations. Much objective information is quickly forgotten even short periods after the evaluation, so further notes and inferences should be quickly recorded immediately after the interview session. With experience, the value of particular sets of observations will become apparent and note taking can be more selective. Helpful suggestions for preparation of the subject for testing, as well as for note taking and report writing are offered by Ross (1959). A further useful treatise of gathering objective data, making inferences, and organizing the written report is given by L'Abate (1964). Other suggestions occur in Hammond & Allen (1953); Lodge (1953); Thorne (1956); and Cuadra & Albaugh (1956), regarding the laboratory method of testing; Jones and Gross (1969) regarding readability of reports.

INTERACTION OF EXAMINER AND SUBJECT. In the two-person setting, aspects both of the subject's behavior as well as those of the examiner interact to produce the data from which inferences are made. Carter and Bowles' (1948) clinical manual is still appropriate in suggesting that testing instruments are not really the measuring instruments, but rather are merely sampling devices for observing behavioral data to compare with norms. Thus the examiner should bear in mind that he is not really measuring entities such as ego or intelligence, which are based more on traditional influences or thinking than from behavioral observations, but rather he is observing particular ways of the organism in responding to various stimulus circumstances. The items composing the tests are objects, things, and events which can be seen, heard, manipulated, and referred to, and the behavior of the child with respect to these objects is the essential datum. These views demonstrate the importance of the examiner's not being test bound, but that he should intentionally observe processes of problem solving and interpersonal interaction within the setting.

Unique situations for behavioral study which the examiner and examinee create together are a most important consideration. Sarason's (1954) collection of research findings is an example of observations of the effects on clinical interaction of age, status, and other attributes of examiner upon the patient. Less in the literature is said about the effects of examinee upon the examiner, and most infrequent is a consideration of how each mutually affects the other and thus affects the diagnostic evaluation. Two single writings discuss this most important area of mutual interaction and will be reviewed briefly here. Engel's (1966) observations direct themselves to testing children, and Schafer's (1954) direct themselves to testing adults. Although Schafer's contributions are highly relevant, some of the relationships described are not applicable to the special problems of testing children. Engel (1966) states that with children not only are technical difficulties of task presentation more difficult (more manipulative, more structured, etc.), but relationships such as empathy and transference are significantly affected or reduced by an adult's tendency to make children targets for aggressive drives and to project their tendencies for relationships with others also upon children.

Among the unique situations or parameters for behavioral study observed by Engel is that of the issue of control. Unlike the clinician, the youngster is seldom aware of his particular role in the diagnostic process. This situation may become altered, however, by actions on the child's part to make demands, alter events in testing, or to be resistive, with the result that the examiner's clinical skills may be temporarily unavailable. The examiner may not be immediately aware of this alteration of roles; he may deny it by ingenious after-the-fact interpretations, or he may successfully recognize and interpret it as a transaction in which he himself is a principal agent. Engel states that the examiner's "dealing with the issue of control in transactional terms can then lead to an understanding of how the child experiences and deals with his needs to control adults in general."

By contrast to this reversal of roles is the one in which the examiner maintains excessive control in the situation. For example, the examiner may insist on an inviolacy of standard test procedures, etc., resulting possibly in much constraint upon the rich data the child is capable of presenting. The child who is perceived by the examiner as a model patient would earmark this situation. In resolving these extreme roles, Engel suggests the most helpful position of control lies in the fluidity of change of active and reactive roles, but with alert awareness on the part of the examiner of the direction of these changes, and the strength and consequences of them in order to make an accurate description and sound explanation of the child and his problem.

The second parameter is the issue of levels and modalities of communication. Evidence is offered that our devotion to words is not crucial to obtaining valuable test information. Excellent examples are given of nonverbal communication enriching clinical diagnosis. Non-verbal communication by the child has a clear interrelationship with control in the setting. The examiner may commit errors of being either over attuned or underattuned to metaphoric communication and thus jeopardize the relationship.

The third parameter is concerned with regressions which can occur during the evaluation. It is seldom that the question is whether or not aggression has occurred; most often the question is, *In whose service aggression?* Engel gives examples of lowered level of psychological functioning in both child and examiner and calls the forces which operate *the regressive pull in the transaction.* The goal is to properly assess regression as it occurs in both examiner and child and let it work to advantage in making final judgments about the case. The examiner's prohibitive or sanctioning attitudes towards displays of regression can seriously affect the child's behavior so as to lead to inappropriate diagnostic inferences.

One type of regression in the examiner is when he operates at the level of stereotyping the child as induced on the basis of referral information or dramatic incidents of regression by the child (as e.g. in encopresis in school age children) . Another type of regression may occur in which the examiner's personal indulgences (e.g. gifts, candy) court behaviors in the child which may then be interpreted without remembering the circumstances initiated by the examiner's needs. Engel suggests regressive tendencies should be allowed reasonably free play, but that it is most important to understand the play between child and examiner in these tendencies.

The fourth aspect of the diagnostic transaction considered is the parameter of time and space. Seeing a child in an evaluation interview over several occasions has an advantage of being able to observe his ability to develop a relationship and to tolerate it. Furthermore, the physical setting matters in the transaction (as in a medical clinic or home) inasmuch as it can help in understanding the meaning of the child's associations and references in the interview. Time-space limits cannot be accepted by hyperactive children with their running about and inability to control; the time-space realm is confused in schizophrenic children with their compulsive touching and frantic explorations. This parameter also, more than any of the others, is expressed in contacts with the parents. They may demonstrate their own inability or confusion in time and space in their handling of appointments, transportation, and reporting. Engel suggests, "Time and space are not only the backdrop of the diagnostic transaction but its very essence."

The second single writing which was mentioned before regarding the interpersonal dynamics of the testing situation is a chapter in Schafer's (1954) book dealing with the interpretation of the Rorschach test. That it refers to the Rorschach and that it applies generally to adults are not serious detractions, however. Anyone involved in psychological testing in the schools will find it an important service in analyzing the demands and complications which can occur between the tester and the subject. Schafer reminds us that the clinical testing situation has a complex psychological structure, and is not "an impersonal getting-together of two people in order that one, with the help of a little 'rapport', may obtain some 'objective' test responses from the other." Both the subject and the tester bring into the test situation many demands and expectations—in reality and in fantasy—with the result that some facts are concealed or ignored. He further suggests that the intricate interpersonal relationship which exists in testing is not an evil and should not be striven against. The relationship should be regarded as inevitable, and a potentially significant influence on the subject's productions, as well as ". . . a possible gold mine of material for interpretation." Schafer's chapter considers both the needs and problems of the tester, as well as the psychological situation existing for the patient being tested. Highlights of these sections are summarized in the following paragraphs.

Sometimes professional role problems exist for the tester such that there arise for him *pushes and pulls* which lower his autonomy in testing and foster disruptive behavior in relation to the subject. In settings where he is consistently overvalued, for example, he may tend toward grandiosity, hedging, propitiation, etc. In settings by contrast where he is consistently undervalued, there may be shifts in the tester toward submission, rivalry, overcompensation, etc. These professional pressures on the examiner will have varying effects upon the testing particularly in regard to the manner in which he attempts to get scorable responses, to obtain frankness from the subject, a verbatim record, and to sustain a *standardized* test administration.

In addition to the professional role problems, the examiner faces four conditions constantly present during interviewing, to which he shows varying reaction tendencies. One condition is that of a voyeur because of his *peeping into the interiors* of individuals. Another is that of an autocrat since there is so little sharing of control in the relationship. In addition, the tester is an oracle, drawing portentous inferences from the signs and symbols of the data given, and he is also a saint with a *power of salvation* as a result of his activities. Each of these constants may seduce or repell the examiner, but he must cope with them in some way. Aspects of his personality may play upon or structure the relationship. He may have an uncertain sense of personal identity, or be socially inhibited or withdrawn. He may show rigid defenses against dependency and hostility, or even manifest sadism and masochism. If not usually dominant, any of these tendencies may become dominant as minor crises occur in the testing relationship.

Schafer also decribes the psychological conditions which exist for the subject. Five major conditions which are constant or ever present for the subject are the following: intimate communication and violation of privacy without a basis in trust; loss of control of the interpersonal relationship; exposure to the dangers of premature self-awareness; regressive tendencies; and the dangers of being given freedom in the situation. Given these challenging and anxiety arousing conditions, the subject must also cope with them in his own way. His reactions to them become a separate set of target data for observation by the examiner, and provide a major portion of the substance from which the evaluation is made. Numerous defensive behaviors in reaction to the testing situation by the subject are analyzed by Schafer. Observation and analysis of these modes by the examiner, together with the actual test responses, form two sets of data which help confirm, amend, and amplify each other, providing a more enriched interpretation. The brief summaries given here to aspects of both Engel and Schafer's writings do not do them the service they deserve, and interested readers should refer to the original articles.

It is not difficult to find examples of testing situations in which examiners are not yet sensitive to aspects of the relationship described by Engel and Schafer. The following experiences of graduate students in training are poignant illustrations of several of the issues. One student with related experience mostly in a college counseling center was to evaluate an intelligent high school student alert to social and political issues, and who was engaging in semi-delinquent activities. In the testing situation the subject responded sometimes in a surly voice with such statements as, "Wait a minute, repeat that again, and a little slower." On occasion he asked the examiner to stop, then he planted his feet firmly on the floor, sat on the edge of his chair, arms on knees and said, "Ready, go ahead." The examiner became extremely uncomfortable, and found it difficult to complete the testing, reporting feelings of threat from his perception of hostility being directed at him by the subject. The supervisor had been told later by the subject that taking an intelligence test was the one threatening experience he had encountered in some time, and generally in every other aspect in his life he sensed self assurance and control.

In another instance a female graduate student was confronted with a handsome, athletic, male high school student with particular willingness to discuss travel and other common interests with the examiner. When the data were discussed with the supervisor afterward, she became aware that she had permitted more than the usual amount of time for responses according to her own norm of testing, and even had solicited additional responses from the subject when unwarranted in such ways as suggesting that the subject try again on particular items, etc.

A graduate student on one occasion rather missed the point of testing when attempting to evaluate a hyperactive, mobile child who responded alternately with aloofness and then moving about the room to manipulate the test items. The examiner felt it necessary to end the testing session and reached a conclusion that the child was *untestable*. In another situation, a late elementary child freely and vividly described to the examiner his problems and negative reactions to school experience. The examiner reacted with seeming indulgence to *get things off his mind* by describing in turn to the subject some of his own experiences as a teacher, relating some of the circumstances, facing a teacher which can become negative for children.

While the discussion above has attempted to analyze and describe factors affecting the relationship between examiner and subject, the research literature has increasingly paid attention to the significance and degree to which these various factors affect the relationship. One study by Masling (1959) demonstrated the raising and lowering, respectively, of intelligence test results by experimentally manipulating *warm* and *cold* interactions in the testing situation. Another line of research has reviewed the phenomenon of experimenter bias, sometimes now known as the *Rosenthal effect* (Rosenthal, 1968). In a study with school children, though attenuated by criticisms of the statistical treatment, Rosenthal (1968) demonstrated that adults' expectations for children can possibly affect the performance of children particular aptitude tests. An extensive review was made by Sattler (1969) into the research literature concerned with the effects of race of the experimenter upon subjects in situations where tests, experiments and psychotherapy occur. Among his conclusions from this review are that the subjects' racial attitudes are significant in affecting the situation as much as the race of the experimenter, and in addition, the following directions emerge: "The overall trend in personality, attitude and preference, interviewing, and psychotherapy studies indicates that Negro subjects tend to perform more adequately and to be less inhibited with Negro experimenters than with white experimenters, whereas in task performance and intelligence test studies no overall trend is evident." (See also Sattler and Thaye, 1967.)

A Set Toward the Emotionally Disturbed Child

In interviewing, it is possible to forget that problems of children and adolescents are not simple versions of the adult conditions. McCandless and Young (1966) illustrate the contrast with comments that the adult will verbalize his feelings of extreme anxiety, discomfort, fear or emotional upheaval. To alleviate his own suffering, he will actively seek the help of a professional worker and be motivated to cooperate in this treatment. The child, on the other hand, almost never seeks out the treatment on his own, and instead is brought to the setting by his parents or some other adult in society. His motivation for behavioral change will be low, either because he doesn't believe there is anything wrong or he is too frightened of what may happen if there is change. An additional factor is that the child's interpersonal relations and psychological processes are constantly changing and being developed. Children do not have the durability and consistency which typifies the adult.

Among interpersonal experiences of children four important aspects are described by McCandless and Young (1966). One aspect is the long period of psychological biological dependency characterizing childhood. The complete dependency of early childhood as contrasted with the intense struggle for independence of the adolescent can lead to inappropriate learnings and thus abnormal behavior. Secondly, interpersonal relationships of children are much more variable than those of the adult, partially due to rapidly developing and changing psychological processes of the child—as evidenced, for example, by their rapidly changing allegiance to friends. A third aspect of these relationships is that a child's social role may vary greatly depending on whether he is a preschooler, a one year old, or a preadolescent. In each instance a markedly different organism is being observed in terms of psychological and biological development. A fourth aspect is a child's extreme vulnerability to both inner and outer stresses, as may easily be seen in outbursts and then cessation of temper and crying. Part of the normal socialization process of the child is to develop adequate self control and inhibitory behavior when confronted with these above stress situations. From McCandless and Young's (1966) comments, it can more easily be seen that highlights of the socialization for some children are adverse and intense. A point of view or shift of set by the examiner toward appreciating and understanding these areas and their intensity is essential when working with children. Some adults possibly never pass this hurdle of developing empathy for children in their professional work (Olden, 1958).

What to Look for

In psychological evaluations the mode of observation as well as the content of observation ultimately reflect the theoretical background and degree of training of the examiner. Although we're *embarrassed by riches* in descriptive categories for observation of children (Wright, 1960), generally these categories can be grouped along the three dimensions of *literal objectivity, psychological specificity,* and *theoretical integration.* Depending upon the skill and the approach used, the examiner may either record his observations at the first dimension and interpret and integrate later, or he may immediately translate these observations into interpretations at the second level. Any number of ways of organizing the material to be gathered may be used: one set of categories by L'Abate (1964) is the following:
1. intellectual, cognitive problem solving abilities
2. learning, educational, vocational deficits
3. neurological dysfunctions
4. emotional, interpersonal, and pathological differences
For most examiners, taking exhaustive notes is critical since

on-the-spot translation of observations into inferences is often difficult. A further critical responsibility is to check the validity of the interpretations by hypothesis testing within the interview and by subsequent confirmaton. By analogy, the examiner is performing much as a story teller; with experience he develops a sophisticated ability to utilize his observations and create a lucid story about the individual; the story teller may ultimately develop eminent skill as a fiction writer; can he write true stories as well?

When the focus of evaluation is emotional problems or a survey of adjustment, emphasis is given to a search for the particular ways in which the child copes with and defends against hurdles in his interpersonal experiences and general development. The child's best asset is an ability to organize and integrate his resources to react to these hurdles. The level of this ability and its efficiency reflect the level of development of his ego and its strength. Important functions of the ego described by Hartman (1958) are the following: the individual's relating to reality; effectiveness of reality testing; organizing and controlling movement and perception; developing a protective barrier between external and internal stimuli, etc.

The term ego development does not have to be limited to a particular theoretical formulation. Halpern (1965) describes disturbances of children by using the term *ego* in an operational sense to cover "all those functions of the organism which enable it to experience itself and act in self-fulfilling yet environmentally acceptable fashion." These functions help the individual attain a state of equilibrium satisfying inner needs and outer pressures, ". . . without producing lasting, pervasive, and crippling anxiety." Halpern (1965) describes styles and responses which typically appear in interviewing children with various types of disturbances. Within the interview observations focus on such areas as intellectual functioning in verbal and reasoning ability, organization and integration of learning and memory, the nature of the perceptual process and richness of emotional and fantasy life, capacity for regression when necessary, interpersonal reactions, etc.

The manner in which we see children coping with and defending against hurdles may be viewed from a different base than merely describing pathology. Lois Murphy's (1960) concept of coping behavior is that children are continually confronted with new situations and challenges which call for new responses not previously crystallized; the process of acting and reacting to these situations is described as coping, and leads ultimately to adaptation as an end. Her book is an excellent sourcebook of descriptive studies of children in whom this process is manifest. Coping includes all efforts at mastery and becomes almost synonymous with problem solving. This broad view is consistent with attempts of ego psychology to consider non-neurotic ways of adaptive functioning and to seek explanations to deal with active, healthy, conflict solution and problem solving. Lazarus (1966) defines coping in the more limited context of the individual's reactions surrounding threat. The observable consequences of threat are many and diverse, including affective experiences, behavioral reactions, and physiological stress. Coping is defined as the strategies adopted by the individual in dealing with threat. Included are those direct actions strengthening the resources of the individual against anticipated attacks and also defensive reappraisals which are psychological maneuvers in which the individual deceives himself about the actual conditions of threat. Defenses may be successful but maladaptive. Kroeber (1963) conceives of general mechanisms of the ego which can take on either coping or defensive functions. Differentiations between either are illustrated by lists of characteristics; coping functions, for example, are flexible, purposive, and allow impulse satisfaction in ordered ways, etc.; defensive functions are more rigid, tend to distort the situation, and permit impulse gratification more by subterfuge and indirection.

With any of these conceptualizations there are some general issues important to consider in the context of an evaluation. The term *defense* (like *ego*) is a theoretical construct and not necessarily an entity. Coping or defensive behavior serves to maintain balance for the individual, as for example, by preventing excesses, and by keeping the person oriented to reality. The behavior may be helpful to the individual if it serves as a way of mediating between internal and external demands, or it may be limiting and detrimental as the defensive behavior becomes exaggerated, distorted, or compounded. Several behaviors may develop in hierarchies and patterns, and thus a particular defensive behavior is not separate from other patterns of behavior. If aspects of behaviors are maladaptive, questions should be considered as to whether they are frequent or infrequent, and if they are deviant from the individual's norms. Is the behavior efficient, or inefficient, i.e., what is the cost in regard to consequences? Is some defensive behavior cutting out experiences in the child's life in certain areas? Do secondary gains sometimes result?

Other important questions refer to age and cultural norms. Is the defensive behavior *age adequate?* Some children may be either immature or precocious in regard to particular defensive behavior. What is considered appropriate for an early age may be defined as pathological when appearing at a later age. Moreover, is the defensive behavior idiosyncratic or does it reflect a subculture? Studies of gangs, minority groups, and other sociological contexts demonstrate that the behavior sometimes serves the individual well in his subcultural setting. Redl (1966) vividly displays instances in which unseen demands play upon particular children which the interviewer must take into account; he says to young psychiatrists ". . . you think you are in a pair situation . . . In reality you have the whole gang lying under the couch."

Observation of the child begins when the examiner first sees him. How the child is introduced to the examiner, and what is said to the child as the reason for the interview may offer important clues to the *set of mind* other adults have toward him. How willingly or not the child is able to accompany the examiner to an interviewing spot, and his own expression of what he thinks the reasons are for his being seen offer information about his insight and style of reacting to his problems. Non-verbal communication by the child may be observed in such behavior as physical posture whether free or constrained; gestures and facial expressions; physiological responses such as blushing; perspiration, muscular tension; characteristics of the language, such as tempo, speed, fluency, and quality of verbal output, etc. Particular tasks which increase fatigue or manifestations of frustration are also important to note.

Not enough emphasis in this commentary can be placed on the

importance of integrating the observational material into a complete study of the individual, and developing a *working image* (Sundberg and Tyler, 1962). Fractionation of the child's behavior into discrete areas of study may be necessary for more intense observation but the goal is to develop a full appreciation of the child's behavior in the context of his interpersonal life under the demands of his school setting and subcultures.

The Joint Family Interview

In many instances a more complete understanding of the learning and emotional problems of the child may be obtained by asking all of the members of the family to meet jointly in an initial interview. This arrangement may be difficult to accomplish in many school situations because of scheduling problems and possibly even because of open defection of members of the family from the child and his problems.

Wherever possible, the joint family interview arrangements nevertheless should be pursued since the implications possible are far greater than just an opportunity for information gathering. For example Pytkowicz (1968) describes some of the treatment beginnings possible within this interview. The purpose for a succeeding evaluation may be clarified and an implied message given to the child that his point of view is worthwhile and that it will be necessary for him to participate in order to resolve the problem. In addition the parents have an opportunity to organize their own perceptions of the need for evaluation and to present them in a straightforward manner. This helps induce in them a sense of responsibility for participation on their part. Three main parts of the interview are defined:

1. Defining the problem with the family. This includes understanding how all members perceive the problem and gives cues regarding the nature of priority in their reactions to the problem.

2. Helping the family experience the mutual discomfort around the learning problem. Discussion may help premature labeling of the problem and possibly cut through denial of existence of the problem. Observations of the

family interacting in the interview offer data for extrapolating about family interaction in general.

3. Establishing a commitment or contract with the family. Initiating subsequent evaluations and remediation requires participation by the family. They should have an opportunity for discussion about what expectations to have and what approaches may be used.

Repertoire of Tests

Assessment of Intellectual Aspects

Psychological evaluation is not solely dependent upon a specific test and its responses *per se*. Selecting any test may be determined by the opportunity it affords to structure an interview for clincial observation as much as for the objective scores obtained. Individual intelligence tests very frequently serve both purposes and are important in the repertoire of tests to consider. Using intelligence tests in personality assessment is a result primarily of changing conceptions about intelligence being separate from personality. As originally conceived, intelligence tests were constructed to measure levels of intellectual capacity as separate from personality. The influence of personality was interpreted merely as an *interference phenomenon* demonstrating deterioration or decline in intellectual functioning. Interest developed in analyzing psychological functions as assessed by various subtests, and as a result conceptions of personality organization were broadened considerably to include aspects of intellectual functioning which may show patterns of ego functioning and integration. At the basis of the rationale for using intelligence tests in assessment of personality is the *projective hypothesis* which infers that each person's personality organization is to some extent reflected in his individual responses, manners, and acts. By observing how a person performs on diverse tasks of an intelligence test the information may be used in assessing ego functions and the manner in which these functions are integrated into various modes of adaptation. Blatt and Allison (1968) show how the projective hypothesis may be applied to intelligence tests from the following three essential types of information:

(1) *The content of responses* may contain personalized concerns and idiosyncratic preoccupations.

(2) *The style of responses* shows the quality and nature of the clinical transaction representing aspects of personality organization.

(3) *The organization of specific cognitive functions* as measured by the subtests is an integral aspect of personality organization.

Sample responses with test behavior exemplifying particular interpretations are given. Rabin (1965) shows in a comparable chapter how intelligence test data may be used diagnostically on the basis of the following four levels: numerical indices, including general level of IQ and changes which occur; variability of subtests such as verbal-performance discrepancies, mean scatter among subtests, special profiles of subtest performance, etc.; scatter within each subtest in regard to failing easy or difficult items; qualitative aspects such as analysis of content of responses and form of responses by the subject to the tasks presented. As the use of information increases in level, the burden of interpretation shifts from test to tester. It seems beyond the scope here to further elaborate on interpretation since learning in this area requires a grounding in personality theory and psychopathology, several academic courses in diagnostic testing, and much further clinical experience with the tests. The following sections briefly mention more frequently used tests which may be used in an evaluation. Tests of intellectual functioning as well as those which attempt to measure other aspects of personality will be described.

THE WECHSLER SCALES. Staples among individual intelligence tests available are the Wechsler Scales. In addition to providing an overall measure of intellectual functioning, they have an appealing feature of showing psychological processes assessed by the ten to twelve various subtests.

The Wechsler Intelligence Scale for Children (WISC) has gained popularity as one of the most useful for psychological evaluation of children (Wechsler, 1949). It covers the ages of five through fifteen. Five subtests and one alternate comprise the Verbal Scale, and another five subtests and one alternate the Performance Scale. The Full Scale is the total of the Verbal and

Performance Scales. Scores on the subtests are converted to standard scores which may be summed and converted to Deviation IQ scores for each of the three scales. The Deviation IQ scores have a distribution with a mean of 100 and standard deviation of 15, making results comparable across all ages.

In addition to the manual the following references are particularly noteworthy for using the WISC. Interpretative rationale for the subtests and suggestions for administering, scoring, and interpreting performance are given in a training manual by Glasser and Zimmerman (1967). Ross (1959) also provides a general description of its use in the practice of child clinical psychology. A review of research with the WISC by Littel (1960) summarizes evidence for the groups, settings, and conditions under which it may most optimally be used. Special notes for the use of the WISC with mentally retarded persons who are sixteen and over are reported by Simpson (1970). Norms for subtest score differences which are significant are reported by Newland and Smith (1967). There is a natural tendency to make interpretations on the WISC which are analogous to those made on the adult form of the test by assuming the same patterns of performance have the same meaning but evidence is not sufficient to warrant this assumption (Littel, 1960).

The Wechsler Adult Intelligence Scale (WAIS) is the form used with persons sixteen and over in age. Twelve subtests make up the Full Scale with six each contributing to the Verbal and Performance Scales. Deviation IQ's for each scale form distributions with a mean of 100 and standard deviation of 15. The WAIS was published as a revision of two earlier forms (Wechsler, 1955). An additional text by Wechsler (1958) elaborates on his conception of intelligence and personality, the theoretical rationale for the scales, standardization data, interpretation of results, and other topics describing factors affecting intellectual functioning.

Further references for interpreting performance from the test occur in several texts dealing with clinical psychology and projective techniques, recent ones by Allison, Blatt, and Zimet (1968), Blatt and Allison (1968), and a revision by Holt of a classic reference by Rapaport, Gill, and Schafer (1968).

The Wechsler Preschool and Primary Scale of Intelligence (WPPSI) is an extension of the WISC for younger children between the ages of four and six and one-half (Wechsler, 1967). There is an overlap with the WISC of ages five to seven. The Full Scale contains subtests with a similar format to the other Wechsler Scales and a similar distribution of Deviation IQ scores.

THE STANFORD-BINET INTELLIGENCE SCALE, FORM L-M. The latest form is a revision composed of selected and altered items from former L and M forms (Terman and Merrill, 1960). Results of the test are reported by a single Deviation IQ score based on a standard score distribution with a mean of 100 and standard deviation of 16. The test is applicable for persons two years of age through adult.

The format of items for the Stanford-Binet is considerably different from that of the Wechsler Scales. Six subtests form each of multiple age groups spread from two years through adult. In administering the test the examiner attempts to start at a baseline level where the subject will pass all six subtests and continue on through more difficult items until a *ceiling* is reached where the subject fails all the subtests. Verbal and nonverbal tasks are mixed together within the age groupings without separation as in the Wechsler Scales.

Reliability of the Stanford-Binet is noteworthy among tests of any kind, but the reliability varies slightly with age and IQ level being highest for adult persons at lower IQ levels, and slightly lower among preschool children at higher IQ levels. The judgment of whether to use the Stanford-Binet Scale instead of the Wechsler Scales is based on the examiner's experience and suitability of the items for the subject. Many prefer the Stanford-Binet for evaluating preschool and early elementary school children and particularly those with mental retardation. The WISC is preferred by many for older children and the WAIS with adults.

The Stanford-Binet theoretically assesses a general factor of intelligence, and maintains the Binet tradition of subtests which cover many activities that occur in the natural life and school experiences of persons. A comprehensive review of research with the instrument was made by Himelstein (1966). Although the manual says it is not appropriate to use individual subtests for pattern analysis and clinical interpretation, style and quality of responses to items on the test are not without meaning. Rabin (1968) shows its use in historical perspective in the assessment of personality. Anderson and Anderson (1951) and Ross (1959) also describe how the Stanford-Binet may be used to better understand the performance of the individual.

Even with the intent to assess general intellectual ability, examiners still tend to describe relative strengths in different areas of cognitive performance. Newland and Meeker (1964), and Meeker (1965) propose a system assigning subtests to categories defined by Guilford's model of intellectual functioning. A profile is thus obtained for each individual showing his baseline level of functioning in all of the intellectual operations, contents, and products. Using this approach assumes that Guilford's categories of intellectual functioning are important information to have about the individual, and that the content of the Stanford-Binet subtests is an appropriate measure of the categories to which the subtests are assigned. Another system for categorizing subtest items is proposed by Valett (1965). An examiner's own experience and preference may dictate further groupings.

OTHER INDIVIDUAL INTELLIGENCE SCALES. Although the Wechsler and Stanford-Binet Scales tend to dominate, other useful supplementary scales are the Leiter International Performance Scale (LIPS), the Columbia Mental Maturity Scale (CMMS), and the Raven Progressive Matrices (RPM). Each of these is particularly useful for persons with speech and language handicaps since verbal responses are not required and the subject may answer merely by pointing on the CMMS and RPM and by arranging blocks on the LIPS. Test stimuli for each of them are presented visually and with a minimum of directions. No words are included in the stimuli and thus they may be considered to be more neutral. Many examiners feel that by using these additional scales it is easier to assess cognitive abilities, particularly concept formation, because of the reduction of interdependence of emotional and language experience within the test stimuli.

The *Leiter International Performance Scale* (Leiter, 1950) requires the subject to match a set of wooden cubes with symbols and drawings on the faces to a stimulus card with a pattern of symbols. Directions may be given by pantomime or at most by asking one question. Four subtests are given at successive age levels including two through eighteen to determine a basal and a ceiling of performance for the individual. Performance is indicated with a summary Mental Age and IQ score. An Arthur Adaptation of the scale is available which is appropriate for children with mental ages of three to eight years and covering difficulty levels of two to twelve (Arthur, 1952). Some examiners find either form particularly useful for *testing the limits* or finding the *edge of ability* by a method of supplying successive clues for various subtest items. Differentiations can sometimes more easily be made by this approach between problems having a more emotional basis as contrasted with a neurological basis.

The *Columbia Mental Maturity Scale* (Burgemeister, Blum, and Lorge, 1959) consists of one hundred large cards with sets of pictures or designs in which one does not belong. The subject can respond merely by pointing, and the test can be completed within half an hour. It has stimuli for children with mental ages of two and one-half to sixteen, but is best used for children between either extreme because of its low ceiling. There was a new form available in 1972.

The *Raven Progressive Matrices Test* (Raven, 1958) is appropriate for children between five and eleven years of age. The test consists of a booklet containing many design patterns with a part missing. The subject is asked to select from several alternative parts the missing portion for each design. Solution to the problems requires the subject to discriminate figure and ground, to analyze and integrate the spatial patterns of the stimuli, and at the more complex end of the scale to form concepts regarding a progression of the symbols. A total score is obtained for the number of matrices completed correctly which may be converted to a percentile for appropriate age groups. For children with problems the stimuli are free from content which may be loaded with sources of emotional and social conflict. The content appears to be more neutral even than that of the LIPS and CMMS and thus some examiners feel this test may more successfully measure conceptual integration ability.

It should be noted that the development of tests for special purposes other than with the general population of children poses a dilemma in establishing validity for the tests. Criterion related validity is often determined by using the Stanford-Binet or Wechsler scales as the standards for judgment. These instruments themselves are criticized for being used inappropriately with special groups and having insufficient construct validity (Himelstein, 1966; Littel, 1960). The instrument under development therefore does not have an adequate standard for judgment. Even if the criterion instruments are altered in such a way as to be more suitable for children with special problems, then the conception of what is being measured becomes ambiguous. This problem occurs, for example, when the Verbal Scale is omitted and only the WISC Performance Scale is used as a standard among children with language problems. The dependence of language on the measure of cognitive performance is reduced, but the conception of intelligence as measured by the Performance Scale is radically changed when compared with that for the Full Scale.

Assessing Non-Intellectual Aspects of Personality

The aim of instruments described in this section is to provide opportunities for the subject to perform in an individualistic way and permit observation by the examiner. The person may react with high or low involvement, passively or assertively, showing discomfort or relative self-assurance. On the tasks presented he may choose to be talkative or not, to create, to fantasize, perceive details or wholes, tell his associations, or otherwise describe the material—all in varying degrees of visibility to the examiner. These instruments present a rich source of information to the observer regarding how the individual chooses to commit himself to the task and what are his preoccupations in doing so. Although they are commonly called projective tests, the issues of whether or not they are tests, and how one defines their reliability and validity are inseparable questions from research and clinical practice with the instruments.

A common feature of these instruments is that rather ambiguous stimuli are presented to the subject and are assumed to permit responses which mirror important and enduring characteristics of

his personality. Lindzey (1961) describes the following characteristics expected of the instruments: "a projective technique is an
instrument that is considered especially sensitive to covert or
unconscious aspects of behavior, it permits or encourages a wide
variety of subject responses, is highly multidimensional, and it
evokes unusually rich and profuse response data with a minimum
of subject awareness concerning the purpose of the test . . . the
stimulus material presented by the projective test is ambiguous,
interpreters of the test depend upon holistic analysis, the test
evokes fantasy responses, and there are no correct or incorrect responses to the test."

The instruments available are so numerous that exercises occur
in how to categorize them. These are not empty exercises however, since they have implications for possible use and criteria of
scoring. Some of the categories are formed on the basis of features
of the material, its administration and scoring, similarities in type
of responses evoked, breadth and type of the target content assessed, based in psychological theory, etc. (Lindzey, 1961; Frank,
1948).

The projective hypothesis tends to be the dominant rationale
for using the instruments in clinical evaluation. Freud's original
use of the word projection dealt mainly with psycho-pathology and
was quite limited when compared with the subsequent conceptual
development of the projective hypothesis. The rationale was
further elaborated into a complex consideration of the processes
by which a person attributes characteristics to others, how he se-
lectively perceives, justifies, and shapes the outer world (Rabin,
1968).

Attempts at describing the place of projective techniques in
psychological evaluation involve complex and multidimensional
issues. Their use is unquestionably on the decline in clinical
evaluatons and training programs. Their development as viewed
by Molish (1972) was a rebellion against the more objective
psychometric techniques in order to return to consideration of the
human as a whole individual, but then subsequent evaluations
accused them of being inadequate on the basis of criteria from the
canons of psychometric methods. Thus Molish questions if the
end is where we started from. Projective techniques are still seen

as a viable approach in clinical evaluations though they are used so variously by examiners. Approaches in interpretation are susceptible to theoretical background of the examiner and highly dependent upon his level of training. Harrison (1965) summarized for one technique that it is as much as anything a test of the tester.

Aside from clinical use the instruments have become more firmly established in research. The volume of studies with them, although going through waves of rise and decline, has tended to be sustained at the same level for the last dozen years. Interest has focused on the instruments as alternative sources of data gathering for a variety of psychological theories. They may be used for observing factors influencing behavior in experimental situations, such as experimenter bias, temporary arousal states of the individual, attitudes toward scenes depicted in the tasks, sociocultural processes of interaction, etc. Attempts are made to conceptualize the techniques within the context of particular psychological theories. Holzberg (1968) reviews how some of the major theories may utilize the instruments and explain behavior observed in testing in ways which rival the projective hypothesis. Responses from the subject, for example, do not have to imply hidden dynamics, but may be viewed according to social learning theory as evidence of direct and purposeful actions which show how the individual has decided to relate himself to the task. Or responses may be viewed as emotional habits predicting behavior according to learning theory, etc. Often these views tell more about the theories than they do the projective techniques, however.

There are a number of issues stemming from research with projective techniques which confront the examiner when considering how they may be used. One set of questions concerns properties and functions of the stimuli. How specific or how general should the stimuli be? Instruments with the most ambiguous stimuli, thus permitting a wide range of responses, increase the ambiguity of interpretation for the examiner. On the other hand, stimuli that are preselected to cover specific areas may reduce the subject's involvement, increase suppression of responses, or otherwise limit opportunities for projection. Do some materials have more of a *stimulus pull* than others for certain conflict areas or themes, or tend more to evoke anxiety, aggression, or other emotional reactions? Other questions refer to the relationship between fantasy and behavior, and the examiner-subject interaction. Whether or not the responses are viewed as *sign* data and reflect personality dynamics, or as "sample" data from the individual's domain of awareness, indicating what he is thinking about as influenced by previous experience, are additional questions. Since responses are readily influenced by temporary internal states induced by emotions, drugs, and physiology, information about circumstances of testing and past experience of the individual may be critical in understanding the responses.

Questions regarding the most effective use of the instruments may be considered from the vantage of decision theory (Cronbach and Gleser, 1965). Their utility should be compared in relation to their cost. Utility varies depending on what decision is made or what is to be done for the subject as a result of gathering the information. In regard to cost, they require extensive time and experience for optimal administration and interpretation. As mostly wideband tests they are able to cover broad content areas of personality but their fidelity or dependability is lower than for narrowband tests. By permitting them to contribute to a whole matrix of data in a sequence of gathering information, they may be used early in the sequence for scanning broad areas where hypotheses may be formulated and which will later be checked. When time is a constraint and there is a priority of needed information from narrowband tests where reliability and validity are higher, then they may be used in a later sequence of data gathering to greatly enrich the eventual clinical picture.

THE RORSCHACH TECHNIQUE. The Rorschach (1942) stands out from other approaches to studying personality because of its frequent use, the demanding level of training and experience necessary for using it, and the large body of literature devoted to it. It is categorized as an association technique, and involves imposing structure on the stimuli which permits observations of how the subject handles objects and events before hm. The instrument consists of various inkblot stimuli to which the subject is asked to respond with what he sees. Klopfer's (1956) aim with the technique is to note which areas of ego functioning are intact or may be impaired, and by how much, and to observe abilities of the subject to test reality, to organize experiences, and to tolerate tension. Hutt (1968) makes a distinction between structural aspects of personality as well as dynamic aspects and lists examples of these aspects observed by the Rorschach. Other projective techniques generally do not cover the same breadth of aspects of personality as the Rorschach.

For use with children the same stimuli cards are used as for adults, but directions given and guidelines for interpretation of results may differ. Usually it is not considered to be appropriate for children before the middle and late elementary age, but Ames et al. (1952) and Halpern (1953) find it useful with younger and even preschool children.

Essential readings for using the Rorschach with children are those of Halpern (1965). Some of the differences in interpretation for children as compared with adults are mentioned by Rabin (1968) and Ross (1959). The very nature of the task requiring the subject to *regress* into a mood requiring imagination and story telling is not necessarily a regression in children; as a result observations of defensive behavior are more limited. Development of personality in children also is more fluid and undifferentiated, making an assessment of structure of personality more difficult. Among children with serious emotional disturbances, however, their exaggerated preoccupations and conflicts may still provide ample responses to the stimuli to support interpretations in clinical evaluations. The instrument may be most helpful when the aim is to determine maturational levels of personality development in children—which often is the primary concern (Coleman, 1968).

The Holtzman Inkblot Technique (Holtzman, 1961) is a modification of the Rorschach developed to respond to such problems as unsatisfactory reliability, lack of agreement in scoring criteria for different variables, variations from examiner-subject interactions, and widely varying responses obtained from the stimuli. Compared to the Rorschach the technique is relatively new and is just now coming into its own. The stimuli are presented in a multiple choice format and may be scored on some twenty-one variables. The influence of the examiner and other situational factors is reduced. It has characteristics of an objective test with reliability data being shown for internal consistency, stability, and a parallel form. Standardization data are available for various populations including normal and psychiatric subjects, and subjects from several cultures. Use of the technique with children has dealt mainly with gathering normative data for the variables at various developmental levels. The Holtzman technique best offers a quantitative approach in clinical application, but since it draws heavily on the Rorschach for its basic method and rationale, Holtzman (1961) suggests a qualitative approach in interpretation may also be appropriate.

PICTURE-STORY INSTRUMENTS. Numerous instruments categorized also as construction techniques have in common a set of cards with pictures on them to which the subject is to make up and tell a story. It is assumed that the fantasies described will help in understanding the individual's mode of adjusting to conflicts as well as indicating the source and intensity of these conflicts. Major differences between these instruments occur from differences in the areas of personality to which the stimuli are oriented, the theoretical approach to personality forming a rationale for the pictures, and depth of interpretation possible.

The Thematic Apperception Test (Murray, 1943) is possibly the most familiar of the picture-story instruments and one which sets a precedent for the development of other thematic methods. Although it is claimed to be appropriate for children, the pictures do not include important interpersonal situations that occur in the lives of children such as scenes dealing with a child's relationship with father, mother, and siblings. Interpretation is based on Murray's theory of needs in personality. Check sheets for scoring a number of variables are available, but interpretation is highly subjective and variable depending upon the examiner. It is used rather widely in research for data gathering in the context of other personality theories.

An instrument developed for more representative data from children is the *Children's Apperception Test* (Bellak, 1949). The cards in the CAT depict scenes with animals rather than humans with the assumption that children from three to ten years of age can more easily identify with animals. They may also be more culture fair. Analysis sheets and suggestions for interpretation on eleven variables are available. A second form was developed for older children using humans in the scenes (Bellak and Hurvich, 1965). Research has questioned the assumption of children's identifying more readily with animals and also whether or not identification tends to limit examples of unprotected impulses, and increase repression, etc. The CAT may also be considered for longitudinal studies in child development. Haworth (1966) has a major text devoted to the CAT.

The Michigan Picture Test (Andrew, Hartwell, Hutt, and Walton, 1953) was designed for children eight to fourteen to observe their emotional reactions to scenes dealing with interpersonal situations inside and outside the family. A formal scoring system was devised for assessing level of adjustment. Extensive standardization data and validation research was acquired and presented at publication, all of which is satisfactory enough to encourage its use as a screening device for maladjustment in children.

The Picture Story Test (Symonds, 1948) was developed for use with adolescent age persons for understanding underlying wishes, impulses, and attitudes. Suggestions for interpretation are not explicit, but include analysis of the content of fantasies and formal characteristics of the way the subject responds such as reaction time, range and consistency of content, etc. The pictures are quite gloomy, draw from limited themes, and normative data are not sufficient.

The Blacky Pictures (Blum, 1950) are a series of cartoons for adolescents and adults showing the dog Blacky in various activities. It is possibly the best example of a projective technique dependent upon a specific theory of personality, in this case psychoanalytic concepts of development. Although the pictures may appeal to children the content may be too subtle to provide the associations desired and the children may respond in stereotyped ways, making differentiation difficult. Standardization data were obtained on college students. More recent developments with the technique have been reported by Blum (1968).

The Make A Picture Story Test (Schneidman, 1947) has very

appealing material for children, permitting them to select human figures to place against various background living environments and then tell a story about each setting. The subject may experience *vicarious psychodrama* with his creations. An extremely broad range of stories and content is possible with this method and the examiner may search widely for styles of behavior and themes. Since the number of permutations possible may become unwieldy for interpretation, however, the examiner may wish to preselect among the materials those figures and backgrounds focusing on particular content areas.

The School Apperception Method (Solomon and Starr, 1968) was developed to assess adjustment of preschool through adolescent children in school situations. The drawings depict a wide range of school interactions which are assumed to elicit responses that reflect specific attitudes, feelings, and behavioral tendencies in the school setting. The authors make a point of indicating the SAM adds a dimension of situational relevance to projective testing. The content of other instruments may provide information from which similarities of response patterns may be inferred to the school setting, but the approach is indirect, the inferences risky, and the differences in response patterns are not evident. The uniqueness of school situations justifies the use of relevant stimuli. The instrument was released on an experimental basis with a later set of pictures and standardization data to follow.

COMPLETION METHODS. In the sentence completion method the subject is given a list of stems of sentences, sometimes a word or sometimes a phrase. He is then to write in words to complete the thought elicited by the stem. The method is used frequently and applies easily to many situations, including individuals and groups. Some forms maintain a status of validity as high or higher than any other technique. Comprehensive reviews by Goldberg (1965a, 1965b, 1968) summarize research with the instruments and indications of areas of success. There are several forms developed which have definite scoring criteria and published norms. These have shown their highest validity in assessing adjustment and severity of disturbance in adults but have not fared as well in assessing other variables. A cautionary note regarding the sentence completion method is that new forms may easily be made up using different bases for selection and composition of the sentence stems. The status of validity for other forms with their particular scoring criteria and standardization data is not at all generalizable to new unvalidated forms. This same note applies to modifying an adult form to become more readable or appealing to children. Each new or modified form must bear the burden of validation procedures as an independent instrument.

FIGURE AND DESIGN DRAWING TECHNIQUES. Instruments described in this category require the subject to draw what he sees on the stimulus card. It is assumed he reflects in the drawings his way of perceiving objects and events and the manner in which he organizes these events in the environment. Perceptions may be limited, distorted, or exaggerated by aspects of personality organization and emotional conflict. Neurological or even biochemical conditions may also affect these perceptions. Poor performance on the drawings may be the result of undifferentiated perception as an aspect of personality development, or distorted by more specific emotional factors. Differentiation must be made also between poor performance due to neurological limitations or to maturation of drawing ability and motor coordination.

The Machover *Draw A Person* technique (Machover, 1949) is frequently used for building rapport with children or for diversion from other activities in the interview in addition to its use as a projective technique. The subject is asked to draw a person, and then after one is drawn, he is asked to draw another person of the opposite sex. He may then be asked to tell something about each figure. Lists of topics for further questioning of the subject about his responses are sometimes used which are oriented to eliciting the subject's associations about real persons and situations. For interpretation of performance Machover (1949) and other researchers describe numerous features of the drawings assumed to be associated with particular aspects of personality. A more recent book by Koppitz (1968) shows an accumulation of sample drawings from children with guidelines and normative data for interpretation. Although the figure drawing technique is so easily administered, so frequently used, and has such broad appeal to children, valid interpretations of the data are much more complex and questionable. Reviews are quite pessimistic about their validity for any purpose other than to show gross cognitive maturity.

The Bender Gestalt Test (Bender, 1938) is rarely omitted from a typical psychological battery. The original set of stimuli were selected by Bender as a visual motor gestalt test for use in a hospital setting with adults. The test was an attempt to assess development of pathology as a result of neurological and personality problems. The subject is asked to copy a series of geometric designs one by one. The task minimally requires visual perception and motor integration, but perception is assumed to be susceptible to influences by aspects of personality organization and development. Pascal and Suttell (1951) propose a system for scoring the test with adolescents and adults as a measure of egostrength and emotional adjustment. Guidelines are given for analyzing each drawing along several dimensions resulting in numerous details for interpretation. Moderately respectable reliability among examiners and stability over time with the same examiners is reported. Other adaptations of scoring and of the stimulus cards have been made but not so widely used.

The Koppitz (1964) system for scoring the original set of drawings is an exemplary attempt to develop objective scoring with standardization data and norms for interpretation. The system applies only to performance of children five to ten. Each design is analyzed along several dimensions described by Koppitz and raw score points assigned when the drawing satisfies each criterion. A total score is obtained which then may be interpreted from the norms to indicate level of development according to maturation and perception and to differentiate performance due to emotional factors.

For children between the ages of eleven and fifteen neither of the scoring systems above has developed norms. Elliott (1968) attempted to see if either system could appropriately be extended over samples within this age range and if one has an advantage over the other. His results indicated successful discrimination of normals from psychiatric patients samples by either method of scoring, although the psychiatric children were not separated out from the neurotic children by either scoring system.

The descriptions of techniques within the various categories above have been necessarily brief and only minimally representative of instruments available. The comprehensive reviews completed by Fisher (1967) and Molish (1972) each cover several hundred references. In addition there are several dozen exhaustive and detailed textbooks for specific methods and instruments for use in clinical evaluation. A comprehensive text by Rabin (1968) describes various techniques and discusses issues relating to theoretical rationale, determining validity, use in research, and professional issues dealing with appropriate use of projective techniques. A textbook for using the techniques specifically with children is by Rabin and Haworth (1960), and for use in schools by Magary (1967).

In evaluating aspects of personality with these projective instruments one cannot escape plethoric views regarding their rationale, utility, and validity. In the light of these views Holt (1967, 1970) has made a plea for reviewing the context of much of this research. He suggests that research is all too frequently oriented to criteria that are specific and short term. The instruments are required to be experimentally isolated from broader clinical settings which have more diverse objectives and information. Moreover, experienced examiners are rare. When the instruments are used for initiating hypotheses and pursuing intuitive hunches, and the data to be integrated with other modes and sources of information, this is a very different use from the research design calling for a terminal assignment and justification of persons into criterion categories on the basis of the instrument alone. Fisher's (1967) review attempts to explain why the techniques continue to hang on rather than show further demise. He recognizes an increasing objectivity and *fair-mindedness* in research strategies with the techniques that are oriented to see both the potentialities and limitations of the methods. He suggests further that the ". . . hard questions which have been raised about projective tests have turned out to apply equally well to the class of so-called 'objective' personality tests." Examples by analogy are the questions of the source or level of *straightforward* responses on a paper and pencil questionnaire, as dramatically illustrated by research in response styles of acquiescence, social desirability, etc. For both approaches to personality assessment the complexity and class of problems are in Fisher's opinion not fundamentally different. Both depend upon adequate theory, need to define criteria more satisfactorily, and are susceptible to sampling variations and influence of examiners, etc.

Our expectations from any set of instruments whether objective or subjective, broad or narrow in their focus, do not necessarily correspond with what success we have in helping procedures for children with mental health problems. The process of making evaluations and arriving at diagnostic formulations is often a distressing activity when it is not pertinent to what decisions and what resources are available. Engel (1966) sees our reluctance to diagnose from several aspects. Expecting test scores to correspond to a particular syndrome of emotional disturbance is actually a fantasy. In addition, our knowing that personality interactions in the interview between examiner and subject have a significant bearing upon the interpretations, ". . . tends at times to send us scurrying in the direction of paper and pencil inventories where we seek safety from the effects of our personality upon the final diagnosis." A third source of reluctance to diagnose is in expecting that a correct diagnosis will somehow guarantee a good cure. A fourth is anxiety that the diagnosis, once given, will become a *verbal shackle,* or an indictment of parents, or an uncomplimentary label lasting the remainder of years for the child. A fifth is that *belief in treatment implies belief in change,* and thus the child becomes a responsibility to the examiner, an obligation uncomfortably ever-present if services are not available and change does not occur.

One set of burdens facing the profession is the paucity of models of personality theory, the complexities of deriving useful and valid interpretations from personality instruments and the inadequacy of systems for classifying children with pathology. But another set of burdens which is equally important, and which indicts more the educational institutions, is to further define categories of teaching methods and varieties of educational strategies, and to conduct research regarding which types of children profit most from these approaches. A conclusion by Engel (1966) implies a rapprochement of these two sets of problems:

Carefully executed studies of children in educational

settings might lead to a re-evaluation of teaching methods, curriculum, forms of discipline; diagnostic studies might, on occasion, show important deficiencies in the school milieu. Thus, psychological examinations may lead to judgments about educational practices that become the mainspring for action affecting many children, not just one. It is seldom entirely clear who is being evaluated.

REFERENCES

Abidin, R. R.: The laboratory method of psychological diagnosis in the schools. *J. Sch. Psychol, 4:* 45–49, 1966.

Achenbach, T. M.: The classification of children's psychiatric symptoms: A factor analytic study. *Psychological Monographs,* 1966, 80 (Whole no. 615).

Allison, J., Blatt S. J., & Zimet, C. N.: *The interpretation of psychological tests.* Evanston, Harper & Row, 1968.

Allport, G. W.: *The nature of personality: Selected papers.* Cambridge, Mass., Addison-Wesley, 1950.

American Psychiatric Association: *Diagnostic and statistical manual of mental disorders.* (2nd ed.) Washington, D.C.: American Psychiatric Association, 1968.

American Psychological Association: Ethical standards of psychologists. *Am Psychol, 18:*56–60, 1963.

American Psychological Association: *Casebook on ethical standards of psychologists.* Washington, D.C., American Psychological Association, 1967.

Ames, L. G., Learned, J., Metraux, R. W., and Walker, R. N.: *Childhood Rorschach responses: Developmental trends from two to ten years.* New York, Hoeber-Harper, 1952.

Anastasi, A.: *Psychological testing.* (3rd ed.) New York, Macmillan, 1968.

Anderson, H. H., and Anderson, G. L.: *An introduction to projective techniques.* (Eds.) Chaps. 19, 20. New York, Prentice-Hall, 1951.

Andrew, G., Hartwell, S. W., Hutt, M. L., and Walton, R. E.: *The Michigan Picture Test.* Chicago: Science Research Associates, 1953.

Arthur, G.: *The Arthur Adaptation of the Leiter International Performance Scale.* Washington, D.C., Psychological Service Center Press, 1952.

Balow, B.: The emotionally and socially handicapped. *Rev Educ Res 36:*120–133, 1966.

Bateman, B.: Learning disabilities—yesterday, today, and tomorrow. *Except Child, 31:*167–177, 1964.

Bellak, L.: *The Children's Apperception Test.* Larchmont, New York, C .P. S., Inc., 1949.

Bellak, L. and Hurvich, M. J.: *Manual for the CAT-H* (Human modifications of the CAT). New York: C.P.S., Inc., 1965.

Bender, L.: *A visual motor gestalt test and its clinical use.* New York, American Orthopsychiatric Association, 1938.

Berecz, J. M.: Phobias of childhood. *Psychol Bull, 70:*694–720, 1968.

Bierman, R.: Dimensions of interpersonal facilitation in psychotherapy and child development. *Psychol Bull, 72:*338–352, 1969.

Blatt, S. J., and Allison, J.: The intelligence test in personality assessment. In A. I. Rabin (Ed.), *Protective techniques in personality assessment.* New York, Springer, 1968.

Blum, G. S.: *The Blacky Pictures: Manual of instructions.* New York, Psychological Corporation, 1950.

Blum, G. S.: Assessment of psychodynamic variables by the Blacky Pictures. In P. McReynolds (Ed.), *Advances in psychological assessment.* Palo Alto, Science and Behavior Books, 1968.

Breger, L.: Psychological testing: Treatment and research implications. *J Clin Consult Psychol 32:*176–181, 1968.

Brill, H.: Psychiatric diagnosis, nomenclature and classification. In B. B. Wolman (Ed.), *Handbook of clinical psychology.* New York, McGraw-Hill, 1965.

Brison, D.: The school psychologist's use of direct observation. *J Sch Psychol, 2:*109–115, 1967.

Burgemeister, B. B., Blum, L. H., and Lorge, I.: *Columbia Mental Maturity Scale.* New York, Harcourt Brace & World, 1954.

Burgemeister, B. B., Blum, L. H. and Lorge, I.: *Columbia Mental* Maturity Scale. (2nd ed.) New York, Harcourt Brace & World, 1959.

Burgemeister, B. B., Blum, L. H. and Lorge, I.: *Columbia Mental Maturity Scale.* (3rd ed.) New York, Harcourt Brace Jovanovich, 1972.

Carter, J. W., and Bowles, J. W.: A manual on qualitative aspects of psychological examining. *Clinical Psychology Monographs, 2:* 1948.

Catterall, C. D.: Taxonomy of prescriptive interventions. *J. Sch Psychol, 8:*5–12, 1970.

Chess, S.: *An introduction to child psychiatry.* New York, Grune & Stratton, 1959.

Coleman, J. C.: Rorschach content as a means of studying child development. *J Proj Tech & Personality Assess, 32:*435–442, 1968.

Cronbach, L. J.: The two disciplines of scientific psychology. *Am Psychol, 12:*671–684, 1957.

Cronbach, L. J.: *Essentials of psychological testing.* (2nd ed.) New York, Harper & Row, 1960.

Cronbach, L. J., and Gleser, G. C.: *Psychological tests and personnel decisions.* Urbana, Illinois, University of Illinois Press, 1957.

Cronbach, L. J., and Gleser, G. C.: *Psychological tests and personnel decisions.* (2nd ed.) Urbana, Illinois, University of Illinois Press, 1965.

Cuadra, C. A. and Albaugh, W. P.: Sources of ambiguity in psychological reports. *J Clin Psychol, 12:* 109–114, 1956.

Dreger, R. M.: Aristotle, Linnaeus, and Lewin, or the place of classification in the evaluative-therapeutic process. *J Gen Psychol, 78:*41–59, 1968.

Elliott, J. A.: A validation study of the Koppitz and Pascal and Suttell systems with eleven through fourteen year old children. Unpublished research report, The University of Michigan, 1968.

Elwood, D. L.: Automation of psychological testing. *Am Psychol, 24:*287–289, 1969.

Engel, M.: Some parameters of the psychological evaluation of children. *A. M. A. Archives of General Psychiatry, 2:*593–605, 1960.

Engel, M.: Time and the reluctance to diagnose. *J Sch Psychol, 4:*1–8, 1966.

Finch, S. M.: *Fundamentals of child psychiatry.* New York, W. W. Norton & Co., 1960.

Fisher, S.: Projective methodologies. *Annu Rev Psychol, 18:*165–190, 1967.

Frank, J. D.: Discussion of H. J. Eysenck, "The effects of psychotherapy." *Int. J. Psychi, 1:*288–290, 1965.

Frank, L. K.: *Projective methods.* Springfield, Thomas, 1948.

Fry, E.: Do-it-yourself terminology generator. *J Read, 11:*428, 1968.

Gamble, K. R.: The Holtzman Inkblot Technique: A review. *Psychol Bull* 77: 172–194, 1972.

Gellert, E.: Review of E. M. Koppitz, Psychological Evaluation of Children's Human Figure Drawings. *Contemporary Psychology, 14:*187–188, 1969.

Girschick, M. A.: An elementary survey of statistical decision theory. *Rev Educ Res, 24:*448–466, 1954.

Glasser, R.: Instructional technology and the measurement of learning outcomes. *Am Psychol, 18:*519–521, 1963.

Glasser, A. J., and Zimmerman, I. L.: *Clinical interpretation of the Wechsler Intelligence Scale for Children.* New York, Grune & Stratton, 1957.

Galvin, J. P., and Quay, H. C.: Behavior disorders. *Rev Educ Res, 39:*83–102, 1969.

Glidewell, J. C., and Swallow, C. S.: *The prevalence of maladjustment in elementary schools.* A report prepared for the Joint Commission on the Mental Health of Children. Chicago, University of Chicago Press, 1968.

Golann, S. E.: Emerging areas of ethical concern. *Am Psychol, 24:*454–459, 1969.

Goldberg, P. A.: A review of sentence completion methods in personality assessment. *J Proj Tech Personality Assess, 29:*12–45, 1965.

Goldberg, P. A.: A review of sentence completion methods in personality assessment. In B. I. Murstein (Ed.), *Handbook of Projective Techniques.* New York, Basic Books, 1965.

Goldberg, P. A.: The current status of sentence completion methods. *J Proj Tech Personal Assess, 32:*215–221, 1968.

Guilford, J. P.: *The nature of human intelligence.* New York, McGraw-Hill, 1967.

Halpern, F.: *A clinical approach to children's Rorschachs.* New York, Grune & Stratton, 1953.

Halpern, F.: Diagnostic methods in childhood disorders. In B. B. Wolman (Ed.), *Handbook of clinical psychology*. New York, McGraw-Hill, 1965.

Hammond, K. R., and Allen, J. M.: *Writing clinical reports*. New York, Prentice-Hall, 1953.

Harrison, R.: Thematic apperceptive methods. In B. B. Wolman (Ed.), *Handbook of clinical psychology*. New York, McGraw-Hill, 1965.

Hartman, H.: *Ego psychology and the problem of adaptation*. New York, Universities Press, 1958.

Haworth, M. R.: *The CAT: Facts about fantasy*. New York, Grune & Stratton, 1966.

Haworth, M. R.: *The TAT and CAT in clinical use*. (2nd ed.) New York, Grune & Stratton, 1971.

Hewett, F. M.: *The emotionally disturbed child in the classroom*. Boston, Allyn Bacon, 1968.

Himelstein, P.: Research with the Stanford-Binet, Form L-M. *Psychol Bull, 65*:156–164, 1966.

Hobbs, N.: Mental health's third revolution. *Am J Orthopsychi, 34*:822–833, 1964.

Hobbs, N.: Ethics in clinical psychology. In B. B. Wolman (Ed.), *Handbook of clinical psychology*. New York, McGraw-Hill, 1965.

Hoch, P. H., and Zubin, J. (Eds.): *Comparative epidemiology of the mental disorders*. New York, Grune & Stratton, 1961.

Holt, R. R.: Diagnostic testing: Present status and future prospects. *J Nerv Ment Dis, 144*:444–465, 1967.

Holt, R. R.: Yet another look at clinical and statistical prediction: Or, is clinical psychology worthwhile? *Am Psychol, 25*:337–349, 1970.

Holtzman, W. H., Thorpe, J. S., Swartz, J. D., and Herron, E. W.: *Inkblot perception and personality*. Austin, University of Texas Press, 1961.

Holzberg, J. D.: Psychological theory and projective techniques. In A. I. Rabin (Ed.), *Projective techniques in personality assessment*. New York, Springer, 1968.

Horrocks, J. E.: *Assessment of behavior*. Columbus, Ohio, Charles E. Merrill, 1964.

Hutt, M. L.: "Consecutive and adaptive" testing with the Revised Stanford-Binet, *J Consult Psychol, 11*:93–103, 1947.

Hutt, M. L.: Psychopathology, assessment, and psychotherapy. In A. I. Rabin (Ed.), *Projective techniques in personality assessment*. New York, Springer, 1968.

Jahoda, M.: *Current concepts of positive mental health*. New York, Basic Books, 1958.

Jones, R. L. and Gross, F. P.: The readability of psychological reports. *Am J Ment Defic, 63*:1020–1021, 1969.

Kanner, L.: Early infantile autism, *J Ped, 25*:211–217, 1944.

Katz, I., Epps, E. G., and Axelson, L. J.: Effect upon negro digit-symbol performance of anticipated comparison with whites and with other negroes. *J Abnormal and Soc Psychol, 69*:77–83, 1964.

Katz, I., Roberts, S. O., and Robinson, J. M.: Effects of task difficulty, race of administrator, and instructions on digit-symbol performance of negroes. *J Personal Soc Psychol, 2*:53–59, 1965.

Katz, M. M., Cole, J. O., and Barton, W. E. (Eds.) : *Classification in psychiatry and psychopathology.* Chevy Chase: Public Health Service Publication Number 1584.

Kelly, G. A.: *The psychology of personal constructs.* Vol. 1, *A theory of personality.* New York, Norton, 1955.

Kessler, J. W.: *Psychopathology of childhood.* Englewood Cliffs, New Jersey, Prentice-Hall, 1966.

Klein, D. C.: Some concepts concerning the mental health of the individual. *J Consult Psychol, 24*:288–293, 1960.

Klopfer, B. (Ed.) : *Developments in the Rorschach technique. II. Fields of application.* Yonkers-on-Hudson, World Book Co., 1956.

Koppitz, E. M.: *The Bender Gestalt Test for young children.* New York, Grune & Stratton, 1964.

Koppitz, E. M.: *Psychological evaluation of children's human figure drawings.* New York, Grune & Stratton, 1968.

Kroeber, T. C.: The coping functions of the ego mechanisms. In R. W. White (Ed.) , *The study of lives: essays on personality in honor of Henry A. Murray.* New York, Atherton Press, 1963.

Kubie, L. S.: Are we educating our maturity? *Nat Educ Assoc J, 48*:58–63, 1959.

L'Abate, L.: *Principles of clinical psychology.* New York, Grune & Stratton, 1964.

Landreth, C.: Playing games. *Am Psychol, 16*:604–607, 1961.

Lazarus, R. S.: *Psychological stress and the coping process.* New York, McGraw-Hill, 1966.

Leiter, R. G.: Part II of the Manual for the 1948 Revision of the Leiter International Performance Scale. *Psychological Serv Cent J, 2*:259–343, 1950.

Levine, D.: Why and when to test: The social context of psychological testing. In A. I. Rabin (Ed.) , *Projective techniques in personality assessment.* New York, Springer, 1968.

Lindquist, E. F. (Ed.) : *Educational measurement.* Washington, D.C., American Council on Education, 1951.

Lindzey, G.: *Protective techniques and cross-cultural research.* New York, Appleton-Century-Crofts, 1961.

Littel, W. M.: The Wechsler Scale for Children: Review of a decade of research. *Psychol Bull, 57*:132–156, 1960.

Liverant, S.: Intelligence: A concept in need of reexamination. *J Consult Psychol, 24*:101–110, 1960.

Lodge, G. T.: How to write a psychological report. *J Clin Psychol, 9:* 400–402, 1953.

Machover, K.: *Personality projection in the drawing of the human figure: A method of personality investigation.* Springfield, Thomas, 1949.

Magary, J. F.: *School psychological services in theory and practice: A handbook.* Englewood Cliffs, New Jersey, Prentice-Hall, 1967.

Maher, B. A. (Ed.) : *Progress in experimental personality research.* Volume II. New York, Academic Press, 1966.

Masling, J.: The effects of warm and cold interation on the administration and scoring of an intelligence test. *J Consult Psychol, 23:*336–341, 1959.

Masling, J.: The influence of situational and interpersonal variable in projective testing. *Psychol Bull, 57:*65–85, 1960.

McCandless, B. R., and Young, R. D.: Problems of childhood and adolescence. In I. A. Berg and L. A. Pennington (Eds.), *An introduction to clinical psychology.* (3rd ed.) New York, Ronald Press, 1966.

McCarthy, D.: A study of the reliability of the Goodenough drawing test of intelligence. *J. Psychol, 18:*201–216, 1944.

McHugh, G.: Changes in IQ at the public school kindergarten level. *Psychological Monographs,* 55, 1943.

Meeker, M.: A procedure for relating Stanford-Binet behavior samplings to Guilford's structure of the intellect. *J Sch Psychol, 3:*26–36, 1965.

Megargee, F. I. (Ed.) : *Research in clinical assessment.* New York, Harper & Row, 1966.

Milliren, A. P., and Newland, T. E.: Statistically significant differences between subtest scaled scores for the WPPSI. *J Sch Psychol, 7:*16–19, 1968–69.

Molish, H. B.: Projective methodologies. *Annu Rev Psychol, 23:*577–614. 1972.

Morse, W. C.: Diagnosis of learning problems with implications for remediation in the classroom setting. Paper presented at the meeting of the Montreal Children's Hospital Conference, 1966.

Morse, W. C., and Dyer, C. O.: The emotionally and socially handicapped. *Rev Educ Res, 33:*109–125, 1963.

Murphy, L. B.: Coping devices and defense mechanisms in relation to autonomous ego functions. Bulletin of the Menninger Clinic, *24:*144–153, 1960. (Reprinted in J. O. Palmer and M. J. Goldstein, *Perspectives in psychopathology: Readings in abnormal psychology.*)

Murphy, L. B.: *The widening world of childhood.* New York, Basic Books, 1962.

Murray, H. A.: *Thematic Apperception Test.* Cambridge, Harvard University Press, 1943.

Newland, T. E., and Meeker, M.: Binet behavior samplings and Guilford's structure of the intellect. *J Sch Psychol, 2:*55–59, 1964.

Newland, T. E., and Smith, P. A.: Statistically significant differences between subtest scaled scores on the WISC and the WAIS. *J Sch Psychol, 5:* 122–127, 1967.

Olden, C.: Notes on the development of empathy. In *The Psychoanalytic Study of the Child*. Vol. 13. New York, International Universities Press, 1958.

Pascal, G. R., and Suttell, B. J.: *The Bender-Gestalt Test: Quantification and validity for adults*. New York, Grune & Stratton, 1951.

Pearson, G. H. J.: *Emotional disorders of children*. New York, W. W. Norton, 1949.

Phillips, L., and Draguns, J. G.: Classification of the behavior disorders. *Ann Rev Psychol, 22:*447–482, 1971.

Pimm, J. B., Quay, H. C., and Werry, J. S.: Dimensions of problem behavior in first grade children. *Psychology in the Schools, 4:*155–157, 1967.

Popham, W. J., and Husek, T. R.: Implications of criterion-referenced measurement. In W. J. Popham (Ed.), *Criterion-referenced measurement*. Englewood Cliffs, New Jersey, Educational Technology, 1971.

Pytkowicz, A. R.: Action-oriented evaluation of learning disorders. In Special Child Publications (Eds.), *Learning disorders*. Vol. 3, Seattle, Special Child Publications, 1968.

Quay, H. C., Morse, W. C., and Cutler, R. L.: Personality patterns of pupils in special classes for the emotionally disturbed. *Except Child, 32:*297–301, 1966.

Rabin, A. I.: Diagnostic use of intelligence tests. In B. B. Wolman (Ed.), *Handbook of clinical psychology*. New York, McGraw-Hill, 1965.

Rabin, A. I. (Ed.): *Projective techniques in personality assessment*. New York, Springer, 1968.

Rabin, A. I., and Haworth, M. R.: *Projective techniques with children*. New York, Grune & Stratton, 1960.

Rapaport, D., Gill, M. M., and Schafer, R.: *Diagnostic psychological testing*. (Rev. ed., edited by R. R. Holt) New York, International Universities Press, 1968.

Raven, J. C.: *Progressive Matrices Test*, London, H. K. Lewis & Co., 1958. (Distributed in the United States by the Psychological Corporation.)

Redl, F.: *When we deal with children: Selected writings*. New York, Free Press, 1966.

Reichenberg, Hackett, W.: Changes in Goodenough drawings after a gratifying experience. *Ann J. Orthopsychi, 23:*501–517, 1953.

Rorschach, H.: *Psychodiagnostics*. (2nd ed.) New York, Grune & Stratton, 1942.

Rosenthal, R., and Jacobson, L.: *Pygmalion in the classroom: Teacher expectation and pupils' intellectual development*. New York, Holt, Rhinehart & Winston, 1968.

Ross, A. O.: *The practice of child clinical psychology*. New York, Grune & Stratton, 1959.

Ross, A. O.: Learning difficulties of children: Dysfunction, disorder, disabilities. *J Sch Psychol, 5:*82–92, 1967.

Ross, R. T., and Morledge, J.: Comparison of the WISC and WAIS at chronological age sixteen. *J Consult Psychol, 31:*331–332, 1967.

Sarason, S. B.: *The clinical interaction, with special reference to the Rorschach.* New York, Harper, 1954.

Sattler, J. M.: Effects of cues and examiner influence on two Wechsler subtests. *J Consult and Clin Psychol, 33:*716–721, 1969.

Sattler, J. M.: Racial *experimental effects* in experimentation, testing, interviewing and psychotherapy. *Psychol Bull, 73:*137–160, 1970.

Sattler, J. M. and Theye, F.: Procedural, situational, and interpersonal variables in individual intelligence testing. *Psychol Bull, 68:*347–360, 1967.

Schafer, R.: *Psychoanalytic interpretation in Rorschach testing.* New York, Grune & Stratton, 1954.

Schneidman, E. S.: The Make-A-Picture Story (MAPS) projective personality test: A preliminary report. *J Consult Psychol, 11:*315–325, 1947.

Scott, W. A.: Research definitions of mental health and mental illness. *Psychol Bull, 55:*29–45, 1958.

Sears, P.: From libido to cognition. *Contemparary Psychology, 14:*218–219, 1969.

Sharma, S. L.: A historical background of the development of nosology in psychiatry and psychology. *Am Psychol, 25:*248–253, 1970.

Shoben, E. J., Jr.: Toward a concept of the normal personality. *Am Psychol, 12:*183–189, 1957.

Simpson, R. L.: Study of the comparability of the WISC and the WAIS. *J Consult Clin Psychol, 34:*156–158, 1970.

Smith, M. B.: Research strategies toward a conception of positive mental health. *Am Psychol, 14:*638–681, 1959.

Society for the Psychological Study of Social Issues. Guidelines for testing minority group children. *J Soc Issues, 20:*127–145, 1964. Supplement.

Solomon, I. L., and Starr, B. D.: *School Apperception Method.* New York, Springer, 1968.

Stutsman, R.: *Mental measurement of preschool children.* Yonkers-on-Hudson, World Book, 1948.

Sundberg, N. D., and Tyler, L. E.: *Clinical psychology: An introduction to research and practice.* New York, Meredith, 1962.

Symmes, E. F.: Some techniques in securing rapport with preschool children. *Am J Orthopsychi, 3:*181–190, 1933.

Symonds, P. M.: *Manual for Symonds' Picture Story Test.* New York, Bureau of Publications, Columbia University Press, 1948.

Szasz, T. S.: The myth of mental illness. *Am Psychol, 15:*113–118, 1960.

Terman, L. M., and Merrill, M. A.: *Stanford-Binet Intelligence Scale: Manual for the Third Revision Form L-M.* Boston, Houghton Mifflin, 1960.

Thorne, F. C.: A view outline for psychological report writing. *J Clin Psychol, 12:*112–115, 1956.

Trippe, M. J.: Review of M. A. White and J. Charry (Eds.), School disorder, intelligence and social class. *Except Child 34:*287–290, 1967.

Tyler, L. E.: Toward a workable psychology of individuality. *Am Psychol, 14*:75–81, 1959.

Ullmann, L. P., and Krasner, L.: *A psychological approach to abnormal behavior.* Englewood Cliffs, New Jersey, Prentice-Hall, 1969.

Valett, R. E.: *A profile for the Stanford-Binet (L-M), item classifications by Robert E. Valett.* Palo Alto, Consulting Psychologists Press, 1965.

Ward, A. J.: Early infantile autism. *Psycholog Bull, 73*:350–362, 1970.

Wechsler, D.: *Wechsler Intelligence Scale for Children: Manual.* New York, The Psychological Corporation, 1949.

Wechsler, D.: *Wechsler Adult Intelligence Scale: Manual.* New York, The Psychological Corporation, 1955.

Wechsler, D.: *The measurement and appraisal of adult intelligence.* (4th ed.) Baltimore, Williams & Wilkins, 1958.

Wechsler, D.: *Wechsler Preschool and Primary Scale of Intelligence: Manual.* New York, The Psychological Corporation, 1967.

Weiner, B. B.: Assessment: Beyond psychometry. *Except Child, 33*:367–370, 1967.

White, M. A., and Charry, J. (Eds.) : *School disorder, intelligence, and social class.* New York, Teachers College Press, 1966.

Wright, H. F.: Observational child study. In P. H. Mussen (Ed.), *Handbook of research methods in child development.* New York, John Wiley & Sons, 1960.

CHAPTER IX

THE GIFTED

JOSEPH L. FRENCH

"**D**EFINE A GIFTED child almost as you wish," wrote Willard Abraham (1958). "You will find some authority to support your point of view." Giftedness is far more than a high score on an intelligence test. In 1951 Wolfle stated, "intelligence alone is not enough for effective intellectual work: To make creative contributions in a scientific or scholarly field, one must also be endowed with interest in it, industry, persistence, strength of character, confidence, and some depth of originality." Certainly the characteristics identified by Wolfle are not measured by intelligence tests, but no matter how much drive, if one does not have enough intellectual power, a high level creative contribution will not be forthcoming. Such things as persistence, competence and even originality are not measured well by tests. These characteristics need to be developed in many youth through educational programming and/or the home environment. Since these characteristics are not well measured and since a minimal level of intelligence is necessary for creative production, the intelligence test has been relied upon widely and appropriately in identifying children and youth for special educational opportunities for the gifted.

The problem of identifying gifted children has been one of the major obstacles in the path of those interested in *doing something for the gifted*. The success of special programs is, in large measure, the result of the appropriateness of the program for the children selected. Some educators pay so little attention to identification that their efforts are wasted. This frequently occurs when educators, often new to the field, plan programs for students of extremely high ability and then find that such a population does not exist in their community. More frequently the problem is at the other extreme. The ability of students is often underestimated or truly bright students are not recognized, even when the planners are in constant contact with them. Other workers spend so much time considering the problems of identification that they neglect plans for a constructive educational program.

One of the reasons that identification of the gifted has been so difficult is that no one definition of giftedness has received universal acceptance. Perhaps more important is the fact that it is frequently assumed that all gifted children will profit from one program or that the content of a program is unimportant in identifying individuals for the program. The program content should influence the plan for selecting participants. It is important, therefore, to see how program personnel define their program and in so doing define giftedness. Another approach is to engage in a thorough and comprehensive process of identifying gifted people, study their needs and then develop a program to better meet the most urgent needs. It is possible that many gifted youth have their educational needs well met. While individuals with general intellectual superiority make up most groups of *gifted* persons, we are often in error trying to apply group statistics or other descriptors to any given individual.

A short time ago a questionnaire was received from professors in seventy-four institutions offering course work about the gifted. About one-third of them defined the gifted in terms of IQ with seventeen indicating an IQ of 130 or more as an essential part of the definition. The other responses were divided roughly into three categories. One major block did not respond. Another major block made some reference to an unmeasurable characteristic such as *potential for outstanding achievement*. Most of the latter group accepted Paul Witty's definition: "One whose performance is consistently remarkable in any potential valuable area of human activity." (Witty, 1940) A few chose the definition offered by Leonard J. Lucito: . . . "students whose potential intellectual powers are at such a high ideational level in both productive and evaluative thinking that it can be reasonably assumed they could be future problem solvers, innovators, and evaluators of the culture if adequate educational experiences are provided." (Dunn, 1963) A few others chose a definition by T. Ernest Newland which is somewhat more operationally oriented: "Gifted children are those children who by virtue of objectively ascertained learning potential (with or without demonstrated superior competence) can be deemed capable of making contributions to society at levels comparable in difficulty and significant to the technological level or above." (French, 1966.) Statements such as those by Lucito and Newland are preferred over a specific IQ for several reasons but the key reason is the latitude the statements allow the professional educator. A child who, by virtue of a comprehensive assessment of his functional ability, seems to fit in the type of learning experiences planned for a particular program can be accepted even if his IQ may fall a point or two or three below a particular cut off score. Another individual who may have an IQ above the specified cut-off but who, after a comprehensive assessment, does not seem to be one who could most advantageously be enrolled in the program need not be included.

Will an IQ alone identify those children appropriately included in a program for the gifted? Indeed it will not. However, it is an essential ingredient in most identification schemes. So far tests of intelligence have not been designed which will measure all of what theoreticians refer to as intellectual capability. However, some tests are much more adequate than others in measuring a reasonably comprehensive portion of general intellectual ability. "Intelligence may be defined as the use of mental ability to function efficiently in the environment. Mental abilities are functioning efficiently when they are used to:

    a. Perceive verbal and numerical symbols and spacial relationships,

    b. Acquire and retain general and specific information in common symbol form for reuse at later times, and

    c. Relate the symbols to each other and manipulate them in the solution of problem situations.

"Ability to learn and comprehend abstract symbols and their relationships is commonly understood to be a function of intelligence. While the previous experience of an individual, to a degree, determines the opportunity to ascertain symbolic relationships, the more intelligent members of a given environment use more symbols and recognize appropriate relationships among them than do the less able. Such capability is a good indication of expected success in future learning situations." (French, 1964B)

A test of general mental ability takes advantage of the fact that various intellectual functions are themselves correlated. Long standing research has established that competency in certain mental functions indicates intellect in efficient operation. These factors include verbal comprehension, numerical computation, perceptual organization, memory and reasoning. The content of some intelligence tests reflect these functions much more than others.

Intelligence tests and achievement tests are similar in that both measure previous learning of the individual being tested on the items selected for the test. The difference between the two types of tests relate to the manner in which the items have been selected. The achievement test items are selected to measure the accomplishment of specific academic objectives stated by the test authors and related to the curriculum in which the individuals have been enrolled. The intelligence test items, on the other hand, have been selected to reflect more generalized accomplishments within the total structure of one's environment rather than the outcome of specific instructional activities. The intelligence test items should reflect more reasoning ability and more ability to select an appropriate process to arrive at a solution rather than mechanical computation or fact or symbol retrival. Since intelligence tests were designed to indicate a rate of general acquisition of knowledge and ability to use it in the solution of new problems associated with the academic world, a degree of academic bias is present. Such bias is necessary to optimize the prediction of future learning in an academic situation.

The definition of intelligence quoted above suggests that individuals developing in some environments may not be able to answer as many questions on a particular intelligence test as individuals developing in another environment but the statement does suggest that those individuals who solve more of the problems on the test than their age mates can be predicted to succeed more rapidly and work more efficiently than their age mates with xx lower scores. This concept is particularly important when there is concern about the identification of gifted individuals from disadvantaged neighborhoods.

Assessment of intellectual ability implies a much broader study of an individual than merely obtaining a test score. To assess the characteristics of an individual in regard to a program for the gifted requires some knowledge of the generally accepted characteristics of the gifted.

A major reason for our lack of knowledge about the gifted is our attempt to adhere too rigidly to a long list of characteristics of giftedness. The gifted as a group are certainly more homogeneous than the entire population and probably more homogeneous than the rest of the population, but within the gifted themselves there is great heterogeneity. Using the average for children of the same sex and chronological age as a base, a composite list of the characteristics of academically talented children follows:

1. Superior physique as demonstrated by above average height, weight, coordination, endurance, and general health
2. Longer attention span
3. Learns rapidly, easily, and with less repetition
4. Learns to read sooner and continues to read at a consistently more advanced level
5. More mature in the ability to express himself through the various communicative skills
6. Reaches higher levels of attentiveness to his environment
7. Asks more questions and really wants to know the causes and reasons for things
8. Likes to study some subjects that are difficult because he enjoys the learning
9. Spends time beyond the ordinary assignments or schedule on things that are of interest to him
10. Possesses one or more special talents

11. Knows about many things of which other children are unaware
12. Is able to adapt learning to various situations somewhat unrelated in orientation
13. Reasons out more problems since he recognizes relationships and comprehends meanings
14. Analyzes quickly mechanical problems, puzzles, and trick questions
15. Shows a high degree of originality and often uses good but unusual methods or ideas
16. Is more adept in analyzing his own abilities, limitations, and problems
17. Performs with more poise and can take charge of the situation
18. Evaluates facts and arguments critically
19. Has more emotional stability
20. Can judge the abilities of others
21. Has diverse, spontaneous, and frequently self directed interests (French, 1964)

While these characteristics describe gifted and talented children in general, they may not apply equally to all such children. There is no such thing as an accurate composite of a gifted child. Generally we expect gifted children as a group to have more positive and fewer negative characteristics, and they may acquire these characteristics both earlier and with more intensity. The intelligence of a child does not determine the degree to which he possesses these traits. Some quite gifted individuals may possess only a few of these characteristics. Such a list will not replace a good intelligence test for identifying a gifted child, but it will help in the assessment process and it might indicate areas where a child is not fulfilling his potential.

The list above can be helpful in trying to identify the gifted in certain unusual or exceptional environments which differ markedly from the traditional educational scene. Items 11 through 21 will be most helpful in non-test assessment of individuals from disadvantaged communities. Tests which can be purchased from publishers will be of little help in developing information for this part of the assessment process. Instead situations may need to be devised so that observation by the identification team can take place. In some instances teachers and other professional people who have an opportunity to observe the individuals under consideration will be helpful in obtaining ratings. The effectiveness and efficiency of teacher ratings will be discussed later.

The purpose of the identification program is to identify those individuals who may or may not be achieving efficiently or at a high level but should center on identifying those individuals who are capable of high achievement. The high achievement may be in general academic proficiency but the high achievement may also be in some special talent field.

In a critique of research trends in the education of gifted children Gallagher (1964) introduces the reader to the problems of the gifted as follows:

The achievement of intellectually superior individuals do not equal the sum of the achievements of any number of less talented people. The definition of a genius as *a person who does easily what no one else can do at all* is appropriate here. One cannot evaluate Michelangelo by saying that he is equal to twenty painters of inferior rank, or Einstein by saying that his work approximates the combined products of thirty run-of-the-mill physicists. These rare individuals are invaluable; they produce something that no other collection of persons can produce. The same generalization holds true at lower intellectual levels. No collection of persons of below average intellectual abilities can match the contribution of the best individual physician, college professor, or executive. Attempts to use to the utmost the intellectual resources of the society can result in incalculable benefits, not only to the individual but to the society as a whole. . . .

Environment can have either an inhibiting or an encouraging effect on the development of intellectual talent. Such an assumption places a heavy responsibility on the culture and the education system, but it is also an exciting one for the educator and the social scientist. The concept of *intelligence* as a genetically determined trait has been replaced by the concept of a pliable and plastic intellect which is responsive to the environment in which it is placed. The place of genetics in intelligence has not been denied; rather, the place of environment and its interaction with genetics has been reaffirmed.

Other implications of this newer concept are that (a) the prediction of future intellectual ability must take into account past environmental and probable future environmental experiences; (b) any classification of giftedness should be tentative and should be used for present educational planning rather than for prediction; (c) the younger the child the more plastic his abilities; (d) prediction of future performance should not be ruled out, but the complex nature and problems of such prediction should be fully realized.

Whereas the most frequently used score in identifying the gifted is IQ from an intelligence test, it is essential that intelligence be considered a multidimensional and involving more than can be measured by existing tests. Until new means of assessing the broader spectrum are validated, however, the IQ from an individually administered test such as a Binet or Wechsler stands as the best single criterion.

Tests of creativity, while holding much early promise, have not been associated with high enough validity indices to warrant use as either a sole indicator of *giftedness* or *creativeness* or as a substantial contribution to prediction formulas. Thorough and systematic evaluations of studies related to creativity raised numerous questions which have toned down much of the enthusiasms of the 1960's. Wallach and Kogan (1966) produced evidence to show that indices of creativity possess little relationship to one another yet they do relate more strongly to standard intelligence test scores than other variables. Such evidence suggests that obtaining a composite score from the *creativity* subtests is a mistake and that the subtests are too weak to stand alone. The assumption that creativity is not related to intelligence is unwarranted.

It is reasonable to assume that some children do develop at rates different from the majority and a real intellectual growth spurt can, when identified, suggest the need for a new or different educational program. In some cases a change in motivational influences can result in a similar need. Because significant changes in the rate of a few individuals have been observed and because motivational influences due bring about significant changes in behavior, it is undesirable to lock students into tracks which prohibit them from either tapering off if the pace is too rapid or complex or moving into stiffer competition should the setting of new academic or vocational goals be appropriate.

Longitudinal studies have been used to demonstrate both the lack of consistency and the consistency of repeated measurements of intellectual ability. The Berkley Growth Study (Bayley, 1955) data revealed that intelligence measured at age one has a zero correlation with intelligence measured at seventeen. However, the reason for such lack of correlation is assumed to be related to the means by which intelligence has been measured. The infant scales are largely motor and physical development tests and differ markedly in content from the test based on verbal reasoning. However, by four years of age the correlations become substantial (Bloom, 1964). In the school years longitudinal studies reveal rather consistent measurements for most subjects.

Enough evidence is on hand to convenience many scholars that intellectual ability can be modified. The environment can inhibit or facilitate development of intellectual talent. Such a belief places heavy responsibilities on the educator who must believe in the fullest development of all students. Classification of giftedness must be used for educational planning. As other students develop to the point where they no longer can be expected to profit maximally from their program and now seem to be gifted, doors should open for them so that in a different program their rate of development can be maintained. For those who find the pace in a program for the gifted too pressing, alternate programs should be available. Identification at one time is not enough. Each student must be monitored periodically to assure that personality, academic and intellectual development continue appropriately.

"It is highly unlikely that any society has developed a system of child rearing in education that maximizes the potential of the individuals who compose it. Probably no individual has ever lived whose full potential for happy, intellectual interests and growth has been achieved. If we could adopt this point of view and offer consistent appropriate opportunities to the gifted people whom we identify, each child's potential for intellectual development would be maximized and untold benefits would accrue to both the individual and the society with which they have contact." (Hunt, 1961)

The use of scores from intelligence tests in operationally defining intelligence seems justified only to the extent that the abilities measured by the test are themselves important and valuable in this culture. Giftedness is inseparable from its social and cultural environment. Socially deprived children are not handicapped by a test; rather their handicap is described, in part, by the test score just as a scale reflects the weight of an undernourished waif.

In the current literature one finds reference to several means of identifying talented students, but only individually administered intelligence tests can identify very intellectually capable students. When group intelligence and achievement tests are used without the individual tests, only academically talented students are located. Many underachievers are missed. The use of tests which can be used with groups of students often merely *certify* able students rather than identify students with high potential. The students with hidden intellectual talent are not located by tests (Wrightstone, 1960) and are not found until an enriched environment helps them bloom. Intelligence tests seldom identify students who have high potential in the performing arts. Torrance (1960) and Getzels and Jackson (1958) have located other significantly high achievers (but perhaps less pleasing students in the classroom) with various tests of creativity. They have found two-thirds of the students with high standardized achevement test scores and high creativity test scores to have lower IQ's than others of similar achievement. These lower IQ's, however, range above 115.

In the foregoing paragraph I have tried to make a case for four groups of gifted students, namely:

1. The intellectually capable but not necessarily academically able,
2. The academically able who must be intellectually capable,
3. The student with hidden talent brought out, not by tests but by opportunity and strong (and often new) desire to produce, and

4. The highly creative student who has the superior intellectual capability (IQ of at least 115), plus an added
factor.

Any classification of talents should be flexible and subject to
revision. But, more than that, those identified must be thought of
as *possessing high potentiality* rather than *assured of achievement*
through membership in a designated group. It is unrealistic for
anyone to expect each member of a *talented group* of children
ultimately to attain extreme success as judged by traditional criteria such as eminence, professional accomplishment, or the production of creative ideas. This reality should not keep us from
searching for programming that will more effectively meet the
unique needs of all children.

The topic of identification of the academically able and intellectually capable is discussed in several other sources (National
Education Association, 1961; Pegnato and Birch; 1959; Gallagher,
1960; French, 1964; and De Haan, 1957).

Some of the problems inherent in identifying the gifted in our
society have been identifyed by Freehill (1961), who reminds us
that brightness is much less obvious than dullness because 1)
gifted people are capable of average performance; 2) many gifted
people do not live in situations that bring forth ingenious verbal
or academic behavior; and 3) gifted responses are marked by *appropriateness* and/or by the fact they are stimulated by *small*
clues which may or may not produce unusual behavior or performance.

Effectiveness of Identification for Academic Aptitude

The best tool for locating academically talented students has
been the individual intelligence test, either the Stanford Binet or
one of the Wechsler Scales. Gallagher and Lucito (1961) and
Thompson and Finley (1962) found gifted subjects to earn
slightly higher WISC scores on the *verbal comprehension* (i.e.,
Similarities, Information, Comprehension and Vocabulary) subtests than on those more related to perceptual organization. They
concluded that WISC verbal IQ's would overestimate full scale
WISC IQ's. Tests which can be administered to groups of children at one time may be economical but in many instances
children with reading difficulties, emotional difficulties, or moti-

vational problems have been missed. Achievement tests have the same limitations of group intelligence tests but have even more difficulty in indicating the capability of the educationally handicapped child.

Achievement test results are often misleading. Most students who are gifted will have grade placements above that expected for their CA—even if they are underachieving. But many very bright students have only slightly above average scores and when only those scores are considered they do not appear to be outstanding. In some instances the brightest students do not have the highest scores. The bright student with diverse interests is often attracted to topics such as navigation, free form writing, photography, or stamp collecting. Such activities may be intellectually challenging and rewarding but the information gained in the study of such enriching topics is seldom reflected in the content of a standard achievement test. On the other hand, the student who labors away on course content specifically related to the objectives upon which the test was built will often earn a higher score. Standard achievement tests are designed to measure the specific content of the prescribed curriculum. Such tests may measure what they are supposed to measure very well but they were not designed to measure the enriching activities offered in the school or found in the community. The bright student who complies with the assigned school tasks but relishes related activities and thrives on extra curricular, academic work is often one whose accomplishments are underestimated by standard achievement batteries.

All intelligence and achievement tests are known as *maximum performance tests*. Such tests require the individual to exert his maximum effort to perform at the upper limit of his ability. As a result it has long been recognized that psychologists and other test administrators often underestimate the maximum level of many students. With an individually administered, reliable test the chances of underestimating the ability of an individual are less. When an individual test is used by a competent psychologist, it is possible to judge whether or not the individual is exerting his maximum effort. However, the individual tests are expensive to administer in terms of the use of trained personnel and it is often impossible to have an individual test administered to every child.

The purpose of a program for identifying gifted children and youth is to enable educators to decide whether special educational provisions should be made for a given child, and, if so what kind of special opportunities should be provided. The purpose of any identification schedule is not to label a child for the rest of his life, rather it is to help diagnose his educational needs. Procedures should be systematic and inclusive.

Screening should be a continuous process. Even if the procedures for identification used at an early educational level are adequate and efficient, efforts to locate other bright children in need of different educational programs should be continuous.

A method has been presented by Pegnato and Birch (1959) for making a judgment in terms of effectiveness and efficiency of various screening instruments. The work of Pegnato and Birch has been supported by several other investigators. As a result, a multidimensional type of screening program seems necessary to efficiently identify the talent reservoir for a school program.

Gowan and Demos (1965) suggest the following measures:

1. Select the approximate percentages of students that you wish to include in a program, presumably not less than one percent nor more than ten.

2. Use a group intelligence test and screen the top five percent and place them in a talent pool.

3. Circulate to each classroom teacher a paper for him to nominate the best student, the child who does the best critical thinking, the able child who is the biggest nuisance, the brightest minority child, etc.

4. Use an achievement battery and cut it at a point that will yield three percent of the students. Make a list of all students in the top ten in numerical skills and add these to the reservoir.

5. Have a principal, curriculum and guidance staff make a list of children who have achieved outstandingly in any skill, held leadership positions, are examples of reading difficulties but believed bright, etc.

All youngsters who have received two or more nominations

should then be given an individual intelligence test. This would be a way of establishing a superior talent reservoir for the school. If the school is developing a special program in a given area then additional identification tests may be needed.

Many people believe that gifted children are not difficult to discover. They themselves have noted some gifted children. It is true that many gifted children reveal themselves by outstanding performance. Such recognition by parents, neighbors, teachers and other children should not be overlooked; however, relying only on such judgment is disastrous if one wants to identify all of those individuals of truly high intellectual ability.

Parents have not proven to be reliable sources of screening information. Whereas some parents are eager for the prestige associated with having a child in a special program and will push too hard for the welfare of the child, other parents subscribe to the belief that people should not publicize their own virtues. Modesty is often the expected behavior and as a result children are reluctant to volunteer for special talent programs and parents are reluctant to push them except for activities involving such talents as athletic, music, and drama.

Parents and children, often fear that such names as *egghead, bookworm,* or even *gifted child* will be thrown up to them. Even senators have been known to favor *mediocrity* in supreme court judges so as to provide better representation for the people. Despite overwhelming research evidence to support average or better than average mental health for the gifted many parents persist in fearing giftedness as similar to insanity. Many parents believe that talent in athletics is good and should be publicized but talent in academics should be mentioned quietly if at all. Such an attitude holds back program development as well. In other areas of exceptionality parents push hard for programs and are very instrumental in establishing and maintaining programs. To push for programming for the gifted—especially for your own child—is almost un-American.

Although the generally negative attitude toward giftedness prevails in many communities, the gifted are relatively popular among their peers when their talents are not touted. Gallagher (1958) related intelligence with the number of friendship choices received in grades two through five in a midwestern community of above average socio-economic status. The children with IQ's of 132 and above obtained an average of six or more friendship choices as opposed to an average of four or less for children with IQ's below 100. While bright children tend to choose other bright children and average children choose average children for their friends, it is also true that average children choose children who have slightly higher intelligence test scores.

Martyn (1957) studies the social adjustment of gifted and highly gifted children in grades four through twelve with the Cunningham Social Distance Scale. The elementary aged gifted children studied were more popular but at the secondary level the gifted were not significantly more socially acceptable than their agemates. Since the attitude of many youth and their parents is adverse as it is to special programming for the gifted, considerable work will be necessary in each community before parent nominations can be used in an identification program. Parent nominations may be used in a program in which some of the gifted in a community are to be certified as gifted. Asking parents for nominations is often helpful in a public relations program as long as there is an *easy way out* for those who do not qualify. Other approaches will most certainly be necessary in a comprehensive identification program.

The general consensus regarding the weakness of teacher ratings can be summarized as follows: The teacher is likely to miss gifted children who are not enthusiastic about the educational program, who are achieving only slightly better than the average child in class, and/or who is belligerent or apathetic toward the school program. Some teachers are much more efficient than others in rating the intellectual ability of children. Generally those teachers with more education, particularly in child development type courses; who have had more teaching experience; and who have had more time to learn about the children they are rating are more efficient than those individuals who have not had as much course work, experience, or opportunity. When ratings are employed it is very important to define in some detail the characteristic to be rated. When teachers are asked to name those children they consider to be very gifted they are not as able to rate the children as effectively as when a more adequate verbal description such as the list of characteristics discussed earlier has been provided or when a rating procedure recommended by Kough and De Haan is employed. Kough and De Haan (1955) provide the list of about ten characteristics and then ask the teacher how a pupil stands out on those characteristics when compared with the rest of the class. Kough and De Haan have provided a list of characteristics for general intellectual ability and a number of talent areas.

With anything less than the rating system suggested above a few children are *certified* and many are misclassified. A study by Lewis (1945) could easily be replicated today if raters were asked only to identify those children they would classify as *extremely mentally retarded* or those they rate as *genius*. Lewis found that while teachers labeled somewhat over seven percent of their pupils as mentally retarded they labeled less than one percent of them as genius and selected slightly more girls than boys in the upper category. In terms of IQ range, approximately twenty-seven percent of the children labeled as *genius* had group intelligence scores of 109 or below and only forty percent of them had IQ's in the 120 and above range. Of those rated as extremely mentally retarded one percent had IQ's of 110 and above and about twenty-five percent had IQ's of 90 or above. Since group intelligence test scores are notably undependable, it may have been the test score rather than the teacher that was incorrect in some instances. Nevertheless these results did raise serious doubt as to the teachers' ability to identify such youngsters without any more directions than were given in this situation.

Some able children can be identified through the use of standardized tests; others through the process of systematic observation of their work. *Work samples* can be rated by panels of experts in the specific fields such as music, art, commerce, mechanics, etc. The judges need instruction and experience in looking for the right characteristics. Those students capable of a high level of performing specific talents have long been sought in some educational circles. Athletic coaches, band directors, and drama coaches have spent considerable energy trying to ascertain which individuals within a school can perform most efficiently in their special field. These special educators have defined the talented behavior they hope to develop and then looked for ways in which they can identify these individuals who can be taught to achieve at a very high level. Some basketball coaches have isolated the various tasks. Among those potential players with keen interest and moderate achievement in the fundamentals of the game some coaches have sought to measure such characteristics as reaction time, ability to jump and reach, and manual dexterity in addition to the ability to put the ball in the basket in identifying those players whose talent they will try to develop more fully. In considering other talents and how a particular educational program might develop them more fully, it is necessary to analyze the essential characteristics necessary for developing that skill and then determining ways of measuring relative ability among those interested in the particular talent.

There are times when identification (or certification) of talent is easy. The boy who is younger than his classmates who excells in athletics, who is on the honor roll even though he spends little time in study and is popular with the boys and girls as well as the faculty is easy. But there are times when the problem of identification is difficult because some popular school leaders obtain above average grades through hard work and personal charm rather than intellectual ability. Without tests these students may be mistakenly identified as academically talented. Placed in situations where they must achieve at higher levels than they are capable of, they incur psychological harm. One instance of this occurred in a community which instituted an accelerated reading program for those who were already considerably above the average of their group. As the group acquired increased responsibility and more complex work, the teacher suddenly discovered that one of the girls was cheating. When group intelligence tests were administered that year for the first time, this girl was found to have an IQ of 109. Further investigation revealed that this was an accurate measure of her intellectual level. Apparently she had been achieving to the very limit of her ability before the speed-up program tempted her so much that she consistently cheated to retain her position as a high achiever.

Although bright children are reported to enjoy better mental health than the average child, they are not free from social and emotional strain. Their mental maturity may spurt ahead of their social development. Such children are often missed in searches for academic talent and perhaps the most appropriate program should be directed at improving their social and emotional development rather than concentrating on an academic program. Which child needs a modified school program? In many instances the child who is socially secure, personally popular and achieving at a splendid academic pace is singled out for a special enriched program and the individual who is his intellectaul peer but who lacks the social, personal, and academic development commensurate with his intellectual ability is required to stay in the same old program in which he has enjoyed less than optimum success. Perhaps the individual most in need of a *gifted child program* is the latter rather than the former. Sometimes these underachievers or individuals with hidden talent are not identified with intelligence tests but can be identified after their performance on tests of spatial perception, of clerical speed and accuracy or their ability to excel in some particular field such as speech or auto mechanics or even *world cultures* suggests high capability. When the program emphasis is on something such as interpretation of current events these students with hidden talent need an enriched or remedial program that may differ from the traditional. With such students, initial identification may be dependent upon teacher, parent, or even peer nomination. Such nominations often come in the form of a concerned individual inquiring about why a particular student is so good in one thing and having such difficulty in many others. Such students are often overlooked when the faculty is asked for nominations of gifted students.

In only the most wealthy districts will psychologists be able to periodically evaluate all children with individually administered tests. Therefore, in the vast majority of school systems a screening procedure will be necessary. At all age levels the general procedure recommended previously by Gowan and Demos but with modifications in keeping with local conditions can be recommended. In pre-school activities the use of individually administered tests will be far more necessary and as individuals progress in chronological age the use of individually administered tests will be less necessary. Throughout the pre-school, elementary and junior high years, the Stanford Binet will often be used in preference to one of the Wechsler Scales because of a higher test ceiling. The Wechsler format has a tendency to restrict the range of scores in the early elementary and early teen years. As students move into senior high school their habit patterns are often so set that programs for the gifted usually require more of a *certification of giftedness program* rather than an *identification of giftedness*. Therefore, group administered tests are used most frequently. Beyond the senior high school group tests are used almost exclusively.

With young physically handicapped children other tests may be more appropriate. With deaf children the Hiskey-Nebraska Test of Learning Aptitude or the Leiter International Performance Scale may be used effectively. Children with cerebral palsy or a relatively severe speech defect who are below the age of eight may be able to show their intellectual superiority more on a test such as the Pictorial Test of Intelligence than on the Stanford Binet or Wechsler.

Individually administered multiple choice tests are sometimes difficult to terminate because the subject is able to answer some questions correctly due to chance. As a result, some children have earned scores considerably above those earned on tests on which the answer must be given verbally or through a manipulation by the child.

Children with auditory or visual perceptual deficits and/or emotional disturbance may show an unusually wide scatter on the most appropriate test for them. Individuals with responses scored at a wide variety of intellectual levels should receive an exhaustive battery of tests and other assessments to identify those areas of relative weakness which need strong educational programming.

In searching for students with artistic talent the *Meier Art Tests* have the best reviews. They are easy to administer and score and possess satisfactory reliability. The *Art Judgement* test is recommended for students in grades seven through sixteen and adults and the *Aesthetic Perception* test is for students in grades nine through sixteen. No measure of performing ability is obtained. By selecting the preferred picture, art judgment and perception are rated. However, most educators prefer the work sample to any test.

Several tests are available in music. The revised edition of the *Seashore Measures of Musical Talents* appears to be favored by music educators for use with young children and those who profess little or no music interest or are not sophisticated in music. The *Seashore* can be used as low as grade four and provides in about sixty minutes of testing six scores: pitch, loudness, rhythm, time, timbre, and tonal memory. The *Drake Musical Aptitude Test* was designed for use with children eight and over but the test is hard for younger children and those naive in musical terminology. The *Drake Test* yields scores in *musical memory* and rhythm. Another test which may be used profitably with samples of children known to be better than average in talent and interest is the *Wing Standardized Tests of Musical Intelligence*. The seven tests in the Wing battery were designed for administration in about one-half hour. Children age eight and over respond to chord analysis, pitch change, and memory. Older children may respond to rhythmic accent, harmony, intensity, and phrasing.

According to some state laws, a particular cut off score is established for eligibility in a program. Such restrictive legislation is not in the best interest of children. If the average IQ in a class is 123, the child with an IQ of 130 is not, in all likelihood, in need of some special programming but in some states only those children with IQ's above 130 are eligible for state reimbursement of excess costs. If the same child (with an IQ of 130) should be located in a class with an average IQ of 110 and a range of 70 or 80 IQ points, it is quite possible that some special programming would be desirable. However, it is also quite likely that a child with an IQ of 120 in a class whose average is 90 would also need some kind of special programming.

When a cut off score does determine eligibility for a program two characteristics of the identifying instruments should be well known: the standard error of measurement and the artificial ceiling imposed by the instrument.

A standard error of measurement always surrounds an IQ. Repeated measurement of an individual will often yield IQ's varying around the first measurement by five to fifteen points in above average populations. When an IQ of 125 is used as a cut off score, not all individuals who earn scores of at least 125 may be eligible for the program. The 125 cut off score insures that most of the persons with IQ's of 130 and practically all of those with IQ's of 135 have been included in the sample. Therefore, several of those students with lower IQ's (125 to 130) usually do not fit the reasons for selection, and other observations are usually needed before a final selection is made.

The *ceiling effect* is most often noted on group tests. A test designed for children in grades three to six may have a very adequate range of items for gifted third grade children but may have very few items for sixth grade children that show the extent of their intellectual functioning. It is quite possible on some tests for a child to have an IQ that would make him eligible for a program in grades three and four but not eligible in grades five and six simply because not enough items existed in the form of the test he was taking to enable him to earn a satisfactory high score.

Martinson and Lessinger (1960) after studying the identification procedures in the state of California charged that group tests are built and normed for the average learner and that they do not have sufficient items to discriminate among gifted pupils.

After reviewing the California program for gifted children and the means by which children were identified, Martinson (1966) (see Curtis) strongly advocated the use of individual intelligence tests. She found that there has been a trend to use short cuts in intellectual assessment and to group measures of dubious value coupled with teacher nominations and an "almost frantic effort to include sundry unvalidated measures in the hope that they will add to the understanding of unknown dimensions of the intellect" Whereas it is hoped by many concerned with the gifted that tests of creativity, problem solving ability, and evaluative thinking will be developed and validated, as yet they are not strong enough to do more than supplement the scores obtained from the more traditional individually administered intelligence test. Such a statement should not prohibit personnel from developing educational programs to encourage the skillful performer or master technician simply because they do not have scores on individual tests of intelligence which would indicate that they are gifted. As programs requiring less enthusiasm for general academic performance and more enthusiasm for the technical skills and the performing arts are developed, procedures for identifying those who will be a success in such programs will need to be developed with them. At the present time the work sample technique seems to offer the most hope.

In summing up conditions conclusive to productive achievement, Pressey (1955) identified six crucial ingredients:

1. a favorable immediate environment which includes a prevalent cultural interest in the accomplishments of the individual,
2. an early opportunity for ability to develop,
3. expert early instruction continuing through the formative years,
4. frequent and progressive opportunities for exercise and the freedom to progress as the individual is able,
5. social facilitation through close association with others of similar interest, and
6. frequent success experiences for which the individual gains the feeling that he is recognized by significant persons.

High level performance in any field requires interaction of capability, opportunity, and personality. In the past too much stress has been placed on *genetic* traits and too little attention has been given to providing facilitating conditions to develop the potentiality. When superior talent is identified, the challenge is to help it develop.

REFERENCES

Abraham, W.: *Common Sense About Gifted Children.* New York, Hayser and Brothers, 1958.

Bayley, Nancy: On the growth of intelligence. *Am Psychol. 10:*805–818, 1955.

Bloom, B. S.: *Stability and Change in Human Characteristics.* New York, John Wiley and Sons, Inc., 1964.

DeHaan, R. F.: Identifying gifted children. *School Review, 65:*41–48, 1957.

Dunn, L. M.: *Exceptional Children in the Schools.* New York, Holt, 179–238, 1963.

Freehill, M. F.: *Gifted Children.* New York, MacMillan, 1961.

French, J. L. (Ed.) : *Educating the Gifted.* New York, Holt, 1954.

French, J. L.: *The Pictorial Test of Intelligence.* Boston, Houghton Mifflin, 1964B.

French, J. L.: Where and how are teachers of the trained? *Selected Convention Papers.* Washington, D.C., Council for Exceptional Children. 1966.

Gallagher, J. J.: Peer acceptance of highly gifted children in elementary school. *Elem Sch J, 58:*365–470, 1958.

Gallagher, J. J.: *Analysis of Research on the Education of the Gifted.* Springfield, Illinois; Office of the Superintendent of Public Instruction, 1960.

Gallagher, J. J. and Lucito, L. J.: Intellectual patterns of gifted compared with average and retarded. *Except Child,* 479–482, 1961.

Gallagher, J. J. (Ch.) *et al.: Research Trends and Needs in Educating the Gifted.* Washington, D.C., U.S. Government Printing Office, 1964.

Getzels, J. W. and Jackson, P. W.: The meaning of giftedness. *Phi Delta Kappan, 40:*75–77, 1958.

Gowan, J. C. and Demos, G. D.: *Guidance of Exceptional Children.* New York, McKay, 1965.

Hunt, J. M.: *Intelligence and Experience.* New York, The Ronald Press, 1961.

Kough, J. and DeHaan, R.: *Teacher's Guidance Handbook.* Chicago, Science Research Associates, 1955.

Martinson, Ruth and Lessinger, L. M.: Problems in the identification of intellectually gifted pupils. *Except Child, 23:*227–31 and 242, 1960.

Martyn, K. A.: *The Social Acceptance of Gifted Students.* Unpublished doctoral dissertation, Stanford University, 1957.

National Education Association and American Personnel and Guidance Association. *Guidance for the Academically Talented Student.* Washington, D.C. National Education Association, 1961.

Pegnato, C. V. and Birch, J. W.: Locating gifted children in junior high school. *Except Child, 25:*300–304, 1959.

Pressey, S. L.: Concerning the nature and nurture of genius. *Scientific Monthly, 68:*123–129, 1955.

Thompson, J. M. and Finley, C. J.: A further comparison of the intellectual patterns of gifted and mentally retarded children. *Except Child,* 379–381, 1962.

Torrance, E. P. *et al.: Assessing Creative Thinking Abilities in Children.* Minneapolis, University of Minnesota, Bureau of Educational Research, 1960.

Wallach, M. E. and Kogan, N.: *Modes of Thinking in Young Children.* New York, Holt, Rinehart and Winston, 1966.

Witty, P.: Some considerations in the education of gifted. *Educ Admin Super, 26:*516, 1940.

Wolfle, D.: Intellectual resources. *Scientific American, 185:*42–46, 1951, as reprinted in French, J. L.: *Educating the Gifted,* New York, Holt, 1964, 19–27.

Wrightstone, J. W.: Demonstration guidance project in New York City. *Harvard Educat Rev, 30:*237–251, 1960.

CHAPTER X

EVALUATION AND ASSESSMENT OF CHILDREN'S LANGUAGE AND SPEECH BEHAVIOR

David E. Yoder

$\mathbf{M}$ AN IS OFTEN referred to as the talking animal, and to date no human group has been found who lacks a spoken language. We know from man's behavior that he is unique in his ability to receive and transmit this complex symbol system which classifies his experiences and allows him to problem solve as well as communicate with his friends. This process is so complicated that Teuber (Darley, 1967) states, ". . . . we simply do not know how the listener manages to analyze the stream of speech, structures it into phonemes and morphemes and comprehends strings of sentences according to syntactic rules. Nor do we seem to know how this understanding of speech, on all levels, is acquired by the normal child . . ." If this is true, one might question the audacity of individuals attempting to explain, evaluate and teach language and speech behavior.

For most individuals the acquisition of language and speech comes about with little thought and/or consideration as to how it developed. However, when the small child does not begin to respond appropriately when spoken to and/or use the speech of his linguistic community he is largely cut off from its activities and its members. Consequently, there is need to investigate the child's use (comprehension and production) of language and speech behavior, as well as other non-linguistic behaviors, for

329

those variables which may be interfering with acquisition and function of his code.

Language Behavior Described

The basic issue discussed in this chapter is that of assessing the language and speech behavior of children. However, before doing so let us briefly look at what the behavior is that we are going to be evaluating. Present day literature in the fields of psychology, linguistics, psycholinguistics, sociolinguistics, speech and language pathology, speech and semantics, to mention only a few, have attempted in their own way to define language and speech behavior. However, to give the reader a definition of this very complex behavior appears to the writer to be useless as well as impossible. It appears more relevant for those of us working with children's language and speech behavior to be cognizant of the common components and processes which make up this complex behavior than to confine ourselves to an inadequate definition. Let us look at some of the things which help us describe langauge structure and behavior.

Langauge components and processes:
    a. An acquired code
    b. A code with structure governed by rules,
       phonology, morphology, syntax
    c. A code which has meaning (semantics)
       meaning may or may not be rule—governed
          e.g., intonation of voice
    d. Used for problem solving, ordering and classifying our
       environment and experiences, communication
    e. Basically acquired in a linguistic environment through
       the sensory modalities of hearing, seeing and touching
    f. Basically expressed through speaking, writing and gestures
This list of possible components and processes which constitute the behavior we are writing about can almost be as infinite as the possible combinations of the symbols which make up the code. This list is not meant to be complete, nor all inclusive, but serves to point out some basic and salient features which need to be taken into consideration when talking about language behavior.

Language is, above all, a code for communicating meaning

from one individual to another. Communication as such involves salient situational dimensions. Initially, there is a *Sender* or composer of the message, usually the speaker himself (but sometimes the mother, brother or sister does the *speaking* for the child). Next, there is the *Receiver*, the person who listens to the sender and usually the person to whom the sender addresses the message. Then the *message* itself—the information which the sender intends to convey to the receiver. The message is put into some type of *code* (here we will concern ourselves only with the spoken language as the code, though sign language, writing, or smoke signals are alternatives) which is transmitted through a *channel* (e.g., air) to the listener, usually the receiver. The message is about something (the *topic*); and the exchange takes place in a particular place or *setting* (physical or psychological).

These situational categories are discussed by Chapman (1972) who characterizes each category by question: "Who said it?" (the sender). "Who'd he say it to?" (the receiver). "What'd he say?" (the message). "Did he phone it or write it?" (the channel). "Was it in English?" (the code). "What'd he talk about?" (the topic). "Where'd he say it?" (the setting). One of the questions which Hymes does not ask in this discussion of situations is "How'd he say it?" which might be logically answered by the listener as (unintelligibly, disfluently, inarticulately, harshly, etc.).

The latter question dealing with *how* the message was expressed is the one with which the speech and language specialist has spent most of his time looking for answers. Thus, he has focused most of his professional energies on the speech behavior (articulation defects) often at the expense of the broader scope of the communicative event. The basic point being made is that objectively describing the *whole* situational milieu allows the clinician to develop a more complete and honest perspective of the child's language behavior.

The Role of Language and Speech Assessment

When the child comes to the attention of the speech and language specialist for an evaluation it is usually because someone in his environment has noticed that he is responding differently with respect to language behavior (comprehension or production) than his peers in the mainstream society. The specialist then employs the tactics of a *detective* to get some answers to some strategic questions which revolve around the child's communication behavior. His primary concern is to evaluate the speech and language behavior of the child in order to establish a baseline communication functioning level and to develop a teaching or modification program when necessary.

The language and speech specialist's multi-faceted evaluation task centers around these basic questions:

1. What is the child's language and speech acquisition history?
2. What is the environment in which the child is being reared?
3. What sensory modalities are available to the child for language acquisition and function; and how are they used?
4. What need does the child have for using language?
5. What is the child's comprehension of the language spoken in his environment?
6. What is the child's production of the language?
7. What is the gap between the child's comprehension and production of the language?
8. What is the gap between the language abilities (comprehension and production) of the child and that of the language users in the community?
9. What related behaviors appear to be interfering with language acquisition and function? (e.g., attention, discrimination, perception, memory, motivation?)
10. What can be done to alleviate the language gap, if one exists, between the child and his peers in the community?

We can see from this list of questions that we need information about the child's current language behavior; the sensory modalities which are most useful to him in receiving linguistic information and producing it, and about the environment in which he exists with respect to the stimulation which he receives and the consequences the child experiences for his speech and language responses.

The Evaluation Process

Within the evaluation process, two primary areas are explored: 1) past development and sequence of acquisition of speech and language behaviors and 2) the child's present repertoire of behaviors (language and related). These are both explored because it is assumed that the information gained from these explorations will be relevant to future efforts of teaching and modification.

The Use of Behavioral History:

In exploring the child's behavioral history, the basic purpose is for determining the sequence in which the behavior was acquired. This is not a simple task, and is one in which language and speech clinicians are frequently not well trained. To acquire a set of complex behaviors presupposes that other behaviors were previously acquired which made possible the current behaviors. For this reason, we can justify spending time in exploring the child's history from pre-birth to the present. This sequential and developmental information with the observations of present behavior repertoires will constitute a baseline of behavior to be used by the clinician in initiating a teaching and modification program.

However, this is not the only purpose for gathering historical data on a child. Usually the language and speech specialist pursues the child's history for purposes of discovering the etiological factors, the causal events which would account for or could be designated as the variables responsible for the child's deficits in language and speech behavior. Etiology used in this manner, refers to causes which can be classified under such factors as physiological, neurological, intellectual, emotional and/or environmental, or any combination of two or more of them.

It is assumed that knowledge of the etiology will in some manner be helpful for specifying a course of teaching or modification procedures. But in fact does understanding the *cause* for the child's deviant behavior provide information on how to proceed to change his behavior? Two children with different *etiological labels* may exhibit similar or different behaviors when presented with a particular stimulus. But the clinician will determine what procedures to use on the basis of the child's behavior in the situation, not on the basis of an etiological category.

All too frequently, a *cause* is defined in terms of a label. Use of the label in this manner results in a circular kind of explanation which presents no information to the clinician. For example, to the question, "Why does he act (talk) like that?" the answer would be, "Because he is mentally retarded." In the response to the question, "Why is he mentally retarded?" the answer would be, "Because he acts (talks) like that." To follow this line of reasoning further, we would predict that when the child *talked right* he would no longer be mentally retarded, which we know is fallacious reasoning. Other variations of causal explanations exist. Frequently the etiology is inferred from the behavior, when for example, an individual suggests that a child must be brain damaged because he acts like a brain damaged child, such explanations may be misleading since there are children with known brain damage who act very little like other children with known brain damage, and other children with no evidence of brain damage who act very much like one would expect a brain damaged child to act, if one had categorized brain damaged children's behavior.

Regardless of the etiology then, with every language and speech impaired child, the clinician works with the same dependent variable—the behavior. The point is, a clinician cannot work with the past history of a child, he works with the present behavior. The clinician cannot work with etiology, he works with the present behavior. If a child lacks language and speech behavior due to an assumed brain damage, the clinician does not work with the damaged brain, he works with the behavior. In a similar manner, if the child is diagnosed as emotionally disturbed, the clinician does not work with the emotional disturbance, he works with the child's behavior. In all cases, the clinician observes what behaviors are present or lacking, and on the basis of these observations, designs procedures which use environmental events to change the child's behavior. The *causes* therefore, are of little help since the clinician bases his work not on the *causal* events, but on the current, observable events.

If in a language evaluation the examiner is interested in determining causal relationships for deviant behavior, this can only be done by making careful observations of the environment in which the child lives. Causes in this sense refer to events in the environment which are operating to maintain the child's deviant behavior. A careful analysis of the functional relationships between the child's behavior and the consequences of the behavior will provide the clinician with specific information as to what changes in the environment can be effective to result in changes in the child's behavior. The observations, to be useful, however, must include only observable events, and not inferences drawn on observations, since a clinician cannot work directly with inference any more than he can work directly on labels. If the observations are objective (free of observer inferences), the clinician will be able to isolate the events to be manipulated in order to effect change in the child's behavior.

With further regard to the past history of the child, what are the behaviors we are specifically interested in? Too frequently we have considered many things in the child's history which have little, if anything, to do with his speech and language function. Much of our attention has been directed toward asking questions of the informants with regard to *length of pregnancy; length of labor; sedatives used during labor* ad nauseam. The writer underscores a point here. *The role of the speech and language specialist is to evaluate and teach language and speech behavior, not to establish medical and psychological labels for children's behavior, or lack of it.*

The writer does not intend to give a case-history outline in the discussion here. There is a plethora of suggested model outlines in the literature (for those interested consult Darley, 1964). These history models place much of their emphasis on questions relating to a medical model which are directed toward organic pathologies with an intent to establish labels. Thus, the point is, do the questions which I ask of the informant give me information which allow for an understanding of the behavior I need to change? e.g., "When Jon was a baby did he make sounds and noises?" "Describe these sounds for me if you can." "Does Jon understand you when you give him a command like 'come'?" etc.

Developmental Scales

Instruments which are frequently used in conjunction with the history, or as extensions of the history, are developmental scales. For the most part we don't consider them as tests because they don't elicit direct samples of behavior to stimuli. This is especially true of the Vineland Social Maturity Scale (Doll, 1965) and the Verbal Language Development Scale (Mecham, 1959). Although the information may be very useful, the examiner needs to keep in mind that the norms originally established on the *VSMS* were done almost thirty years ago and as such may be somewhat out of date.

Vineland Social Maturity Scale (1965)

Purpose: The scale evaluates a progression of detailed social performances demonstrated by children as they mature toward independence as adults.

Age Range: 3 months of age to adulthood (25 years of age +).

Description: The scale is organized into one year age intervals, containing descriptions of behavior drawn from the following categories; self-help general, self-help eating, self-help dressing, self-direction, occupation, communication, locomotion, socialization. The examiner, in an interview setting with either the subject or a third person discusses the presence or absence of particular behavior at a given age level.

The scale can be administered to a third person, the subject need not be present. One of the major values of the scale is in parent interviewing. A double scoring procedure is available for situations influenced by factors extraneous to intelligence (such as motor crippling, emotional disturbances, situation factors).

Standardization: Standardization data has been obtained from 10 normal subjects, of each sex, for each age level from birth to 30 years of age. The sample was not large, instead the evaluation of the measure was based in a large part on the internal consistence of the scale.

Critique: The 1965 revision of the Vineland provides "new age" scores, reformulation of items, substitution of new items for those found unsatisfactory, and a clarified definition of items. In general the scale has not been changed; it has been refined and improved.

References: Doll, Edgar A. *Vineland Social Maturity Scale—Condensed Manual of Directions—1965 Edition.* Circle Pines, Minnesota: American Guidance Service, Inc., 1965.

Verbal Language Development Scale (1959)

Purpose: To assess a child's verbal language ability progressively.

Age Range: One month to 15 years.

The method of administrating this test is the informant-interview method. The informant may be anyone who knows the child intimately; however, the parent or the teacher is the preferred informant. The interviewer scores the informant's responses.

The total score for any given child is the sum of all full and half points. The total score can be converted to language age equivalent by referring to the conversion table in the back of the manual.

Description: There are 50 items which the informant is interviewed on, i.e., crows, laughs, or smiles at one month; expressive vocabulary of at least two words at age one; and, etc., until at age 15 he reads on own initiative; follows current events and discusses them with others.

Standardization: Item calibration and tentative normative scores were derived from a sample of 120 normal speaking children selected randomly from urban and rural areas. The sample included five boys and five girls on each of the 12 age levels on the scale.

Critique: The *E* has to rely entirely on the informant for the information. The *E* has to be somewhat subjective in scoring the test with plus, plus and minus, and minus.

References: Mecham, J. Merlin, *Verbal Language Development Scale,* American Guidance Service, Inc., Publisher's Building, Circle Pines, Minnesota, 1959.

Evaluation of Present Language and Speech Behavior

The second basic area explored in speech and language assessment, is the child's present behavioral repertoire. It is here that we are establishing a baseline of current behavior from which we will work with regard to teaching new behaviors, and modifying others. Language behavior is comprised of observable and recordable physical events; consequently, it is important that these events themselves be carefully observed and recorded, but it is also important to note under what circumstances they were ob-

Table X.1. Selected Tests of Language Behavior to Assess
the Structure and Content of Language

Language Structure	Tests
Phonology—Speech sounds	a. Templin-Darley Screening and Diagnostic Tests of Articulation b. Goldman-Fristoe Articulation Test c. The Deep Test of Articulation (McDonald) d. Developmental Articulation Test (Hejna) e. Fisher-Logeman Test of Articulation
Morphology—Word forms tenses, plurality possessive, comparative pronoun changes, prefixes, suffixes and Syntax—Word order phrase structure transformations	a. Test of English Morphology (Berko) b. Exploratory Test of Grammar (Berry & Talbot) c. Auditory Test for Language Comprehension (Carrow) d. Northwestern Syntax Screening Test (Lee) e. Evaluation of Grammatical Capacity (Menyuk) f. Grammatic Closure—subtest of ITPA (Kirk & McCarthy) g. Grammatical Comprehension Test (Bellugi-Klima) h. Analysis of spontaneous language samples i. Selected items from Peabody Language Development Kits (Dunn & Smith)

Semantics—Word meaning vocabulary (choice, variety and number) concepts (classifications, relational and logical)	a. Peabody Picture Vocabulary Test (Dunn)
	b. WISC: Vocabulary & Similarities subtest
	c. Binet: Vocabulary subtest
	d. ITPA: Auditory reception (Kirk & McCarthy)
	    Visual reception
	    Verbal expression
	    Manual expression
	    Auditory vocal association
	    Visual Motor association
	f. The Basic Concept inventory (Engelman)
	g. Boehm Test of Basic Concepts
	h. Analysis of spontaneous language samples
	i. Selected items from Peabody Language Development Kits (Dunn & Smith)

served. There are two types of observations which speech and language specialists usually make: (1) standardized and (2) non-standardized.

Standardized Observations

Standardized observations, which usually consist of formal tests, assess speech and language behavior, as well as some behaviors demonstrated in various psychological tests. Table X.1 categorizes some of the current (1972) and commonly used standardized assessment tools according to the particular aspect of the language structure and content assessed by the test. In the assessment session we ask the child to respond to some language tasks. These tasks have been arranged according to a language structure model. The child's responses (comprehension and production) need then to be compared to an established norm or criterion which gives information with respect to how different his language comprehension and production is from his peers in his language community. This information will help us to answer in part the questions regarding current language functioning. It is not the intent of the author to imply that all these tests be given each child. However, information from any one of the tests listed does assist us in establishing baseline information with regard to the child's performance in the areas specified.

Templin-Darley Screening and Diagnostic Test of Articulation

Purpose: The purpose of the diagnostic test is to obtain a detailed evaluation and description of a child's articulation. The purpose of the screening test is to assess the general adequacy of a child's articulation.

Age Range: From point of verbal identification of visual stimuli upward.

Description: The diagnostic test consists of 176 items; 50 of these may be used for a screening test. Spontaneous or, if necessary, imitated, production of all English consonants in initial, medial, and final positions in words, and of blends, diphthongs and vowels, is elicited by the presentation of 57 picture cards. In the diagnostic test, for each sound misarticulated, the child is given a clear auditory pattern of the sound in isolation, in isolation in a syllable, and in a word, and is asked to imitate it. Responses are scored as correct, substitution, omission, distortion, or *no response*. Errors are simply noted in the screening test. A final evaluation is made of the child's intelligibility in conversational speech, and instructions for analysis of results are provided.

The inclusion of norms and cut-off scores with the test enables the examiner to decide whether a child needs speech correction (diagnostic test) or to prescribe the nature of speech correction for children with articulatory problems (diagnostic test) .

Standardization: 480 children, ages 3–8 established norms and cut-off scores. Validity demonstrated by Jordan with 150 children ages 5–10. Test—retest reliability coefficients for the screening test ranged from .93 to .99.

Critique: Although the test does not consider coarticulation of speech sounds, it is a valuable screening and diagnostic tool, especially in its extensive normative data against which results can be analyzed.

Reference: Templin, M., and Darley, F. *The Templin-Darley Tests of Articulation.* Division of Extension and University Services, the University of Iowa, Iowa City, Iowa (1964) .

Goldman-Fristoe Test of Articulation (1969)

Purpose: To assess an individual's articulation of the consonant sounds.

Age Range: Three to six years.

Description: The test consists of thirty-five pictures depicting objects familiar to young children. In addition to naming the pictures, the children reply to questions about eight of them, resulting in a total of forty-four responses. All but one (zh) of the single consonants in English are evaluated in all positions, in which they are found, with a few exceptions. Although the test is not designed specifically to study vowel and diphthong production, all vowels and all but one diphthong (I) are present in the test responses, and deviations can be noted. Responses are scored in code as correct, substitution, omission, mild or severe distortion, dentalized production, or nasalized production. Stimulability is tested for defective sounds in isolation. There is a Sounds in Sentences Subtest to provide the clinician a systematic means of assessing speech sound production in a situation similar to conversational speech.

Standardization: Data not reported.

Critique: The test meets its criteria of accuracy, quick administration and high interest value. It has been found useful with children who have low attention spans.

Reference: Goldman, Ronald, and Fristoe, Macalvane, *Goldman-*

Fristoe Test of Articulation. American Guidance Service, Inc., Circle Pines, Minnesota. 1969.

The Deep Test of Articulation (1964)

Purpose: To assess articulatory adequacy in various phonetic contexts.

Age Range: From point of verbal identification of visual stimuli upward.

Description: The Picture Test consists of two sets of pictures mounted side by side, such that each picture can be turned individually. The child is to pronounce the adjacent pictures' names as one word. In this way articulation of each consonant sound is tested as it is followed by a vowel and preceded by every other consonant, and as it is preceded by a vowel and followed by every other consonant. There is also a Sentence Deep Test which utilizes reading responses to test articulation of speech sounds in various phonetic contexts.

Permits evaluation of overlapping, ballistic speech by testing articulation of speech sounds in representative phonetic contexts.

Standardization: Correlations between four different forms of a deep test ranged from .61 to .97. Validity and norms have not been established.

Critique: Despite the fact that it is time consuming to administer, the Deep Test permits a uniquely thorough evaluation of articulation of speech sounds in many phonetic contexts.

Reference: McDonald, Eugene T., *The Deep Test of Articulation.* Stanwix House, Pittsburgh, Pa. 1964.

Developmental Articulation Test (Revised, 1959)

Purpose: To assess consonant sounds on a developmental scale, testing them according to the various chronological age levels by which approximately 90 percent or more of children use sounds correctly.

Age Range: Three to eight years.

Description: There are one or more pictures on each card. These are presented to the child individually. When the *E* points to the picture the child is asked "What's this?" The test gives a composite picture of each child's use of sounds and assists the clinician in determining the child's age level relative to articulatory development.

Standardization: The information is not given.

Critique: The test makes no attempt to look at coarticulation of speech sounds. The pictures are dated and produced in poor color. Other tests of articulation are more free of stimuli variables.

References: Hejna, Robert F., Ph.D., *Developmental Articulation Test* (Revised, 1959), Speech Materials, Box 1713, Ann Arbor, Michigan.

The Fisher-Logemann Test of Articulation Competence (1971)

Purpose: To assess individual's phonological system by means of a distinctive feature analysis of articulation errors.

Age range: From point of verbal identification of visual stimuli upward.

Description: 109 picture stimuli are displayed on 35 cards. A single word response is evoked to demonstrate the child's articulation for each English phoneme, in each syllabic position and phonetic context to be tested. Each stimulus word contains the phoneme being tested, in conformity with the phonology of standard dialects. The occurrence of the phoneme in the stimulus word is systematized on the basis of syllabic function. The test words are common to the vocabulary of the age of the individual being tested. There is a screening form designed for rapid identification of children with articulatory difficulties, when only minimal time is available for testing.

A sentence test consists of 15 sentences which can be quickly administered to individuals who read. It tests every singleton consonant, in all syllabic functions compatible with English phonology, and every vowel phoneme of English.

Standardization: No data available.

Critique: The stimulus materials are well packaged. The record forms are easy to follow and record data on. The manual furnishes less experienced clinicians with a list of all phonic symbols and modifiers, with accompanying descriptions. Sample record forms illustrating specific procedures are included for both standard and dialect speakers. Considered by the writer as one of the best on the market for assessing articulation responses.

Reference: Fisher, Hilda B. and Logemann, Jerilyn A. *The*

Fisher-Logemann Test of Articulation Competence. Boston: Houghton-Mifflin Co. 1971.

Exploratory Test of Grammar (1966)

Purpose: To assess the child's production of morphological features.

Age Range: Five to eight years.

Description: The test involves using pictures of nonsense characters, animals, etc., with the examiner reading sentences which contain nonsense words. The examiner reads the sentences for each picture and the child is instructed to finish the last sentence (i.e., he is to give the nonsense word with the appropriate morphological feature added). E.G. "This is a nad. Now there is another one. There are two of them. There are two _____." (Correct response: *nads*). The morphological features tested are:

1) The plural and the two possessives of the noun.
2) The third person singular verb.
3) The progressive and the past tense verb forms.
4) The comparative and superlative of the adjective.

Standardization: Norms are not yet established. From preliminary studies the authors predict that the average five year old will complete successfully items I–V; the six year old, I–XIV (with one error); the seven year old, I–XX (with one error); and, allowing for one error, the average child of eight should be able to complete successfully all items.

Critique: The test is almost directly taken from Berko's *Test of English Morphology* (1961), with no obvious improvements. The plates have nonsense pictures which are in black and white and are not too exciting for young children. The test has little, if any, validity when used with mentally retarded children.

References: Berko, J., The Child's Learning of English Morphology, In *Psycholinguistics: A Book of Readings*, S. Saporta Ed., Holt, Rinehart, Winston, 1961.

  Berry, M., and Talbott, R., *Exploratory Test of Grammar.* 4332 Pinecrest Road, Rockford, Illinois. 1966.

Grammatical Comprehension Tests (1968)

Purpose: This test is designed to investigate a child's understanding of the syntax of language. Syntax being defined as the particular patterns of words, regularities, and relationships of words in a sentence.

Age Range: No particular age range is indicated by the author. The materials would appear to be appropriate for a child approximately two years of age to five or six years of age.

Description: The test consists of a series of pairs of statements. The child is asked to listen to a statement and then manipulate objects to demonstrate his understanding of the syntax of the statement. Key lexical elements are unchanged in the sentence pairs. Meaning of the statement is, however, different, due to syntactic, or word order, variations. Key lexical items are defined by showing the child appropriate objects prior to giving him the test. This test proposes a method of investigation syntax which the examiner can adapt to the specific diagnostic needs of a variety of situations.

Standardization: There is no standardization data.

Critique: The author asks that the measure be considered as a proposal. It is based on linguistic theory, psycholinguistic research and developmental studies of children's speech, but not all of the tests have been adequately explored nor have the tests been standardized. This measure represents an initial version of a tool for exploring a child's ability, as a listener, to understand syntactical relationships.

References: Bellugi-Klima, Ursula. *Evaluating the Child's Language Competence.* Urbana, Illinois: Illinois University National Coordination Center, National Laboratory on Early Childhood Education. 1968.

Auditory Test for Language Comprehension (1968).

Purpose: To assess auditory comprehension of language structure by children and to obtain information about the sequence in which children learn to comprehend the lexical and grammatical aspects of language.

Age Range: Three to seven years.

Description: The test consists of a set of plates, each of which contains one to three black and white line drawings. The pictures represent referential categories and contrasts that can be signaled by form classes and function words (nouns, verbs, adjectives, adverbs and prepositions), morphological constructions (er and ist to free morphs), grammatical categories (case, number, gender, tense, status, voice and mood), and syntactic structure (predication, complementation, modification and coordination).

The present form of the test comprises 123 items; each item assigned a point value of one for the purpose of scoring. The total score being the number of items passed. The manual has the stimulus items in Spanish as well as in English.

Standardization: 159 monolingual children seven to nine years of age, with I.Q.'s above 80, free from severe speech and hearing problems were administered the test. Their performance data was charted by dividing them into nine age groups each representing a six-month age span, and recording the age levels at which 60 percent of the children passed each item. The test was also administered to 40 children between the ages of two-six and six-six in order to standardize the procedure, revise specific items and to determine the order of presentation of the items.

Critique: Several of the pictures do not effectively illustrate the desired concept. When a child fails an item, the tester does not know if it is lack of knowledge of the item on the test, or factors such as perceptual problems. No guidelines for interpreting results are given, other than standardization data. The examiner is responsible for deriving a pattern of the child's errors by comparing the child's responses with the norms Carrow presents.

Reference: Carrow, Elizabeth, *Auditory Test for Language Comprehension.* (Exp. Edition) Austin, Texas, 800 Brazos Street, Southwest Educational Development Laboratory. 1968

Northwestern Syntax Screening Test (NSST) (1969)

Purpose: The NSST is a screening instrument designed to give a quick estimate of a child's syntactic development. Measures both receptive and expressive use of syntactic forms.

Age Range: Three to eight years of age.

Description: The NSST consists of forty pairs of sentences, twenty of which test receptive syntactic ability by having the subject listen and identify an appropriate picture, and twenty of which explore expressive syntactic skills by having the subject listen to a pair of statements and then at the presentation of a stimulus picture, repeat one of them. Materials consist of stimulus pictures and test forms.

Because the test is short it is appropriate for speech clinicians and diagnosticians who are screening large numbers of children. *Standardization:* The NSST was standardized on 344 children, ages zero to three and seven to eleven. The standardization population spoke only a Standard American dialect and were from middle and upper middle income communities only. No differences in males and females were noted in the standardization sample.

Critique: The examiner must be sure that the subject knows what the individual words in the stimulus sentence mean. He must know this before he can infer that a child's inability to select the correct stimulus picture is due to a lack of understanding the syntactic variables in a sentence pair as opposed to inability to understand the individual words in the sentence. The basic assumption that a child repeats only those syntactic forms that he can use is equivocal.

Reference: Lee, Laura L. *Northwestern Syntax Screening Test.* Evanston, Illinois: Northwestern University, 1969.

Illinois Test of Psycholinguistic Abilities—Revised

Purpose: The revised edition, as well as the original ITPA, was conceived as a diagnostic rather than a classificatory tool. Its object is to delineate specific abilities and disabilities in children in order that remediation may be undertaken when needed. Thus, the ITPA provides: a) a framework within which tests of discreet and educationally significant abilities have been generated; b) a base for the development of instructional programs for children. With this dual purpose the diagnostic teaching model serves not only as a model for evaluating learning problems but also as a model for selecting and programming remedial procedures. (The theoretical basis for such a measurement grew out of Osgood's language theory, 1957a, 1957b).

Age Range: Two-six to ten years of age.

The examiner should be qualified to administer intelligence tests or to follow the rigorous steps presented in the manual and observed giving the test at least ten times.

Description: The 1963 edition taps essentially the same abilities as the original ITPA but incorporates several additions as well as modifications in format and content. The following changes will be noted:

1. An additional ability has been tapped—Visual Closure Test, which fills a gap (visual-motor automatic function) in the experimental edition of the ITPA.

2. The new edition provides two tests which give supplementary clinical information. These are an auditory closure test and a Sound Blending Test, which supplement the grammatical closure test in tapping the auditory-vocal automatic function.

3. New norms extend the use of the battery up to ten years.

4. With the addition of the new tests and the increase of items in the subtests, the time required to administer the complete battery of tests has been somewhat extended, requiring from 45 to 60 minutes for an experienced examiner.

5. Changes in format and content have simplified the administration, reduced the number of objects to manipulate, and made it possible to package the materials in a smaller space.

6. Some terms have been changed to give more commonplace labels for the various functions examined. The following changes will be noted: a) the term "reception" has been substituted for the term "decoding" "auditory reception" for auditory decoding; visual reception for visual decoding; b) the term "organizing process" has been substituted for *association* which now applies only to the organizing, process at the representational level; c) the terms "visual sequential memory" and "auditory sequential memory" have been substituted for *visual sequencing* and *auditory sequencing;* d) the term "automatic level" has been substituted for automatic sequential level.

Description of the subtests of the ITPA. The twelve tests of the ITPA are described below:

1. Functions tested at the representational level.

   a. The receptive process (decoding).

      There are two tests at this level which assess the child's ability to comprehend visual and auditory symbols.

      (1) Auditory reception (auditory decoding). This is a test to assess the ability of a child to derive meaning

from verbally presented material. Since the receptive rather than the expressive process is being sampled, the response is kept at a simple level of *yes* or *no* or even a nod or shake of the head. The vocabulary becomes more and more difficult while the response remains at a two-year level. Similarly the automatic function of determining meaning from syntax has been minimized by retaining only one sentence form. The test contains fifty short, direct questions printed in the manual, i.e., Do dogs eat?

(2) Visual reception (visual decoding). It is a measure of the child's ability to gain meaning from visual symbols. In this test there are 40 picture items, each consisting of a stimulus picture on one page and four response pictures on a second page. The child is shown the directions, "See this?" Then the page of response pictures is presented with the directions, "Find one here." The credited choice is the picture which is conceptually similar to the stimulus. The other choices include pictures with varying degrees of structural (rather than functional) similarity or pictures which are associated with the stimulus or with the acceptable choice.

b. Organizing Process (association). At the representational level this process is represented by the ability to relate, organize and manipulate visual or auditory symbols in a meaningful way.

(1) Auditory-vocal association. This test taps the child's ability to relate concepts presented orally. The organizing process of manipulating linguistic symbols in a meaningful way is tested by verbal analogies of increasing difficulty (auditory receptives and vocal expressive is kept minimal). A sentence completion test is used; there are 42 orally presented analogies such as, "I cut with a saw; I pound with a _____."

(2) Visual-motor association. This is tapped by a picture association test with which to assess the child's ability to relate concepts presented visually. The child is presented with a single stimulus picture surrounded by four optional pictures, one of which is associated with the

stimulus picture. The child is asked, "What goes with this?" (sock is stimulus picture) "Which one of these?" (pointing to four optional pictures). The test is expanded at the upper level to provide visual analogies. "If this goes with this (pointing to each of a preliminary pair of pictures) then what goes with this?" (pointing to the central picture as before). The test consists of twenty items of the simpler form and twenty-two visual analogies.

Expressive Process (encoding). This process at the representational level involves the child's ability to use verbal or manual symbols to transmit an idea. There are two subtests, one requiring vocal and the other manual responses.

1. Verbal expression (vocal encoding). The purpose of this test is to assess the ability of the child to express his own concepts vocally. The child is shown four familiar objects one at a time (a ball, block, envelope, and button) and is asked, Tell me all about this. The score is the number of discreet relevant and approximately factual concepts expressed.

2. Manual expression (motor encoding). The test taps the child's ability to express ideas manually. In this test 15 pictures of common objects are shown to the child one at a time and he is asked to, Show me what we do with a _____. The child is required to pantomime the appropriate action, such as dialing a telephone or playing a guitar.

Functions Tested at the Automatic Level. The following subjects are basically "whole level" tests which measure the child's ability to perform automatic, nonsymbolic tasks. Two abilities are tested:

1. Closure. The following tests assess the child's ability to fill in the missing parts in an incomplete picture or verbal expression (the ability to integrate discreet units into a whole).

    a. Grammatic closure. This test assesses the child's ability to make use of the redundancies of oral language in acquiring automatic habits for handling syntax and grammatic inflections. There are 33 orally presented items accompanied by pictures which portray the content of the verbal expressions. The pictures are included to avoid contaminating the test with difficulty in the receptive process. The examiner points to the appropriate picture as he reads the given statements, i.e., Here is a dog; here are two _____.

b. Supplementary Test 1. Auditory closure. It assesses the child's ability to fill in missing parts which were deleted in auditory presentation and to produce a complete word. It is an automatic process. In this test the child is asked, "what am I talking about bo/le? There are 30 items ranging in difficulty from easy words such as "airpla/" to difficult ones such as "ta/le/ oon."

c. Supplementary Test 2. Sound Blending. This test provides another means of assessing the organizing process at the automatic level in the auditory-vocal channel. The sounds of a word are spoken singly at half-second intervals and the child is asked to tell what the word is applicable to younger children by including pictures, thus making the task less open-ended. At the upper levels the test has been extended by including nonsense words.

d. Visual Closure. This test assesses the child's ability to identify a common object from an incomplete visual presentation. There are four scenes, presented separately, each containing 14 or 15 examples of a specified object. The objects are seen in varying degrees of concealment. The child is asked to see how quickly he can point to all examples of a particular object within thirty seconds.

2. Sequential Memory. There are two tests to assess the child's ability to reproduce a sequence of auditory or visual stimuli.

a. Auditory sequential memory. This test assesses the child's ability to reproduce from memory sequences of digits increasing in length from two to eight digits. The examiner gives this at a rate of two per second instead of one per second on the Stanford-Binet and WISC and he is given a second trial. Two points are given if he gets it correct the first time and one if on the second trial.

b. Visual sequential memory. This test assesses the child's ability to reproduce sequences of nonmeaningful figures from memory. The child is shown each sequence of figures for five seconds and then is asked to put corresponding chips of figures in the same order. The sequence increases from two to eight figures and he is given two trials.

Standardization: The ITPA was normed on seven hundred children in five communities in the midwest. Only children whose I.Q.'s were between 84 and 116 (one standard deviation above and below the I.Q. norm) were used. No black or physically handicapped children, or students in parochial schools were used.

Critique: Test items are supposed to measure processes which must be intact and developed to a definite level for language to be forthcoming. But as Spradlin (1963) has pointed out, language itself is used to assess these processes. The value of the ITPA appears to be in the fact that various subtests explore different modalities semi-independently (auditory, visual, motor, vocal) at different points in processing (reception, expression). With exception of Grammatical Closure Sub-test it measures little with respect to language structure.

References: Kirk, S., McCarthy, J. and Kirk, W. *Illinois Test of Psycholinguistic Abilities* (Rev. Ed.) University of Illinois Press, Urbana, Ill. 1968.

Kirk, S., and McCarthy, J. The Illinois test of Psycholinguistic Abilities—an approach to Differential Diagnosis. *American J Ment Defic,* November 1961, 66, 3, 399–412.

The Houston Test for Language Development—Part I

Purpose: The present test was constructed to measure the development of language in children up to three years of age.

Age Range: Part I—Six to thirty-six months.

Description: At each age level items are presented that represent the various aspects of language, both from the broad classifications of reception, conceptualization, and expression to the more specific categories of melody, rhythm, accent, gesture, articulation, vocabulary, grammatical usage and dynamic content.

This test can be administered by speech clinicians by following the specific instructions in the manual.

Standardization: The test was administered to 113 white children, located in the greater metropolitan area of Houston, who were within a month of a critical birthday. They were equated as to age and sex. The study avoided bilingualism in the home, multiple births, institutionalized cases and observable mental or physical defects. The items were scored on a percentage basis and rearranged according to difficulty. Items were discarded that were too easy or too difficult, except retained if necessary to cover the range to be tested.

References: Crabtree, M., *The Houston Test for Language Development.* 10133 Bassoon, Houston 25, Texas, 1958. Part I.

The Houston Test for Language Development—Part II

Purpose: The purpose of Part II is to establish a basis for objective evaluation of language functioning in children.

Age Range: Part II—Three to six years.

Description: The following items are tested:

      I. Self-identity (Name and age)

     II. Vocabulary (Naming nouns, action words, adjectives and colors).

   III. Body Parts (Point to body parts named and also asked questions like "What do you hear with?"

   IV. Gestures (Show me your teeth; clap your hands)

    V. Auditory Judgment (Which is bigger, mother or baby?)

   VI. Communicative Behavior (Child uses miniature furniture and tells a story about it while playing with it)

  VII. Temporal Content (Based on material recorded in the preceding item)

 VIII. Syntactical Complexity (Use material recorded in Item VI)

   IX. Sentence Length (Material in Item VI)

    X. Prepositions (Take the rabbit and chair used in VI and have the child put the rabbit *in, under, behind, and in front of the chair*)

   XI. Serial Counting (Have child count)

  XII. Counting Objects (Have child count cards in front of him)

 XIII. Repetition of Speech Patterns (Say a word or sentence and have the child repeat it)

 XIV. Repetition of Melody Patterns (Child repeats vocal rises in pitch and loudness after the examiner)

XV. Geometric Designs (Have the child draw a circle, square, triangle, and diamond after the examiner)

XVI. Drawing (Have the child draw a house, tree, and person)

XVII. Verbalization While Drawing (Record all verbalizations of the child while he does items XV and XVI)

XVIII. Tells about Drawing (Have the child tell about the pictures he has drawn in item XVI)

Standardization: 215 white children located in the greater metropolitan area of Houston. (The rest is the same as Part I of this test under standardization).

References: Crabtree, M., *The Houston Test for Language Development.* 10133 Bassoon, Houston 25, Texas, 1958. Part II.

Peabody Picture Vocabulary Test (PPVT) 1965

Purpose: To assess an individual's comprehension vocabulary of single words.

Age Range: Two and one-half years to adult.

Description: Selected nouns and verbs are assessed by having the examiner ask the subject to choose one of the four pictures that best illustrates the key word in the phrase *show me* _____. The results show comprehension of single words without requiring a verbal response. There are two comparable forms of the PPVT; they can be administered and scored easily by a reasonably naive examiner. Results from raw scores can be converted to I.Q., percentile, and mental age by tables in the manual.

Standardization: Standardization was carried out on 4,012 white children in Nashville, Tennessee between the ages of two-six and eighteen years. The PPVT is a better indicator of current functioning than it is a predictor, and for speech and language specialists should be used only as a measure of comprehension vocabulary rather than as a measure of intelligence.

Critique: The PPVT can be easily and quickly administered. It is especially good for handicapped individuals, including M.R.'s and can be administered to any individual who can signal *yes* or *no.*

Reference: Dunn, L. M. *Peabody Picture Vocabulary Test Manual.* Minneapolis, Minnesota: American Guidance Service, 1965.

Full-Range Picture Vocabulary Test (1948)

Purpose: To assess comprehension vocabulary skills as indicated by simple pointing or verbal responses to verbal and picture stimuli.

Age Range: Two years to adult.

Description: The examiner shows one of sixteen picture cards (4 cartoon-like drawings per card) and says a test word. The subject is then to indicate the picture which best illustrates what the word means. If the subject is unable to point he is asked to indicate *yes* or *no* as the examiner points to each drawing. The test can be used with anyone then who is able to signal an interpretable *yes* or *no*. Each word is assigned a point-level representing approximately the mental age at which 50 percent of the individuals in a representative population would fail the word. There are two comparable forms.

Standardization: 589 individuals from two years of age to the adult level comprised the sample. The sample was drawn from the metropolitan Denver areas, as well as rural Nebraska. The population consisted mainly of white children, however, 80 Spanish and 80 Black children were also included in the norm sample.

Critique: The picture stimuli are considered very poor and children who have any visual perceptual difficulties will be penalized. From that stand point the PPVT is better, however, both have limitations related to its use with bilingual groups.

References: Ammons, R. B. and Ammons, H. S. *The Full-Range Picture Vocabulary Test.* Missoula, Montana: Psychological Test Specialists, 1948.

The Basic Concept Inventory (Field Research Edition) (1967)

Purpose: The basic purpose of this measure is to determine whether or not children are familiar with several basic concepts used in instruction and explanation in the first grade.

Age Range: Primarily preschool and very early elementary grade children, although it can be used with children as old as ten years of age.

Description: The Inventory consists of three basic parts. The examiner asks the subject to: (1) identify the various parts and aspects of pictures, (2) repeat statements and answer questions about those statements, (3) identify correct and incorrect hand patterns, phoneme (sound) patterns, and the repetition of digit patterns. In each case a model was demonstrated prior to asking the child to make the discrimination.

The Inventory is designed to be used with culturally disadvantaged preschool and kindergarten children, slow learners, emotionally disturbed children, and mentally retarded children. A teacher can administer the inventory if the purpose is to help design a remediation program; however, it is recommended that a trained person give the test if the results are to be used in formulating a diagnosis.

Standardization: There is no validity or reliability information published with this test. There are no age norms with the test. The author argues that this is a criterion-referenced measure, not a norm referenced achievement test. It measures whether a child does or does not have a skill; it does not evaluate the appropriateness of his having or not having that skill.

Critique: The criterion reference rationale makes this an excellent tool for use in designing a remediation program. The lack of validity or reliability information limits its usefulness at present as a diagnostic instrument.

In regard to the subjects for whom this test was designed, it should be noted that the language dialect of culturally disadvantaged, slow learners, emotionally disturbed and mentally retarded subjects *may* not be the same dialect as used in the test. In such a case the results of the Inventory mean only that the ability to express or understand a given concept is not present in a child's Standard English repertoire. This test does not, therefore, answer the question of whether or not the child understands or can use these concepts, but only can he handle them within his standard English repertoire.

References: Engelmann, Siegfried. *The Basic Concept Inventory-Field Research Edition.* Chicago, Illinois: Follett Educational Corporation, 1967.

Boehm Test of Basic Concepts (1970)

Purpose: To identify individual children whose overall level of concept mastery is low as well as to identify individual concepts with which large numbers of children may be unfamiliar.

Age Range: Kindergarten through second grade.

Description: The instrument consists of fifty pictorial items arranged in approximate order of difficulty and divided evenly between two booklets (25 items per booklet). Booklet 2 is more difficult than Booklet 1. Each item consists of a set of three pictures, about which statements are read aloud by the examiner. The statements (in sentence form) briefly describe the pictures and instruct the children to mark the one that illustrates the concept being tested.

This test was designed for use with groups of children in the classroom. However, it can also be used with prekindergarten age children and, in this case, it is suggested that it be administered individually and that the child be requested to point to the correct picture stimulus rather than marking it with a pencil.

Concepts can be grouped into context categories of: space, quantity, time and miscellaneous. The child's raw score can be converted to a percentile equivalent according to his grade level, socio-economic level and whether the test was administered at the beginning or middle of the year.

Standardization: The sample which served as a basis for the norms consisted of 3,517 kindergarten children, 4,659 first graders, and 1,561 second graders from 16 cities located across the United States. There was an attempt to include all socio-economic levels in the sample.

Critique: The test items were selected from relevant curriculum materials and represent concepts basic to understanding directions and other oral communications from teachers at the preschool and primary-grade level. It is easy to administer and allows the clinician to gain some information about basic language and concept comprehension through auditory stimulus presented in sentence form rather than in single words.

Reference: Boehm, Ann E. *Boehm Test of Basic Concepts.* New York: The Psychological Corporation, 304 E. 45th Street. (1970)

Concerns Relative to Vocabulary Testing

Most vocabulary tests select a small number of words which represent different levels of difficulty. Thus, subjects are ranked on their capacity to perform on these words. The words themselves are selected usually, only as representatives of all words at that level of difficulty. Miller and Yoder (1972) advocate assessing the vocabulary which is to be used in a particular teaching program. This attitude they believe to be quite wise when the setting is a preschool program or one involving children living in an institution. Vocabulary items used in a test should be organized into conceptual categories found to be necessary for general vocabulary development based on the functional needs of the child in his living environment.

There are some limitations to the current vocabulary and concept tests available today. The first is that all these tests, test vocabulary as a single item of information. Scoring is usually all or none with little opportunity to assess the type of error made. Some consideration to approximations to the totally correct response should be given. Tests need to be constructed which give consideration to the semantic features which constitute a lexical item. The construction of such a test is difficult, and probably is why there isn't any such instrument available today; consequently, it is best to use an informal testing procedure.

A second problem with current vocabulary tests is that not all children have the same experience and understanding of the conventions of pictorial (graphic) stimuli. Thus the use of three dimensional objects may in many cases be more appropriate than two dimensional stimuli.

One further comment which I have toward vocabulary testing is that all tests to date, test the meaning of a word in isolation, yet words are greatly affected by their use within a sentence. Whether this should be tested in the area of grammar or the area of vocabulary is an open question.

Nonstandard Observations:

In the nonstandard task, free language and speech samples may be tape recorded and evaluated through processes described by Loban (1963); Williams (1969); Labov (1970) and Lee & Canter (1971). The information from these non-standard measures are compared to the standardized tasks which have already been discussed. Recording the child's verbal interactions with his peers and adults in the environment provides information in the way language and speech are used in unstructured and non-stimulus specific situations. If the child is recorded in his *natural environments* and in the presence of familiar and unfamiliar persons, the clinician can determine how the child uses the language he has. This provides different information than that derived from standardized tests which are designed to tell us what the child knows about his language. If it is not possible to tape-record language samples, then the clinician can take random handwritten samples of the child's utterances. This type of sampling should be done in several settings, i.e., play with peers, interacting with an adult and so on. These types of observations are usually less reliable than those which are taken from a taped recording. When one has a tape recorded to refer to, it is possible to check unfamiliar constructions and usage more carefully, and the examiner is less likely to bias the sample with his own linguistic system, i.e., unconsciously correcting or filling in the child's utterances.

It is necessary to caution the individual who uses the less structured approach to gather language samples about some of the problems which might exist. Some children are shy of talking in the presence of a microphone and consequently may do less talking under these conditions than normally. They may also use a more formal style of talking that when they are unaware of a recording being made. Consequently, it is advised that little attention be drawn to the fact that the language and speech behavior is being recorded if this is at all possible. Another problem which frequently arises with analyzing recorded speech samples has to do with the accuracy of writing the protocols from the recordings. The adult speaker is prone to filter what he is hearing through his own language system. Therefore, he too frequently will write down what he thinks he hears, or what he thinks he should hear, rather than what the child has actually said.

The information which we can get from the recorded speech and language samples allows us to make comparisons with the information which we have from the structured and standardized test materials. The way in which a child may use various grammatical contrasts when asked to respond to stimuli in a structured test situation does not mean that he may be using these contrasts the same way in his conversational speech with his peers or his parents. There are times when children who are referred to the clinician for evaluation by a teacher or parent because of unusual language patterns, will perform within the expected range on the test materials presented. However, when examining the connected speech and language samples recorded in various situations and environments one finds many unusual patterns which may indicate that the child has learned some patterns appropriately for structured situations, but that the system he has available for use is not yet governed by the grammatical rules used by the mainstream speakers in his environment.

Another very valuable use of the conversational and free speech sample is that from these situations it is possible for the clinician and parent to establish information about the semantic intent of the spoken message given by the child. This has been brought to our attention most recently by Lois Bloom (1968) who investigated the syntactic development of young children. Judgements of semantic intent of utterances are based on observation of contextual cues (i.e., whom is the child addressing, objects he is playing with and other antecedent events to the utterance) and the child's behavior in speech events (i.e., sitting, running, throwing, etc.). By not taking the intent of the message into account the clinician too frequently loses valuable information about the child's communication abilities. For example, one might hear the child utter one word *Mama* a number of times. However, upon close observation we find that this word has multiple meanings in relation to some aspect of the child's experience. e.g.,

1. *Mama* used to point Mama out.
2. *Mama* said when looking at or pointing to objects associated with Mama.
3. *Mama* used in reference to events in which Mama is the agent. ("Mama cooking pudding.")
4. *Mama* used in reference to events in which Mama is the object. ("closing the door to hide Mama in the kitchen.") Bloom, 1968.

We can see from this illustration that a mere word count of this child would indicate that, in terms of vocabulary, we have one (1) word being used, and that it has occurred four (4) times. However, when we examine the situations in which the word was emitted we find the word "Mama" was used to communicate four different things. This type of information can be very helpful in establishing a language teaching program. For more information in this respect see Miller and Yoder (1972).

Analyzing Nonstandard Language and Speech Behavior

Several systems do exist for the evaluation of free speech samples. Myklebust (1965) has published the *Picture Story Language Test* which measures the adequacy of written responses, but with some modifications has applicability to spoken language as well. Three scales are used for this analysis:

(1) A productivity scale which involves the total amount of words in the protocol, the number of sentences and the mean length of each sentence.

(2) Syntax Scale which measures the correctness of the production in terms of syntax and morphology.

(3) Abstract-Concrete Scale—this is a scale which measures the content of the passage. Scoring is in relation to "meaning" with meaningless language being the lowest and abstract-imaginative language being the highest. Norms for this test run from seven years to seventeen years.

Johnson, Darley and Spriestersbach (1963), following in the tradition of McCarthy (1954) propose using the mean length of response as an index of linguistic complexity. Such a measure along with its companion, the mean length of the five longest utterances, is a very gross estimate of the level of language development. Brown (1968) claims that such a measure is a relatively accurate measure of complexity up to five morphemes. Again, though, sentence length does not tell the clinician where the child is having problems in his development of linguistic structure.

Also existing is the system for analyzing the structure of the child's utterances based upon an immediate constituent framework developed by Williams (1969). This procedure will give the examiner more information about the structure the child is using and is not using. Again, as in most linguistic analyses of free speech, this analysis takes a great deal of time.

Lee and Canter (1971) have devised very recently an effective way of measuring a child's syntactic development which is not as cumbersome as those mentioned above and will be discussed below.

Developmental Sentence Scoring (1971)

Purpose: To assess a child's syntactic performance in spontaneous speech.

Age Range: Three to seven years.

Description: A sample of the child's spontaneous speech is tape-recorded and analyzed. Fifty consecutive utterances are scored. An utterance is considered a sentence if it contains a subject and predicate, i.e., fifty complete, different, consecutive, intelligible, non-scholastic, utterances evoked from a child in conversation with an adult using stimuli such as pictures and toys which interest the child.

Since scoring every individual feature of a child's language sample would be so time-consuming as to be impractical, eight features would have been selected, based upon their early appearance in children's language and their developmental progression. Weighted scores are assigned to later developing forms. The eight features scored are: 1) indefinite pronouns and/or noun modifiers, 2) personal pronouns, 3) main verbs, 4) secondary verbs, 5) negatives, 6) conjunctions, 7) yes/no questions, 8) who questions. To account for unscored grammatical items (articles, plurals, possessives, prepositional phrases, adverbs, word order, etc.) an additional sentence point is added to the total sentence score, if the sentence is correct in all respects.

Standardization: Norms were established on a sample of 160 children between three and 6–11 years of age. They came from white, monolingual families. All children obtained I.Q. scores between 85 and 115 on the PPVT.

Critique: The DSS is a technique which can be easily learned and effectively applied. It allows for a qualitative description of children's language behavior and to date, is the best thing available for describing linguistic information taken from free speech samples.

Extra-Linguistic Variables Related to Language Use

Up to this point we have discussed the value of the case history and various standardized and non-standardized procedures to assess the child's current level of language functioning. The child's inability to perform well on a task presented to him may not be due to his not knowing the information asked for, but rather because of a break down of one of the following variables:

Attention
Memory
Perception
Discrimination
Motivation

Because of the importance of these variables to the results obtained on any evaluation procedure (standardized or non-standardized), each of these needs to be discussed relative to the assessment results.

One characteristic of many speech and language disordered children is failure to attend to stimuli. Preoccupation with irrelevant stimuli, daydreaming, withdrawal, and inability to recall what has been presented often interferes with the child's ability to function adequately in communication activities as well as acquisition processes. Since paying attention to the clinician and the learning task is fundamental if the child is going to learn language, describing his attending responses (or lack of) in descriptive terms relative to the stimuli and in terms of frequency of occurrence of such allows us to establish a baseline of attending behavior. Hewett (1968, p. 32) presents an *Attention Level Inventory* which may be helpful to clinicians in recording the attending behavior of the child they are evaluating. Extensive information on this subject can also be taken from Haring (1968). The examiner usually does not need to have a list of questions in front of him regarding the attending behavior of the child since these are usually relatively obvious. However, the author appeals to the examiner to record his observations well, so that he is able to make some specific comments with regard to the child's attending behavior. The observations made in this respect will often direct us to examine other variables which may account for the inattentiveness, e.g., hearing loss, visual problems, short memory span, and so on.

Assessing Perception, Discrimination and Memory via the Sensory Channels.

In looking at variables such as perception, discrimination, and memory as they relate to language and speech behavior, it appears reasonable to assess their function within the context of the sensory modalities. This means assessing the child's ability to process incoming and outgoing stimuli by way of auditory, visual, and tactile channels.

It is always necessary and important to have a child evaluated by an audiologist, otologist, ophthalmologist, neurologist, or other specialists to make a valid assessment of suspected sensory acuity problems. However, the child who has not performed well on stimulus tasks presented through various sensory channels may not have done so because of a break-down in end-organ sensory functioning. That is to say, he received the stimulus but was unable to understand it or he was unable to differentiate it from a similar or related stimulus. The first is related to perception and the latter to discrimination ability. This is true of visually, auditorially and tactually presented material. A child who is not blind is able to see what is presented to him, but may not be able to structure the visual stimuli in a meaningful way or visually discriminate between two similar stimuli.

Take for example the child, who when asked to *please bring me the book from the table,* brings a book from a chair beside the table. From previous observation we know he understands the lexical item *book* and the verb *bring.* The fact that he brought a book to the examiner rather than the other adult in the room leads us to believe he comprehends the personal pronoun *me,* although we cannot be completely sure about this. The child may have brought the book to *me* because I (the examiner) was the sender of the message. This, however, could be checked out in other ways and in other circumstances. There are two things which we will need to check out with regard to the child's incorrect response. The first, is whether he perceives tables and chairs differently or the same. Secondly, whether his inability to carry out the command was due to a memory problem.

To check out the first question will require our asking him to do various tasks in which the only variable changed will be the items *table* and *chair*. If we find that he does not perceive these as different we will have information upon which to make a judgement relative to his ability to discriminate between these two items of furniture which have four legs and are both made of wood. This can be checked out further by setting up situations which allow the child to make a discrimination between a table and a more different item of furniture such as a *piano*. It is crucial to future program planning to find out what variable is interferring with the child's ability to comprehend the task.

If the child readily differentiates between table and chair we will seek to explore the area of memory abilities. That is, did the original command list more information than the child was able to retain in memory storage. To check this out we will need to reduce the number of auditory stimuli until the child is able to respond correctly, i.e., simplify the command to fewer pieces of information. Consequently, the examiner will have information with regard to the number of items the child is processing (comprehending) correctly via the auditory channel.

Memory per se can be further tested in other ways. There are subtests of the *ITPA* and *WISC* for example for assessing both auditory and visual memory. These sub-tests of memory, like many others, ask the child to repeat a sequence of digits or arrange a set of geometric designs in a certain order. These tests, which are assessing basically non-linguistic information, have no sequential dependence between items. Sequential dependence between items is both characteristic and critical of language and speech behavior. If we are concerned about the child's memory abilities as they relate to language then it certainly appears more reasonable to assess this ability with linguistic material. Differences have been demonstrated for different kinds of material used in assessing memory span, i.e., digits, random words and sentences (Kluppel and Bernthal, 1970).

The type of material used for assessing memory then becomes important. Kluppel's work indicates that sentences are remembered best. This is due to the facilitation effect of the grammar. Digits are remembered next best due to the restricted set (i.e., a 1–9 range). Random words are most difficult to remember and this is undoubtedly due to the fact that this represents an open set (i.e., an unlimited number of items).

At this point there is little clear-cut information relating memory deficits to language impairment, although it appears obvious that memory must play a large part in comprehension and production of language. It is therefore important that when we suspect the child is having difficulty performing various language tasks because of reduced memory capacity, that we check out his memory facilities both through auditory and visual modalities. Secondly, we must use the materials which will prove most valid to the behavior we are assessing.

The examiner must structure the testing situations carefully in order to insure that he is not confusing either the information received from the specific modalities he is assessing or the psychological variables within the modality. If, for example, the examiner commands the child to *come here* while at the same time giving him a beckoning gesture, he does not know whether the child is responding to the verbal-auditory stimulus or the motor-visual stimulus. Or as in the earlier example, the command *bring me the book from the table,* if given while pointing to the specific book on the table and then gesturing toward himself. The child may not have comprehended one auditory signal, but because of careful visual attending was able to carry out the command correctly.

The child's inability to perform certain tasks because of an auditory processing break-down does not mean that he may not use some auditory cues when accompanied by certain visual cues. Consequently, when the child has been checked out for his performance level on a single modality we should also check him for responses to combined or associated modality use. Most of us have learned our language through multiple modalities and function well this way. Who of us has not heard the remark by an individual who has worn corrective lenses most of his life say, "I can hear better with my glasses on."

Although we have talked mostly in this section about the child's

Table X.2. Systematic Record of Behavior

Stimulus: A-uditory V-isual M-otor	Specific Stimulus	Response: V-ocal N-one M-otor	Specific Response	Consequences: S-ocial C-onsumable O-bject N-one	Specific Consequence
Example #1					
V	Picture—boy playing with dog	V	Boy—doggie	S	Yes—a boy is playing with his dog
A-V	Picture & statement—The boy is playing with his dog	V	Boy play doggie	S	Very good—the boy is playing with his dog
Example #2					
A	Command—Please come here	M	Child sits on chair	N	Ignores response
A-V-M	Command with appropriate gesture	M	Child goes to clinician	S-O	Hug and plastic trinket
Example #3					
A	[V] sound produced	N	Child just stares at clinician	N	Fine—let's try again
A-V-M	"Do this"—puts teeth on lower lip	M	Child puts incisors on lower lip	S	

A-V-M	Put your teeth on your lower lip again and make the sound [V]	V-M	Child produces sound correctly	S	Fine
A-V	[V] Sound produced, visual model present	V	Child produces sound correctly	S-C	Very good—gives child sip of orange drink
A	[V] Sound—no visual model	V	Child produces sound correctly	S-C	Very Good—pat on the head with orange drink
Example #4					
A	[θ] Sound produced	N	Child stares at clinician	N	
A-V-M	"Do this"—puts tongue between teeth	M	Child protrudes tongue between teeth	S	Good—that was just right
A-V-M	Put your tongue between teeth again and make this sound [θ]	V-M	Child produces sound correctly	S	Very good
A-V	[θ] Sound produced with visual model	V	Child produces sound correctly	S-C	Very good—gives child sip of orange drink
A	[θ] Sound—no visual cues	V	Child produces sound correctly	S-C	Fine—sip of orange drink

comprehension of auditory and visual stimuli we are, nonetheless, interested in his *response mode* to these stimuli. The following table shows what we have been discussing with respect to modality assessment. We are looking at this from the standpoint of both information intake, and expression. We, therefore, look at comprehension through response modes as well as record what consequences may have come about as a result of the response.

In looking at the modality of input in Table X.2, the kind of input (stimulus) needs to be recorded with regard to the complexity of the material and the number of trials to success. With regard to response mode we are interested in the channel of output as well as type of output behavior, e.g., sounds, words, sentences spoken; gestures; written words, etc.

Additional Comments on Auditory Discrimination:

The effect of auditory discrimination ability on speech (articulation) and language behavior has long been questioned. For years, however, the speech and language specialist has assessed the child's auditory discrimination abilities and on the basis of his behavior has concluded that his inability to distinguish between certain phonemes could account for deviant speech patterns (Cohen and Riehl, 1954; Schiefelbusch and Lindsey, 1958; Prins, 1963; Wepman, 1960; Aungst and Frick, 1964; and others) but the findings have been regarded as equivocal at best. Weinler (1967) concluded from his work that a meaningful positive relationship exists between children who have severe articulation defects and auditory discrimination. Citing several standardization studies (Templin, 1943, 1957; Wepman, 1958), Weinler also concludes that the ability to distinguish between speech sounds auditorily and the development of articulatory skills are age-related variables, and that a positive relationship between auditory discrimination and articulation is found almost invariably in studies of children below nine years of age. There is still a great deal of research which needs to be done in this area. The tests which are presented for the reader's investigation are Wepman, 1960; Templin, 1957, and Goldman, Fristoe and Woodcock, 1970. There are other tests of auditory discrimination; however, those listed have been selected because of their most common usage. Baratz 1969, 1970 indicates that a cultural bias prevails among tests of auditory discrimination as well as other language tests; consequently, this needs to be kept in mind when testing children who speak a dialect other than standard English.

Auditory Discrimination Test (1958)

Purpose: To identify those children from five to eight years of age with auditory discrimination deficits.
Age Range: Five to Eight years.
Description: Each form of the test contains 40 items comprising 40 three-to-five letter words of the CVC variety. On each form the vowel is identical in 36 of the word pairs. The examiner reads the word pairs and the child indicates whether the words in each pair are the same or different. Ten word pairs are identical as false positive choices to determine test validity.
Standardization: Calculations of phoneme difficulty on the two forms resulted in a rank order correlation of .67 for 214 cases.
Critique: The test provides a quick and accurate assessment of auditory discrimination among children from five to eight years of age.
References: Wepman, Joseph M. Auditory Discrimination, Speech, and Reading. El. Sch. J., 1960, *60*, 325–333

Test of Auditory Discrimination (1970)

Purpose: To assess speech-sound discrimination ability.
Age Range: Three years, eight months to seventy years and over.
Description: The test provides a measure of auditory discrimination under various listening conditions considered to be ideal. It is comprised of three parts. The training procedure familiarizes subjects with the word-picture associations to be used in the two subtests and permits the examiner to establish the presence of these associations. The Quiet Sub-test provides a measure of auditory discrimination in the absence of background noise. The Noise Subtest provides a measure of auditory discrimination in the presence of distracting background noise. The Training Pro-

cedure is presented orally by the examiner. However, a magnetic tape player is used, to present the instructions and stimulus statements for the two subtests.

Standardization: The sample included 745 subjects ranging from three to eighty-four years of age. Performance differences were noted as a function of subject age and sex and between the two types of tests. The differences due to sex were not expected and are of small magnitude. Consequently, only a single set of norms for both male and female subjects is used.

Critique: The test allows for finding the types of listening environments which may present problems to individuals. The recorded stimuli have been found to present problems to young subtests. The child may give erroneous information based on the task rather than because of true discrimination problems.

References: Goldman, Ronald, Fristoe, Macalane and Woodcock; Richard W., *Test of Auditory Discrimination.* American Guidance Service, Inc., Circle Pines, Minnesota 1969.

Assessing Environmental Consequences

Related to the observations and records we make regarding the child's sensory modalities, we need to look at what environmental consequences have been brought about through the language responses of the child. Human behavior customarily occurs in the presence of a specific, although complex, stimulus, and does not occur when the stimulus is absent. A man, for example, will not stop his car at the corner if the light is green, but will stop if the light is red. Both lights are stimuli in the presence of which different responses are emittted; a child will not ask for a toy placed on a high shelf if he is alone in the room. However, if one introduces another stimulus, and in this case, another individual, the probability of his asking is quite high. The evaluation of the environment for language and speech behavior should, therefore, be structured to maximize the probability that the specific behaviors of interest will occur. For a complete description of behavior, the clinician will need observations pertaining to the kinds of events which follow the omission of behavior as well, for example, the consequences of behavior. Using the example above of the child who would request a toy from an adult, reveals the possibility of several consequences. For instance, the child's request might be followed by the adult's reaching for the toy and giving it to him. This consequence might increase the probability that in future similar situations the child will emit a similar request. On the other hand, if the child's request has been followed by no consequence, that is, no response from the adult, or an aversive response such as telling the child to *shut up*, the probability that the request behavior will occur in future similar situations is decreased.

The point here is that the emission of behavior is a function of both antecedent and consequent events. Thus, for developing teaching and modification procedures, information on what antecedent and consequent events decrease and increase the frequency of emission of language and speech behavior, is of prime importance. Observations of effects of consequent events should be made apart from the base behavior. That is, it is extremely difficult to observe and record accurately both the antecedent and consequent events as well as the child's speech and language behavior. It is necessary, therefore, to set up multiple observational sessions to record the effects of antecedent and consequent events. These observations are particularly relevant for determining what events in the environment are acting to maintain the child's present behavior repertoire. Once the behaviors have been accurately identified and described, the clinician will have specified which behaviors need to be trained, which behaviors are present and can be used as a basis for beginning training and teaching, and which behaviors are present but need to be eliminated because they are incompatible or interferring with the teaching and modification of language behaviors.

Assessing Production Variables

The child's inability to communicate effectively with his peers may be due to certain physiological reasons. Due to malfunctioning of the oral musculature (lips, tongue and velum) brought about through paralysis or mal-development, the child may not be able to produce the sounds and/or sound combinations necessary to form well-articulated words. It may also be that the child is not capable of building up sufficient breath pressure for producing sustained vocalization. To adequately assess these abilities, the clinician should and must use the services of other allied professions. Giving simple acoustic descriptions will not suffice with regard to setting up a remedial or teaching program for most children who have a dysarthria or post surgical insufficiencies as a result of a cleft of the lip and/or palate. There are devices available today which assist the clinician in assessing the physiological components necessary for speech.

For the clinician and teacher interested in the instrumentation and protocol needed for assessing glottal and supra-glottal valving, diadochokinesis, prosodic elements and pulmonary functions during speech for dysarthric individuals, read Netsell and Hixon, 1971. For the most part the evaluation should be conducted by an individual who has the objective data-gathering equipment available to him. Even though the clinician has an idea of what may or may not be involved as the interfering variable with respect to the dysarthric patient, it is best to seek the advice of the specialist in order to maximize patient service, and minimize time and effort on the part of the clinician and subject receiving treatment.

The child who has a sizeable vocabulary, good syntactic structure, along with adequate articulation may still have communication difficulties with his peers because of problems connected with speech dysfluency. In some cases the dysfluent responses are quite severe and have been referred to as stuttering. Evaluating the child's speech responses and establishing the number, type and frequency of dysfluencies as well as under what conditions the child is dysfluent appear to be the most reliable measures available today.

However, the literature in this area remains equivocal today. VanRiper (1971) considers stuttering to be *primarily a disorder of the temporal aspects of speech and not of the articulatory, phonatory or symbol functions.* His review of the state of the art in dysfluency is recommended for the clinician who is concerned with the exploration of how best to describe and measure the complex of symptoms which are inherent within the ruberic stuttering.

Language Deviancies vs. Differences

Increasingly, persons concerned with educational intervention programs of handicapped children have turned to the speech and language clinician for advice or assistance on problems associated with handicapped children. The speech and language specialist has basically been involved in the past with disorders or deviances in language (structure and content) and speech (articulation, fluency, voice). Quite recently he has also been called upon to assist with what might be done for the language development and function of the Bi-cultural child, apart from the types of detailed disorders we have discussed so far.

In evaluating the speech and language behavior of the child who lives in a culture different from that of the mainstream society, one should not expect that he will respond to and use the language of the mainstream society, but that his language behavior will reflect the differences of his personal community. With the speech and language specialist's primary experiences in disordered or delayed, language behavior, it is not surprising that he has been prone to look at the child from a different culture as having deficient speech and language behavior. However, the mistake which the specialist has made in coming to this conclusion is that he has not recognized that our standard speech and language tests are subject to cultural biases (Severson and Guest, 1970; Baratz, 1970).

This issue of deficiency-difference interpretation, has been a major challenge when the speech and language specialist has tried to formulate a viewpoint on the language behavior of poverty children. How can one best differentiate deficiencies from differences? If deficiencies do exist, how can they be dealt with? If differences are the key problem, who is trained adequately to identify and deal with them?

One position that may reduce some of the confusion raised by the deficiency-difference issue is to insist upon a more rigorous definition of what qualifies as a language deficiency. This can be done, as discussed elsewhere in this chapter, by assessing the child's language functioning abilities with standardized and non-standardized tasks. If he does not meet the functioning criterion established by his own community of speakers he can be considered as having a deficient language system. This may be reflected in both comprehension and production of the demands for using some mainstream version of a language (as standard English would be), but can meet the demands of another community (such as the use of *Black* English; see Labov, 1970) ; this, then, is a case of language difference.

It is clear that a different set of assumptions would underly our work with the linguistically different as compared to the linguistically deficient child. Our focus on the deficient language is primarily a developmental one. What so-called *basics* of language does the child possess, and what level of achievement might we hope to gain relative to his entrance into some speech community? This is the thinking which we most typically exercise with the mild to moderately retarded child, when the aim is to teach him enough language so that he can get along in society. The linguistically different child on the other hand, already possesses the basics of language and has a normally developed system to meet the demands of his primary speech community. Thus, our goal, rather than being one of basic development, is one of parallel development along the lines of an additional linguistic system. To understand the basic capabilities of the language deficient child one needs information about the etiologies of language deficits, development of language, and how to modify and change behavior. By contrast, perhaps the most important thing for the specialist in language differences is a knowledge of the contrasts between a target language or dialect and the child's existing language or dialect. This calls for knowledge and information about the existing dialect being used by a child and the understanding that dialects by their very genesis may have evolved to accomplish different communicative tasks, and thus are to be preserved.

Obviously, this line of reasoning presents a formidable challenge, since the specialist in language differences will have to become knowledgeable (but not necessarily a user) of the details of one or more language communities other than his or her own.

Thus, we need to know more of the contrasts between the communicative aspects of standard English and, say, the language of New York Puerto Ricans, of Chicanos, of American Indians, and inner-city children, to name a few. The implication for recruiting minority group members as speech specialists seems obvious here.

Although persons such as Labov (1970), Baratz (1970), and Severson and Guest (1970) have pointed out that most of our strategies for language assessment are culturally biased, a careful consideration of the deficiency-difference contrast will enable us to use some of these strategies with less error. If, say, an articulation test were carefully used, it would allow us to see what linguistic differences on this level exist in a Bi-cultural group, thus helping the specialist to plot the course of instruction. Moreover, such tests could be used at various stages of instruction as an index of progress in developing the additional language or dialect system. Ironically, the more culturally biased such tests are, the more benefit they will be in this case, *as long as they are used as a basis for describing differences instead of deficits.* For further discussion of this issue see Yoder (1970).

Over and above what has already been said about the assessment and evaluation process there are some points which the examiner of language and speech behavior should keep in mind.

1. Children, especially the very young, respond inconsistently in testing situations. Consequently, it is necessary to evaluate their language and speech responses on a test-retest basis, keeping conclusions and interpretations tentative.

2. It is most important, above all, to observe and record the way in which the child we are evaluating goes about solving the task which we have presented him, as well as keeping a good record of what response he gave to a given stimulus. Too frequently the examiner is only concerned with whether the response is correct or incorrect, rather than what the response was, e.g., to the stimulus question which appears on the *WISC* "How many in a dozen?" the response *eggs* rather than the correct number or even an incorrect number response, may be giving us information about associations and processing behavior. Nonverbal problem solving tasks may be much more easily accomplished than verbal tasks; this needs to be noted.

3. Evaluation and assessment of speech and language behavior is an ongoing process even after the examiner believes he has established relatively reliable baseline information upon which a teaching program may begin. The child is always measured against his own baseline as well as the norm of the society in which he lives. A realistic target behavior must be kept in mind, based on the child's need for communicative skills.

REFERENCES

Ammons, R. and Ammons, H.: *The Full-Range Picture Vocabulary Test.* Missoula, Montana, Psychological Test Specialists, 1948.

Aungst, L. and Frick, J. V.: Auditory discrimination ability and consistency of articulation of /r/. *J Speech Hear Dis, 29:*76–85, 1964.

Baratz, J.: A Bi-Dialectal Task for Determining Language Proficiency in Economically Disadvantaged Negro Children. *Child Development 40:* 889–901, 1969.

Baratz, J.: Teaching Reading in an Urban Negro School System. In F. Williams (Ed.) *Language and Poverty: Perspectives on a Theme.* Chicago, Markham Publishing Co. 1970.

Bellugi-Klima, Ursula: *Evaluating the Child's Language Competence.* Urbana, Illinois, Illinois University National Coordination Center, National Laboratory on Early Childhood Education. 1968.

Berry, M., and Talbott, R.: *Explanatory Test of Grammar.* 4332 Pinecrest Road, Rockford, Illinois. 1966.

Berko, J.: The Child's Learning of English Morphology, In *Psycholinguistics: A Boook of Readings,* S. Saporta Ed., Holt, Rinehart, Winston, pp. 359–377, 1961.

Bloom, L.: *Language Development: Form and Function of Emerging Grammars.* Doctoral dissertation, Columbia University, 1968.

Boehm, A.: *Boehm Test of Basic Concepts.* New York, The Psychological Corporation, 304 E. 45th Street. 1970.

Brown, R.: The development of questions in child speech. *J. Verbal Learning Verbal Behavior. 7:*279–290, 1968.

Carrow, E.: *Auditory Test for Language Comprehension,* (Exp. Edition) Austin, Texas, Southwest Educational Development Laboratory. 1968.

Chapman, R. S.: Some Simple Ways of Talking About Normal Language and Communication. In McLean, J. E., Yoder, D. E. and Schiefelbusch, R. L.: *Language Intervention With the Retarded: Developing Strategies.* Baltimore, University Park Press, 1972.

Cohen, J., and Riehl, C.: Relations of speech-sound discrimination ability to articulation-type speech defects. *J Speech Hear Dis, 28:*187–190, 1963.

Crabtree, M.: *The Houston Test for Language Development* Part I and II 10133, Bassoon, Houston 25, Texas. 1958.

Darley, F.: *Diagnosis and Appraisal of Communication Disorders*. New Jersey, Englewood Cliffs, Prentice-Hall, Inc. 1964.

Darley, F. L. (ed.) : *Brain Mechanisms Underlying Speech and Language*. New York, Grune and Stratton, pp. 204–205, 1967.

Doll, E. A.: *Vineyard Social Maturity Scale-Condensed Manual of Directions— 1965 Edition*. Circle Pines, Minnesota, American Guidance Service, Inc., 1965.

Dunn, L. M.: *Peabody Picture Vocabulary Test Manual*. Minneapolis, Minnesota, American Guidance Service, 1965.

Dunn, L. and Smith, J.: *Peabody Language Development Kits* Minneapolis, American Guidance Service 1965, 1967, 1968, 1969.

Englemann, S.: *The Basic Concept Inventory-Field Research Edition*. Chicago, Illinois, Follett Educational Corporation, 1967.

Fisher, H., and Logemann, J.: *The Fisher-Logemann Test of Articulation Competence*. Boston, Houghton-Mifflin Co. 1971.

Goldman, R., and Fristoe, M.: *Goldman-Fristoe Test of Articulation*. American Guidance Service, Inc., Circle Pines, Minnesota, 1969.

Goldman, R., Fritoe, M. and Woodcock, R.: *Test of Auditory Discrimination* American Guidance Service, Inc., Circle Pines, Minn. 1970.

Haring, N.: *Attending and responding*. San Rafael, California, Dimensions Publishing Co., 1968.

Hejna, R., Ph.D.: *Developmental Articulation Test* (Revised) Speech Materials, Box 1713, Ann Arbor, Michigan, 1959.

Hewett, F.: *The Emotionally Disturbed Child in the Classroom*. Boston, Allyn and Bacon, Inc. 1968.

Hymes, D.: The Ethnography of Speaking. In T. Gladwin and W. Sturtevant (eds.) , *Anthropology and Human Behavior*. Washington, D.C., Anthropological Society of Washington, 1962.

Johnson, W., Darley, F., and Spriestersbach, D.: *Diagnostic Methods—Speech Pathology* New York, Harper and Row, 1963.

Kirk, S., and McCarthy, J.: The Illinois Test of Psycholinguistic Abilities— an Approach to Differential Diagnosis. *Am J Ment Defic, 66*:399–412, 1961.

Kirk, S., McCarthy, J. and Kirk, W.: *Illinois Test of Psycholinguistic Abilities* (Rev. Ed.) Urbana, University of Illinois Press, 1968.

Kluppel, D., and Bernthal, J.: Auditory Short-term Memory and Children's Language Behavior. Paper presented at American Speech and Hearing Association, November, 1970.

Lee, L.: *Northwestern Syntax Screening Test*. Evanston, Illinois, Northwestern University, 1969.

Lee, L., and Canter, S.: Developmental Sentence Scoring: A Clinical Procedure for Estimating Syntactic Development in Children's Spontaneous Speech. *J Speech Hear Dis, 36*:315–340, 1971.

Loban, W.: The Language of Elementary School Children. *Nat'l Council of Teachers of English, Research Report No. 1*, 1963.

Labov, W.: The Logic on Nonstandard English. In F. Williams (ed.) *Language and Poverty: Perspectives on a Theme.* Chicago, Markham Publishing Co. 1970.

McCarthy, D.: Language Development in Children. In L. Carmichael (Ed.) *Manual of Child Psychology.* New York, John Wiley and Sons, Inc. 1954.

McDonald, E.: *The Deeep Test of Articulation.* Pittsburg, Stanwix House, 1964.

Mecham, M.: *Verbal Language Development Scale,* Circle Pines, Minnesota, American Guidance Service, Inc., 1959.

Menyuk, P.: *Sentences Children Use.* Research Monograph No. 52. Cambridge, Mass., The M.I.T. Press, 1969.

Miller, J. and Yoder, D.: A Snytax Teaching Program. In J. E. McLean, D. E. Yoder and R. L. Schietelbusch, *Language Intervention with the Retarded: Developing Strategies.* Baltimore, University Park Press, 1972.

Myklebust, H.: *Picture Story Language Test* New York, Green and Stutton. 1965.

Netsell, R., and Hixon, T.: Speech Res. Lab., Prog. Rep. No. 1, Neurol. & Rehab. Hosp. Univ. of Wis. 1971.

Osgood, C. E.: In *Contemporary Approaches to Cognition.* Cambridge, Mass., Harvard University Press, 1957 A.

Osgood, C. E.: Motivational Dynamics of Language Behavior. In *Nebraska Symposium on Motivation* Lincoln, University of Nebraska Press, 1957B.

Prins, D.: Relations among specific articulatory deviations and desponses to a clinical measure of sound discrimination ability. *J Speech Hear Dis 28:*382–389, 1963.

Schiefelbusch, R., and Lindsey, M.: A new test of sound discrimination, *J Speech Hear Dis, 23:*153–59, 1958.

Severson, R., and Guest, K.: Toward the standardization assessment of the language of Disadvantaged Children. In F. Williams Ed. *Language and Poverty: Perspectives on a Theme.* Chicago, Markham Publishing Co. 1970.

Spradlin, J. E.: Assessment of Speech Language of Retarded Children: The Parsona Language Sample. In R. L. Schiefelbusch (ed.) Language studies of Mentally Retarded Children. *J Speech Hear Dis,* Monogr. Suppl. *10:*8–31, 1963.

Templin, M.: *Certain Language Skills in Children.* Institute of Child Welfare, Monograph Series, No. 26 Minneapolis, University of Minnesota Press, 1957.

Templin, M.: A study of sound discrimination ability of elementary school pupils. *J Speech Dis, 8:*127–132, 1943.

Templin, M., and Darley, F.: *The Templin-Darley Tests of Articulation* Division of Extension and University Services, The University of Iowa, 1964.

Van Riper, C.: *The Nature of Stuttering.* Englewood Cliffs, New Jersey, Prentice Hall, Inc., 1971.

Weinler, P.: Auditory discrimination and articulation. *J Speech Hear Dis,* *33*:19–29, 1967.

Wepman, J.: Auditory discrimination, Speech, and Reading. *Elementary School Journal, 60*:325–333, 1960.

Wepman, J. *Auditory Discrimination Test* (Manual of Directions). Chicago, Language Research Associates 1958.

Williams, F., and Naremore, R.: On the functional analysis of social class differences in modes of speech. *Speech Monographs, 36*:77–102, 1969.

Yoder, D.: Some viewpoints of the Speech, Hearing and Language Clinician. In F. Williams, *Language and Poverty: Perspectives on a Theme.* Chicago, Markham Publishing Co. 1970.

Appendix

FORMULAS

2.1 $IQ = \dfrac{MA}{CA} \times 100$

2.2 $MA = \dfrac{IQ}{100} \times CA$

2.3 $EQ = \dfrac{EA}{CA} \times 100$

2.4 $AQ = \dfrac{EA}{MA} \times 100$

2.5 $P_p = L = \left(\dfrac{pn - cf}{fi}\right)h$

2.6 $PR = \dfrac{100 \times R - 0.5}{N}$

2.7 $PR = 100 \times \dfrac{fc + \left(\dfrac{RS - L}{i}\right)fw}{N}$

2.8 $SD = \sqrt{\dfrac{\Sigma\,(X - \overline{X})}{N}}$

$$2.9 \quad SD = \sqrt{\dfrac{\Sigma\ X^2 - \dfrac{(\Sigma\ X)^2}{N}}{N}}$$

$$2.10 \quad SD = i\ \sqrt{\dfrac{\Sigma fd^2}{N} - \left(\dfrac{\Sigma\ fd}{N}\right)^2}$$

$$2.11 \quad \text{Z-score} = \dfrac{X - \overline{X}}{SD}$$

$$2.12 \quad \text{T-score} = 50 + 10\left(\dfrac{RS - M}{SD}\right)$$

$$2.13 \quad \text{Stanine score} = 5 + 1.96\left(\dfrac{X - \overline{X}}{SD}\right)$$

$$2.14 \quad SDc = SD^2 - \dfrac{i}{12}$$

$$3.1 \quad n \geqq \dfrac{(2k + 1) + \sqrt{8k - 1}}{2}$$

$$3.2 \quad \sigma^2_t = \sigma^2_{co} + \sigma^2_s + \sigma^2_e$$

$$3.3 \quad \sigma^2_t = \sigma^2_a + \sigma^2_b + \sigma^2_c + \cdots + \sigma^2_n + \sigma^2_s + \sigma^2_e$$

$$3.4 \quad h^2 = \sigma^2_a + \sigma^2_b + \sigma^2_c + \cdots + \sigma^2_n$$

3.5 $\quad r_{xy} = \dfrac{\sigma_t^2}{\sigma_t^2} - \dfrac{\sigma_e^2}{\sigma_t^2}$

3.6 $\quad r_{xy} = 1 - \dfrac{\sigma_e^2}{\sigma_t^2}$

3.7 $\quad r_{xy} = a_x\, a_y + b_x\, b_y + c_x\, c_y + \ldots + n_x\, n_y$

3.8 $\quad X_t = X_\infty + X_e$

3.9 $\quad \dfrac{\sigma_t^2}{\sigma_t^2} = \dfrac{\sigma_\infty^2}{\sigma_t^2} + \dfrac{\sigma_e^2}{\sigma_t^2} = 1.00$

3.10 $\quad \sigma_e^2 = \sigma_t^2 \left(1 - r_{xy} \right)$

3.11 $\quad SE_{mea} = \sigma_e = \sigma_t \sqrt{1 - r_{xy}}$

3.12 $\quad r_{xy} = \dfrac{2\, r_{ab}}{1 + r_{ab}}$

3.13 $\quad r_{xy} = \dfrac{n r_{ab}}{1 + (n - 1)\, r_{ab}}$

3.14 $\quad n = \dfrac{rn\, (1 - r_{xy})}{r'_{xy}\, (1 - rn)}$

$$3.15 \quad r = \left(\frac{n}{n-1}\right) \left(\frac{\sigma_t^2 - \Sigma pg}{\sigma_t^2}\right)$$

$$3.16 \quad r_{xy} = 1 \quad \frac{\frac{\Sigma d^2}{N}}{\sigma_t^2}$$

$$3.17 \quad \Sigma T_f = \Sigma P_i = G$$

$$3.18 \quad Ssb = \frac{\Sigma P_i}{k} - \frac{G^2}{kn}$$

$$3.19 \quad \frac{SS_b}{n-1} = MS_b$$

$$3.20 \quad r = \frac{MS_b - MS_r}{MS_b}$$

$$3.21 \quad r_{xy} = \frac{n\, r_{ab}}{1 + (n-1)\, r_{ab}}$$

$$3.22 \quad n = \frac{r\,(1 - r_{xy})}{r_{xy}\,(1 - r)}$$

NAME INDEX

385

SUBJECT INDEX

A

Academically talented, 316
Achievement quotient, 35
Achievement tests, 21, 317
   deaf and hard of hearing, 205
   retarded subjects, 140
Actuarial vs. clinical prediction, 253
Adaptive behavior
   behavior scales, 134
   retarded subjects, 146, 133
Adolescent Emotional Factors Inventory, 173, 186
Aesthetic Perception Test, 324
Age scores, 32
Alathena Smith's Test for Preschool Deaf Children, 200
American Association of Mental Deficiency, 102
American Foundation for the Blind, 188
American Printing House for the Blind, 172, 188
American Psychological Association, 297
Analyzing nonstandard language and speech behavior, 360
Aptitude tests, 20
   deaf and hard of hearing, 207
Artistic talent, 324
Art Judgement Test, 324
Assessment techniques, 221
   discrimination and memory via sensory channels, 363
   functions of, 247
   non-intellectual aspects of personality, 285–297
   perception, 363
Attention Level Inventory, 362
Attitudes towards emotionally disturbed children, 273
Audiological reports
   deaf and hard of hearing, 208
Audiologist
   deaf and hard of hearing, 207
Auditory Discrimination Test, 369

Auditory perceptual deficits, 324
   discrimination, 368
Auditory Test for Language Comprehension, 344
Ayres Space Test, 224

B

Basal age, 32
Basic Concept Inventory, 354
Bayley's Infant Scales of Motor and Mental Development, 129, 221
Behavioral history, 333
Bender-Gestalt, 294
   deaf and hard of hearing, 203, 205
Bender Visual Motor Gestalt Test, 223
Benton Visual Retention Test, 130
Berry-Buktenica Visual-Motor Integration Test, 223
Binet, A.
   intelligence evaluation, 10
Blacky Pictures, 291
Blindness
   definition, 159–160
   problems in testing, 162
   school age evaluation, 170
   selecting correct test, 167
Boehm Test of Basic Concepts, 355
Braille answer sheets, 164
Brain dysfunction
   etiologies, 215
   symptoms, 215

C

C—score, 51
Cain-Levine Social Competency Scale, 136–137
   use with retarded subjects, 136, 147
California Occupational Interest Inventory, 174
California program for gifted, 326
Case History
   deaf and hard of hearing, 208
Cattell Infant Intelligence Scale, 129, 222